D1552697

CHILD SOLDIERS

Practice, Law and Remedies

CHILD SOLDIERS
Practice, Law and Remedies

Wg Cdr (Dr) U C Jha

Vij Books India Pvt Ltd
New Delhi (India)

Published by

Vij Books India Pvt Ltd
(Publishers, Distributors & Importers)
2/19, Ansari Road
Delhi – 110 002
Phones: 91-11-43596460, 91-11-47340674
Fax: 91-11-47340674
e-mail: vijbooks@rediffmail.com

Copyright © 2018, *Wg Cdr (Dr) U C Jha*

ISBN: 978-93-86457-52-3 (Hardback)

ISBN: 978-93-86457-54-7 (ebook)

Price in India: ₹ 995/-

Printed and Bound in India

Contents

Preface

In every society down the ages, children have been held as man's most precious resource and the most important national asset. The future of a nation hinges on the health and all round development of its children. Since children are the weakest and most vulnerable section of society, it is the duty of the society to protect them from exploitation of all forms and ensure their development in a healthy environment. Unfortunately, the ongoing armed conflicts in many regions of the world, coupled with acute poverty, discrimination, exploitation, corruption, and lack of education, health and social welfare has resulted in grave violations of the rights of children. A large number of non-state armed groups (NSAGs) have recruited children to perform various tasks during armed conflicts. Irrespective of the roles they perform, child soldiers are exposed to acute levels of violence – as witnesses, direct victims and as forced participants. Some are injured and have to live with disabilities for the rest of their lives.

The use and recruitment of children as soldiers is not a phenomenon restricted to a particular region, conflict situation or continent. It is a global issue that demands a measured global response. There are approximately 300,000-350,000 child soldiers worldwide. Most of them are victims of illegal recruitment practices. They work as combatants, spies, cooks, porters, messengers and also as sex slaves for adult soldiers. They are increasingly being used as human shields, for carrying out acts of terror, including as suicide bombers, and even as executioners by NSAGs. Besides, several countries still recruit individuals below 18 in their armed forces under the pretext that they would be undergoing military training and would not be deployed until attaining the age of 18. For instance, the British armed forces recruited 2,250 children (under the age of 18) in the financial year 2015-16. Researchers have established that children in the age group of 16-17 are emotionally underdeveloped and should not be put through military training, which conditions them psychologically to obey all orders without question, including the order to kill. The Indian armed forces also recruit persons below 18 years of age.

In spite of the many international treaties, agreements and conventions on safeguarding children, child soldiers are extensively used in many parts of the world. The international community views the abuse of children as a tragedy, but has failed to put an end to this practice. The UN Committee on the Rights of the Child, in its concluding observations published in July 2016, expressed grave concern that in Pakistan, children continue to be targeted for recruitment and training by armed groups for military activities, including suicide bombing and the detonation of landmines, and that they are transferred to the frontlines of conflict areas where they are exposed to mortal danger, and that the State party has taken insufficient measures to prevent such recruitment.

The UN Secretary-General's annual report on children in armed conflict lists the States and non-state actors responsible for the recruitment and use of child soldiers. In the past two years, civil society organizations and the media have exposed the undue pressure (including threats to withdraw funding) exerted on the UN by some Member States to avoid being listed, despite credible evidence pointing to violations. In 2015, then UN Secretary-General Ban Ki-moon succumbed to pressure from the US to prevent the listing of the Israeli Defence Forces, in spite of a recommendation from his Special Representative to do so. In 2016, the Secretary-General faced pressure from Saudi Arabia, to remove the Saudi-led coalition from his list. The coalition forces had been listed for the grave violations of killing and maiming of children and attacks against schools and hospitals in Yemen.

This book about child soldiers contains six chapters. Chapter I gives a historical account of the use of children in war, defines the term "child soldier", describes the modes of recruitment of children and seeks to find an answer as to why recruiters prefer children. The Second chapter deals with the recruitment and use of child soldiers in 14 countries, namely Afghanistan, the Central African Republic, Colombia, the Democratic Republic of Congo, India, Iraq, Myanmar, Nigeria, Pakistan, Palestine, Israel, Somalia, South Sudan and Yemen. The UN Security Council has focused on six grave violations against children in current warfare: killing and maiming, sexual violence, recruitment and use, denial of humanitarian access, abduction, and attacks on schools and hospitals. These are discussed in the Third chapter.

The international child rights movement has prompted the development of international law, policies and programmes concerning the use of child soldiers. In the Fourth chapter, the issue of child soldiers has been discussed in the context of international humanitarian law (IHL) and international human rights law (IHRL). International criminal law (ICL) relating to child soldiers has been covered in the Fifth chapter, which analyses the extent to which international and "mixed" or "hybrid" criminal courts, in particular the Special Court for Sierra Leone (SCSL) and the International Criminal Court (ICC), have focused on crimes against children and dealt with children as victims. Chapter six is the concluding chapter, containing certain recommendations addressed to the United Nations, international community and the States that may serve as future guidelines to protect children in situations of armed conflict. The documents relating to child soldiers are placed at the end of the book (Appendices A to N).

I am thankful to my wife, Ratna, for her constant support, and to Medha and Chandana for editorial assistance. I would also like to thank Vij Publications Pvt Ltd, New Delhi, for their cooperation in bringing out this volume.

– U. C. Jha

1 Introduction

In 1924, the Geneva Declaration on the Rights of the Child enunciated a set of principles aimed at ensuring the well-being and protection of the child.[1] It provided a moral benchmark for the evaluation of the special position of the child. Exactly 90 years later, in 2014, the Third Optional Protocol to the Convention on the Rights of Child [2] set out an international complaint procedure for child rights violation. The Third Protocol allows children from states that have ratified it to bring complaints directly to the UN Committee on the Rights of the Child if they cannot find a solution at the national level. According to the Office of the United Nations High Commissioner for Human Rights, the ability of children, in their individual capacity, to complain about the violation of their rights in an international arena has brought real meaning to the rights contained in the human rights treaties.

1　In 1924, the Assembly of the League of Nations adopted the Geneva Declaration on the Rights of the Child, which was the first international instrument dealing with children's rights. It proclaimed that 'mankind owes to the child the best it has to give' and set out the following social and economic entitlements of children: (1) The child must be given the means requisite for its normal development, both materially and spiritually. (2) The child that is hungry must be fed; the child that is sick must be nursed; the child that is backward must be helped; and the orphan must be sheltered and succoured. (3) The child must be the first to receive relief in times of distress. (4) The child must be put in position to earn a livelihood, and must be protected against every form of exploitation. (5) The child must be brought up in the consciousness that its talent must be devoted to the service of its fellowmen.

2　On 19 December 2011, the General Assembly adopted a new Optional Protocol to the Convention on the Rights of the Child that established a communications procedure for violations of children's rights. This quasi-judicial mechanism applies to any violation of any right in the Convention and its protocols, including the Optional Protocol on the Involvement of Children in Armed Conflict. On 14 April 2014 this Optional Protocol entered into force following ratification by the required ten countries.

When children's rights are being incrementally expanded in the international and domestic arenas, one wonders how a child can be exploited as a soldier, used as a human bomb or abused as a victim of human trafficking. Despite the advances in international law, technology, and human rights consciousness, we are witnessing the dreadful abuse of children in armed conflicts globally. These abuses are directly related to the denigration of the respect for international humanitarian and human rights law by parties to conflicts. There have been most disturbing reports of sexual exploitation and abuse of children by United Nations peacekeepers and civilians and non-United Nations international forces.

The 2016 Annual Report of the United Nations Special Representative for the Secretary General on Children and Armed Conflict listed nine state armed forces and nearly fifty non-state armed groups (NSAGs) that currently recruit and use children in fifteen countries around the world.[3] The question arises: Who is a child soldier? In layman's language, child soldiers are children under 18 years of age, who are used for military purposes. Some child soldiers are used for fighting – they're forced to take part in armed conflicts, to kill, and commit other acts of violence. Some are forced to act as suicide bombers. Some join 'voluntarily', driven by poverty, a sense of duty, or the force of circumstance. Some children are used as cooks, porters, messengers, informants, spies or anything their commanders want them to do. Child soldiers are sometimes sexually abused. Whilst some may be in their late teens, others are as young as four years old.

Child Soldiers in History

Child soldiers are not a recent phenomenon. On the contrary, it was formerly commonplace for children to be enrolled in field regiments in Europe, although society was then substantially different. During the Age of Sail, children were assigned to man naval cannons, carry gun powder to the cannons and clean the cannons. These children were the so-called "Powder Monkeys." In France, under Napoleon's regime, "drummer boys" under Napoleon's personal direction helped the army to play the drums in the communication systems on the battlefield. By the end of the eighteenth century, in certain regions of France, up to a third of children were killed or abandoned, in particular in towns and in times of famine or hardship. Many

---

3   Children and armed conflict: Report of the Secretary-General, UN Doc A/70/836-S/ 2016/360 dated 20 April 2016.

abandoned children joined regiments, and the youngest child in large families was often entrusted to the army. These so-called "lost children", often served in the front ranks and in the most exposed positions. In this way, they "paid their debt" to society.

The American Civil War (1861-1865) could be considered the epitome of underage children at war. Although no concrete figures exist, according to conservative estimates, more than 200,000 soldiers of the Civil War, i.e., 10 to 20 per cent of the fighting force were sixteen and under. One of the youngest was Avery Brown, aged 8 years, 11 months, and 13 days. Brown lied about his age to join the service, claiming he was a full twelve years old. Although young soldiers performed the traditional role of drummers and later buglers, many underage volunteers engaged in combat and served with distinction during the war.[4]

All armies in the First World War used child soldiers. In the beginning of the war, the enthusiasm to join the battle was so great that young boys and even girls could hardly be stopped from enlisting. The officers responsible for recruitment closed their eyes when eager children clearly under the required age (18 years) showed up to join their armies. Hardly trained in military skills, the kids were sent to the trenches in Belgium, France, Russia and Turkey, where they mingled with the older soldiers and died with them. As many as 250,000 boys under the age of 18 served in the British Army during the First World War. Technically the boys had to be 19 to fight, but the law did not prevent 14-year-olds and upwards from joining in droves. They responded to the Army's desperate need for troops and recruiting sergeants were often less than scrupulous.

---

4 John Lincoln Clem is perhaps one of the most famous child soldiers of the Civil War. At the age of nine, accepted as an unofficial drummer boy for the 22nd Michigan, he was more of a camp follower than a soldier and appeared on no official muster rolls. At Pittsburg Landing, Clem's drum was smashed by a cannonball yet he stood his ground as Confederate forces routed the men in blue. He was spotted by General Ulysses Grant in the midst of the melee. The general reportedly cried out, "Johnny Shiloh won't run! Don't let a boy and his general stand here and fight alone!" The Union held its position long enough for reinforcements to arrive the following morning and emerged victorious. For his valiant stand, the "Drummer Boy of Shiloh," was rewarded with a valid enlistment in the US Army. He was ten years old. He went on to fight in many of the most grueling campaigns of the war. At twelve he was promoted to the rank of sergeant, and after the war was nominated for West Point by the former general turned President. Refused admission for deficient education, Grant commissioned him a lieutenant in the US Army. Major General John Clem retired in 1915.

Describing the training of a boy soldier in the First World War, Wilfred Owen wrote in 'Arms and the Boy':

Let the boy try along this bayonet-blade
How cold steel is, and keen with hunger of blood;
Blue with all malice, like a madman's flash;
And thinly drawn with famishing for flesh.
Lend him to stroke these blind, blunt bullet-heads
Which long to muzzle in the hearts of lads.
Or give him cartridges of fine zinc teeth,
Sharp with the sharpness of grief and death.

When the Second World War started in 1939, very few countries were prepared for a protracted conflict. The drafting age was thus lowered repeatedly to ensure a steady supply of soldiers to the armies. Both Germany and the Allied countries resorted to the mobilization of their population for the war effort and almost every country recruited children below 18 years in their armed forces. In the years immediately preceding the Second World War, the US Navy, Marine Corps, and Coast Guard allowed enlistment at age seventeen with parental consent, and at age eighteen without. Many lied about their age and concocted stories about their birthdates and their true identities. [5]

The Cold War saw an almost systematic resort to conscription – massive or selective. However, child soldiers in this period were essentially an issue in the wars of decolonization. The use of child soldiers increased with the increasing number of internal armed conflicts in the 1990s. Children are vulnerable to both forced and voluntary recruitment by non-state armed groups. The breakdown of the protection mechanisms during conflicts makes it easier for such groups to access children, who in some cases, join armed groups as a survival strategy.[6] Children are also among the first to be affected

---

5 Calvin Graham joined at age 12 and served with distinction in the US Navy. He was awarded the Bronze Star for valour and a Purple Heart. When an executive officer learned his true age, Graham was stripped of his medals, his military record, and even his uniform. Almost 32 years after World War II, his medals were reinstated, with the exception of the Purple Heart. Forty years after the War, he received his disability benefits. Two years after his death, the Navy presented his widow with his Purple Heart. Pollarine Joshua, Children at War: Underage Americans Illegally Fighting the Second World War, professional paper, The University of Montana, 2008, pp. 105.

6 Gogg Charu Lata, Child recruitment in South Asian Conflict: A Comparative Analysis of

by internal conflicts. In South Asia, a large number of children have been killed and maimed during the conflicts in Nepal[7] and Sri Lanka.

Children and terrorism have long intermixed in the modern era and in 2013 alone, the United Nations documented 4,000 cases of child recruitment, with thousands more likely undocumented. Although the number of states deploying children in their national armies has declined, children are deeply entrenched in armed conflict in the Middle East and Africa. At present, at least 1 in every 10 soldiers in armed conflicts is a child. These children not only carry weapons, but are also deployed in other ways such as porters, cooks, spies, guards or sex slaves.

Defining "Child" and "Child Soldier"

There are numerous challenges in defining the term 'child soldier'. One of these is that the term may apply to a wide range of people with varying experiences and roles. For example in Uganda, some children were taken mainly for sexual purposes, while others served mainly as porters. In Syria, the ISIS [8] has allegedly recruited children and trained them as suicide bombers.

The definition of a child soldier can be deduced only indirectly from international conventions, treaties and national legislation. Although there are differences in the age threshold for taking part in hostilities and being recruited by the armed forces, all international instruments generally consider the age limit to be 18, some explicitly while others as an advisory. According

---

Sri Lanka, Nepal and Bangladesh; Chatham House: The Royal Institute of International Affairs, 2006, p. 52.

7   From 1996 to 2006, Nepal was gripped by a conflict between the government and the Communist Party of Nepal (Maoist). The Maoists abducted tens of thousands of schoolchildren for 'political education'. Many were used as messengers, porters, cooks and fighters by the Maoist army.

8   In Syria, numerous parties have been involved in child recruitment. This includes the Islamic State in Iraq and Sham (ISIS), the Syrian government, Free Syrian Army (FSA)-affiliated groups, the Kurdish People Protection Units (YPG), Ahrar Al-Sham, and Jabhat al-Nusra. Until January 2015, more than 1,100 Syrian children under the age of 16 had joined the Islamic State of Iraq and al-Sham (ISIS); out of which 52 children had been killed, with 8 acting as suicide bombers. The United Nations Committee of the Rights of the Child further reported that as of 22 January 2015, ISIS has abducted 858 children since June 2014. *Maybe We Live and Maybe We Die*, Human Rights Watch, 2015; Report of the Secretary-General on Children and Armed Conflict in the Syrian Arab Republic, Secretary General of Children and Armed Conflict-The United Nations Security Council, 2014.

to the Convention on the Rights of the Child, a child is "every human being below the age of 18 years unless under the law applicable to the child, majority is attained earlier".[9]

The definition of child soldier used by the UNICEF is based on the Cape Town Principles (1997), which state: A child soldier "is any person under 18 years of age who is part of any kind of regular or irregular armed forces in any capacity, including but not limited to cooks, porters, messengers, and those accompanying such groups, other than purely as family members. Girls recruited for sexual purposes and forced marriage is included in this definition."

Child soldiers are also often referred to by child protection agencies as "children associated with armed groups and forces". The Paris Principles (2007) state, "A child associated with an armed force or armed group" refers to "any person below 18 years of age who is or who has been recruited or used by an armed force or armed group in any capacity, including but not limited to children, boys and girls, used as fighters, cooks, porters, messengers, spies or for sexual purposes. It does not only refer to a child who is taking or has taken a direct part in hostilities." [10] The Paris Principles have changed the phrase "child soldier" to "a child associated with an armed force or armed group", but the essence of the definition is the same.

The UN Convention on the Rights of the Child (CRC) recognized the conscription of children as detrimental to the rights contained in the convention. In Article 39 it stated that the state parties shall take all appropriate measures to promote the physical and psychological recovery of a child victim of....armed conflict. Although the CRC highlighted the prevention of child conscription as important, the earliest appropriate age of recruitment mentioned in the CRC at that time was 15 years.[11] In a gross contradiction, the definition of a child in the same document was an individual under the age of 18.[12] The document remained unchanged until 2000, when the UN

---

9   The Convention on the Rights of the Child 1989, Article 1(1).

10 UNICEF, The Paris Principles: the Principles and guidelines on children associated with armed forces and armed groups, February 2007, p. 7.

11 Article 38 (2) of the Convention on the Rights of Child (CRC) provides: "State parties shall take all feasible measures to ensure that persons who have not attained the age of 15 years do not take a direct part in hostilities." Article 38 (3) provides, "State parties......"

12 Article 1 of the CRC provides: "For the purposes of the present Convention, a child means every human being below the age of 18 years unless under the law applicable to the child,

adopted the Optional Protocol to the CRC on the Involvement of Children in Armed Conflict, now ratified by 166 member nations. The Protocol raised the age of compulsory recruitment to 18 for the State armed forces and non-state armed groups (NSAGs).[13]

The Optional Protocol requires states parties to make a binding declaration upon ratification, setting the minimum age for voluntary recruitment in the armed forces at 16 years or above. [14] The Protocol lays down four safeguards related to the voluntary recruitment of those aged at least 16 into government armed forces and who will not in any circumstances be deployed in combat. These safeguards require that (i) the recruitment is genuinely voluntary; (ii) the recruitment is carried out with the informed consent of the potential recruit's parents or legal guardians; (iii) the potential recruit is fully informed of the duties involved in such military service; and (iv) provides reliable proof of age prior to acceptance.[15] In practice, most of the states that have become parties to the Optional Protocol have specified a minimum age of 18 or more. The age norms for recruitment in the armed forces under various treaties are shown in the following table.

---

majority is attained earlier."

13 Article 2 of OP to the CRC provides "States Parties shall ensure that persons who have not attained the age of 18 years are not compulsorily recruited into their armed forces." Further Article 4, para 1 of the Protocol states: "Armed groups that are distinct from the armed forces of a State should not, under any circumstances, recruit or use in hostilities persons under the age of 18 years." From this wording, Article 4(1) imposes a legal obligation on NSAGs not to recruit or use in hostilities persons under 18.

14 Article 2 of the Optional Protocol reads: Article 3(1) of the same Protocol reads: "States Parties shall raise in years the minimum age for the voluntary recruitment of persons into their national armed forces from that set out in article 38 (3), of the CRC, taking account of the principles contained in that article and recognizing that under the Convention persons under the age of 18 years are entitled to special protection." Article 3(3) provides that state parties that permit voluntary recruitment into their national armed forces under the age of 18 years shall maintain certain safeguards contained therein. Article 4 (1) provides:

15 Article 3(2) of the Protocol reads: "Each State Party shall deposit a binding declaration upon ratification of or accession to the present Protocol that sets forth the minimum age at which it will permit voluntary recruitment into its national armed forces and a description of the safeguards it has adopted to ensure that such recruitment is not forced or coerced."

Age Norms for Child Soldiers

S. No.	Treaty	Compulsory Recruitment	Voluntary Recruitment
1.	Optional Protocol to the Convention on the Rights of the Child on the Involvement of Children in Armed Conflicts, 2002	18	16*
2.	ILO Convention 182 concerning the Prohibition and Immediate Action for the Elimination of the Worst Forms of Child Labour (1999)	18	N/A
3.	African Charter on the Rights and Welfare of the Child, 1990	18	18
4.	Protocol to the African Charter on Human and Peoples' Rights on the Rights of Women in Africa, 2003	18	18
5.	Convention on the Rights of the Child, 1989	15	15
6.	Protocols I and II Additional to the Geneva Conventions of 12 August 1949 (1977)	15	15
7.	Rome Statute of the International Criminal Court, 1998	15#	15#
8.	Statute of the Special Court for Sierra Leone, 2002	15#	15#

* The Optional Protocol Article 3, para 2, requires states parties to make a binding declaration setting the minimum age for voluntary recruitment at 16 years, and specifying safeguards to ensure that such recruitment is not forced or coerced.

\# Recruitment below this age would become a war crime.

Why Children Are Preferred as Soldiers

Armed groups see a number of benefits in recruiting children rather than adults. For example, in Mozambique, NSAGs preferred to recruit children because they were thought to have more stamina, be better at surviving in the bush, did not complain and followed orders more readily. Other reasons for the recruitment of child soldiers may be that children (i) work for lower pay; (ii) can be easily manipulated, intimidated and brainwashed; (iii) normally constitute no threat to leaders; (iv) may pose a moral challenge to enemy forces attacking them; (v) can be easily pressured into illicit activities such as trafficking or be exploited as sex slaves; and (vi) can replenish ranks and/or ensure long-term survival of the cadre.[16] Children can also take extreme risks in battle, which makes them valuable fighters, especially when they are under the influence of drugs.

The proliferation of small arms, such as AK-47, handguns, light machine guns, and revolvers has contributed significantly to the use of child soldiers. The widespread availability of these weapons is an important factor that enables children to participate as combatants in armed conflict. Small arms are light-weight, cheap and easy to use.[17] There could be other peculiar reasons for the recruitment of children by armed groups. For instance, Hamas used children to build tunnels because of their nimble bodies. In Colombia, child soldiers are known as "little carts" because of their ability to sneak hidden weapons through military checkpoints without arousing suspicion.[18]

Some factors which make children more vulnerable to recruitment by an armed group are: (i) Impoverishment; (ii) Travelling unaccompanied; (iii) Orphan-hood; (iv) Homelessness; (v) Living in an IDP or refugee camp; (vi)

16 Al Qaeda Expanding Recruitment of Children, CBS News, 4 July 2008. Available at: http://www.cbsnews.com/news/al-qaeda-expanding-recruitment-of-children/; Rashid Najm, Life under ISIL Caliphate: Recruitment of Child Soldiers, Al-Shorfa, 15 July 2015.

17 They call them the "cubs of the caliphate" and one of them, a French national who looked like a 12-year-old, was filmed shooting an accused spy in the forehead, then pumping additional rounds into his body. In the execution video posted by the extremists a new militant song can be heard playing in the background: "We have come, we have come, we have come, as soldiers for God. We have marched, we have marched, we have marched, out of love for God. We know religion, we live by it; we build an edifice, we ascend it. We deny humiliation we have experienced; we put an end to idolatrous tyranny." Jamie Dettmer, How ISIS Schools Little Boys to Be Suicide Bombers, 16 March 2015.

18 Horgan John G, Max Taylor, Mia Bloom, and Charlie Winter, From Cubs to Lions: A Six Stage Model of Child Socialization into the Islamic State, *Studies in Conflict and Terrorism*, 2016, p. 1-20.

Being female; (vii) Illiteracy or lack of basic education; (viii) Relationship or friendship with someone who has joined an armed group; (ix) Relationship or friendship with someone who has been maimed or killed in conflict (x) Engaging in forced labour (e.g. in a mine, factory, crop field, etc.); (xi) Birth into an armed group; (xii) Belonging to a community that hosts a "community protection militia"; (xiii) Belonging to an ethnic or religious minority; (xiv) Being in conflict with the law; (xv) Addiction to drugs and/or alcohol.[19]

Mode of Child Recruitment

'Recruitment' is a general term covering any means, whether voluntary, forced or compulsory, by which a person becomes part of an armed force or NSAG. The manner in which children are recruited varies. Voluntary recruitment refers to cases where children take the initiative of joining armed groups themselves, without being under immediate physical threat. Forced recruitment is commonly associated with abductions (individually or in groups), death threats (to the children or their family and peers) as well as severe punishment for desertion, a logical step as forced recruitment would be pointless without such a deterrent. It is estimated that 40 percent of the Revolutionary Armed Forces of Colombia (FARC's) child soldiers were forced into service, and 60 percent joined of their own volition. A survey in East Asia found that 57 percent of the children had volunteered.[20] A survey of child soldiers in four African countries found that 64 percent joined under no threat of violence.[21]

A. Voluntary Recruitment

According to a study undertaken by the ILO,[22] there are five major factors that influence a child's decision to join armed forces or armed groups voluntarily. These are: armed conflict, poverty, education, employment and

---

19 Whitman Shelly, Tanya Zayed and Carl Conradi, *Child Soldier: A Handbook for Security Sector Actors*, The Roméo Dallaire Child Soldiers Initiative, UNITAR, October 2013, p. 30.

20 Adult Wars, Child Soldiers, UNICEF, Geneva, 2003, p. 19.

21 International Labour Office, Wounded Childhood: The Use of Children in Armed Conflict in Central Africa, Geneva, 2003.

22 The research project was jointly undertaken by the Quaker United Nations Office, Geneva, and the International Labour Organisation. The research entailed in-depth interviews with 53 individuals from 9 countries who identified themselves as having volunteered to join armed forces or armed groups before the age of 18. Bret Rachel, Adolescents volunteering for armed forces or armed groups, *International Review of the Red Cross*, December 2003, Vol. 85, No. 852, p. 857-866.

family. Other factors, such as ideology, ethnicity, a struggle for liberation or against oppression, and friends can also play a part. The five major factors can have different influences and they do not operate in isolation from each other. The impoverished child in a conflict zone, without access to school or employment and whose family has been destroyed or torn apart, is the most at risk of joining the military or an armed group.

Armed Conflict: Armed conflict itself helps to create or exacerbate the other major factors mentioned, for example by forcing the closure of schools, causing the dispersal or death of family members, resulting in the loss of income and the lack of alternative employment. Most children get involved in an armed conflict because they happen to live in a conflict zone. It creates an opportunity for employment (be it formal employment with the army or an informal source of financial income or food via armed groups); for an escape from an oppressive family situation or from humiliation at school; and for adventure, to emulate military role models or to serve the cause (whether religious, ethnic, or political). In such a situation, children may join the military because of family traditions or because they see no other alternative to protect themselves or other members of their family.

Poverty: Poverty is the single most easily identifiable common characteristic of child soldiers. In other words, it is rare for children who are not living in poverty to become soldiers. Poverty is both a direct and an indirect cause for young people to volunteer to become soldiers.

Education: In all situations, whether during an armed conflict or not, the proportion of poor children not attending school is greater.[23] Their job prospects are limited due to the lack of education. Since many such youngsters have nothing else to do, they are perceived by recruiters to be available and are thus targeted. Some get involved in violence or crime and join an armed group as a form of protection. Others may see the military as a role model. Even when education is available, many adolescents drop out of school if education is unlikely to lead to employment, or if the school environment denigrates or humiliates them either as individuals, or for belonging to a specific group. At the same time, schools may serve as centres for military recruitment — whether directly by the government armed forces or armed opposition groups, or indirectly in response to an ethnic, religious or political

---

23 "If I Could Go To School..." Education as a tool to prevent the recruitment of girls and assist with their recovery and reintegration in Democratic Republic of Congo, Child Soldier International, p. 7.

dimension of the conflict.[24]

Employment: Adolescents are acutely aware of their prospects of formal employment or other gainful economic activity. They are at a critical juncture in the transition between school and work, and between economic dependence and self-sufficiency. Many are aware that a lack of education, appropriate schooling or vocational training leaves them with very few choices. Many also know all too well that the choices available are limited, whatever their level of schooling. Where they perceive the military or armed groups as the only employer, they opt for this "alternative" either on a regular basis or as a last resort to support themselves or their family.

Family: When their parents have been killed or their families disrupted, children may not only have to fend for themselves, but may have to assume the additional responsibilities of the head of a household and provide financial maintenance and physical protection for other members of their family. Thus they become an easy target for recruitment in the military or armed groups. Others join armed forces or groups because they are running away from an abusive or exploitative domestic situation. The family can also be a "pull" factor: some girls join to assert their equality (for example when the male members of the family are in armed forces or groups), while some boys feel pressured into joining because it would reflect badly on their father if they did not.[25]

The Geneva Centre for the Democratic Control of the Armed Forces has reclassified the factors responsible for children joining the armed forces or NSAGs voluntarily as follows:[26]

> ➢ **Political and security:** abuse by state or non-state forces, conflict, invasion or   occupation

> ➢ **Economic and social:** economic destruction, poverty, unemployment, lack of education, domestic violence or exploitation

> ➢ **Protection:** loss of family or home, harassment and discrimination of individuals or their families

---

24 Bret Rachel, Adolescents volunteering for armed forces or armed groups, *International Review of the Red Cross*, December 2003, Vol. 85, No. 852, p. 861.

25 Bret Rachel, Adolescents volunteering for armed forces or armed groups, *International Review of the Red Cross*, December 2003, Vol. 85, No. 852, p. 861.

26 Child Soldier, The Geneva Centre for the Democratic Control of the Armed Forces (DCAF) Backgrounder series 10/2016.

> ➤ **Cultural:** value systems that glorify military life, peer pressure

> ➤ **Ideological:** fighting for what is believed to be a 'just' cause

> ➤ **Personal:** gaining of military privileges, an education, money or status.

Though one may classify the factors under different heads, the fundamental reason behind children joining armed groups is that they are driven to do so by forces beyond their control. Hunger and poverty are endemic in conflict zones. Children, particularly those orphaned or disconnected from civil society, may volunteer to join any group if they believe that this is the only way to procure regular meals, clothing and medical attention. As one young boy in the Democratic Republic of Congo (DRC) explained, "I joined [President Laurent] Kabila's army when I was 13 because my home had been looted and my parents were gone. As I was then on my own, I decided to become a soldier."[27] In Sierra Leone, economic, educational and socio-political factors have been the most recognized driving forces that influence the decision of children to join the armed forces.[28] According to Schmidt (2007), the lack of food, income and education, in addition to the prevalence of war, gives rise to what some authors call "push and pull factors" that lead children to become soldiers.[29] According to Machel (2001), low education levels due to school desertion and closures, high unemployment rates, unsatisfied material needs, and the prevalence of war are constant factors in the lives of child soldiers. Under these circumstances, it would be misleading to consider the recruitment of children in armed forces and NSAGs as voluntary, because their choice is not exercised freely.[30]

Some NSAGs take deliberate advantage of the fact that adolescents are at a stage in life where they are still defining their identity. These groups hold out promises of a glamorous role, as well as membership and acceptance in a group. These messages are particularly seductive in areas where children

---

27 Save the Children, "Children of the Gun," Children in Crisis project report, September 2000.

28 Maria Paula Ballesteros Duarte, Understanding the Context of Voluntary Child Soldiers: Why did they choose to join the Irregular Armed Forces? The Case Study of Sierra Leone, unpublished dissertation, Barcelona, 2010.

29 Schmidt, A, Volunteer Child Soldiers in Africa: A Development Issue for Africa, *New School Economic Review*, Vol. 2(1) , 2007, p. 49-76.

30 Machel, G, 2001.The impact of war on children: A review of progress since the 1996: United Nations report on the impact of armed conflict on children. New York: Palgrave.

feel the most powerless or victimized.[31] One survey of child soldiers in Africa found that 15 percent volunteered because they were fascinated by the prestige and thrill of serving in a unit and having a gun.[32] Many children personally experience or are witness to extreme violence, including massacres, summary executions, ethnic cleansing, death squad killings, bombings, torture, sexual abuse, and destruction of home or property. Thus, vengeance can also be a reason for joining an armed conflict voluntarily.[33] Another reason for young people to take up arms is that guns are often seen as keys to a world of wealth and power. As one former child soldier explains: "I joined the army when I was young (at 15) without thinking much. I admired soldiers, their guns and crisp, neat uniforms. I just wanted to fight the way they did in the movies and so I joined the army."[34]

B. Forced Recruitment

Forced recruitment is enlistment into armed forces or NSAGs by means of abduction and/or the threat or use of violence or other reprisals.[35] Forced recruitment accounts for the vast majority of child soldiers. Children who are forcefully recruited are usually abducted from their homes or schools and beaten into submission.[36] In some cases, parents are forced to sell or give their

---

31 Surveys, interviews, and focus groups conducted in Nigeria in 2013 suggested that poverty, unemployment, illiteracy, and weak family structures contributed in making young men vulnerable to radicalization. Itinerant preachers capitalize on the situation by preaching an extreme version of religious teachings and conveying a narrative of the government as weak and corrupt. NSAGs such as Boko Haram could recruit and train youth for activities ranging from errand running to suicide bombings. Onuoha Freedom C., Why do Youth join Boko Haram, United States Institute of Peace, Special Report, June 2014.

32 *Wounded Childhood: The use of Children in Armed Conflict in Central Africa*, International Labour Office, April 2003, p. 31.

33 Singer PW, Child Soldiers: New Faces of War, available at: https://www.brookings.edu/wp-content/uploads/2016/06/singer20051215.pdf, accessed 25 April 2017.

34 *Children of Conflict*, BBC, UK, 2002.

35 Case studies indicate that in the majority of conflicts, a widely used method of recruitment of children is some form of abduction. Typically, recruiting parties are given conscription targets that change according to the group's needs and objectives. For example, the Union of Congolese Patriots for Reconciliation and Peace (UPC/RP), a militia led by Thomas Lubanga in eastern Congo, had a policy that each family within its area of control must provide a cow, money, or child to the group. The LRA in Uganda sets numeric goals for child recruits and sends raiding parties into villages to meet them.

36 The decision of where groups carry out their operations to find their recruits is also based on planned efforts to maximize the efficiency of their efforts. The most frequent targets are secondary schools or orphanages. The Liberation Tigers of Tamil Eelam (LTTE) in

children under threat. Armed groups sometimes demand a certain number of children from a village as a whole. The villagers usually comply to avoid being attacked or raided by the armed group. In all such cases, children are faced with extreme violence and witness the unthinkable atrocities of war. Fatima, a 15-years-old girl in northern Sierra Leone narrates her ordeal: "The rebels—they came and attacked my village. They burnt many homes and took many like me as wives. I was 12 years old, just a young girl. I was so scared. They made me carry supplies--really heavy things--on my head, and I thought we would be shot. My captor (husband)….he beat me and had sex with me. I got pregnant and had my baby in the bush. Now I have AIDS and my baby too….I am too poor to buy medicines…What will happen to me and my baby?"[37]

Child soldiers are almost exclusively from communities that suffer from extreme poverty. Orphans are much more likely to be recruited, and some forced recruits become orphans in the process. In some cases, abductors force children to kill their own parents. Armed groups also raid orphanages and abduct all the children. Other groups that are in danger of child recruitment are refugee and internally displaced populations. In many instances, families on the run become disconnected. Armed groups then target the unaccompanied and thus more vulnerable minors.

C. Compulsory recruitment

Also known as conscription, this is service in regular state armed forces required by statute. The compulsory recruitment of child soldiers is primarily conducted to fulfil a state's need for soldiers in times of conflict, though in principle it could be used to sustain a large peacetime army. Compulsory recruitment of persons younger than 18 years is forbidden by the Optional Protocol to the CRC on the Involvement of Children in Armed Conflicts.

However, the line between voluntary and forced recruitment of child soldiers is getting blurred. For instance, one self-defined volunteer in Sierra

---

Sri Lanka even took to setting up a unit formed exclusively of orphans, the elite Sirasu Puli (Leopard Brigade). The Congolese Rally for Democracy-Goma (RCD-Goma) and Rwandan Patriotic Army (RPA) also targeted schools almost exclusively, using kidnapping or coercion to pull in kids. Another common target area is the marketplace. In Sudan, the government set up camps for street children. These camps served as reservoirs for army conscription.

37 Wessells Michael. 2006. *Child Soldiers: From Violence to Protection*, London: Harvard University Press, p. 1.

Leone described the circumstances in which he joined: "One of my friends…
was shot in his head because he refused to join them. He was killed straight in
front of me." Research undertaken to investigate the methods of recruitment
may not be reliable because current and former child soldiers are unlikely to
disclose the "truth" behind their recruitment. Former child soldiers are more
likely to say that they had been abducted or recruited by force. This could be
because of the fear of reprisals from those who remain with armed groups. It
could also help them gain more sympathy during the reintegration process.
While analysing the methods of recruitment, it must also be remembered that
only survivors can tell their stories.[38]

Distribution of Child Soldiers

In the post-World War II era, child soldiers have been serving in significant
numbers on every continent. In fact, they have become integral parts of the
state armed and paramilitary forces as well as the rebel and terrorist groups.
They serve as combatants in a variety of roles — as infantry troops, raiders,
sentries, spies, trench diggers, and recently as suicide bombers.

In the Americas since 1990, child soldiers have fought in Colombia, Ecuador,
El Salvador, Guatemala, Mexico (in the Chiapas conflict), Nicaragua,
Paraguay, and Peru. The majority of child soldiers in Europe have fought
in opposition groups in the east, serving in Chechnya, Daghestan, Kosovo,
Macedonia, and Nagorno-Karabakh.

Africa is often considered to be at the epicenter of the child soldier
phenomenon. It has experienced not only the fastest growth of child soldiering
but also the rapid decline in the age of recruitment. Armed groups using
child soldiers cover the entire continent.[39] The affected countries are Angola,

---

38 In a study of Ethiopian women who had been recruited into the Tigrean People's
Liberation Front (TPLF) as children and were demobilized as adults in 1992/1993, a
variety of reasons for volunteering were cited, including political motivations, inspiration
by peers or family members, loss of family members due to droughts, escaping unwanted
marriages, educational opportunities, or being brought up in the fighter camps (and
attending kindergarten and school there). In Mozambique's war between Frelimo and
Renamo, forced recruitment was predominant; 90 percent of all rank and file combatants
of Renamo were recruited by force. Schmidt, A, Volunteer Child Soldiers in Africa: A
Development Issue for Africa, *New School Economic Review*, Vol. 2(1) , 2007, p. 49-76.

39 Africa combines two important factors that help explain the high rate of participation
of young people as combatants. It is not only the poorest continent, but the youngest in
terms of the demographic composition where children represent the absolute demographic
majority. Schmidt, A, Volunteer Child Soldiers in Africa: A Development Issue for Africa,

Burundi, the Central African Republic, Cote d'Ivoire, the Democratic Republic of Congo (DRC), Eritrea, Ethiopia, Liberia, Rwanda, Sierra Leone, Somalia, Sudan, South Sudan, Tanzania and Uganda. To cite one example, at the beginning of the Sierra Leone conflict (1991 to 2002), 70 per cent of the fighters were under the age of 18 and more than half were between the ages of 7 and 14 when recruited. [40]

Child soldiers have also become an integral part of the conflicts in the Middle East. They have been engaged in fighting in Algeria, Azerbaijan, Egypt, Iran,[41] Iraq, Lebanon, Syria, Tajikistan, and Yemen. Young teens are also at the centre of fighting in Palestine. It has been alleged that Palestinian children are also been used by Israel. Children have been engaged in insurgencies in Cambodia, East Timor, India, Indonesia, Laos, Myanmar, Nepal, Pakistan, Papua New Guinea, the Philippines, Sri Lanka, and the Solomon Islands. The details of recruitment and use of child soldiers in a few states has been discussed in the next chapter.

How Many Child Soldiers Are There?

It is difficult to estimate accurately the number of children associated with armed forces or armed groups throughout the world. No one has ever made a serious attempt at surveying the world's child soldier population. The popularly cited number of 300,000 was projected by members of several child advocacy groups in the mid-1990s as a way to attract attention to the

New School Economic Review, Vol. 2, No. 1, 2007, p.49-76.

40 Maria Paula Ballesteros Duarte, Understanding the Context of Voluntary Child Soldiers: Why did they choose to join the Irregular Armed Forces? The Case Study of Sierra Leone, unpublished dissertation, Barcelona, 2010, p.2.

41 The first modern use of child soldiers in the region was actually during the Iran-Iraq war in the 1980s. Iranian law, based on the Koranic Sharia, had forbid the recruitment of children under 16 into the armed forces. However, a few years into the fighting, the regime began to falter in its war with its neighbour, Iraq. So it chose to ignore its own laws, and in 1984, Iranian President Rafsanjani declared that "all Iranians from 12 to 72 should volunteer for the Holy War. Thousands of children were pulled from schools, indoctrinated in the glory of martyrdom, and sent to the front lines only lightly armed with one or two grenades or a gun with one magazine of ammunition. Wearing keys around their necks (to signify their pending entrance into heaven), they were sent forward in the first waves of attacks to help clear paths through minefields with their bodies and overwhelm Iraqi defenses. Iraq, in turn, enrolled child soldiers in that conflict and more recently, under Saddam Hussein, built up an entire apparatus designed to pull children into conflict. Singer PW, Child Soldiers: New Faces of War, available at: https://www.brookings.edu/wp-content/uploads/2016/06/singer20051215.pdf, accessed 25 April 2017.

plight of child soldiers.[42] But if this figure were ever true, it cannot be so now. Some armed conflicts employing child soldiers, such as those in Angola, Nepal and Sri Lanka have ended; however, in the ongoing conflicts in Syria, Iraq, Afghanistan, Myanmar, Pakistan, South Sudan and Thailand children as young as 14 have been used by armed groups. While armed rebel groups have made extensive use of child fighters, their use is by no means limited to non-state actors. The number of children associated with armed forces or armed groups would be higher than the figure estimated in the 1990s as over 30 states actively recruit children into their military forces. They justify this on the ground that a child recruited at the age of 16, spends at least two years in training before being formally inducted into active military service.

According to Graca Machel (1996), who has served as a special expert for the United Nations on the issue of child soldiers, "These statistics are shocking enough, but more chilling is the conclusion to be drawn from them: More and more of the world is being sucked into a desolate moral vacuum. This is a space devoid of the most basic human values; a space in which children are slaughtered, raped, and maimed; a space in which children are exploited as soldiers; a space in which children are starved and exposed to extreme brutality. Such unregulated terror and violence speak of deliberate victimization. There are few further depths to which humanity can sink."[43]

Girl Child Soldiers

It is estimated that since 1990, girls have participated in armed conflict in 58 countries, with the proportion of girl combatants in African conflicts rising to about 30 to 40 per cent. Girls perform additional duties over and above many of the duties of boy soldiers. For instance, during the armed conflict in Sierra Leone, girl soldiers not only fought, mined for diamonds and fulfilled other duties such as spying, but also cooked, cleaned and performed sexual services.' Similar duties were performed by girls in Burundi, Uganda, Liberia, the Democratic Republic of Congo, and Angola. It has been reported that providing sexual services is inevitably part of a girl's 'duty' within armed

---

42 There are currently over 300,000 children in the world today being used as child soldiers. Wainryb, C, "And so they ordered me to kill a person": Conceptualizing the impacts of child soldiering on the development of moral agency. *Human Development*, Vol. 54(5), 2011, p. 273-300.

43 Promotion and Protection of the Rights of Children: Impact of armed conflict on children, United Nations, Report of the Expert of the Secretary General (Ms. Graca Machel), UN doc A/51/306, 26 August 1996, para 3.

groups. Girls are subjected to various kinds of sexual violence, including gang rapes, sexual torture, and serial rapes by individual male members of the group. They are also given as 'wives' to men or boys in 'bush marriages' as a reward for good fighting. In conflicts in Sierra Leone, 60 per cent of the girls involved with fighting forces were bush wives.[44] The factors responsible for the recruitment of girls into armed groups could be: (i) interruption of education, (ii) need for protection, (iii) seeking revenge for a killing or sexual assault, and (iv) poverty.

Children as Suicide Bombers

Child-bombs are new weapons in the hands of NSAGs. Children have been used to carry out suicide missions for armed groups in Afghanistan, Iraq, Israeli-Palestinian land, Nigeria, Pakistan, Saudi Arabia, Syria, Turkey and Yemen.[45] A child can be easily indoctrinated and can be used for suicide missions within the country or across the border because children are less likely to arouse suspicion. They can also remain unnoticed for a long period of time. A child-bomb can cause massive, precise, and lethal destruction. Faced with abject poverty, parents can be coerced to send their children to help non-state actors,[46] who could then indoctrinate and use them as suicide bombers. Children can be encouraged, tacitly or otherwise, to volunteer to kill themselves and others in the name of religion. Children are easily persuaded by others to lay down their lives to defend their communities, or redress inequalities or discrimination. They are less likely to disobey or attempt to leave and could also be punished for such acts.

In some cases children may not be aware of what they are carrying and explosives may be set off remotely without their knowledge. Non-state organizations may not have to pay any financial compensation to the suicide

---

44 "If I Could Go To School..." Education as a tool to prevent the recruitment of girls and assist with their recovery and reintegration in Democratic Republic of Congo, Child Soldier International, p. 7.

45 Suicide attacks have played a key part in ISIS's military tactics, particularly in Syria and Iraq. The group has also claimed responsibility for suicide attacks in five countries: Yemen, Kuwait, Saudi Arabia, Turkey and Libya.

46 The Taliban in Afghanistan and Pakistan have also forced people to give up a child. They have been demanding either a large amount of money or one of the kids. Because the families are quite large, the parents have no option but to surrender one of the children to the Taliban, thus sacrificing one child for the wellbeing of the family. Boghani Priyanka, Why Afghanistan's Children Are Used as Spies and Suicide Bombers? *Frontline*, 17 November 2015.

bombers' family. When a child suicide bomber is wounded or killed in a failed attempt, the opposing government could be painted as heartless and cruel in the eyes of the world. Child suicide bombing has more shock value and receives greater media coverage because children are considered less likely to commit acts of mass violence.

The ISIS has been using children in suicide missions. Children are trained in suicide attacks and are told to wear suicide vests while performing other jobs, such as guard duties. Children used specifically as suicide bombers have been known to wear vests or drive vehicles full of explosives into target areas and detonate them on arrival. According to the Syrian Observatory for Human Rights, in July 2015 there were as many as 19 cases of child suicide bombings.[47] Children are valuable to IS leaders as suicide bombers because they are generally less fearful than adults, and do not over-analyse situations based on previous experience. For someone who truly believes in the Islamic State and its ideology, killing themselves in a suicide mission is considered the greatest honour.[48]

The use of suicide terrorism has also become a major weapon in the hands of Pakistani militant groups. Children, normally around the age of 15, are indoctrinated and prepared to sacrifice their lives to advance the political agendas of militant groups.[49] Most of the banned organizations in Pakistan such as the Al-Qaeda, TTP and Lashkar-e Jhangvi use suicide bombers. One Pakistani recruiter of child suicide bombers described these children as "tools provided by God". Another Muslim cleric in a *madrassa* stated that it is "a gift from Allah that we have an unlimited number willing to be sacrificed to teach Americans a lesson".[50]

47 Johnlee Varghese, Syria Report: 52 ISIS Child Soldiers Died Fighting in 2015; 19 Under-16 Jihadists Used as Suicide Bombers, *International Business Times*, 16 July 2015.

48 Benotman Noman and Nikita Malik, *The Children of Islamic State*, London: Quilliam, 2016, p. 44.

49 In July 2014, *Newsweek* (Pakistan) interviewed the family of an Uzbek national who moved along with his family to North Waziristan "after he joined Al-Qaeda." When the man was killed in a drone strike, *Newsweek* interviewed his 8-year-old son who declared: "My father is a martyr who sacrificed his life in the path of Allah. America is the enemy of Muslims....I will also fight against them." Nazar Ul Islam, Stranger in a Strange Land, *Newsweek* (Pakistan), 25 July 2014.

50 Franklin, Lawrence A., Children as Suicide Bombers in Islamic Countries, 18 September 2014, available at: http://www.gatestoneinstitute.org/4701/child-suicide-bombers, accessed 10 February 2016.

Militant organizations adopt this inhuman practice for many reasons. It costs little, causes huge damage to the target, makes it difficult for law enforcement agencies to trace the initiator of the crime, and creates despondency among masses. The high casualty rate of suicide bombings attracts media attention, which has a huge psychological impact. By creating a shock effect through suicide bombings, terrorists hope to gain sympathy and legitimacy.[51] In comparison to boys, girl suicide bombers are less likely to be searched.[52] They can avoid military checkpoints or police posts and reach as close to the target as possible with greater ease. A girl who is a victim of rape, physical abuse and torture can be easily recruited as a suicide bomber to take revenge.

International Day against the Use of Child Soldiers

The Optional Protocol to the Convention on the Rights of the Child on the involvement of children in armed conflict entered into force on 12 February 2012. February 12 is now known as the International Day against the Use of Child Soldiers.

Despite a set of binding treaties, the recruitment and use of child soldiers is a deliberate and systematic choice currently being made the world over. There are various factors that contribute to child recruitment. While some children actively seek to join armed groups or armed forces, others are brutally abducted and forced to serve as soldiers. They are used to fight, lay mines and explosives, and as spies, messengers, guards, scouts, cooks, porters, servants and for sexual purposes. They are all at risk of getting wounded, maimed or disabled and extremely vulnerable to health problems including HIV/AIDS or sexually transmitted diseases.

Children who grow up in the midst of war usually lack the basic necessities of schools and health care. They face disrupted family relationships, and family violence. NSAGs may target children with a specific psychological profile depending on their organizational strategy and goals. Children in

---

51 Masood, Major General Talat, Pakistan's Fight Against Terrorism, *Defence Against Terrorism Review*, Vol. 4, No. 1, Spring & Fall 2012, p. 13-30.

52 According to Karen Jacques and Paul J. Taylor, who have studied biographical accounts of 30 male and 30 female suicide bombers; female suicide bombers are more associated with personal motivating factors, such as revenge, whilst male suicide bombers are considerably more associated with religion and nationalism. Jacques, Karen & Taylor, Paul J., Male and Female Suicide Bombers: Different Sexes, Different Reasons? *Studies in Conflict & Terrorism*, Vol. 31 (4), 2008, p. 304-320.

turn may be more susceptible to be recruited by one or the other group as a result of their developmental and psychological needs. For instance, ISIS starts indoctrination at an early age; children as young as 12 are engaged in military training and at 14 they may become suicide bombers. Technological advances in "small arms" now permit the transformation of children into fighters just as lethal as any adult.[53] The NSAGs that recruit and use child soldiers view them simply as malleable and expendable assets. It is difficult to estimate accurately the number of children associated with armed forces or armed groups throughout the world. However, we can say with certainty that many tens of thousands are currently involved. Hundreds of thousands have suffered the same fate during the last decade or so. Regardless of how children are recruited and of their roles, child soldiers are victims.

---

53 These "small arms" include rifles, grenades, light machine guns, light mortars, land mines, and other weapons that are "man-portable", a term often used by the military. Even though they represent less than 2% of the entire global arms trade in terms of cost, small arms are perhaps the most deadly of all weapons to society. They are the weapons most often used both in battle and in attacks on civilians and have produced 60 to 90 per cent of all casualties in recent armed conflicts. Not only have these small arms become easier to use and far more deadly, but they have also proliferated in number. There are an estimated 500 million small arms present on the global scene, one for every 12 persons on the planet.

2   Child Soldiers: Worldwide

The impact of armed conflict on children must be everyone's concern and is everyone's responsibility: governments, international organizations and every element of civil society.[1]

The world has been witnessing the proliferation of light weapons and ammunition, combined with the availability of children—the child soldier being a cost-effective and renewable weapon—as a result of overpopulation in poor and developing countries. These child soldiers are faceless and are considered expendable.[2] Children have proven excellent as soldiers: they are less demanding; can be abducted or coerced to join; can also serve as sex slaves and bush wives; or can be used in a variety of other roles in an armed conflict.[3] A large number of non-state armed groups (NSAGs) have recruited children, both boys and girls, in their armed forces. These children are drawn from the poorest, least educated and most marginalized sections of society. Children who are especially at risk are those with a disrupted family background, refugee and internally displaced children, children living in conflict zones and garrison towns, children from a particular ethnic, racial or religious group, and former child soldiers. Some children join voluntarily to ensure their survival and as an alternative to unemployment, or because they believe in the cause they are fighting for: a holy war, religious freedom, ethnic

---

1   Promotion and Protection of the Rights of Children: Impact of Armed Conflict on Children: Note by the Secretary-General, UN Doc. A/51/306, 26 August 1996.

2   Dallaire Romeo. 2011. *They Fight Like Soldiers: They Die Like Children*, London: Arrow Books, p. 3.

3   The recruited children are used in variety of roles: to fight, lay mines and explosives and as spies, messengers, guards, scouts, cooks, porters, servants and for sexual purposes.

or political liberty, or social justice.[4]

Unfortunately, the use of child soldiers is not confined to NSAGs. Many state armed forces also recruit children in the military when they are below 18 years of age. A number of states prohibit or claim to prohibit persons under the age of 18 years from joining their armed forces and/or from taking part in hostilities. However, when put to the test, these commitments often do not translate into effective protection for children. The fact remains that when states are involved in armed conflict, directly or indirectly through their support of proxy armed groups, they are still likely to use child soldiers. Of the 19 NATO members, 13 countries recruit children under 18 years of age into their military forces. Of the five permanent members of the UN Security Council, only Russia does not recruit children below the age of 18. The US accepts volunteers from the age of 17 years and has deployed 17-year-old combatants in recent operations, such as in Afghanistan and the Gulf War. The UK accepts voluntary recruits from the age of 16 and there are currently between 6000 and 7000 soldiers under 18 years of age in the British armed forces. The UK is also the only European country, which has sent soldiers under the age of 18 years into battle, including the battles fought during the Gulf War.

Today, it is less common than earlier for states to deploy soldiers under 18 years of age in hostilities as part of national armies (army, navy, air force). However, during the period between January 2010 and June 2012, ten states, namely, Chad, Cote d'Ivoire, the Democratic Republic of the Congo, Libya, Myanmar, Somalia, South Sudan, Sudan, the UK and Yemen, deployed soldiers below the age of 18 years. In addition, seven others used child soldiers in state armed forces and state-allied armed groups. These are Afghanistan, Central African Republic, Eritrea, Iraq, the Philippines, Rwanda and Thailand. In another three states (Colombia, Israel and Syria), children were not formally recruited but were nevertheless reported to have been used for military purposes, including intelligence gathering and as human shields.[5] Therefore, child soldiering is a reality in many parts of the world today.

---

4   Peters Lilian, War is no Child's Play: Child Soldiers from Battle Field to Playground, The Geneva Centre for the Democratic Control of Armed Forces (DCAF), Occasional Paper No. 8, 2005.

5   Louder Than Words: An agenda for Action to end state use of child soldiers, Child Soldier International, 2012, p. 11.

How Many Child Soldiers in the World?

It is not possible to establish with absolute certainty the exact number of child soldiers in the world. Certain organizations claim that the number is about 250,000–300,000.[6] Mass displacement and turmoil caused by armed conflicts make it very difficult to arrive at a fixed figure. Moreover, identifying children as former or serving child soldiers may place them at risk. Many children do not wish to be identified or labeled as former child soldiers and girls do not like to be singled out as such because of stigmatization. Therefore, all figures regarding child soldiers must be treated as provisional.

Distribution of Child Soldiers

The Coalition to Stop the Use of Child Soldiers (CSUCS) released Child Soldier Global Reports in 2001 and 2008. These reports published a global account of the geographical and temporal distribution of child soldiers. Both reports addressed the issue of child soldiers on a country-by-country basis. According to Child Soldiers International (CSI),[7] over 30 countries across the globe are currently using child soldiers. These countries include: Afghanistan, Burma, Burundi, Central African Republic (CAR), Chad, Democratic Republic of the Congo (DRC), the Philippines, Somalia, Sudan, South Sudan, Thailand, Yemen, Uganda, Sierra Leone, Iraq, India, Indonesia, Israel, Ethiopia, Liberia, Rwanda, Chechen Republic, Colombia, Cambodia, Sri Lanka, Mozambique, Mexico, Honduras, Peru and Myanmar.[8]

During the last decade, the recruitment and/or use of children by official state forces have been documented by the United Nations in the following

---

6   The first global study on the prevalence of child soldiering, the 1996 UN study, *Impact of Armed Conflict on Children* (Machel 1996), indicated that there were approximately 250,000 child soldiers. Subsequent reports, such as Child Soldiers Global Report 2001 of the International Coalition to Stop the Use of Child Soldiers, estimated that there were about 300,000 child soldiers at any point in time. The UNICEF website does not mention the exact number of child soldiers around the world, but states that since 2013, when fighting first erupted in South Sudan, 17,000 children have been recruited by the armed forces and armed groups. See: www.unicef.org/media_94185.html, accessed 06 February 2017. Also see: **Waschefort Gus. 2015.** *International Law and Child Soldiers*, **Oregon:** Oxford and Portland, p. 27.

7   During 2011, the Coalition to Stop the Use of Child Soldiers (CSUCS) transitioned from being a coalition of different NGOs to becoming an NGO in its own right. With this came a change in name, to Child Soldiers International.

8   *Who are child soldiers?* Child Soldiers International, 2015, available at: http://www.child-soldiers.org/about_the_issue.php, accessed 10 March 2017.

13 countries:

> Afghanistan (Afghan National Police and Afghan Local Police);

> Algeria (Legitimate Defence Force [GLD]);

> Chad (the Principle Security Service for State Institutions, DGSSIE);

> DRC (Republican Guard);

> India (Special Police Officers);

> Iraq (Awakening Councils);

> Libya (Revolutionary Guards, Revolutionary Committees and paramilitary force);

> Myanmar (Border Guard Forces [BGF]);

> Peru (Self-defence Committees [CAD]);

> Philippines (Citizen Armed Force Geographical Units and Civilian Volunteer Organizations [CVO]);

> Sudan (Popular Defence Force and police forces, including Central Reserve Police, Border Intelligence Forces and Camel Police);

> Thailand (Village Defence Volunteers); and

> Yemen (Central Security Forces and Republican Guard).

In 2012, the CSI issued a report, *Louder than Words: An Agenda to End State Use of Child Soldiers*. This 162-page report focuses on the recruitment and use of child soldiers only by the state. According to it, 20 states have used children in hostilities during the period 2010–12 in various capacities.[9] The

---

9   Afghanistan (Afghan National Police, Afghan Local Police and Afghan National Army) have used them at checkpoints, including as messengers and tea boys; (2) Central African Republic, in self-defence militias; (3) Chad, in the Chadian National Army and Sudan armed opposition group(Justice and Equity Movement); (4) Colombia,used for intelligence purposes in the Colombian National Army; (5) Cote d'Ivoire, in the Former Defence and Security Forces, Republican Forces of Cote d'Ivoire,and armed militias and "self-defence" groups instituted by supporters of the President; (6) in the DRC, in the armed forces, paramilitary force(Republican Guard); (7) Eritrea, in the Somali armed opposition group (*Al-Shabaab*); (8) Iraq, in the civil defence force/militia(Awakening Councils); (9) in Israel,alleged use of Palestinian children as human shields; (10) Libya,

2016 report of the UN Secretary-General on children and armed conflict includes a "list of shame", which identifies armed forces and groups that recruit and use children. The list includes the states that recruit children and use them in armed conflict. These are Afghanistan, CAR, DRC, Iraq, Mali, Myanmar, Somalia, South Sudan, Sudan, Syria, Yemen, Colombia, Nigeria and the Philippines. There are reports that in addition to the parties formally listed above, India, Pakistan, Israel/Palestine, Libya and Thailand are also recruiting and using children.

Currently, there is some form of armed conflict in over 40 nations in the world. These conflicts have created instability and exposed children to unfavourable environments. In recent cases of armed conflict, children have been increasingly victimized both as targets and agents of violence. International organizations, policy-makers and humanitarian actors have raised the issue of child soldiers, making it one of the most contended humanitarian issues.[10] This chapter covers the recruitment and use of child soldiers in the following 14 countries.

> Afghanistan

> Central African Republic

> Colombia

> Democratic Republic of Congo

---

in pro-Qadhafi forces, Libyan Armed Forces Paramilitary force (The Kata'eb State armed forces—use of children as human shields); (11) Myanmar, in the national armed forces, paramilitary force(Border Guard Forces); (12) the Philippines, in the paramilitary forces(Citizen Armed Forces Geographical Units), Armed Forces of the Philippines—use of children as informants, guides and porters; (13) Rwanda, in DRC armed opposition groups, including the "M23"; (14) Somalia, in the Transitional Federal Government State-allied militias; (15) Republic of South Sudan, in the Sudan People's Liberation Army; (16) Sudan, in the Sudan Armed Forces, police forces, including the Central Reserve Police and Border Intelligence Forces, and paramilitary forces (Popular Defence Forces; Pro-government militias and Chadian armed opposition groups); (17) Syrian Arab Republic, in the Syrian armed forces and allied armed group, Shabbiha militia—use of children as human shields; (18) Thailand, in the civil defence force (Village Defence Volunteers); (19) United Kingdom, in the British Army; and (20) Yemen, in the Armed Forces of Yemen, paramilitary forces (Central Security Forces and Republican Guard; pro-government tribal militias).

10 Nduwimana Donatien, Reintegration of Child Soldiers in Eastern Democratic Republic of Congo: Challenges and Prospects, Occasional paper series 4, Number 2, International Peace Support Training Centre, Kenya, 2013.

> India

> Iraq

> Myanmar

> Nigeria

> Pakistan

> Palestine and Israel

> Somalia

> South Sudan

> Syria

> Yemen

Afghanistan

Afghanistan has been involved in armed conflict for nearly four decades. Among the factors contributing to the voluntary or coerced military recruitment of children is the highly unstable environment in the country, as arms have infiltrated the very psyche of the Afghan. The very first US service man to die in Afghanistan was shot by a fourteen-year-old sniper.[11] The report of the Secretary-General to the Security Council on children and armed conflict in Afghanistan demonstrates that children bear the brunt of the conflict in Afghanistan and their sufferings have increased over time. Children continue to be recruited and deprived of their rights to education and health care.[12]

Afghanistan is a party to the 1949 Geneva Conventions and its Additional Protocols. It ratified the Convention on the Rights of the Child (CRC) in 1994, and is bound to respect, protect and fulfil the rights of children, including protecting them from taking direct part in hostilities. In 2003, the country also ratified the Optional Protocol to the CRC on the involvement of children in armed conflict. Aimed at ending the recruitment

---

11 The US Army Special Forces Sergeant Nathan R Chapman was gunned down by a 14 years old Afghan boy. D.E. Sanger, 'Bush, On Offence, Says He will Fight to Keep Tax Cut', *New York Times*, 6 January 2002.

12 UN Doc. S/2015/336 dated 15 May 2015(Reporting period: 1 September 2010 to 31 December 2014).

and use of children, it contains an extensive set of obligations applicable to states. A presidential decree criminalizing underage recruitment into the Afghan National Security Forces (ANSF) was passed and signed by the President in February 2015. Afghanistan has not ratified ILO Convention 29 concerning forced labour, but it is a party to ILO Convention 138 concerning the Minimum Age for Admission to Employment and ILO Convention 182 concerning the Prohibition and Immediate Action for the Elimination of the Worst Forms of Child Labour. Afghanistan is also a party to the Rome Statute of the International Criminal Court (ICC), which codifies the war crime of conscripting or enlisting children under the age of 15 years or using them to participate actively in hostilities.

Recruitment to the Afghan security forces is voluntary and the minimum age for joining is 18 years.[13] The ANSF are composed of all government security forces, including the Afghan National Army, the Afghan Air Force, the Afghan National Police (ANP), the Afghan Local Police (ALP) and the National Directorate of Security. In 2011, the Government of Afghanistan entered into an action plan with the United Nations to end and prevent the recruitment and use of children by the ANSF. However, the ANP[14] and the ALP have recruited and used children in armed conflict. Weak implementation of vetting procedures and the formation of unofficial ALP units continue to result in underage recruitment.

The recruitment and use of children by the ANSF is related to a number of factors, like honour and patriotism. However, the primary reason that children join is economic difficulty. On an average, an ALP officer receives a monthly salary of 6,000–9,000 Afghanis (US$103–155), as well as 4,000 Afghanis (US$69) for food and training. An ANP officer may receive a

---

13 Afghanistan's national law prohibits the recruitment of children under 18 years of age into the armed forces through Directive no. 30 of 2008, which states that the age of conscription to the armed services is a minimum of 18 years of age. The other legal provisions prevents the recruitment of underage children to the police force; and a decree 2003, which prohibits the recruitment of children below the age of 18 years into the armed forces. In February 2015, President Ashraf Ghani signed a decree that criminalizes underage recruitment into the ANSF.

14 Placed under the Ministry of the Interior, the Afghan National Police is the primary law enforcement agency. It also takes part in military operations with other elements of the Afghan National Security Forces. The Afghan National Police comprises five pillars: uniformed (civilian) police, national civil order police, border police, anti-crime police and enabling forces. By the end of 2014, there were 156,751 Afghan National Police, against a target of 157,000.

monthly salary of 10,000–18,000 Afghanis (US$172–310).[15] The absence of educational opportunities and alternative vocational avenues and a steady source of income compels children to join the ANSF. Children are also attracted to the status that comes with having access to motorcycles, guns and walkie-talkies, a fact which is known to often be exploited by commanders. Formal recruitment apart, the informal association of children with the ANP often begins with volunteering as support staff, sometimes to support the work of their older male siblings who are official police officers. These children perform a range of functions, such as working as cooks and orderlies.[16]They are provided basic weapons training before being allowed to handle weapons.

It was reported that 159 children were recruited and used by the ANSF during the period 1 September 2010 to 31 December 2014. Children were recruited formally into the ranks of the ANP and ALP or were used in various support roles, including as porters, messengers and spies, often endangering their lives. For example, in March 2013, a 15-year-old boy was wounded in the district of Sirkani in Kunar province in an improvised explosive device (IED) explosion while carrying water to an Afghan National Army checkpoint. In November 2012, in the district of Shah Joy in Zabul province, Afghan National Police forced two boys, of the ages of 12 and 14 years, respectively, to inspect a suspicious bag for possible explosives. The bag contained an IED that killed both children.[17]

The NSAGs consisting of Taliban forces and affiliated groups, including the *Tora Bora* Front, the *Jamat Sunat al-Dawa Salafia* and the *Latif Mansur* Network, have been involved in the recruitment and use of children.[18] These

---

15 Ongoing Recruitment and Use of Children by Parties to the Armed Conflict in Afghanistan, Child Soldier International, March 2016, p. 4-5.

16 Michael Vinay Bhatia and Mark Sedra, *Afghanistan, Arms and Conflict: Armed Groups, Disarmament and Security in a Postwar Society*, Contemporary Security Studies, 2008.

17 UN Doc. S/2015/336 dated 15 May 2015, para 22.

18 The UN Secretary-General's 2014 annual report on children and armed conflict lists the *Haqqani* network, *Hezb-e-Islami* of *Gulbuddin Hekmatyar* and the *Taliban* forces, including the *Tora Bora* Front, the *Jamat Sunat al-Dawa Salafia* and the *Latif Mansur* network, as parties that recruit and use children in hostilities. These armed groups are considered persistent perpetrators since they have been continually named since 2010. Nearly 30,000–35,000 Taliban fighters are active in most provinces of Afghanistan. In most provinces, the Taliban has established shadow administrative structures. With the withdrawal of the International Security Assistance Force (ISAF) in 2014, the group has shifted tactics to assaults of a larger scale, primarily targeting the Afghan National Security Forces and government officials.

groups are considered to be relentless perpetrators of grave violations against children. They have been responsible for the killing and maiming of children, and have used them for attacks on schools and hospitals. In 2014, the NSAGs recruited and used 556 boys and four girls. Most of them were used to manufacture, transport and plant IEDs. For example, in September 2013, in Gardez city in the province of Paktya, six boys were wounded when the IED they were assembling detonated inside a madrassa. In a separate incident, on 23 August 2014, in Ghazni city, the Taliban used three boys, aged six, eight and ten, to unknowingly transport pressure-plate IEDs in a wheelbarrow. Two boys were killed and one injured when the IEDs detonated prematurely.

The Taliban and other armed opposition groups also recruited and used children to conduct suicide attacks. Twenty boys have been killed carrying out suicide attacks since September 2010. For example, on 9 February 2014, in the province of Paktika, a 14-year-old boy detonated his explosives near a police checkpoint, killing himself and injuring five ANP officers and six civilians. The Taliban claimed responsibility for the attack in the local media. In October 2012, according to witnesses interviewed by the United Nations in the district of Tirin Kot in the Uruzgan province, a suspected member of the Taliban forced a boy to push a bicycle-borne IED towards an Afghan National Army vehicle, killing himself and eight civilians. On 11 December 2014, a 16-year-old boy was killed when he detonated his suicide vest at the French Institute inside a high school in Kabul, an attack for which the Taliban claimed responsibility.[19] In January 2014, a 10-year-old Afghan girl named Spozhmai was apprehended wearing a suicide vest. She had been beaten by her father and brother, who was a member of the Taliban, and was forced to carry out the attack after being told that she "would not die".[20]

In April 2007, the Taliban released a video of a 12-year-old boy beheading a Pakistani man accused of spying. Asked why they had used a boy, a Taliban official was reported to say, "We want to tell the non-Muslims that our youngsters are also *Mujahideens* [holy warriors] and fight with us against you.... These youngsters will be our Holy War commanders in the future and continue the jihad for freedom. Islam allows boys and women to do jihad against occupying non-Muslim troops and their spies and puppets."[21]

---

19 UN Doc. S/2015/336 dated 15 May 2015, para 21.

20 Suicide Vest Nine-year-old tells her Story, *BBC*, 13 January 2014, available at: http://www. bbc.uk/news/magzine-25711953.

21 Taliban video of boy executioner causes anger, Reuters, 26 April 2007, available at: www.

In Afghanistan and Pakistan, suicide bombers are recruited in a number of ways, but one of the most common is through madrassas linked to militant groups. A number of reports suggest that Pakistani madrassas are a common recruiting ground for the Taliban and other militant groups. In fact, the Taliban has been the product of Pakistani madrassas and the latter have periodically provided large numbers of recruits to replenish the Taliban's ranks. In addition to madrassas, other schools, refugee camps and orphanages have been recruitment targets.[22] The members of the NSAGs and the ANSF have abducted children for various purposes, including reprisal, ransom, punishment of the victim's family members, sexual abuse, and recruitment and use as child soldiers. During the reporting period of September 2010 to December 2014, 111 incidents of abduction, involving 242 children, who included seven girls, were reported. During the same period, the Taliban and other armed groups were responsible for 44 incidents of abduction, involving 80 boys and five girls. A number of these children have been victims of sexual abuse by members of the ANP, ALP, as well as the Taliban and the Haqqani Network.[23] In addition, the NSAGs have been responsible for a large number of attacks against hospitals and persons associated with hospitals. The number of abductions of humanitarian personnel increased in 2014, when nearly 100 de-miners, 22 health personnel and four humanitarian staff members were abducted. The members of the Taliban and the Haqqani Network were also responsible for indirect and targeted attacks on the convoys and compounds of humanitarian agencies, including the UN. Sexual abuse of children has been reported in the context of *bacha bazi* (dancing boys) and is considered a deeply ingrained cultural tradition in some areas in Afghanistan.[24]

---

alertnet.org. Also see: *Child Soldiers: Global Report 2008*, The Coalition to Stop the Use of Child Soldiers, p.41.

22 Wilkey Nicholas, Suicide Attacks in Afghanistan and Pakistan, unpublished thesis, University of Adelaide, April 2014, pp. 52–53.

23 For example, in March 2014, the ANP arrested a member of the ALP for allegedly raping a 7-year-old boy. The primary court sentenced the perpetrator to 10 years' imprisonment. In June 2014, the appellate court in the same province confirmed the decision of the primary court, but the sentence was reduced to five years of imprisonment by the Supreme Court in November 2014. In a separate incident, in December 2014, two members of the ALP abducted and raped a 15-year-old girl in Kapisa province. UN Doc. S/2015/336 dated 15 May 2015, para 36.

24 The UN has expressed serious concern over the practice of *bacha bazi*, generally associated with sexual exploitation of and various forms of sexual violence against boys as young as six years old by men in positions of power. In August 2014, following a national inquiry into its causes and negative consequences, the Afghanistan Independent Human Rights Commission recommended that the impunity with which the practice was carried out be

The state's responsibility to protect children from involvement in armed conflict does not end with its official armed forces or with those armed groups that are "associated" with or "allied" to the state. Article 4.2 of the OP to CRC defines the responsibility of states to prevent recruitment by armed groups. Specifically, states are required to "take all feasible measures to prevent" the recruitment and use of children by such groups. In addition to the international law obligations binding on states, international human rights law increasingly recognizes that where non-state actors, such as the *Taliban*, exercise *de facto* control over territory, they are bound by certain international human rights obligations.

The Central African Republic

The CAR is rich in diamonds, gold, oil and uranium, but its population of 4.6 millions is one of the world's poorest. The CAR is a landlocked, geographical region of the African continent, surrounded by countries that have seen prolonged armed conflict, including Sudan, Chad and the DRC. Having endured five coups and multiple rebellions since independence from France in 1960, violence in the CAR is complex. The CAR is currently experiencing a quasi-sectarian conflict between Muslims and non-Muslims, primarily Christians and animists. Terrorist groups, such as the Lord's Resistance Army (LRA) and the militant Islamist group, Boko Haram, operate along the borders of the CAR and within the CAR. There have been a number of unsuccessful efforts to build a sustainable peace, such as the Liberville agreement in January 2013 and the Brazzaville agreement in July 2014.[25]

In March 2013, the country descended into chaos when a mainly Muslim Seleka rebel alliance ousted the President.[26] Since the overthrow of the

---

urgently addressed. UN Doc. S/2015/336 dated 15 May 2015, para 39.

25 Tranchik Rachel, Child Soldiers: Creative Disruption and Reintegration, p. 3, available at: https://american.edu/sis/practica/upload/S15-AfP-Creative-Disruption_Child-Soldiers. pdf.

26 The successful 24 March 2013 overthrow of President Bozize marked the end of the first phase of the crisis. Despite the presence of a reinforced MICOPAX peacekeeping force and Chadian soldiers, the Seleka encountered little resistance in their final drive towards the capital. The rebels passed Damara, which had previously been declared a "red line" on the way to Bangui by a MICOPAX commander, without a fight. As they entered Bangui on 24 March, the Seleka engaged South African forces, deployed as part of a security pact between Bozize and South African President Jacob Zuma, and killed 13 soldiers. Twenty-three South African soldiers allegedly did not engage with the Seleka as a result of the large number of child soldiers in their ranks. The result of the losses was that the South African government immediately withdrew its military presence. Cinq-Mars Evan, Too little, too

government by the Seleka rebel movement, the northern and western regions of the country have seen intense and unprecedented violence against civilians and minorities. Violence in and around Bangui escalated in December 2013, when the anti-balaka militia attacked the ex-Seleka. Children were critically affected by a new outbreak of violence in September 2015 between former Seleka elements, anti-balaka elements and members of the former Central African military. According to Save the Children, an estimated 6,000–10,000 Central African children were associated with many of the armed groups as of December 2014.[27]

The United Nations documented 40 cases of the recruitment and use of children in the year 2015 by the LRA, the former Seleka faction and Union for Peace in Central Africa (UPC). There were also reports of abduction of children by the armed groups.[28] Children have been used as combatants, messengers, informants and cooks. Girls were also used as sex slaves. A number of children were used for manning checkpoints and barricades alongside armed individuals. In addition, suspected anti-balaka elements used children as shields as they fired at the United Nations Multidimensional Integrated Stabilization Mission in the CAR (MINUSCA) forces.[29] Amid renewed clashes, some one million people were internally displaced between September 2016 and February 2017. Violence continues, in spite of the presence of a UN peacekeeping force in the country.

The Special Representative of the Secretary-General for Children and Armed Conflict has reported that during the period January 2011 to

---

late: Failing to prevent atrocities in the Central African Republic, Global Centre for the Responsibility to Protect, Occasional Paper Series, No. 7, September 2015.

27 Children are involved in conflict for a number of intertwined economic, social and political reasons. In many conflict-affected areas, there are a number of orphaned and vulnerable children due to years of violence, disease, and death. With no one caring for these children, they may be forced into participating through coercion, kidnapping, false promises, or drugs. CAR: Four times More Children Associated with Armed Groups, Two Years after the Outbreak of the Crisis, Save the Children International, 18 December 2014.

28 According to a UN report, a total of 52 children were verified as having been abducted in 2015: 25 by the LRA, 15 by anti-balaka elements and the remainder by unidentified armed men. More allegations involving LRA were received but could not be verified. While the children abducted by LRA were used as porters or looters or for sexual purposes, abductions by anti-balaka elements were mainly for ransom. Report of the Secretary General on Children in Armed Conflict, UN Doc A/70/70-S/2016/360 dated 20 April 2016, para 38.

29 Report of the Secretary General on Children in Armed Conflict, UN Doc. A/70/70-S/2016/360 dated 20 April 2016, para 34-43.

December 2015, children suffered serious violations and abuses in the armed conflict in the CAR at the hands of the parties to the conflict. There has been a significant increase in the recruitment and use of children by armed groups, the killing and maiming of children in brutal reprisal attacks, and the occurrence of rape and other forms of sexual violence against children. In addition, there have been numerous cases of the abduction of children, committed largely by the LRA. There were a few allegations of sexual exploitation and abuse by United Nations peacekeepers and non-United Nations forces against children in the CAR.[30]

On 5 May 2015, 10 armed groups,[31] including factions of the ex-Seleka and anti-Balaka, signed an agreement to end and prevent the recruitment and use of children, release all children associated with them, and develop and implement action plans in cooperation with the United Nations. It has been reported that command orders issued by the RPRC and the UPC factions of the ex-Seleka to prohibit the recruitment and use of children have led to the release of children from their ranks.

The CAR is a state party to the Rome Statute of the ICC. On 30 May 2014, the national authorities referred the situation in the CAR (since 1 August 2012) to the ICC. The Office of the Prosecutor of the ICC announced on 24 September 2014 that an investigation had been initiated into the alleged perpetration of war crimes and crimes against humanity, including the use of children in armed combat, by all parties (including the ex-Seleka and anti-Balaka groups). The government of the CAR must strengthen the national justice system and establish a special criminal court to prosecute those responsible for committing crimes against children in armed conflict.

Colombia

The Colombian armed conflict, which started in the mid-1960s between the Colombian government, paramilitary groups, crime syndicates and several

---

30 Working Group on Children and Armed Conflict, Conclusions on children and armed conflict in the Central African Republic, UN Doc. S/AC.51/2016/3 dated 19 December 2016.

31 The 10 groups which signed the commitment were the anti-Balaka faction; the Front Démocratique pour le progrès de la Centrafrique (FDPC); Front populaire pour la renaissance de la Centrafrique (FPRC); Mouvement des libérateurscentrafricains pour la justice (MJLC); Rassemblementpatriotique pour le renouveau de la Centrafrique (RPRC); Révolution et justice (RJ); Selekarénovée; Unité du peuplecentrafricain (UPC); Union des Forces républicaines (UFR); and Union des forces républicainesfondamentales (UFRF).

guerilla groups, has resulted in countless human rights violations and war crimes. Despite its duration and destructiveness, there is no consensus on the 'causes' of the Colombian conflict. There has been a transformation in the armed conflict over time and it does not revolve around a single issue or two opposing sides, but has instead been defined by changing local, regional and national dynamics and different historical processes. Violence carried out by leftist guerrilla groups, illegal right-wing paramilitary groups, and Colombia's armed forces have led to the death and displacement of tens of thousands of people. Terror attacks, kidnappings, killings, the recruitment of children for combat, rape and sexual assault, and countless other crimes have been common war tactics in the history of this armed conflict.[32]

In the Columbian conflict, out of every four irregular combatants, at least one has been a child soldier. These children, mostly from poor families, fight an adult war. Often, child combatants have only the barest understanding of the purpose of the conflict. They fight against other children whose background is very similar to their own, and whose economic situation and future prospects are equally bleak. With much in common in civilian life, children become the bitterest of enemies in war.[33] There are no precise data on the number of child combatants in Colombia. In 2003, the Human Rights Watch collated information provided by the child soldiers and concluded that the total number of child combatants in Colombia was likely to exceed 11,000.[34]

---

32 The victims of crimes in Colombia are mostly vulnerable groups of women, farmers, unionists, and indigenous and Afro-Colombian communities. They often find themselves caught in the middle of armed conflict, and must choose between supporting or joining one of the armed groups for protection and survival, or fleeing to urban slums where they encounter massive unemployment. Human rights defenders, judges, lawyers and political leaders who fight and speak out against these terrorizing groups are also common targets: this impedes vocal opposition against the militant groups and delays the process of seeking justice. It is not always clear who the perpetrators of crimes are since the members of guerilla groups, paramilitary groups and Colombian armed forces all commit human rights violations, and often collaborate with each other. Officially, the members of the Revolutionary Armed Forces of Colombia (FARC) and the National Liberation Army (ELN) are the main perpetrators of the human rights violations. Right-wing paramilitary groups, who have also contributed significantly to abuses, have been losing power in recent years after being demobilized by former President Uribe's administration.

33 You Will Learn Not to Cry: Child Combatants in Colombia, Human Rights Watch, 2003, p. 4.

34 Although no official statistics exist about how many children have been recruited by illegal armed groups in Colombia, the debates range on numbers between 5,000 and 14,000 children. Saenz Margarita Maria, Reintegration of Children Associated with Armed

Child soldiers in Colombia have been nicknamed "little bells" by the military, which uses them as expendable sentries, and "little bees" by the FARC guerrillas, because they "sting" their enemies before the enemies know they are under attack. In urban militias, they are called "little carts", as they can sneak weapons through checkpoints without suspicion. These child guerrillas are used to collect intelligence, make and deploy mines, and serve as advance troops in ambush attacks against paramilitaries, soldiers and police officers.[35]

National Recruitment Law and Practice

The minimum age for recruitment to the armed forces is 18 years, established by Law 418 of 1997 for conscription and Law 548 of 1999 for voluntary recruitment. However, the government's 2005 declaration on the ratification of the Optional Protocol to the CRC mentioned an exception to recruitment legislation. The declaration stated that "minors in age" could be recruited with the consent of their parents. The recruitment of children into illegal armed groups was an offence under the criminal code, with prison sentences of between 6–10 years, in addition to a fine. Law 418 of 1997 (Article 14) also prohibited the recruitment of children by armed forces or armed groups, with a penalty of up to five years' imprisonment.[36] Government security forces did not officially recruit children under 18 years of age, but continued to use captured children for intelligence-gathering, despite the legal prohibition of the practice.

Laws on the membership of armed groups and the use of children for intelligence-gathering appeared to be contradictory. The Childhood and Adolescence Code expressly prohibited the use of demobilized children for intelligence-gathering activities. However, Decree 128 of 2003 stated that

---

Groups in Colombia, Harvard Graduate School of Education, 2012, p. 4.

35 Singer PW, Child Soldiers: New Faces of War, available at: https://www.brookings.edu/wp-content/uploads/2016/06/singer20051215.pdf, accessed 25 April 2017.

36 In Colombia, 16-year-olds could enter air force training programs and 17-year-olds could train with the national army as non-commissioned officers in the infantry. Students could also enrol as cadets in military secondary-schools, where they carried out "special" military service from years 4 to 6, including 1,300 hours of military training and participation in military exercises. Government programs such as "soldiers for a day" and "peasant soldiers" aimed to familiarize children with the "war dynamic". The Committee on the CRC considered Colombia's Third Periodic Report on the Convention on the Rights of the Child in June 2006. In its concluding observations the Committee called on the government to take effective measures to prevent the recruitment and involvement of children in armed groups. Child Soldiers: Global Report 2008, Coalition to Stop the Use of Child Soldiers, p. 99–105.

children could be used for activities related to intelligence work (Article 22), and could be financially rewarded for supplying information (Article 9). Law 782 of 2002 stated that a child could be recognized as belonging to an armed group only by the spokesperson of the group in question or as a result of evidence provided by the child (Article 53). Laws and the implementation of regulations on demobilization treated children recruited by illegal armed groups primarily as victims of violence, requiring special care and protection. Law 782 of 2002 defined children involved in armed groups as victims of the armed conflict rather than as combatants (Article 15). In March 2005, the Constitutional Court handed down Judgment 203, which revoked another provision of Law 782 that allowed the prosecution of minors involved in armed groups (Article 19). However, under the Childhood and Adolescence Code, prosecution for the membership of, or for acts committed during the membership of, an armed group could be waived for all but the most serious acts—those "which may constitute grave breaches of international humanitarian law, crimes against humanity or genocide under the Rome Statute".

At a February 2007 ministerial meeting in Paris, Colombia endorsed the Paris Commitments to protect children from unlawful recruitment or use by armed forces or armed groups and the Paris Principles and guidelines on children associated with armed forces or armed groups. In Colombia, children are not formally recruited into the armed forces, but there are reports that they have been used for military purposes, including intelligence-gathering and as human shields.[37]

Armed Groups Responsible for Recruitment of Child Soldiers

In Colombia, three main armed groups are known to have used children and youth as informers and in other combatant roles.

(a) Revolutionary Armed Forces of Colombia-People's Army (FARC-EP): The FARC-EP is the oldest and largest group among Colombia's left-wing rebels, and one of the world's richest and most powerful guerrilla armies. The group was founded in 1964, when it declared its intention to use armed struggle to overthrow the government and instal a Marxist regime. But its tactics changed in the 1990s, as right-wing paramilitary forces intensified their attacks on the

---

37 For more details see: Louder than Words: An agenda for Action to End State Use of Child Soldiers, Child Soldier International, 2012.

guerrilla group, and the FARC-EP became increasingly involved in the drug trade and other illicit activities to raise money for its military campaign. The FARC is governed by a secretariat and is estimated to have 18,000 fighters. The group is known to actively recruit child soldiers, although the precise number is unknown. In 2016, the FARC-EP has made public a commitment to ending the recruitment of children under 18 years of age.

(b) Camilist Union-Army of National Liberation (UC-ELN): This left-wing group was formed in 1965 by intellectuals inspired by the Cuban revolution. The ELN is behind many kidnappings in Colombia, and abducts hundreds of people each year to finance its operations. The group has focused on hitting infrastructural targets, such as the oil industry, because it has been unable to take on the security forces directly, like the FARC. Members justify kidnapping as a legitimate way of fund-raising for what they say is their campaign for improved social justice and human rights. The group is not involved in the drug trade to the same extent as the FARC, partly because of the moral objections of an influential former leader. The ELN reached the height of its power in the late 1990s, but in recent years, has been hit hard by the paramilitaries and Colombian armed forces. The group is thought to have between 3,000 and 5,000 fighters, including child soldiers, although the exact numbers are unknown.

(c) United Self-Defence Groups of Colombia (AUC): This right-wing umbrella group was formed in 1997 by drug-traffickers and landowners. The main aim of the AUC has been to combat kidnapping and extortion by guerrillas and to maintain the economic and political status quo in the country. The AUC has its roots in the paramilitary armies built by the drug lords in the 1980s, and it claims that it took to arms in self-defence, in the place of a powerless state. However, many see it as a violent drugs cartel in charge of a significant chunk of the illegal drug trade. The AUC has grown in strength and influence over the years due to its links with the army and financing from business interests and landowners. The group has carried out numerous massacres and assassinations in Colombia, often targeting left-wing activists who speak out against them. Negotiations have resulted in the demobilization of nearly 32,000 fighters of the AUC. The other armed groups in Colombia are the Casanare Self-Defence Group (ACC) and Peasant Self-Defence Groups of Cordoba and Uraba (ACCU).

In 2016, the United Nations verified 289 cases of child recruitment and use by armed groups, the majority of which were associated with the FARC-EP (182), ELN (74), and other armed groups (33).[38] A survey among former child soldiers in Colombia indicated that as many as 80 percent had voluntarily enlisted themselves into the armed groups (UNICEF, 2005). However, making a sharp distinction between 'voluntary' and 'coerced' recruitment is not an easy task. In reality, most cases of recruitment take place in the grey zone between voluntary and forced recruitment, and the children make their choice on the basis of the information available at the time of recruitment. In some villages where the guerilla or/and the paramilitary were in control in Colombia, 'voluntarily forced' recruitment was the order of the day. The families were expected to send their sons into combat and the children were told that it was their duty as citizens to protect their local areas.[39]

The Human Rights Watch has interviewed children who were as young as eight when they started to fight. These children had special duties, like ferrying supplies and information, acting as advance early warning guards, or even carrying explosives. By the time they were 13, most had been trained in the use of automatic weapons, grenades, mortars and explosives. In the guerrilla forces, children learn how to assemble and launch gas cylinder bombs. Among the guerrillas and paramilitary forces both, they study the assembly of land mines, known as "foot-breakers", then apply that knowledge by planting deadly killing fields. Usually, their first experience of combat comes soon after.

Children do not risk their lives only in combat. They are also expected to participate in the atrocities that have become a hallmark of the Colombian conflict. From the beginning of their training, both guerrilla and paramilitary child recruits are taught to treat the other side's fighters or sympathizers without mercy. Adults order children to kill, mutilate and torture, conditioning them to commit the most cruel abuses. Not only do

---

38 Children and armed conflict: Report of the Secretary-General, UN Doc. A/70/836-S/2016/360 dated 20 April 2016.

39 Bjorkhaug, I., *Child Soldiers in Colombia: The Recruitment of Children into Non-state Violent Armed Groups.* MICROCON Research Working Paper 27, 2010, Brighton: MICROCON, p. 2.

children face the same treatment should they fall into the hands of the enemy, many fear it from fellow fighters. Children who fail in their military duties or try to desert can face summary execution by comrades, who are sometimes no older than themselves.[40]

Internal armed conflict has a devastating impact on civilians in Colombia. They have been victims of extrajudicial executions, enforced disappearance, death threats, anti-personnel mines, indiscriminate attacks and forcible displacement in large numbers. Children formed a high proportion of the victims, in part because fighting forces at times operated in and near schools and other places where children were likely to gather. In one case, in March 2006, army troops took up positions in a village school near Puerto Asis, Putumayo, causing families to leave their homes after the FARC announced that it would attack the site. In June 2006, the Representative of the UN Secretary-General on the Human Rights of Internally Displaced Persons observed that "the armed forces had installed their headquarters in the middle of the village [of Toribo, Cauca], next to a primary school, and had erected posts in the central square of town immediately next to a playground and a church centre".[41]

The situation in Colombia has been changing in the recent past. Armed violence between the FARC-EP and the government forces reached its lowest level in 50 years and displacement decreased following the unilateral ceasefire declared by the FARC-EP and the suspension of aerial bombings by the government. Nevertheless, the activities of the ELN and post-demobilization armed groups continued to cause forced displacement. Substantial progress has been made in the peace talks between the Government of Colombia and the FARC-EP. In February 2016, the group announced that it would stop recruiting children under 17 years of age and intended to release children

---

40 Adriana, a child soldier in Colombia, as stated to Human Rights Watch: "I escaped one day during the day. I had left all my weapons behind. I was on guard duty and I snuck away. They caught me after an hour. The militia recognized me, even though I had changed into civilian clothes. I cried when they caught me. I begged them to let me go. They chained me up with a metal chain. I couldn't move my arms. At the war council, I wasn't allowed to talk. But luckily, they voted not to kill me. Instead, they made me dig twenty meters of trenches, make twenty trips to get wood, and ordered me tied to a pole for two weeks. I had to give a talk in front of everyone, explaining why I had tried to desert, why I had made this mistake." You Will Learn Not to Cry: Child Combatants in Colombia, Human Rights Watch, 2003, p. 4.

41 Child Soldiers: Global Report 2008, Coalition to Stop the Use of Child Soldiers, p. 99–105.

under 15 years of age from its ranks.[42] The Special Representative of the Secretary-General for Children and Armed Conflict has been in contact with the Government of Colombia and the FARC-EP. In May 2016, she witnessed the signing of an agreement on the separation of children from conflict and the commitment to develop a comprehensive special care programme. Through this agreement, the parties have shown their commitment to prioritizing the principles of the best interest of the child and ensuring their treatment as victims. [43]

Democratic Republic of the Congo

The DRC[44] has been at war since 1996. The civil war started from the leftovers of the war in Rwanda. More than 20 years after the beginning of the civil war, the use of child soldiers in that area is not a topic much debated in international forums. The DRC is one of the five countries in the Great Lakes region[45] that are seriously affected by armed conflict. In the DRC, the

---

42 Children and armed conflict: Report of the Secretary-General, UN Doc. A/70/836-S/2016/360 dated 20 April 2016.

43 After the results of the plebiscite on the final peace agreement, the parties reiterated their commitment to continuing to implement confidence-building measures of a humanitarian nature, including the separation of children from the camps of the FARC-EP. Since the signing of a revised agreement on 24 November 2016, efforts have continued to ensure prioritization of the separation and reintegration of all underage children associated with the FARC-EP and to put in place guarantees of non-repetition to prevent re-recruitment by other armed actors. As requested by the parties, the Office of the Special Representative continues to act in support of the process as an observer and guarantor. Considering the political and practical challenges ahead, the Special Representative will pursue her advocacy to emphasize the urgent need to bring protection and peace to the children of Colombia. Annual Report of the Special Representative of the Secretary-General for Children and Armed Conflict, UN Doc A/HRC/34/44 dated 22 December 2016.

44 The DRC has had a tumultuous history that is categorized by conflicts and the many times that the name of the country has changed. It was formerly a Belgian colony from 1908 that led to independence in 1960 and political and social instability came along. In 1965, Colonel Joseph Mobutu declared himself president through a coup, changed the name to Zaire, and stayed president for 32 years. In 1994 the well-known ethnic cleansing in Rwanda took place, which led to many refugees coming to Zaire. In May 1997 Mobutu was removed in a rebellion led by Laurent Kabila with support from Rwanda and Uganda; he renamed the country to its current name. In August 1998 Kabila was attacked himself by a rebellion again with support from Rwanda and Uganda. Troops from Angola, Chad, Namibia, Sudan and Zimbabwe backed Kabila's regime, but in 2001 he was assassinated and his son Joseph Kabila was named as the new president. The constitutional mandate of Kabila was due to expire on 20 December 2016, but has been extended until the end of 2017.

45 The other countries are Burundi, the CAR, Rwanda and Uganda.

governments as well as NSAGs are responsible for the recruitment and use of children in armed conflict. Most armed groups involved in the conflict have had children in their ranks and in certain groups, children may even make up the majority. According to an estimate, 30,000–35,000 Congolese children, from small children to young adults of the age of 17 years, have directly participated in the conflict in the DRC. Many children have been abducted and forced to join the NSAGs. Economic exclusion is also responsible for others to join of the armed forces.

Legal Obligations

The military recruitment and use of children in hostilities in the DRC is prohibited under national laws. Under the Constitution, all forms of exploitation of children are prohibited and the maintenance of "youth armies" is forbidden. The Child Protection Act, 2009, has strengthened legal protection for children, including in relation to their involvement in armed conflict. The Act specifically prohibits and criminalizes the recruitment and use of children in armed forces or armed groups. The Child Protection Act also proscribes a range of abuses to which children associated with the Mai Mai, a NSAG, are routinely subjected, such as abduction; incitement to acts of violence; torture; sexual violence and sexual slavery. In addition, the Act defines the State's responsibility for separating children from armed forces or armed groups, facilitating their reintegration, and for guaranteeing protection, education and care to all children affected by armed conflict.

A range of other national laws also prohibit the involvement of children in armed conflict. These include the Defence and Armed Forces Law No. 04/023, 2004 and the Labour Code, 2002. The former prohibits the maintenance of a subversive group of youth or a youth army, while the latter proscribes the worst forms of child labour, including the forced or obligatory recruitment of children with a view to using them in armed conflicts.

The DRC is party to international human rights instruments, including the Convention on the Rights of the Child and its Optional Protocol on the involvement of children in armed conflict, which prohibits the recruitment or use in hostilities of persons under the age of 18 years by armed groups. The DRC has also ratified International Labour Organization (ILO) Convention No. 182 on the Worst Forms of Child Labour, which prohibits and abolishes the use of children in armed conflict. While the legal framework is broadly in place, the political will to implement it is lacking and the institutional capacity too weak to protect children from exploitation. A number of cases relating to child recruitment and use and other serious abuses against children in the context of armed conflict have been brought to trial. However, the investigations and prosecutions have remained ineffective.

Recruitment and Use of Child Soldiers

According to the Secretary General's report, various actors in the conflict including foreign armed groups and the local militia have recruited or abducted children and deployed them as soldiers. The list of State armed forces and NSAGs includes the: (i) Allied Democratic Forces (ADF), (ii) Armed Forces of the Democratic Republic of the Congo, (iii) Democratic Forces for the Liberation of Rwanda (FDLR), (iv) Forces de résistance patriotiquesen Ituri (FRPI), (v) Lord's Resistance Army, (vi) Mayi Mayi Alliance des patriotes pour un Congo libre et souverain "Colonel Janvier", (vii) Union des patriotescongolais pour la paix (UPCP), also known as MayiMayi "Lafontaine", (viii) Mayi Mayi Simba, (ix) Mayi Mayi Kata Katanga, (x) Nduma Defence of Congo/Cheka, (xi) Mayi Mayi Nyatura, and (xii) Raia Mutomboki.[46] A number of the NSAGs have been responsible for subjecting children to rape and other forms of sexual violence. Some of these parties are considered persistent perpetrators. Once abducted, the children are brutalized and forced to serve as soldiers, porters, and in the case of girls, sex slaves.[47] More than 35,000 children have been demobilized from Congo's battlefields. It is estimated that nearly 8,000 may still be with armed groups in the DRC. Approximately 40 per cent of child soldiers in the DRC are estimated to be girls.[48]

---

46 Children and Armed Conflict: report of the secretary General, UN Doc A/70/836-S/2016/360 dated 20 April 2016.

47

48 The dire situation of returning girl soldiers and their children has been consistently documented for nearly 15 years. Girl soldiers have almost inevitably been subjected to sexual violence or slavery. Some of them have had children while with the armed group. Many girls are subsequently stigmatized or excluded by their community for "having known men"; many are not accepted back into their homes and schools. A large proportion of these girls receive little to no assistance in rehabilitation. "If I Could Go To School..." Education as a tool to prevent the recruitment of girls and assist with their recovery and reintegration in the Democratic Republic of Congo, Child Soldier International, p. 2. Also see: Nduwimana Donatien, Reintegration of Child Soldiers in Eastern Democratic Republic of Congo: Challenges and Prospects, Occasional paper series 4, Number 2, International Peace Support Training Centre, Kenya, 2013, p. 8.

According to a UN report, the security situation in eastern DRC was volatile in 2015, and was marked by military operations by the armed forces of the DRC (FARDC) against the FDLR, the ADF, the FRPI and other armed groups. The situation deteriorated further owing to the activities of armed groups and inter-communal clashes. The UN verified that there were 2,549 violations against children in the year 2015. It also verified that 488 children (26 girls) were newly recruited. Of these, 30 per cent were under 15 years of age when recruited. In 2015, at least 80 children were killed and 56 maimed, with most incidents occurring in North Kivu and Ituri. Armed groups were responsible for the 254 incidents of sexual abuse against children. Allegations of sexual exploitation and abuse of children involving members of MONUSCO military contingents from South Africa and the United Republic of Tanzania were also reported.[49]

During the period 1 January 2012 to 31 August 2013, MONUSCO documented the recruitment of 996 children, including 79 girls, into more than 25 armed groups in the DRC. In the majority of cases, children were abducted and forced to join the group. Others joined voluntarily after they were promised money, education, jobs or other benefits by the recruiters. The children were used as porters, cooks, spies, sex slaves, guards or combatants, and were reportedly often subjected to intensive military training. Minors formerly associated with certain NSAGs were deployed to bury the bodies of adults and children who died on the battlefield during clashes with the FARDC or other armed groups. Girls faced specific challenges during their association with armed groups. Many were subjected to rape and other sexual violence, making them vulnerable to early motherhood and sexually transmitted diseases. Their status as concubines of armed group combatants upon their return to their communities prevented many from escaping the group and returning home.[50]

LRA and Child Recruitment

The LRA usually separated children from the adult abductees soon after capture and forced them to undergo military training. Through mind control methods, sheer brutality and instilling fear, the LRA has been able to turn

---

49 Children and Armed Conflict: report of the secretary General, UN Doc A/70/836-S/2016/360 dated 20 April 2016, para 44-57.

50 Martin Kobler, Child Recruitment by Armed Groups in DRC period: 2012 – 2013, The United Nations Organization Stabilization Mission in the Democratic Republic of the Congo (MONUSCO), 24 October 2013.

nine- to 15-year-old boys and girls into killers. The children are dabbed with "magic" oils, which they are told will make them a member of the LRA and will prevent them from being harmed by bullets. One of the most brutal forms of violence used by the LRA is to force children to kill other children. Usually the victim is a child who has disobeyed the rules. Other children are then ordered to surround the victim in a circle and take turns beating the child on the head with a large wooden stick until the child is dead. Girls abducted by the LRA are often forced to become the "wives", or sexual slaves, of LRA combatants. They usually stay with the same combatant during their entire time in captivity. Regular LRA combatants are allowed one "wife", while commanders have numerous "wives" and are given first pick after an abduction operation.[51]

Mai Mai and Child Recruitment

In eastern DRC, the Mai Mai[52] are among the most prolific recruiters and users of children. Their use of child soldiers has remained unaffected in spite of successive peace agreements, and attempts to disarm them or their integration into the armed forces have failed.[53] International initiatives aimed at halting the recruitment and use of children have also failed due to certain firmly established practices among these groups. Many myths surround the Mai Mai, including a belief that their members possess magical protective powers as a result of the performance of rituals such as tattooing and taking hallucinatory potions. This also has particular implications in relation to the recruitment and use of children who, being young and therefore "pure", are regarded as particularly suitable for preparing and administering potions. Commanders use young children as bodyguards because the former are believed to have special powers of protection. The young children are

---

51 Trail of Death: LRA Atrocities in Northeastern Congo, Human Rights Watch, 2010, p. 39-40.

52 The Mai Mai – a collective term referring to a range of local militias. They have been active throughout the Congo's two wars. Mai Mai Child Soldier Recruitment and Use: Entrenched and Unending, Coalition to Stop the Use of Child Soldiers, February 2010, p. 1.

53 The following statement from an armed group leader demonstrates the prevalence of child recruitment and use as entrenched in social attitudes towards children: "They are available as they have nothing else to do, they are extremely obedient to orders, they make few demands which are easy to satisfy and many of them join as virgins which help us preserve the rituals as children perform these on adults." Nduwimana Donatien, Reintegration of Child Soldiers in Eastern Democratic Republic of Congo: Challenges and Prospects, Occasional paper series 4, Number 2, International Peace Support Training Centre, Kenya, 2013, p. 7.

sent into battle to intimidate the enemy by shouting and screaming, or by invoking their so-called powers of magical protection. This naturally exposes them to extreme danger. Children are also made to collect unofficial taxes from the population and to fulfil a range of functions, such as gathering firework, preparing food and carrying water.[54] Girls are frequently abducted, raped and used for sexual purposes by the Mai Mai. Rape of civilian women and children by the Mai Mai during and after armed encounters has also been well documented by the UN and human rights organizations.[55]

Sexual Abuse of Child Soldier in DRC

Currently, the DRC is among those countries in the world that has the largest number of child soldiers, who have been fighting for all armed forces in the civil war since it began. Sexualized violence against boys, including rape, sexual torture, sexual humiliation, mutilation of the genitals, sexual enslavement and forced incest, have been reported in the DRC. Rape and sexual exploitation[56]have become so prevalent in the country that virtually no family has been left untouched. Almost all girls and some boys have reported being raped or sexually exploited by their commanders or other soldiers in the armed group.[57] The rape of young boy soldiers is often accompanied by acts of extreme violence, such as the inflicting of bayonet or gunshot wounds to their genitals.[58] Although very few boys have given detailed accounts of such attacks, several victims have sought treatment at centres assisting victims of sexual violence, such as the MSF clinic, which has several branches throughout the DRC.

The conflict in the DRC is not a classic inter-state conflict because many of the armed groups have foreign roots and have goals that do not

---

54 Mai Mai Child Soldier Recruitment and Use: Entrenched and Unending, Coalition to Stop the Use of Child Soldiers, February 2010.

55 Democratic Republic of Congo: North Kivu, No end to war on women and children,Amnesty International, (AFR62/005/2008), 29 September 2008.

56 'Child sexual exploitation' is defined as a situation in which an individual takes "unfair advantage of some imbalance of power between themselves and another person under the age of 18 in order to sexually use them". O'Connell Davidson, The Sex Exploiter, NGO Group for the Convention on the Rights of the Child, 2001, p. 4.

57 Jessica Nann Madsen, The Sexual Exploitation of Child Soldiers in the DRC: A Victim-Centered Approach Utilizing Human Trafficking Principles, ftp://ftp.repec.org/opt/ReDIF/RePEc/rau/clieui/FA09/CLI-FA09-A8.pdf .

58 DRC: Arming the East, Armed Sexual Violence, Amnesty International, AFR 62, 2005.

necessarily apply to the DRC. There is a blur between war, organized crime and a violation of human rights. It is not a traditional war anymore. New technologies have changed the complexion of the conflict and the use of children is not a taboo in the DRC. Children can perform many tasks and are cheaper than adults, so it is a win–win situation for the leaders of the armed groups.

On 4 October 2012, the government of the DRC and the UN signed an action plan to "halt and prevent the recruitment and use of children, in addition to sexual violence against children, by the national armed forces and security forces". Both agreed on working together through a technical working group in four areas: (i) the separation and protection of children associated with armed forces and groups; (ii) response to child victims; (iii) the prevention of grave violations against children; and (iv) efforts to combat the impunity of the perpetrators. Attempts are being made to resolve the issues in the DRC; however, the NSAGs and the government forces and militia continue to recruit children. The crimes of the recruitment and use of children remain unpunished by the DCR's justice system.[59]

India

The use of children as soldiers by NSAGs (insurgents, rebel groups, extremists, terrorists, Maoists, Naxals, etc.) and government forces is a reality in India. The recruitment of children by various NSAGs and their use in conflicts in the north-eastern states, Jammu and Kashmir, Chhattisgarh, Jharkhand, Orissa and Andhra Pradesh has been a matter of deep concern.[60] Children as young as 8–10 years of age have been kidnapped, forcibly

---

59 The conviction of Thomas Lubanga by the International Criminal Court (ICC) and the ongoing trial of Bosco Ntaganda in the ICC constitute positive developments towards accountability for the crimes of child recruitment and use. However, at the national level, no member of armed forces or groups has been convicted for child recruitment or use.

60 In India, the State of Jammu and Kashmir (J&K) has been affected by terrorist and secessionist violence, sponsored and supported from across the border, for more than two decades. Left Wing Extremism (LWE) remains an area of concern for the internal security of the country. A hundred and six districts in 10 states are affected by LWE to varying degrees, and 35 districts in 7 states are the worst affected. The CPI (Maoist) continues to be the most potent among the various LWE outfits in the country and accounted for more than 80 per cent of all violent incidents and resultant deaths perpetrated by left-wing extremists. Nineteen major extremist/insurgent organizations in the North-east have been declared "unlawful associations" and "terrorist organizations" under the Unlawful Activities (Prevention) Act, 1967. Ministry of Home Affairs, Government of India, Annual Report 2015-16, p. 5, Annexure IV at p. 307.

recruited, and coerced and induced to become child soldiers. One of the most alarming trends is that these children have been used as combatants.

In Jammu and Kashmir, NSAGs have reportedly recruited under-18s and deployed them as combatants.[61]Extremists have used children as suicide bombers to attack police and security forces, and also as shields during stone-pelting. On 19 April 2000, 17-year-old Afaq Ahmed Shah got into a vehicle filled with explosives and drove to the Indian Army command centre in Srinagar, Kashmir. When stopped by guards at the entrance, the teenager detonated a bomb inside the car, wounding four people. He was the first homicide bomber of the Jammu and Kashmiri conflict.[62]In another case, 17-year-old Mohammad Abdulla, along with an accomplice – both members of the extremist group, Lashkar-e-Taiba – carried out an attack on a crowded residential housing complex in Jammu. Within minutes, the two emptied four AK-47 assault rifle magazines – containing 32 rounds each –and detonated five hand grenades, killing 28 people, including eight women and 10 children. When apprehended and questioned by the Indian police, Abdulla replied, "I was not happy about it, but my controllers in Pakistan said it was necessary to establish terror. I had my orders and had to follow them. It was not a question of liking the job but simply executing it."[63]In August 2003, two Kashmiri Muslim boys of the ages of 13 and 17, respectively, were kidnapped at gunpoint by the Lashkar-e-Taiba. The boys are among hundreds of Muslim youths who have been forcibly recruited and trained by various extremists' organizations in the state to commit acts of terror against the Indian military and civilian populations.[64]

The insurgents and terrorists in the north-eastern states have committed serious abuses, including numerous cases of kidnapping, torture, rape,

---

61 India's Child Soldiers: A shadow report to the UN Committee on the Rights of the Child on the Involvement of Children in Armed Conflict, Asian Centre for Human Rights, 2013, p. 9.

62 Robert Marquand, New Faces Join Fray in Kashmir, *Christian Science Monitor*, May 2, 2000. The term suicide bombings could be more aptly called 'homicide bombings' or 'genocide bombings' if one examines the intent of the bombers and their handlers.

63 Rahul Bedi, Schoolboy Recruit who Killed 28 in First Operation, *Telegraph*, 2002, available at: www.newsstuff.0catch.com/article13.htm.

64 Praveen Swami, Jehadi Groups step up Recruitment of Children, *The Hindu*, 9 September 2003, available at: http://www.hinduonnet.com/thehindu/2003/09/20/stories/2003092001231300.htm.

extortion, and the use of child soldiers.[65] There were reports that in 2012, suspected insurgents in Manipur abducted three teenaged boys. Despite a missing-person complaint and a police search, they were never found. In 2012, five teenaged girls laid down arms before the police in the eastern Indian state of Orissa, a stronghold of Maoist rebels. The Ministry of Home Affairs has reported that Maoist groups conscripted boys and girls of the ages of 6–12 years into specific children's units (*Bal Dasta* and *Bal Sangham*) in the states of Bihar, Jharkhand, Chhattisgarh and Odisha.[66] The Maoist groups used the children in combat and intelligence-gathering roles. The insurgents trained them as spies and couriers, as well as in the use of arms, planting explosives and intelligence gathering.

It has been reported that children as young as twelve were members of Maoist youth groups and allied militia. They reportedly handled weapons and improvised explosive devices. The Maoists reportedly held the children against their will, warning them of the prospect of severe reprisals, including the threat of killing their family members, if they attempted to escape. There were reports of girls serving in Maoist groups. The government claimed, on the basis of the statements of several women formerly associated with Maoist

---

65 Many child soldiers have surrendered before the higher authorities of the Government of India. About 568 cadres of the United People's Democratic Front surrendered on 14 December 2011 and about 1,695 members of various armed opposition groups surrendered before the Home Minister and Assam Chief Minister on 24 January 2012. India's Child Soldiers: A shadow report to the UN Committee on the Rights of the Child on the Involvement of Children in Armed Conflict, Asian Centre for Human Rights, 2013, p. 3.

66 Typically, children recruited by such groups would be used to perform supporting roles, as lookouts, messengers, porters, cooks and cleaners, which expose them to risk and hardship. The Naxalites recruit children between ages six and twelve into children's associations called Bal Sangams, where children are trained in Maoist ideology, used as informers, and taught to fight with non-lethal weapons (sticks). Naxalites typically promote children above age 12 to other wings...In sangams, jan militias, and dalams, Naxalites give children weapons training with rifles and teach them to use different types of explosives including landmines...Children in jan militias and dalams participate in armed exchanges with government security forces. ...Children recruited into dalams may not be permitted to leave, and may face severe reprisals, including the killing of family members, if they surrender to the police. Human Rights Watch, Dangerous Duty: Children & the Chhattisgarh Conflict, September 2008, p.6; Also see: Protection of Children's Rights in Areas of Civil Unrest, National Commission for Protection of Child Rights (NCPCR), 2010. The UN Secretary-General's May 2013 Annual Report on 'Children and Armed Conflict' notes that there has been reports of "Naxalites" resorting to "large-scale recruitment of children aged between 6 and 12 years into their so called children's units (*Bal Sanghatans*) in the affected states". UN Secretary-General, Secretary-General's Annual Report on Children and Armed Conflict, UN Doc. S/2013/245, 15 May 2013.

groups, that sexual violence, including rape and other forms of abuse, was a practice in some Maoist camps. According to government sources, Maoist armed groups used children as human shields in confrontations with security forces. The Maoists' attacks on schools continued to affect children's access to education in the affected areas. There are authentic reports that armed groups recruited children from schools in Chhattisgarh.[67] NGOs estimate that at least 2,500 children were associated with insurgent armed groups in Maoist-affected areas.[68] Another report estimates that up to 90,000 children are involved in the ongoing insurgency in Chhattisgarh;[69] the figure, however, appears unrealistic and exaggerated. In the absence of a comprehensive assessment of the scale of recruitment and use of children by armed groups, it is impossible to determine the number affected.[70]

A visit by the members of the National Commission for Protection of Child Rights (NCPCR) to areas of civil unrest revealed that children are recruited by militant groups in different ways. Some are kidnapped, while others are intimidated into joining. Older children may join armed opposition groups after experiencing harassment from government forces. Faced with violence and chaos all around, they decide they are safer with guns in their hands. In some cases, children "choose" to join insurgent groups because it provides them with a livelihood. Children who are poor and marginalized are the ones most likely to be recruited or forced into militant groups or State-supported groups. Adolescent boys are a particular target. The fear

---

67 India 2015, Human Rights Report, Country Reports on Human Rights Practices for 2015, Bureau of Democracy, Human Rights and Labour, United States Department of State, p. 17-18.

68 India 2015, Human Rights Report, Country Reports on Human Rights Practices for 2015, Bureau of Democracy, Human Rights and Labour, United States Department of State, p. 50.

69 Siddiqui A. B. and Siddiqui Nabila, Child Soldiers in India, *International Journal of Advanced Research in Management and Social Sciences*, Vol. 4, No. 4, April 2015, p. 32-44, at p. 38.

70 Lost Childhood: caught in Armed Conflict in Jharkhand, Child Soldier International and HAQ Centre for Child Rights, 2016, p. 20. According to Asian Centre for Human Rights, it is believed that at least 5,000 children i.e. about 1,000 in the North East India and Jammu and Kashmir and about 4,000 in the Left Wing Extremism (LWE) affected areas are involved in the conflicts. This is excluding those who have become adult since their recruitment. All the insurgent groups irrespective of their ideology or origin and place of operation recruit children, not necessarily only for combat purposes. India's Child Soldiers: A shadow report to the UN Committee on the Rights of the Child on the Involvement of Children in Armed Conflict, Asian Centre for Human Rights, 2013, p. 3.

of retaliation prevents them from leaving once they have been involved.[71] Typically, children recruited by such groups are used to perform supporting roles, such as those of lookouts, messengers, porters, cooks and cleaners, which expose them to risk and hardship.[72]

Child Soldiers International documented 40 cases of the recruitment of children by the CPI (Maoist) in Jharkhand from July 2014 to December 2015. In addition, they documented six cases of the rape and sexual abuse of girl child soldiers by CPI (Maoist) cadres in 2015. Their research found that left wing armed groups in Jharkhand were responsible for the following grave violations against children: killing and maiming, recruitment and use as soldiers, abduction, sexual violence and attacks on schools. These constitute five of the 'six grave violations' against children in armed conflict that have been identified by the UN Security Council as requiring priority attention to ensure the protection of children during war.[73]

Left wing armed groups in Jharkhand have killed children, usually those suspected of being police informers, and admit that children as young as ten are recruited into their ranks. Although NSAG leaders have consistently claimed that they do not permit children under 16 to take part in combat operations, the evidence suggests that children as young as 12 take an active part in hostilities, either through direct combat or in support roles. Formal recruitment follows after an undetermined period of working as "informers" comes to an end. Once recruited, the children are brought to camps for weapons training with a promise that they will receive good food and better

---

71 Guddi (a pseudonym) escaped from the CPI (Maoist) after one of her superiors accused her of collaborating with police informers, a 'crime' that the group punishes with death. She was seventeen in 2015, and was recruited in 2004, at barely seven years of age: "I grew up in the organization learning language, science, mathematics and Mao's ideology. Soon I learnt computers and began typing press releases, revolutionary poems, revolutionary messages for posters and banners. As I crossed the age of 12, I was given a chance to choose the weapon I would like to train with. I preferred INSAS [automatic] rifles and carbines," she said. This 17-year-old girl had already spent over a decade in one of the several left wing armed groups operating across 10 states in central India. She ran away after an altercation with one of her superiors, who suspected that she had been communicating with police informers. Terrified that she or her family would face reprisals from the group, she was in hiding at the time of the interview. Lost Childhood: Caught in Armed Conflict in Jharkhand, Child Soldier International and HAQ Centre for Child Rights, 2016, p. 19.

72 Protection of Children's Rights in Areas of Civil Unrest, National Commission for Protection of Child Rights (NCPCR), 2010, p. 40.

73 Lost Childhood: Caught in armed violence in Jharkhand, Child Soldiers International, and HAQ Centre for Child Rights, 2016.

clothes. Children are trained to lay IEDs, the logic being that their relatively small fingers are better able to handle the electronic circuits that trigger bombs. They are provided weapons training and used as porters, lookouts and intelligence gatherers during military operations. The forcible recruitment of children amounts to abduction, with parents too scared to report their children missing for fear of reprisals. The child soldiers are also subjected to sexual abuse. Young girls recruited into the ranks of left wing armed groups are used to entice boys into joining with the promise of opportunities for sexual gratification.[74]

According to the UN report, NSAGs, including the Naxalites, have recruited and used children as young as six years of age in Bihar, Chhattisgarh, Jharkhand, Maharashtra, Odisha and West Bengal. These children were coerced to join children's units (*Bal Dasta*), in which they were trained and used as couriers and informants, to plant IEDs and serve in front-line operations against national security forces.[75] For example, in April, the Bharatiya Communist Party (Maoist) reportedly forced the inhabitants of

---

74 Lost Childhood: Caught in Armed Conflict in Jharkhand, Child Soldier International and HAQ Centre for Child Rights, 2016, p. 5.

75 In India, Maoists have been responsible for the abduction of children and using them as soldiers to fight against the government forces. In reply to a Parliamentary Question, the Ministry of Home Affairs has informed that the Left Wing Extremist (LWE) groups, particularly the CPI (Maoist), has been recruiting minors, both boys and girls, from the tribal belt of LWE affected areas in the states of Bihar, Chhattisgarh, Jharkhand, Maharashtra and Odisha. In Bihar and Jharkhand, these children are enrolled in 'Bal Dasta' and in Chhattisgarh and Odisha, the children's squad is known as 'Bal Sangham'. The idea behind recruiting tribal children is to wean them away from their rich traditional cultural moorings and indoctrinate them into Maoist ideology. Such children are asked to perform multifarious tasks such as acting as informers, fighting with non-lethal weapons like sticks etc. Subsequently, after attaining the age of 12 years, they are branched into other children units like 'Chaitanya Natya Manch', 'Sanghams', 'Jan Militia' and 'Dalams'. In 'Sanghams', 'Jan Militia' and 'Dalams', the CPI (Maoist) provide training to children on weapons handling and on use of different types of Improvised Explosive Devices. The children recruited to 'Jan Militia' and 'Dalams' also participate in armed exchanges with the security forces where they are tactically pushed to the forefront. This is to derive propaganda mileage by the CPI (Maoist) in case of casualties of minors. The children recruited in 'Dalams' are not permitted to leave. They face severe reprisals including killing of family members, if they surrender to security forces. However, the government has no precise estimates of total number of children recruited by the CPI (Maoist). As per the intelligence reports, in the year 2014, incidents of Maoists forcing at least one child from each family to join the outfit has been reported from areas under Police Stations Senha (district Lohardaga), Bishunpur (district Gumla) in Jharkhand and Police Station Ambabeda (district Kanker) in Chhattisgarh. Lok Sabha Unstarred Question No. 1597 for 02 December 2014.

seven villages in Gumla district in the state of Jharkhand to hand over five children per village to join their ranks. To avoid such forcible recruitment, families have resorted to sending children away from home at a young age, which results in children dropping out of school. Abducted children are subjected to grave violations and abuses, and have been forced to serve in combat functions, exposed to sexual violence and, reportedly, used as human shields.[76]

Child Soldiers International has reported that while NSAG commanders sexually exploit women, most of the time it is projected as consensual sex. Abortions are a routine affair as female commanders cannot become mothers. The commanders have the first claim over a new girl in the camp. A 14-year-old informed Child Soldier International: "Right from the first day, one of the male members began targeting me for sex. I tried my best resisting and running away but couldn't succeed. What happened thereafter was a nightmarish experience. I was raped almost every day. As my condition deteriorated, they administered locally procured medicines but the treatment didn't work. Finally, they left me near a nursing home and ran away. I do not want to go back to the hell again."[77]

A major lacuna in India is the absence of guidance or specific rules of engagement for the security forces when they either confront or detain child soldiers.[78] The police and security personnel face a serious dilemma when they encounter children working with insurgent groups because they have little practical guidance on what steps to take in such a situation. A recent report from an NGO recounts an incident in which the police found two girls, who were 13 and 15 years of age, during an armed encounter in Chhattisgarh:

> The girls were frightened when the shooting started, and hid in a small ditch...According to the police, the two girls looked visibly

---

76 A few children were killed and injured as a result of violence and fighting between armed groups and national security forces. In June 2015, 12 Communist Party of India (Maoist) fighters, including four children dressed in uniforms, were killed in a joint police operation in Bhalwahi village in Jharkhand. In April 2015, Maoists reportedly abducted five girls between the ages of 10 and 13 years from Karcha village, West Bengal, and their whereabouts remain unknown. Children in Armed Conflict, Report of the Secretary-General, UN Doc. A/70/836-S/2016/360 dated 20 April 2016, para 184-186.

77 Lost Childhood: Caught in armed violence in Jharkhand, Child Soldiers International, and HAQ Centre for Child Rights, 2016, p. 30-31.

78 Sinha Samrat and MahantaUpasana, Disjuncture in Law, Policy and Practice: The Situation of Child Welfare in India's Conflict Affected Regions, *Asian-Pacific Law & Policy Journal*, Vol. 17, 2015, p. 1-70.

frightened and started crying and pleaded for mercy. They explained to the police that Naxalites had forcibly inducted them into the dalam. Since they were children, the police decided to make them complainants and asked them to file a case against the Naxalite commander who recruited them. The police said, however, that they could not assist the girls because the government had no scheme to rehabilitate and protect such children. They traced the girls' parents and sent the girls home, even though the parents begged that their children should not be sent back — they would be re-recruited or killed.[79]

Armed Forces

In India, the minimum age for recruitment into the armed forces varies between 16 years and six months for the Navy and Coast Guards, 17 years and six months for the Army and 17 years for the Air Force. Individuals recruited into the three wings of the armed forces are sent for compulsory training and inducted personnel are sent to operational areas only after they attain 18 years of age. The period of training required before recruits are ready to participate in military operations is sufficiently long to preclude the direct involvement of under-18s in hostilities.[80]It is only in an extreme emergency that there is a remote possibility of under-18s being militarily deployed prior to the completion of training. As for the Central Armed Police Forces (CAPF), which includes the Central Reserve Police Force (CRPF), Border Security Force (BSF), Indo-Tibetan Border Police (ITBP), Sashastra Seema Bal (SSB), Central Industrial Security Force (CISF), Railway Protection Force (RPF) and National Security Guards (NSG), only over-18s are recruited.

Special Police Officers

Section 17 of the Police Act, 1861, empowers local magistrates to temporarily appoint residents of the neighbourhood as special police officers (SPOs) to perform the role of officers of police.[81]The regulations for the appointment

---

79 Human Rights Watch, Dangerous Duty: Children & the Chhattisgarh Conflict, September 2008, p. 42-49.

80 Ministry of Women and Child Development, Government of India, State party report on the Optional Protocol to the Convention on the Rights of the Child on the Involvement of Children in Armed Conflict, 2011.

81 The designation of SPOs was created in Chhattisgarh in June 2006, followed by Jharkhand, Orissa, Andhra Pradesh and Maharashtra, tostrengthen the intelligence network and lend support to the security forces in anti-Naxal operations. In addition, village defence parties,

of SPOs do not specify the minimum age at which SPOs can be recruited. The state governments have recruited children as SPOs and used them as guards, besides deploying them in anti-Naxal operations, including armed encounters. Since no qualifications were prescribed for the appointment, preference was given to those who had passed the fifth standard, were over 18 years of age and had knowledge of the local geography.

A PIL was filed in the Supreme Court against the appointment of SPOs in 2007.[82] The petitioners alleged that the lives of thousands of untrained tribal youth appointed as SPOs were being placed in grave danger due to their employment in counter-insurgency activities against the Maoists/Naxalites in Chhattisgarh. The Court observed that tribal youth were appointed by the state of Chhattisgarh, with the consent of the Union of India, to engage in armed conflict for which they were inadequately trained. In view of the large number of casualties among SPOs in the conflict, the Supreme Court observed that the young tribals had literally become cannon fodder in the killing fields. The Court held that employing ill-equipped, barely literate youngsters in counter-insurgency activities, and thus placing their lives in danger, was violative of Articles 14 and 21 of the Constitution.[83]

The new Special Police Officers (Appointment, Training and Conditions of Service) Regulatory Procedure, 2011 failed to convince the Supreme Court that the situation would improve, the role has been extended from guides

---

village guards and SPOs have been deployed in Maharashtra, Assam, Meghalaya, Manipur, Nagaland, Tripura and Jammu and Kashmir.

82 *NandiniSundar v. State of Chhattisgarh,* Writ Petition (Civil) No. 250 of 2007, order dated 5 July 2011.

83 The Supreme Court held that Article 14 of the Constitution is violated because subjecting such youngsters to the same levels of danger as members of the regular force, who have better educational backgrounds, receive better training, and who, because of a better educational background possess a better capacity to benefit from training that is appropriate for the duties to be performed in counter-insurgency activities, would be to treat unequals as equals. Moreover, youngsters, who have low educational qualifications and consequently, the scholastic inability to benefit from appropriate training, cannot be expected to be effective in engaging in counter-insurgency activities; therefore, the policy of employing such youngsters as SPOs in counterinsurgency activities is irrational, arbitrary and capricious. Article 21 is violated because ... youngsters with such low educational qualifications cannot be expected to understand the dangers that they are likely to face, the skills needed to face such dangers, and the requirements of the necessary judgment while discharging such responsibilities. Consequently, appointing such youngsters as SPOs with duties that would involve any counter-insurgency activities against the Maoists, even if it were claimed that they have been put through rigorous training, would be to endanger their lives. *Nandini Sundar v. State of Chhattisgarh,* 2007, para 61 and 62.

to a direct combat with terrorists/extremists.[84] The Supreme Court ordered that the State of Chhattisgarh immediately desist from using SPOs, in any manner or form, in any activities, directly or indirectly, aimed at controlling, countering, mitigating or otherwise eliminating Maoist/Naxalite activities in the state. The report of the National Commission for Protection of Child Rights confirms that the state government has stopped the practice of employing SPOs.[85]

There is no doubt that NSAGs have been more responsible for the recruitment/involvement of children in armed conflicts than the State forces in India. Reports by international and national NGOs have highlighted the widespread use of children by NSAGs; however, the government maintains that these localized conflicts only have a socio-economic impact on children, namely, lack of access to education, health and other basic services.[86] In case a child soldier is killed in an encounter, the government claims that the child was a member of a NSAG, while the NSAGs disown the child. In several cases, child soldiers' bodies have been mutilated in order to make it difficult to ascertain their age and identities. The deaths of such children are frequently said to have been a result of their being caught in the crossfire of an armed encounter.[87]

The Government of India perceives the issue of child soldiers as one of merely law and order. The 2015–16 Annual Report of the Ministry of Home Affairs does not mention the term child soldiers anywhere. The Juvenile Justice (Care and Protection of Children) Act was recently amended and came into effect from 15 January 2016. Section 83(1) of the Act now criminalizes the use of children by militants groups stating: "Any non-State, self-styled militant group or outfit declared as such by the central government, if recruits or uses any child for any purpose, shall be liable for rigorous imprisonment for a term which may extend to seven years and shall also be liable to fine of five lakh rupees." If any adult or an adult group uses children for illegal activities will also be liable for the same punishment. In March 2017, the

---

84 Chakraborty Ananya, Child Soldiers in India—A Case of Continuing Indifference, available at: http://ssrn.com/abstract=2485770.

85 Protection of Children's Rights in Areas of Civil Unrest, National Commission for Protection of Child Rights (NCPCR), 2010, p. 40.

86 Saxena Mukul, Left Out By the Pied Piper: The UN Response to Children in Localized Conflict Settings, *Nw. J. Int'l Hum. Rts.*, Vol. 9, No. 1, 2010, p. 59-81.

87 Ferrao Ranjana, Prohibition on the use of Child Soldiers: How Real, *ISIL Yearbook of International Humanitarian and Refugee Law*, 2009, p .288.

government has ratified the ILO Convention No. 182 on the Worst Forms of Child Labour.[88]

Iraq

After the first Gulf War, Saddam Hussein, the President of Iraq, created *Ashbal Saddam* (Saddam's Lion Cubs), a paramilitary force of boys between the ages of 10 and 15 years. The members of *Ashbal Saddam* received training in small arms and light infantry tactics. They were also trained in hand-to-hand combat and learned how to rappel from helicopters. They were the feeder organization of the paramilitary force, *Saddam Fedayeen*. More than 8,000 young Iraqis were members of this group in Baghdad.[89]

The United States' invasion and subsequent occupation of Iraq began on 19 March 2003. During the war that ended Saddam Hussein's regime, American forces engaged with Iraqi child soldiers in the fighting in the three cities of Nasariya, Mosul and Karbala. There were many instances of children being used as human shields by Saddam Hussein loyalists during the fighting. After the regime of Saddam Hussein was toppled on 9 April 2003, the Coalition Provisional Authority (CPA) ordered the complete dismantling of the Iraqi army, the demobilization of all enlisted soldiers and the indefinite suspension of universal conscription. The August 2003 CPA order creating the new armed forces specified that the minimum age of recruitment was 18 and that recruitment was voluntary. There has been no report of any person

---

88 On 13 June 2017, India has ratified two core Conventions of International Labour Organisation (ILO) on child labour: Convention 138 regarding admission of age to employment and Convention 182 regarding worst forms of Child Labour. The Central government had enacted a new law — Child labour (Prohibition and Prevention) amendment Act, 2016 – banning employment of child labour below 14 years of age in all occupations and processes. It further prohibits employment of adolescents (14-18 years of age) in hazardous occupations. However, children are allowed to "help" families in running their domestic enterprises only after school hours. The new law linked the age of employment for children to the age of compulsory education under Right to Education Act (RTE), 2009.

89 The military officers who supervised the camps noted that the children participating in the program were held under the physical and psychological strain of training sessions that lasted as long as 14 hours per day. At times, there were not enough children to fill all of the vacancies in the camp, and as a result, families were threatened with the loss of food ration cards if they refused to enroll their children in the course. In addition, authorities reportedly withheld school examination results from children unless they registered with the military training camps. Anna-Liisa Jacobsen, Lambs into Lions: The Utilization of Child Soldiers in the War in Iraq and Why International and Iraqi Laws are Failing to Protect the Innocent, *Rich. J. Global L. & Bus*, Vol. 8, 2008, p. 164.

under 18 serving in the Iraqi armed forces since.[90]

During 2004, child soldiers were serving not only Saddam Hussein's loyalist forces, but also radical Shi'a and Sunni insurgent groups. In the battle to retake the city of Fallujah in November 2004, US Marines recounted numerous instances of being fired upon by 12-year-old children with assault rifles. The US detained more than 100 Iraqi juveniles at Abu Ghraib prison.[91] The hanging of Saddam Hussein on 5 November 2006 did not put an end to the use of child soldiers by militant Islamic groups in Iraq. By mid-2007, around 800 children between the ages of 10 and 17 were held in a multinational forces (MNF) base in Baghdad for making and planting roadside bombs for armed groups. Others had been caught while acting as lookouts or carrying guns. The US military considered these children high-risk security threats as they were captured while actively engaged in activities against US forces.[92] The British forces had also detained more than 60 juveniles during their operations in Iraq. In addition to the many instances of children being used as human shields by Saddam loyalists, a number of anti-Saddam paramilitary groups also utilized children. For example, the Free Iraqi Forces that were linked to the US-backed exiled leader, Ahmed Chalabi, also recruited children as young as 13 years of age.[93]

Non-State Armed Groups

Various armed groups have allegedly used child soldiers. The two main child recruiters are al-Qaeda in Iraq and Jaysh al-Mahdi (Army of the Mahdi). These groups reportedly used money to entice children into the group. Children orphaned since the US-led invasion in 2003 were allegedly used by the group as spies, or sent to gather information or distract troops while the

---

90 Child Soldiers: Global Report 2008, p.178-181.

91 Detained children at Abu Ghraib prison subjected to forced nudity, stress positions, beating and in a few cases of rape. Amnesty International, USA: human dignity denied: torture and accountability in the 'war on terror', October 2004.

92 In April 2003, during the war with Saddam Hussein's government in Iraq, American soldiers were forced to fire on and kill Iraqi child soldiers in at least two separate instances. Some of these child soldiers were as young as ten years old. Incidents with child soldiers continued during the guerilla campaign that followed the invasion. The US Army briefings warned of the threat from child soldiers, ranging from child snipers to a fifteen-year-old who tossed a grenade in an American truck, blowing off the arm of an Army trooper. Singer P.W., Talk in Cheap: Getting serious About Preventing Child Soldiers, *Cornell International Law Journal*, Vol. 37, 2004, p. 562.

93 Singer P.W. 2005. *Children at War*, New York: Pantheon Books, p. 22-23.

group prepared to detonate bombs nearby. Reports indicated that al-Qaeda recruited children to carry out its attacks, but the number involved was not known. Child soldiers, some as young as 12, were allegedly used by the al-Mahdi militias during the fighting.[94]

Mentally disabled children were allegedly sold to or abducted by al-Qaeda in Iraq and used by the group in night raids and as decoys to divert the attention of the US or Iraqi forces in the run-up to attacks in cities such as Diyala, Ramadi and Fallujah.[95] The US invasion, downfall of Saddam Hussein and subsequent occupation of Iraq has not been successful in preventing the use of child soldiers by militant Islamic groups.

In the recent past, the recruitment and use of children by NSAGs in Iraq has been rampant. In particular, during the current armed conflicts in Iraq and Syria, the widespread use of children by terrorist groups, especially the Islamic State of Iraq and the Levant (ISIL), has been shocking. Iraq has been facing serious challenges at all levels. Terrorist groups had taken control of several areas and have perpetrated war crimes and genocide. Forced recruitment of children, particularly from refugee camps in Iraq, the disappearance of children and sexual slavery against them are not uncommon. The situation has led to the displacement of children, and affected their rights to access to education and health.[96]

The recruitment of children by the ISIS from the countries neighbouring Syria and their use in the war zone is not properly documented. Recent reports on ISIS activities from the conflating conflict zones between Iraq and Syria indicate that ISIS fighters encourage children to take part in combat in order to train for and take part in atrocities. In ISIS-controlled areas of Iraq, boys

---

94 Peter W. Singer, "Young Soldiers Used in Conflicts Around the World", Washington Post, 12 June 2006.

95 On 21 March 2007, mentally disabled children were allegedly used by al-Qaeda in Iraq operatives in a suicide attack on a market in Baghdad. According to a spokesperson for the Iraq Ministry of Interior, "they were put in the back of a car with another two adults in the front. The military let their car pass through the checkpoint since it had children as passengers. When they reached the market, the adults left the car with the children inside and detonated a bomb in the vehicle, killing the children and another five Iraqis."

96 Iraq is facing tremendous challenges due to the emergence of terrorist armed groups. The recruitment of children by armed groups, particularly in refugee camps in Iraq, and the use of children, including children with disabilities, for terrorist acts are worrisome. Iraqi law has certain gaps in terms of punishing the enrolment of children by NSAGs. Committee on Rights of Child: Reports of Iraq under Convention on the Rights of Child, on children in armed conflict and sale of children, 22 January 2015.

of the age of 15 years and above who have escaped from the ISIS after being forcibly recruited have reported to their families that they were forced to form the front line for ISIS fighters during combat. They also had to donate blood to injured fighters.[97] A joint report of the United Nations Assistance Mission for Iraq (UNAMI) and Office of the United Nations High Commissioner for Human Rights (OHCHR) has stated that the ISIS recently kidnapped 800–900 children in Mosul for religious and military training. In 2016, government-backed tribal militias, known as Hashad al-Asha'ri, also recruited at least 10 children from the Debaga IDP camp in the Erbil governorate to fight against the ISIS.

Myanmar

The conflict in Myanmar dates back to its independence from the United Kingdom in 1948 and has been described as one of the world's longest civil wars. Myanmar has remained under military rule for over half a century and has been marred by armed conflicts. Under the military regime, unsuccessful attempts were made to neutralize armed opposition groups through both direct offensives and ceasefire agreements. Since 2009, efforts by Myanmar's military government to incorporate various armed ethnic groups into a Border Guard Forces (BGF) by disarming them, providing them with government weapons and making their troops subordinate to regional Tatmadaw Kyi commanders has met with limited success. Armed conflict between the State forces and numerous armed ethnic groups forms the violent background against which widespread recruitment and use of children by the State armed forces and NSAGs has been occurring. Children have been drawn into participation in armed conflicts, not just as a result of the militarization of society, but also socioeconomic compulsions. The pressure to maintain and strengthen the number of troops in the armed forces and armed groups is among the primary reasons for the ongoing recruitment of underage children.[98]

In 2011, the new government restarted ceasefire talks with 14 armed groups. This resulted in a significant decrease in military clashes in a number of regions.[99] March 2014 saw the creation of a joint drafting committee of

---

97 Tone Sommerfelt and Mark B. Taylor, The big dilemma of small soldiers: Recruiting children to the war in Syria, Norwegian Peace-building Resource Centre, Report, February 2017.

98 Under the radar: Ongoing recruitment and use of children by the Myanmar army, Child Soldiers International, January 2015.

99 Since the incumbent Myanmar government was established in 2011, the country has seen

the government and NSAGs on a ceasefire. However, a nationwide ceasefire was not successful. Military operations against armed opposition groups continued and intensified in the Kachin and northern Shan states.[100]

Myanmar Armed Forces

The Myanmar armed forces (Tatmadaw) consist of the army (Tatmadaw Kyi), navy (Tatmadaw Yay), and air force (Tatmadaw Lay), but are dominated by the army. The country's forces are a volunteer force. The recruitment of individuals below 18 years of age is prohibited under the Regulation for Persons Subject to the Defence Services Act, 1974.[101] Due to the ongoing armed conflict, the military has been under pressure to maintain its troop strength. There have been reports that the army forcibly recruits persons below the age of 18 years,[102] though representatives from the Myanmar military deny the prevalence of this practice.[103] According to Child Soldier

---

its most intense armed conflicts in decades. However, the incumbent administration has also achieved ceasefires with twelve ethnic armed groups. None of these agreements have mandated any form of parallel administration or led to the official designation of areas under exclusive armed group authority. Many of them, however, permitted certain areas for groups to be based and to carry arms, allowing them a certain degree of local authority. Jolliffe Kim, Ethnic Armed Conflict and Territorial Administration in Myanmar, The Asia Foundation, June 2015,p.85.

100   In the Kachin state, there has been fierce fighting between the Kachin Independence Army (KIA) and the Myanmar military over the past three years. Clashes escalated during 2014. In addition, there have been routine clashes between the Myanmar military and armed groups in the Shan state, particularly with the Shan State Army (South) and Shan State Army (North). Under the radar: Ongoing recruitment and use of children by the Myanmar army, Child Soldiers International, January 2015, p. 5.

101 Under the military instruction of 2 October 1997, the recruitment of individuals below 18 years of age is deemed to constitute forced labour. Further, under Order 1/99 and Supplementary Order 1/99, forced labour is illegal and is a crime under Section 374 of the Myanmar Penal Code.

102 The retirement age from the Tatmadaw Kyi is 60 years. Unofficially, however, in order to seek early retirement, military personnel are required to bring in new recruits. Interviews with confidential sources show that in non-military government offices, employees seeking early retirement have to pay a large amount of money, estimated at approximately US$5,000, in order to leave their jobs. This amount of money depends upon their years of service and training received as it has to cover the costs the state has invested in human resources that will not be serving the nation anymore. Under the radar: Ongoing recruitment and use of children by the Myanmar army, Child Soldiers International, January 2015, p. 9.

103 Under the radar: Ongoing recruitment and use of children by the Myanmar army, Child Soldiers International, January 2015, p. 9.

International, it is virtually impossible to know the number of child soldiers in the Tatmadaw Kyi. Representatives of the Myanmar government have informed Child Soldiers International that they had discharged 587 children between 2004 and 2012 through the Committee for the Prevention of Military Recruitment of Underage Children.[104]

Soldiers who are below the age of 18 years can be deployed in hostilities. Thus, they are exposed to death and injury, and face greater risks of physical and mental trauma because of their lack of experience and relative immaturity. Children deployed in the front line have been used to carry weaponry, detonate landmines and work as porters to carry goods and rations. In the process, they have been exposed to active fighting and often sustained serious or lethal injuries as a direct result of the fighting or landmines. Field research conducted by Child Soldiers International in March 2011 indicated that children recruited by the Tatmadaw Kyi had been deployed in frontline battalions. This practice continues: in 2014, children forcibly recruited by the Tatmadaw Kyi continued to be deployed in the frontline of the Kachin conflict, although it was difficult to determine the precise number.

The exact number of child soldiers currently in the Tatmadaw and NSAGs is difficult to estimate.[105]A total of 357 cases of child recruitment and use by the Tatmadaw were reported during 2015.[106] At least 27 of the

---

104 In rural Myanmar, children have been recruited while on their way to school or when they leave their homes in search of work. In urban areas, unaccompanied children are reported to have been recruited at busy locations, such as railway stations, bus terminals, markets and outside temples. Underage recruitment is carried out by civilian brokers, non-commissioned soldiers and junior police officers. This kind of recruitment affects mostly poor and uneducated children.

105 In 2002, Human Rights Watch report provided a rough estimate, based on interviews with former Burmese child soldiers, which placed the number of child soldiers in the Tatmadaw at 70,000 and the total number in non-state armed groups at 6,000–7,000. Current estimates of the number of child soldiers in the Tatmadaw are often not given; rather, numbers of children released through the International Labor Organization's forced labour complaint mechanism are referenced. Chafin Haley Elizabeth, Stolen Innocence: The United Nations' Battle against the Forced recruitment and Use of Child Soldiers in Myanmar, *GA. J. INT'L & COMP. L.*, Vol. 43, 2014, p. 185-223.

106 The Myanmar Government has intimated that action had been taken against 382 military personnel, including 73 officers, for failing to adhere to recruitment procedures. A civilian was also sentenced to a year's imprisonment for aiding underage recruitment. The United Nations verified three cases of sexual violence against girls, aged between 5 and 10 years, by Tatmadaw soldiers. In a grievous case, an 8-year-old girl was raped by a soldier and died after being taken to hospital. The perpetrators were court-martialled for being absent from duty and intoxicated, and two were convicted of rape by civilian courts. Children in

children—as young as 14 years of age—had been newly recruited in 2014. The children were either enlisted owing to their economic circumstances and family problems, or were deliberately tricked or forced into joining. Those who attempt to escape from the Tatmadaw Kyi are detained and treated as adult deserters. According to the current laws, a child soldier who deserts the military may face a higher penalty than someone who recruits a child soldier. A number of child soldiers who tried to escape the army have been declared 'deserters' and sentenced to imprisonment.

Main Non-State Armed Groups

Myanmar consists of many different ethnic groups, each with their own territory and military. These are the (i) Karen National Liberation Army (KNLA), the military wing of the Karen National Union (KNU); (ii) Kachin Independence Army (KIA), which was formed by the Kachin rebels in 1988 and is the military wing of the Kachin Independence Organization (KIO); (iii) Karenni Army (KA), the military wing for the Karenni National Progressive Party (KNPP), which was created after the Burmese government incorporated the Kayah state into the Union of Burma in 1951; (iv) Chin National Front (CNF), founded in March 1988 as a coalition of several Chin opposition groups to push for greater autonomy; (v) armed wing of the New State Mon Party (NSMP), which has fought the government since 1949, when military forces entered Mon territory; (vi) Shan State Army (SSA), formed in 1964 as the Burmese military began to move into the Shan State; and (vii) Arakan Liberation Army (ALA), which was set up with the help of the KNU in the 1950s, but became defunct after most of its leaders were arrested. In the 1970s, the latter reassembled, but is still one of the smallest ethnic armies. The SSA later split into two factions, creating the Shan State Army-North, which signed a ceasefire with the government in 1964, and the Shan State Army-South, which continued to fight the State until an initial ceasefire in December 2011. The United Wa State Army (UWSA), created after the fall of the Community Party Burma in 1989, is one of the country's most powerful ethnic armies and receives military resources, infrastructure and support from neighbouring China.

According to the UN report, the NSAGs in Myanmar that recruit and use children are the (i) Democratic Karen Benevolent Army, (ii) KIA, (iii)

Armed Conflict, Report of the Secretary General, UN Doc. A/70/836-S/2016/360 dated 20 April 2016, para 101-104.

KNLA, (iv) KNLA Peace Council, (v) KA,(vi) SSA-South, and (vi) UWSA.[107] Children continue to be recruited and used by NSAGs, including through abduction. There are confirmed reports that NSAGs have used children in hostilities.[108]Owing to access issues and limited capacity, the UN has been unable to monitor the presence of children in armed groups.[109]

In 2012, the Government of Myanmar and the UN signed an action plan to prevent the recruitment and use of children by the Tatmadaw and allow for the release of underage recruits.[110] The recruitment of child soldiers has fallen in recent years, but much more needs to be done. Most of the armed groups still use child soldiers today. In October 2015, the government signed a nationwide ceasefire agreement with eight armed groups, including four listed parties. The ongoing peace process offers opportunities to strengthen the government's engagement in the area of protecting children affected by conflict. There has been steady progress in the implementation of the Joint

107 Children in Armed Conflict, Report of the Secretary General, UN Doc. A/70/836-S/2016/360 dated 20 April 2016.

108 In meetings with Child Soldiers International in November 2015, KIA officials admitted that children continued to be recruited, and in some instances deployed to front-line posts, despite official policies prohibiting underage recruitment. They also stated that violations related to the recruitment and use of children tended to occur in posts located in more remote areas that were farfrom the central headquarters.

109 Credible information indicated that children were recruited and used by armed groups; however, five reported incidents could not be verified owing to limited access to the areas. Reports of recruitment involved the Karen National Liberation Army, the Kachin Independence Army, the Shan State Army-South and the Ta'ang National Liberation Army in Kachin, Kayin and Shan States. In one incident a 12-year-old boy was allegedly used as a combatant by KIA and was injured during a firefight with the Tatmadaw in Namkhan. Children in Armed Conflict, Report of the Secretary General, UN Doc. A/70/836-S/2016/360 dated 20 April 2016.

110 The practice of falsifying age documentation continues to be reported. Some military personnel and civilian recruitment brokers reportedly forge documents before bringing children into recruitment centres. In other cases, recruiters are reported to have taken children to a different state to the one they are registered in and had a second Citizenship Scrutiny Card or National Registration Card issued in which the recruit is registered as 18 years old. Age verification documents are easily falsified at local photocopy shops, where templates of birth certificates, family lists and school registration forms are readily available. In 2014, the Myanmar government admitted that the falsification of documents remained an ongoing problem but denied that this led to the recruitment of children since recruitment only took place once the documents were checked and approved by officials from the Ministry of Immigration. Child Soldier International, Ongoing Underage Recruitment and Use by the Myanmar Military and Non-State Armed Groups: Briefing for the UN Secretary General's Annual Report on Children and Armed Conflict - March 2016.

Action Plan. Nearly 800 child soldiers (including young people recruited as children) have been released from the Tatmadaw since the Joint Action Plan was signed in 2012. [111] ILO Convention 182 on the Worst Forms of Child Labour (1999) came into force in Myanmar on 18 December 2014, following its ratification by the Myanmar government in 2013. In September 2015, Myanmar signed the Optional Protocol to the Convention on the Rights of the Child.

Nigeria

On 16 March 2016, two young female suicide bombers walked into a mosque in the Borno state of Nigeria and detonated their suicide vests, leaving 22 dead. The attack was one of the many unleashed by extremists linked to the Boko Haram terror group, founded in Nigeria in 2002.[112]The group has employed diverse violent tactics, such as assassination, ambush, drive-by shootings and suicide bombings, in its attacks against security agents, religious and traditional rulers, worship centres, schools,[113] traders and lately, all non-members of the group. Suicide bombings have remained a key element of its violent campaign. In April 2014, Boko Haram militants kidnapped more than 250 school girls from Chibok in the Borno state. The girls were reportedly hidden in remote areas of Nigeria, Cameroon, Chad and

---

111 Myanmar army frees 46 child soldiers: state media, 13 March 2016, available at:http://www.abc.net.au/news/2016-03-13/myanmar-army-frees-46-child-soldiers-state-media/7243216.

112 Boko Haram was created in 2002 in Maiduguri in the Borno state of Nigeria by the Islamist cleric, Mohammed Yusuf. Although widely referred to as the Boko Haram (Western education is forbidden), it prefers to be called by its original name Jama'atu Ahlissunnah Lidda'awatiwal Jihad, meaning "People Committed to the Propagation of the Prophet's Teachings and Jihad". Its ideology is based on extreme Islamic teaching which rejects most Western ideas and institutions as un-Islamic. The group seeks to impose Sharia, or Islamic law, in Nigeria. Since stepping up its activities in 2009, Boko Haram has killed over 15,000 people and nearly 1.5 million displaced by the insurgency. Onuoha Freedom C. and Temilola A. George, Boko Haram's Use of Female Suicide Bombing in Nigeria, Report: Al Jazeera Centre for Studies, 17 March 2015, p. 1-9.

113 Since 2014, an estimated 1,500 schools have been destroyed in north-east Nigeria, including 524 in the Borno state. This has prevented access to education for more than 400,000 children. Five schools have reportedly been used for military purposes by Boko Haram in the Bauchi state, and three by the Nigerian security forces since April 2014 in Maiduguri and Chibok Local Government Area, Borno state. To strengthen the protection of education, Nigeria endorsed the Safe Schools Declaration, agreeing to use the Guidelines for Protecting Schools and Universities from Military Use during Armed Conflict. Children in Armed Conflict, Report of the Secretary-General, General Assembly/ Security Council Doc. A/70/836-S/2016/360 dated 20 April 2016, para 193.

the Central African Republic.

The first Boko Haram female suicide bomber in Nigeria attacked a military barracks in February 2014. She detonated her suicide vest shortly before she could go through the security checkpoint. One soldier was killed. Since then, Boko Haram's new tactic has involved enlisting dozens of women and girls to carry out suicide missions, some of the girls being as young as 10 years old. Two female suicide bombers of the Boko Haram group were responsible for killing 58 people in an internally displaced persons camp (IDP) located in the state of Borno. On 10 January 2016, two female suicide bombers killed 10 people in an attack in Cameroon. No country in West Africa is secure from these suicide attacks.

The Boko Haram group has intensified its operations, including suicide attacks, which have spread from north-east Nigeria to Cameroon, Chad and the Niger, causing a significant number of casualties among civilians and large-scale displacement. Over the past three years, Boko Haram has kidnapped more than 10,000 boys and trained them in boot camps in abandoned villages and forest hideouts. In these training camps, children as young as five years of age learn to handle assault rifles and march through the woods in flip-flops; sometimes under a 15-year-old trainer. For even minor infractions, the militants beat the boys nearly unconscious, or deny them food and sleep for days.[114]

The UN has verified that over 2000 children were recruited by Boko Haram in the year 2016.[115] Twenty-one girls, some of them as young as seven or eight years of age, were used in suicide attacks in 2016. The UN has verified the killing of 244 children (109 boys and 135 girls), mostly in Borno, Adamawa and Yobe. Thirteen suicide attacks claimed the lives of 65 of the children. A total of 112 children (54 boys and 58 girls) were maimed. It has been reported that children have also been recruited and used by the Civilian Joint Task Force of the Nigerian government. These children were used to man checkpoints and worked as messengers and spies.[116]

---

114 Drew Hinshaw and Joe Parkinson, The 10,000 Kidnapped Boys of Boko Haram, *Wall Street Journal*, 12 August 2016, available at: https://www.wsj.com/articles/the-kidnapped-boys-of-boko-haram-1471013062.

115 Ed Adamczyk, Boko Haram recruited 2,000 child soldiers in 2016: UNICEF, 21 February 2017, available at: http://www.upi.com/Top_News/World-News/2017/02/21/Boko-Haram-recruited-2000-child-soldiers-in-2016-UNICEF/8831487689926/.

116 Children in Armed Conflict, Report of the Secretary-General, General Assembly/

Many of the abducted girls have been forcibly married to their captors and raped, often by different men, over months and become pregnant. Girls who have been subjected to sexual violence have been returning to their communities in the IDP camps and host communities, or to their local government areas (LGAs). Some are returning with the children who were born to them as a result of sexual violence. A significant proportion of them face stigma and rejection from their communities. Many are marginalized, discriminated against and rejected by their family and community members due to social and cultural norms related to sexual violence. There is also a growing fear that some of these girls and women were radicalized in captivity. Children born of sexual violence are at an even greater risk of rejection, abandonment and violence.[117]

Nigeria is currently going through its worst political and human rights crisis in years. It is extremely divided, and entangled in violence triggered by ethnic and religious conflict. Children across the country are being denied their human rights, such as their right to education. They are recruited into the armed forces. These child soldiers are subjected to the death penalty, are punished by cruel, inhumane methods, and suffer many other forms of violence. Children involved in armed conflict are frequently killed or injured during combat or while performing other military tasks. They are forced to engage in hazardous activities, such as laying mines and using explosives, besides serving as suicide bombers. Some are also illegally used as spies, messengers, porters and servants. Children have also been recruited into paramilitaries, the civil militia and a variety of other armed groups.

Pakistan

In Pakistan, the recruitment and use of child soldiers by NSAGs is a reality and a growing phenomenon. There are thousands of seminary schools (*madrassas*) across Pakistan that provide religious education, food and shelter free of charge to children from poor families.[118] However, a number of such

---

Security Council Doc. A/70/836-S/2016/360 dated 20 April 2016, para 187-195.

117 Many perceive these victims of conflict as being partly responsible for the violence and losses suffered by entire communities during the insurgency. As a result, children and newborns as well as their mothers are being increasingly ostracized and are at risk of further violence. "Bad Blood": Perceptions of children born of conflict-related sexual violence and women and girls associated with Boko Haram in northeast Nigeria, Research Summary, UNCEF Nigeria and **Borno State Ministry of Women Affairs and Social Development, 2016.**

118 The USAID has given millions of dollars to reform the education in *madrassas*. Despite

schools have developed links with NSAGs, which have unleashed violence across the country. The militant groups that are responsible for carrying out suicide attacks in Pakistan claim that they are waging *jihad*, which is one of the basic tenets of Islam. However, these militants follow neither Islamic, nor international rules of war. The militants have not hesitated to use innocent children as suicide bombers in their attacks on places of worship like mosques and shrines, hospitals, markets, hotels, bakeries and all kinds of public places.[119] It is reckoned that nearly 90 per cent of the estimated 5,000 suicide bombers trained in Pakistan are under the age of 16.[120]

In March 2013, the Pakistani police arrested a group of 11 children who were of the age of 11 to 18 years, and were suspected to be involved in a series of bombings in Quetta, the capital of the province of Baluchistan. The local police later revealed that some of the children claimed that they did not know what the packets contained and what they are doing, and that they were merely content to receive a small amount of money for dropping the packets. These children received Rs 2000–5000 (US$ 20–50) per blast. The

---

this huge expenditure, only a few registered with the Government, and most continue with their own system of education, and indoctrination. The system is so entrenched that the Government is literally helpless, and quite a few of the current suicide bombers are children from the *madrassas*. Alternative Report on the State of Child Rights in Pakistan by Civil Society of Pakistan, Save the Children UK (Pakistan office) and the Society for the Protection of the Rights of the Child (SPARC), March 2009, p. 25.

119 Not all *madrassas* directly educate their pupils in Jihadi violence. About a third provide military training, the rest may send their pupils on to other establishments for training in the use of weapons and insurgency tactics. Thus whilst there is a strong link between *madrassas* and militarization, with *madrassa* pupil being fed into military training camps, it cannot be assumed that all *madrassa* pupils will end up as combatants. In addition, not all young fighters for the Kashmiri jihad or the Afghan war are recruited through *madrassas*. Some volunteer straight to training camps. The reasons behind their volunteering are both economic - an interview with a young carpenter in Karachi, for example, revealed his dissatisfaction over his earnings of Rs 300 a day and his intent to earn better money through fighting in Afghanistan- and ideological. The relationship between ISI support for militants in Kashmir and *madrassa* education in Pakistan is unclear. There are, however, reports that the ISI is active in recruiting from schools in Indian-held Kashmir and bringing boys over the border to receive military training in Pakistan. Other Pakistan-based militant outfits may offer large cash inducements for boys to go for military training. Berry Jo de, Directly Affected by Armed Conflict in Pakistan, Discussion document prepared for UNICEF Regional Office South Asia & Save the Children Fund (USA), Pakistan and Afghanistan Field Office, p. 20-21.

120 Crimi, F., Al-Qaeda's Female Suicide Bomber Death cult, Frontpage Mag, 6 November 2012, available at: http://www.frontpagemag.com/2012/frank-crimi/al-qaedas-female-suicide-bomber-death-cult/. Iqbal Khuram. 2015. *The Making of Pakistani Human Bomb*, London: Lexington Books, p. 112-113.

children, who came from extremely poor families, had been attracted by a Baluch militant organization that directed them to place packages containing home-made bombs in markets, dustbins and on routes used by the police and security forces. The police also seized anti-personnel mines, explosives, and other arms and ammunition from the children.[121]

In the late afternoon of 3 April 2011, in the Pakistani city of Dera Ghazi Khan, twin suicide bomb attacks killed over 50 people and left more than 120 wounded at an annual Sufi Muslim religious festival at the shrine of the 13th century saint, Ahmed Sultan. The bombers struck a few minutes apart, instantly turning the atmosphere of festivity and prayer into one of carnage and horror. As crowds of worshippers fled in terror, an elderly woman ran into a young boy, out of whose hands dropped a grenade. His name was Umar Fidai, a 15-year-old, and he was the third intended child suicide bomber that day. Umar's explosive vest had failed to detonate and as his handlers had instructed, he was attempting to kill himself and as many others as possible with the grenade that they had provided him as a back-up.

Umar was shot and wounded by the police and failed in his mission, but he is only one of the hundreds of other children believed to have brainwashed and utilized by the Pakistani Taliban (TTP) as suicide bomber in their ongoing war with the State. Most children recruited for suicide bombing are from poor families and are indoctrinated through networks of *madrassas* that provide the only hope of advancement in isolated regions poorly served by the Pakistani government. Many are also procured through abduction, kidnapping or coercion by armed gangs. A significant majority of suicide bombers in Pakistan are believed to be between the ages of 12 and 18, with some studies putting the percentage at around 90 per cent. The TTP commander, Qari Hussain, has stated that his organization recruits children as young as five years old for suicide attacks, because, in his words, "Children are tools to achieve God's will, whatever comes your way you sacrifice it."[122]

There are nearly 2,000 *madrassas* in the border regions of Afghanistan and Pakistan. A significant percentage of these *madrassas* are believed to be involved in brainwashing and indoctrinating young boys into militancy. The students in these schools receive free board and education. This, on the face

---

121 RalucaBesliu, Police detain child 'bombers' in Pakistan, available at: http:/www. digitaljournal.com.article/345621.

122 Murtza Hussain, Pakistani Taliban's indoctrinated child bombers, available at: http:// www.aljazeera.com/indepth/opinion/2012/10/20121014102539659862.html

of it, appears to be a remarkable opportunity for poor and isolated children, whose parents cannot afford to send them to good schools, but ultimately, it comes at a terrible price to both them and Pakistani society. The following are a few other examples.

> On 19 August 2011, at least 51 people were killed and 105 injured in a suicide attack inside Mandokhel Masjid in the Jamrud area of Khyber Agency. A young boy, who was 15–16 years old, had entered the mosque through a window and exploded himself in the main hall during the Friday prayers.

> In 2008, Aitezaz Shah, 15, was detained in the northern town of Dera Ismail Khan. He told investigators how he had been recruited by extremists after dropping out of school in Karachi in May 2007. He said he had been assigned to act as a "back-up" bomber in the assassination of Benazir Bhutto, the chairperson of Pakistan's populist People's Party, who was killed in a suicide bombing on 27 December. Aitezaz had been trained at a *madrassa* in the tribal area of South Waziristan and was preparing to carry out other attacks.

> In 2007, another 15-year-old Pakistani suicide bomber, Hainullah, who had been trained in Waziristan, was arrested in neighbouring Afghanistan, where he had been sent to carry out an attack on US troops. He said a preacher had offered him a "way out of a life of boredom" at a seminary in the area and had held out visions of paradise, where rivers of milk and honey flowed, if, in exchange, he gave up his life by becoming a suicide bomber.

> In 2007, a 14-year-old would-be bomber, Rafiqullah, was pardoned by Afghan President Hamid Karzai and sent back to Pakistan after he was arrested for wearing a "suicide vest" packed with explosives.[123]

Evidence from Pakistan suggests that child suicide bombers come from the vulnerable groups of society, and they appear to be participating due to subtle or blatant forms of coercion. Militants purposely recruit ill-educated, timid children who are easily manipulated into performing acts that they may not comprehend. The targeting of children is a part of a broader strategy of

---

123 Child suicide bombers "victims of the most brutal exploitation", available at: http://www. irinnews.org/feature/2008/02/12/child-suicide-bombers-%E2%80%9Cvictims-most-brutal-exploitation%E2%80%9D.

the militants, who employ children for a variety of tasks.

Interviews of rescued child suicide bombers have revealed that isolated and impressionable young children were highly susceptible to intensive brainwashing by Taliban militants. The latter would make the young recruits spend weeks watching videos of atrocities and of foreign troops raping women and girls—a fate which they said would await their own female relatives if they did not carry out suicide operations on behalf of the TTP. Cut off from parental contact, the young children are easily influenced by surrogate authority figures, such as the religious clerics in the *madrassas*. Many such child soldiers are told that they are acting in the name of Islam and if they carry out their missions successfully, they will be rewarded with heaven.

A new boarding school has been established in Swat Valley in Pakistan to rehabilitate and deradicalize former child militants. The army-sponsored centre currently houses nearly 100 young boys who are between the ages of 15 and 18 years, and were either captured by the military or brought in by their families. Some of these children were trained by insurgent groups as slaves or thieves, and some as bombers. The rehabilitation of these boys and studying them gives us a deeper insight into the indoctrination of child militants in Pakistan.[124]

Recruitment in the Armed Forces

The age for enlistment in the armed forces of Pakistan is between 17 and 22 years for officers and between 16 and 25 for soldiers.[125] Fighter pilots can be admitted for training at the age of 16 years. The Pakistani government claims that although under-18s are recruited, there are adequate safeguards to ensure that they are not involved in armed conflict till they reach the age of 18 years.[126] There are a number of cadet colleges that admit children from

---

124 Kalsoom Lakhani, 29 March 2010, Pakistan's Child Soldiers, *Foreign Policy*, available at: http://foreignpolicy.com/2010/03/29/pakistans-child-soldiers/

125 Article 39 of the 1973 Constitution of Pakistan provides that the State shall enable people from all parts of Pakistan to participate in the Armed Forces of Pakistan. There is no conscription in Pakistan. The 1952 Pakistan Army Act allows compulsory military service to be introduced in times of emergency, but this provision has never been applied, as the number of voluntary recruits has been sufficient.

126 In Pakistan, the minimum age for voluntary recruitment is set at 18 years, with the possibility of beginning two years earlier (at 16) for training. However, according to the official website of Pakistan's air force (http://www.joinpaf.gov.pk), an individual may join as an aero-technician from the age of 15 years (one year below internationally accepted standards). According to the website, training for aero-technicians lasts a minimum of 46

the age of 10 years. However, these colleges focus exclusively on academic pursuits and no military training is imparted. The students do not receive any stipend. They are not considered members of the army, and may choose whether or not to join the army after completing their schooling and attaining the age of 18 years.

While the Pakistan armed forces do not officially deploy children for active military combat, there are ancillary forces that do not follow these regulations. There are serious allegations that some within Pakistan's security establishment are affiliated to NSAGs. While it is difficult to confirm these links, some groups also recruit children. The Taliban and other armed groups, such as the Lashkar-e-Taiba, are widely believed to recruit children, although their numbers remain unknown. Once recruited, child soldiers are required to perform a range of tasks, which include front-line combat, exploding landmines, detonating bombs, scouting, spying, guarding camps, cooking and other support functions. They are transferred to the front lines of conflict areas, where they are exposed to the grave risk of physical harm. Whilst the primary responsibility for ensuring that children are not recruited and used in hostilities rests with the relevant armed groups, the government has a responsibility to take all feasible measures to prevent the recruitment and use of children by such groups, and promote and facilitate their release and reintegration. This is particularly crucial in cases where State agencies provide overt or covert support to armed groups. However, the government does not appear to prioritize the release of children from these groups.[127]

The most striking form of child abuse is visible in Pakistan, where *jihadi* extremists are involved in the recruitment and indoctrination of children and their transformation into child soldiers and suicide bombers. These children are shown brightly coloured paintings meant to depict the heavenly delights, including rivers of milk and honey and female virgins, which await them.[128] In the past two decades, Pakistan has made very little

---

and a maximum of 143 weeks, depending on the trade and skills requirements. In theory, it would, therefore, be possible for aero-technicians to be fully trained and qualified for active service before their sixteenth birthday. In these circumstances, it is unclear whether additional safeguards exist to prevent them from being deployed in situations of armed conflict.

127 Alternative Report to the Committee on the Rights of Child on the occasion of the Pakistan's fifth periodic report on the Convention on the Rights of Child: Child Soldiers International NGO report, July 2015, p. 8-9.

128 Franklin Lawrence A., Children as Suicide Bombers in Islamic Countries, 18 September 2014, available at: http://www.gatestoneinstitute.org/4701/child-suicide-bombers, accessed 12 January 2016.

progress towards recognizing child rights. It has ratified the Convention on the Rights of the Child (CRC) and signed the CRC's Optional Protocols related to the recruitment of child soldiers and child pornography (the ratification is pending). It has also ratified the ILO Conventions 182 and 138. Only one major law relating to child labour has been introduced during the past 18 years, i.e., the Employment of Children Act 1991. Laws for making primary education compulsory have been introduced in all provinces and areas, except the province of Baluchistan, the Northern Areas and Pakistan-Occupied Kashmir, but have yet to be enforced. There are no laws relating to child rights in the North-West Frontier Province (NWFP), the province of Baluchistan, the Federally Administered and the Provincially Administered Tribal Areas, the Northern Areas and Pakistan-Occupied Kashmir.[129] In fact, there are no legal provisions in Pakistan to safeguard the rights of children under 18 years of age, in particular, by prohibiting and criminalizing their recruitment and use in hostilities by armed forces and NSAGs.[130] On the whole, the legislative environment is ineffective and inadequate to provide effective protection to children.

Palestine and Israel

Children in Palestine continue to suffer daily human rights abuses. Palestinian armed groups have been accused of recruiting children for direct or indirect participation in combat, including suicide missions. In June 2002, Issa Bdir, a 16-year-old Palestinian boy, was dispatched by the Al-Aqsa Martyrs Brigade to Rishon Letzion, a suburb of Tel Aviv. His hair dyed blond so that he should appear European, he entered a crowded pedestrian mall packed with elderly people and foreign workers and blew himself up, killing two Israelis (including a teenager) and wounding over 30 others. Bdir became the youngest person at the time to have completed a suicide mission in Israel.[131]

There are allegations that the Israel Defence Forces (IDF) have also recruited Palestinian children as informers and used them as human shields

---

129 Alternative Report on the State of Child Rights in Pakistan by Civil Society of Pakistan, Save the Children UK (Pakistan office) and the Society for the Protection of the Rights of the Child (SPARC), March 2009, p. 3.

130 Alternative Report to the Committee on the Rights of Child on the occasion of the Pakistan's fifth periodic report on the Convention on the Rights of Child: Child Soldiers International NGO report, July 2015, p. 4.

131 Ha'aretz Staff and Agencies, 16 Year-Old Rishon Bomber was Youngest to Strike in Israel, *Ha'aretz*, 9 June 2002.

during military operations.[132]Human rights organizations have documented 17 cases of Palestinian children being used as human shields by the IDF from April 2004 to August 2010. The children were tied to the bonnet of an IDF military jeep for hours during clashes; forced to walk at gunpoint in front of Israeli soldiers and enter an abandoned house in search of combatants; or detained close to military operations for a few days during war in Gaza. The use of children as human shields is violative of the rules of IHL.

Palestinian Authority

The Palestinian Authority (PA) does not have a system of universal conscription for its security services, which include the Presidential Guard (Force 17), the Preventive Security Force associated with Fatah and the Executive Security Force associated with Hamas.[133] Recruitment for all government service is on a voluntary basis, starting from the age of 18 years.[134]Article 46 of the Palestinian Child Law of 2004 prohibited the use of children in armed conflicts. The amended Basic Law of 2005 also prohibited the abuse of children.[135] According to the Child Soldier Global Report 2008, children have been given military training by armed Palestinian groups.[136]

The military wings of Palestinian political groups – Hamas, Fatah,

---

132 In 2011, the UN reported that Palestinian children had been used as human shields by the Israeli security forces for the third consecutive year, with three new cases documented in three separate incidents in the West Bank during 2010. See Children and armed conflict, Report of the Secretary-General, UN Doc A/65/820-S/2011/250, 23 April 2011, paragraph 122.

133 Hamas, or the *Haraka al-Musallaha al-Islamiya*(Islamic Resistance Movement), organizes its functions into political, welfare and military wings in Palestine. The number of actual fighters or people engaged in support functions in the military wing is not known.

134 Both the UN Committee Against Torture and the Human Rights Committee have recommended that all interrogations of Palestinian children held in Israeli custody be audio-visually recorded. The UN Committee Against Torture, Concluding Observations, Israel (14 May 2009), CAT/C/ISR/CO/4 – paragraph 16; and the UN Human Rights Committee, Concluding Observations, Israel (29 July 2010), ICCPR/C/ISR/CO/3 – paragraph 22.

135 UN Committee Against Torture, Concluding Observations, Israel (14 May 2009), CAT/C/ISR/CO/4; UN Human Rights Committee, Concluding Observations, Israel (29 July 2010), ICCPR/C/ISR/CO/3; Report of the Special Rapporteur on the situation of human rights in the Palestinian territories occupied in 1967, Richard Falk, 10 January 2011, A/HRC/16/72.

136 Child Soldier: Global Report 2008, The Coalition to Stop the Use of Child Soldiers, p. 258-259.

Islamic Jihad and the Popular Front for the Liberation of Palestine (PFLP) – have recruited children as young as 11–13 years of age for various tasks, like smuggling of explosives and weapons and acting as suicide bombers. It has been reported that thousands of Palestinian children from the Gaza Strip are receiving military training as part of Hamas' summer camps on a regular basis. The camps, which are held under the banner "Vanguards of Liberation", are aimed at preparing children to fight against Israel. According to Hamas officials in the Gaza Strip, more than 25,000 children joined its camps for training in 2015. Families are not hesitant to send their children for training as future *jihadis* in the war against Israel. On the contrary, many are proud to see their children being taught how to use various types of weapons.

The summer camps are held in bases belonging to Hamas' armed wing, Ezaddin al-Qassam, throughout the Gaza Strip. The declared goal of the camps is to "prepare a new generation of Palestinian youths spiritually, mentally and physically for the battle to liberate Palestine". These Palestinian children are being educated and trained to prepare for joining the war aimed at destroying Israel. The children are taught that their role models are the Hamas suicide bombers and terrorists responsible for the death of hundreds of Israelis over the past few decades.[137]

Once trained and indoctrinated, the child suicide bombers are sent into action by Hamas. Hamas typically lets the bombers choose their targets themselves. The target might be a bus or workplace. A large number of suicide bombing attacks have been carried out by children since the Israel–Palestine conflict flared up again in 2000. Knowing that the soldiers of the Israeli Defence Forces (IDF) have been ordered not to shoot live ammunition at children, Palestinian snipers hide among and behind groups of children, on rooftops, in alleys or orchards, often using the kids as shields when aiming at exposed IDF soldiers. Hamas has also been accused of kidnapping and murdering three Jewish boys in Israel.[138]

Palestinian children and teenagers are directly involved in terror attacks, especially suicide bombings. On 30 March 2002, Ayat Akhras, a 16-year-old Palestinian girl, walked into a Jerusalem supermarket and detonated

---

137 Toameh Khaled Abu, Hamas's Child Abuse Camps, 30 July 2015, available at: https://www.gatestoneinstitute.org/6259/hamas-camps-child-abuse, accessed 10 February 2017.

138 Franklin Lawrence A., Children as Suicide Bombers in Islamic Countries, 18 September 2014, available at: http://www.gatestoneinstitute.org/4701/child-suicide-bombers, accessed 12 January 2016.

a bomb hidden under her clothing, killing two Israelis and wounding 22 others. In May 2002, a 16-year-old Palestinian boy was arrested at an IDF roadblock near Jenin as he had a suicide bomb on his body. On 13 June 2002, a 15-year-old Palestinian girl, arrested for throwing a firebomb at IDF soldiers, admitted during interrogation that she had previously been recruited as a suicide terrorist. On 24 March 2004, 14-year-old Hussam Abdu was caught at an IDF roadblock with an explosive belt wrapped around his chest. He told investigators that he had been paid 100 shekels (approximately USD $25) to carry out a suicide bombing.[139] Possibly the most tragic example is that of a semi-retarded 16-year-old, who was convinced by Hamas to strap himself with explosives. He was caught by the Israeli police in the town of Nablus, just before he was to blow himself up at a checkpoint.[140] The children are also employed in other areas of terrorist activity. They carry ammunition and explosives or are left behind to trigger booby-traps that terrorists set for troops.[11]

After the operation has been carried out, the group concerned is usually quick to claim credit. The success of an operation is seen both as an achievement of the group's wider goal to spread fear, as well as an aid in its recruiting strategy. For example, Hamas and Palestinian Islamic Jihad typically notify the local media right after an attack and distribute copies of the attacker's final video or audio message. After this, the action is extolled in local organizations affiliated with the group, such as mosques or schools. The heroism of the youth might also be praised through graffiti and leaflets that are posted (usually depicting the bomber in Paradise under a flock of green birds, referring to a belief that the soul of a martyr is carried to Allah upon the wings of a green bird of Paradise).

Television and radio stations, Internet websites, religious sermons, school textbooks, newspapers and magazines, and even summer camp curricula are all directly or indirectly controlled by the PA, which uses them to glorify martyrdom and convince Palestinian children to engage in life-threatening behaviour. Television programmes of all kinds displaying images of blood and dead children are frequently broadcast, followed by scenes of children

---

139 Amos Harel, Palestinians: Policeman Hurt in IDF Raid in Gaza Refugee Camp, *Ha'aretz*, 25 March 2004.

140 Gul Luft, The Palestinian H-Bomb, *Foreign Affairs*, July 2002; Coalition to Stop the Use of Child Soldiers (CSC), 1379 Report (www.child-soldiers.org), 2002, p. 54; Suzanne Goldenberg, A Mission to Murder, *The Guardian* (London),11 June 2003; and Johanna McGeary, Inside Hamas, *Time*, 28 March 2004.

playing, captioned with the slogan, "Seek Death – The Life will be Given to You". Calendars that even have illustrations of the "martyr of the month" are distributed.

For many Palestinian children, incitement begins at home. Many parents believe that the death of their child for the sake of holy *jihad* and Islam will guarantee him or her everlasting life and bliss in the hereafter. This type of sacrifice has become a badge of pride in certain segments of Palestinian society. The father of a 13-year-old says, "I pray that God will choose him to become a *shahid*."[141] The mother of a 13-year-old, who perished as a result of his participation in the *Intifada*, told a journalist: "I am happy that he has been martyred. I will sacrifice all my sons and daughters (12 in all) to Al-Aqsa and Jerusalem."[142] Another reason why Palestinian parents allowed and even encouraged their children to get involved was the financial incentive offered to the families of the 'martyrs'. Thus, the Palestinian authorities furnished a cash payment—USD $2,000 per child killed and USD $300 per child wounded. From the beginning of the *intifada*[143] until the capture of Baghdad

---

141 Chris Hedges, The Glamour of Martyrdom, *New York Times*, 29 October 2001.

142 Sam Kelly, A Deadly Game, *The Times (London)*, 19 October 2000.

143 The first Palestinian *intifada* ("uprising" or "shaking off") officially began on 9 December 1987 as a response to a deadly collision in the Jabaliya refugee camp between an Israeli military truck and a Palestinian car in which four Palestinians were killed. Over the course of the *intifada* (1987–93), an estimated 1,100 Palestinians were killed by Israeli forces and 164 Israelis were killed by Palestinians. In addition, 120,000 Palestinians were arrested and an estimated 1,000 Palestinians were killed by Palestinians themselves as alleged collaborators. The second *intifada* began in late September of 2000 in East Jerusalem. Although the actual cause of this *intifada* is still not well known, it started right after Ariel Sharon, the leader of Israel's right-wing Likud Party, who was running for Prime Minister, visited *al-Haram al-Sharif* or the Temple Mount in Jerusalem on 28 September 2000. Apparently, his visit inflamed some Palestinian nationalist sentiments as it was viewed as a deliberately provocative symbol of Israeli control over all of Jerusalem, east and west. The following day, a large number of young Palestinians demonstrated against Sharon's visit and began clashing with the Israeli police force. The second *intifada* was typified by armed conflict, guerilla warfare and terrorist attacks. The majority of the suicide attacks were carried out by Hamas and the Islamic Jihad, although the military wing of *Fatah*—the al-Aqsa Brigades—participated in a few. By the end of 2004, there had been 135 Palestinian suicide bombings, which had killed 500 Israeli civilians and brought the war right to the centre of Israel's cities. According to the summary of data released by the Israeli Information Centre for Human Rights, a total of 6,371 Palestinians (including 1,317 minors) were killed by the Israeli forces. The Palestinian suicide bombs and rockets killed 1,083 Israelis inside Israel and in the Occupied Territories. Of these fatalities, 741 were civilians, 124 being minors and 342 being members of the security forces.

by allied forces in April 2003, the Arab Liberation Front, a Palestinian group loyal to former Iraqi President Saddam Hussein, paid generous bounties to the injured and the families of the Palestinian dead ($500 for a wound; $1,000 for disability; $10,000 to the family of each martyr; and $25,000 to the family of every suicide bomber).[144]Given the chronic unemployment and poverty of the Palestinians residing in the West Bank and Gaza Strip, this amount is a huge incentive for the families of future child soldiers.[145] However, on a few occasions, Palestinian families have publicly blamed the loss on the militant organizations.[146]

The PA and NSAGs have been denying that they use children as suicide bombers. The youngest Palestinian suicide bomber, 14-year-old Hussam Abdo, was caught during a security check at the Hawara check point in the West Bank in March 2004. The personnel at the IDF checkpoint stopped Hussam after noticing the bulk under his sweater. The security personnel then patiently removed the explosives from his body. If Hussam had detonated the device, he could have killed the Israeli soldiers and 200–300 Arabs awaiting security checks. At first, Al Aqsa Martyrs Brigades claimed responsibility for Hussam's heroic attempt to martyr himself. However, when the media revealed that the bomber was a 14-year-old child, Al Aqsa denied having sent him and claimed that the previous information was a fabrication of Israeli propagandists.[147]

Israeli Defence Forces

The IDF[148] employs a number of techniques to maintain control over the

---

144 Justus Reid Weiner, Children on the Frontlines: Palestinian and Pakistani Child Abuse, 1 January 2010, http://jcpa.org/article/children-on-the-frontlines-palestinian-and-pakistani-child-abuse/.

145 Hassan Fattah, Saddam Rewards Palestinian Martyrs, *Jerusalem Post*, 14 March 2003.

146 In November 2003, a 16-year--oldboy, Sabih Abu Saud,had strapped himself with explosives. He detonated the device when cornered by Israeli soldiers. Fortunately, it inflicted only a minor injury on an Israeli soldier. Sabih was unfortunately killed in the blast. It was reported that he had been sent by the Al Aqsa Martyrs' Brigade, a group that has ties with Yasser Arafat's Fatah movement. Sabih's father did not declare his son a hero; instead, he said that the group responsible should have left his son alone and that he was only a "little boy".

147 Lt Col Lillian A. James-O'Neal, Suicide Bombers--Some Were Merely Children, US Army War College, unpublished thesis.

148 All Israelis are required to perform military service from the age of 18 years. Men are expected to serve for 36 months and women for 24 months. Children are assessed and

Occupied Palestinian Territory, including the recruitment of Palestinians as informants. The task of the informant is to monitor the movement and activities of people living in his or her neighbourhood and to pass this information onto the Israeli forces. The types of activities monitored range from involvement in armed resistance and political activism to children throwing stones. The primary means by which Israeli forces seek to recruit Palestinians, including children, as informants appears to occur during their interrogation following arrest. Each year, Israeli forces arrest and interrogate approximately 500–700 Palestinian children from the West Bank, after which the children are prosecuted in military courts. The majority of these children are accused of throwing stones. It is estimated that since 2000 alone, around 7,500 Palestinian children, some as young as 12 years of age, have been detained and prosecuted in the system. Under this military detention system, children are frequently arrested from the family home by heavily armed soldiers in the middle of the night. They are tied and blindfolded before being placed in the back of a military vehicle and transferred to an interrogation and detention centre. It is rare for a child, or his/her parents, to be told the reason for arrest or where the child is being taken. The arrest and transfer process is frequently accompanied by both physical and verbal abuse.[149]

As alleged, children are questioned by the Israeli forces in the absence of a lawyer or family member. Few children are informed of their right to silence at the time of arrest or prior to being questioned. During the interrogation, children are frequently threatened and physically assaulted, which often results in a coerced confession or the signing of documents that the child has not been given a chance to read or understand. It is also at this point that attempts to recruit children as informants occur. These attempts usually involve a combination of inducements and threats.[150] The

---

interviewed for service in the armed forces from the age of sixteen-and-a-half years, and at 17, they are issued formal call-up notices. Voluntary recruitment is allowed from the age of 17 years, although the armed forces state that "frontline" duties are possible only from 18. Exemption is possible on medical grounds and at the discretion of the Minister of Defence. Only women can state religion or family status as grounds for exemption.

149 DCI-Palestine, In their own Words: A report on the situation facing Palestinian children detained in the Israeli military court system, 19 July 2011, available at: http://www. dcipalestine.org/documents/submission-situation-facing-palestinian-children-detained-israelimilitary-detention.

150 A few examples of the types of threats and inducements used in attempts to recruit children as informants include: (i) offering early release, (ii) offering money in return for

body primarily responsible for recruiting Palestinian children as informants is the Israel Security Agency (ISA), also known as the Shabak. The Shabak is Israel's domestic agency responsible for gathering intelligence; it carries out covert operations in the Occupied Palestinian Territory, conducts some interrogations and reports directly to the Israeli Prime Minister.[151] However, the prohibition against coercing persons to become informants has been endorsed by the Israeli High Court of Justice.[152]

Similar to Afghanistan and Pakistan, the disturbing practice of deadly child abuse is on the rise in Palestine also. Two factors have led Palestinian groups to use children during the two *intifadas*. The first motivating factor was strategic, in that having children take part in the violence (whether it be burning tyres or throwing Molotov cocktails) was a way to attract television cameras, which would give visibility to the Palestinian cause on the world's screens. The second factor was tactical. Israeli troops had a standing order not to shoot live ammunition against children under the age of twelve. So Palestinian gunmen began to work in tandem with children, using them to draw out Israeli troops as well as provide a screen for their sniping.[153]

For the PA, suicide bombing serves as an efficient method for weaker forces to strike at an otherwise well-prepared opposition. Even if they lack the technology for guided missiles or other "smart bombs", the inclusion of the human element allows groups to create a thinking bomb that can adjust to changing circumstances. According to a Hamas leader, "We do not have tanks or rockets, but we have something superior—our exploding Islamic human bombs. In place of a nuclear arsenal, we are proud of our arsenal of believers."[154] Compared to the typical costs of guided weaponry, the human child bomb is cheap. According to Palestinian experts, the total cost of a typical operation is about $150, with the most expensive part often being the bus fare paid for the

---

information, (iii) offering to provide a car or a house in return for information, and (iv) threatening the child with imprisonment if the child does not become an informant.

151 Recruitment and Use of Palestinian Children in Armed Conflict, Defence for Children International – Palestine Section (DCI-Palestine), February 2012.

152 *Adalah v Military Commander of the West Bank* (HCJ 3799) (2005), the then Chief Justice, Aharon Barak, paragraph 24.

153 Jack Kelley, Street Clashes Now Deliberate Warfare, *USA Today*, 23 October 2000; Herb Keinon, Israel to the UN: Keep Palestinians from Using Kids as Shields, *Jerusalem Post*, 8 November 2000; and D. Kuttab, A Profile of the Stone Throwers, *Journal of Palestine Studies*, Vol.17, 1998, p. 14–23.

154 Nasra Hassan, "An Arsenal of Believers," *The New Yorker*, 19 November 2001.

transport of the bomber to his/her target. and the child bomber is then able to kill or wound all individuals within an area of 25–50 metres.[155]

Somalia

Somalia has experienced both political fortunes and misfortunes since independence from European rule in 1960. In 1960, Somaliland and Somalia were brought together by passionate nationalism, coupled with ambitions to extend the resulting Somalia republic to include the entire nation and other Somali-speaking persons from the neighbouring Africa region. However, political misfortunes extinguished these nationalist ambitions.[156] The Somali people have suffered from long-standing oppression and violence at the hands of their fellow Somalis. Between 1992 and 1996, Somaliland experienced two civil wars.[157]

Underlying the Somali conflict is a multifaceted array of causes, including political, economic, cultural and psychological. Various peripheral and internal actors have played different roles during various stages of the conflict. The lawlessness in Somalia not only affects the people within Somalia, but also has a number of negative effects on the neighbouring countries. In mid-2015, the African Union Mission in Somalia (AMISOM)[158] and the Somali

---

155 GehudAuda, *Palestinian Suicide Bombing: Description and Evaluation*, Ahram Strategic Papers, no. 114 (Cairo, Egypt: Al-Ahram Center for Political and Strategic Studies, 2002); and Hassan, "Arsenal of Believers."

156 Somali gained independent in 1960 when the British Somaliland protectorate was united with the Italian-administered United Nations territory of Somalia. During the self-governing era (1960–1969), self-rule and newly established state institutions failed to meet the people's expectations.

157 From December 1991 to March 1992, the country was torn apart by clan-based warfare, and factions plundered the remnants of the state and fought for control of rural and urban assets. Four months of fighting in Mogadishu in 1991 and 1992 killed an estimated 25,000 people, 1.5 million people fled the country, and at least 2 million were internally displaced. A limited UN peacekeeping mission – the UN Operation in Somalia (UNOSOM) – was unable to stem the violence or address the famine. In December 1992, the outgoing US administration authorized the deployment of US forces to support the beleaguered UN mission in Somalia. Under US leadership, UNOSOM mustered a multinational force of some 30,000 troops. UNOSOM dominated Somali politics for the next three years. However, the mission failed to mediate an end to hostilities. UNOSOM became embroiled in the conflict, leading to the infamous shooting down of US Black Hawk helicopters in Mogadishu and the subsequent withdrawal of US forces. UNOSOM's humiliating departure from Somalia was followed by international disengagement and a decline in foreign aid.

158 AMISOM is an active, regional peacekeeping mission operated by the African Union

National Army launched a joint military operation, code-named "Operation Juba Corridor", against Al-Shabaab. With the loss of its strongholds and the weakening of its forces, al-Shabaab increasingly resorted to asymmetrical attacks against the Somali National Army, AMISOM and soft targets, including through ambushes, hit-and-run attacks, suicide bombings and the use of improvised explosive devices. These attacks often resulted in heavy civilian casualties, including women and children.[159]

Somali Armed Forces

The Federal Government of Somalia Armed Forces (SNAF) comprise the Somali National Army (SNA), the Somali Air Force, the Somali Navy, the Somali Police and prison forces. Additionally, various entities have operated in different combinations in support of the Somali National Army, including clan militias and regional security forces. Somalia has ratified the Convention on the Rights of the Child in October 2015. Earlier, in March 2014, it ratified the International Labour Organization Worst Forms of Child Labour Convention, 1999 (No. 182), which includes provisions on child recruitment in armed conflict.

Non-State Armed Groups

Al-Shabaab emerged as an independent militant group in 2006 after breaking away from the Union of Islamic Courts. While the group's activities focused on targets within Somalia, it also carried out deadly strikes in the region. Al-Shabaab remained a major threat to Somalia and the region despite significant territorial losses. ASWJ is a Somali militia that controls parts of Galmudug, including its capital, Dhuusamarreeb. It joined forces with the Transitional Federal Government in 2010 to fight Al-Shabaab, presumably in exchange for positions in the government.

In Somalia, Al-Shabaab and the ASWJ are responsible for the recruitment and use, as well as killing and maiming of children in armed conflict. The

---

with the approval of the United Nations. The AMISOM forces are supported by troops from Burundi, Djibouti, Ethiopia, Kenya, Sierra Leone and Uganda, and police forces from Ghana, Kenya, Nigeria, Sierra Leone and Uganda. These forces are referred to as government-friendly forces.

159 According to the International Committee of the Red Cross (ICRC), in the year 2010, 43 percent of patients admitted to the two main referral hospitals in Mogadishu with war-related injuries were women and children. Somalia: ever higher numbers of war-wounded in Mogadishu hospitals, ICRC news release, 27 January 2011.

government armed forces are also responsible for the recruitment and the use of children.[160]

Recruitment and Use of Children

The UN verified that between 2014 and 2016, there were 6,163 cases (5,933 boys and 230 girls) of the recruitment and use of children in Somalia.[161] A recurrent pattern of child recruitment and use by the Somali National Army[162] and armed groups was observed during this period. It is estimated that children may constitute more than half of AlShabaab. For example, at least 60 per cent of the AlShabaab elements captured in Puntland in March 2016 were children. Children were trained and used in combat, with some as young as nine years of age reportedly being taught to use weapons and sent to the front line. Children were deployed in operations that included the use of explosive devices, and in support roles, such as carrying ammunitions or performing domestic chores. They were also used as spies during intelligence operations and counter-terrorism activities. In addition to using children in its more conventional combat operations, Al-Shabaab has also used them as suicide bombers.[163]Children have been exposed to other grave violations, including killing and maiming, during military operations and air strikes targeting Al-Shabaab. Further, they have been subjected to arrest and detention by the Somali security forces during military or search operations. In September 2016, a number of children, between the ages of 15 and 17

---

160 Report of the Secretary-General on children and armed conflict in Somalia, UN Doc. S/2016/1098 dated 22 December 2016.

161 The main perpetrator was al-Shabaab, with 4,313 verified cases, followed by the Somali National Army (920), ASWJ (346), regional security forces consisting of Galmudug Interim Administration, Interim Jubba Administration, Somaliland and Puntland forces (193) and unknown armed elements. The use of 40 children by AMISOM in support roles was also verified. Report of the Secretary-General on children and armed conflict in Somalia, UN Doc S/2016.1098 dated 22 December 2016, para 15.

162 Notwithstanding an action plan signed in 2012, the Somali National Army continued to recruit and use children for various tasks, including manning checkpoints and as bodyguards. Recruitment and use by the Somali National Army were verified throughout the reporting period, with 179 cases in 2012, 209 in 2013,197 in 2014 and 218 in 2015. During the first half of 2016, 117 children were recruited and used by the Somali National Army. While many children were believed to have joined the Somali National Army because of lack of livelihood opportunities and extreme poverty, others were abducted for recruitment purposes. Report of the Secretary-General on children and armed conflict in Somalia, UN Doc S/2016/1098 dated 22 December 2016, para 23-24.

163 No Place for Children: Child Recruitment, Forced Marriage, and Attacks on Schools in Somalia, Human Rights Watch, 2012, p. 33.

years, were sentenced to 10 to 20 years of imprisonment by a military court in Garoowe. Earlier, in June 2016, 12 children were sentenced to death by a military court and transferred to Boosaaso, where they were held together with adults. The UN has also verified that there were 1,023 cases of abduction of children between 2014 and 2016. Abductions were used primarily as a tactic for recruitment. They were also linked to rape, sexual violence and forced marriage.[164]

With an estimated population of 11,332,000 as of April 2017, Somalia is counted as one of the least developed countries in the world. More than 2 million people in the country are displaced and 5 million need humanitarian assistance. Due to the long-standing state of conflict in Somalia, children remain vulnerable, as both government and non-state parties continue to be involved in violations against them. There has been an increase in the recruitment, use, killing and maiming of children.[165] An increase in the detention of children for association with armed groups has also been documented. A child protection unit has been established in the Somalia Armed Forces, and mechanisms have been put in place for handing over children found in their ranks to the United Nations.

South Sudan

The South Sudan government has enacted legislation criminalizing the recruitment and use of children under 18 by the armed forces.[166] South

---

164 Young girls are often taken as wives for Al-Shabaab militiamen without consulting or asking for their parents' consent on the marriage of their daughters. Asha, a mother whose daughter was brainwashed by the Al-Shabaab teachers in the Madrassas and was married to an Al-Shabaab fighter, said how it happens: "The girls, who are still very young, like 15 years of age, are taken by the Al-Shabaab fighters. Some of the girls agree to marry the armed men and others are forced into these marriages. The girls who agree to marry the Al-Shabaab militia men are the ones who were brainwashed in the Madrassas and who are lured by the stories and the future promises made to them by the Al-Shabaab militia. On the other hand, those who are married by force are told that an Al-Shabaab fighter wants to marry you and he is a good man who can take care of you. If the girl refuses, she is said to have betrayed a fellow brother who is fighting for the religion. In the process, the girl's father is talked to and threatened with death. Fearing for his life, he agrees to the marriage." Martin Okwir, Children at Risk: Protection of Children in Somalia, Occasional paper series 4, No 5, 2013, International Peace Support Training Center (IPSTC), p. 52.

165 Ibid, p. 52.

166 Article 17 of the Transitional Constitution of South Sudan (2012) defines a child as anyone under the age of 18 years and specifies that every child has the right "not … to be required to serve inthe army".

Sudan's Child Act, 2008, defines a child as anyone under the age of 18 and protects children from service with the police, prison or military forces. The Act clearly states that the "minimum age for conscription or voluntary recruitment into armed forces or groups shall be 18 years". Further, "No child shall be used or recruited to engage in any military or paramilitary activities, whether armed or un-armed, including but not limited to work as sentries, informants, agents or spies, cooks, in transport, as labourers, for sexual purposes or any other forms of work that do not serve the interests of the child."[167] This law also explicitly penalizes those for the recruitment or use of a child in an armed force with imprisonment for a term not exceeding 10 years or with a fine, or with both.

The Child Act also provides that all children, including those with disabilities, have the right to free education at the primary level. This education should be compulsory. South Sudan has acceded to a number of important international treaties that ban the use of child soldiers.[168] Individuals who commit serious violations of IHL can be prosecuted in domestic or international courts for war crimes. NSAGs and their allies also have a legal obligation to respect IHL, and leaders have a responsibility to ensure that commanders and combatants abide by its requirements. The South Sudanese government and rebel armies maintain that they do not recruit child soldiers.[169]

In spite of the fact that South Sudan has ratified a number of IHL and IHRL treaties, the tragedy is that both the government forces as well as NSAGs have recruited and used children in armed conflict. It has been

---

167 The Child Act 2008, sections 17, 25, 31 and 36: The law also states that the government must "ensure that children do not take part in hostilities, are not recruited into armed forces and provide rehabilitation, protection and care for child victims or armed conflict". The law also provides that "every child has the right to express his or her opinion freely and to have that opinion taken into account in any matter or procedure affecting him or her".

168 In January 2013, South Sudan became a party to the Geneva Conventions of 1949 and their additional protocols of 1977. It has also ratified the Convention on the Rights of the Child (CRC), the UN Convention against Torture and the Convention on the Elimination of Discrimination Against Women (CEDAW).

169 It is estimated that 50,000 civilians have died and millions have been displaced as a result of fighting which has ravaged South Sudan for at least four years. James Elder, a representative for UNICEF, said that UNICEF and other UN agencies have an abundance of evidence that both parties in the conflict have been recruiting child soldiers. Available at: https://www.alaraby.co.uk/english/indepth/2016/12/15/child-soldier-recruitment-skyrockets-in-south-sudan, accessed 07 April 2017.

reported that there was widespread recruitment and use of child soldiers in South Sudan's recent war, which began in December 2013. Both the Sudan People's Liberation Army (SPLA) (government) and its allies, and the rebel Sudan People's Liberation Army (Movement)-in-Opposition (opposition) and its allies have enlisted the services of children.[170]It is estimated that nearly 16,000 child soldiers have been recruited in South Sudan so far.[171]According to a UN survey, a total of 2,342 children have been killed or maimed since fighting broke out in 2013, and a further 1,130 have been sexually assaulted.

The UN has verified 159 incidents of the recruitment and use of children, in which2,596 children have been affected. Nearly 70 per cent were attributed to the SPLA, other government security forces and allied forces, including the Cobra faction of the South Sudan Democratic Movement/ Army, which was integrated into the SPLA in 2015. Also responsible for the recruitment and use of children were the SPLM/A-in-Opposition, Johnson Olony's armed group, the Arrow Boys and the White Army. Children wearing military uniforms were spotted throughout the country, especially in the greater Upper Nile region, where they were used in direct hostilities and support roles. First-hand reports were received of children being ordered to kill civilians and loot properties in Unity State. It was reported that girls were being gang-raped and used for sexual purposes. According to the UN, the SPLM/A-in-Opposition recruited some 400 South Sudanese children from the Kharasana refugee camp, western Kordofan, in October.[172]

The SPLA has long had a policy of taking boys away from their homes for education and military training. During the protracted conflict, such boys lived in large camps, segregated from their adult counterparts. During the north–south war in Sudan, lasting from 1983 to 2005, thousands of child soldiers were used by southern rebel groups, including the SPLA, which became South Sudan's official military after the 2005 peace deal.[173] In order

---

170 We Can Die Too: Recruitment and use of child soldiers in South Sudan, Human Rights Watch, December 2015, p. 1.

171 The number of children who have fought in South Sudan's conflict is not known, but UNICEF has estimated that nearly 16,000 children may have been recruited by armed groups on both sides of the conflict.

172 Children and Armed Conflict, report of the Secretary-General, General Assembly/ Security Council Doc. A/70/836-S/2016/360 dated 20 April 2016, para 123.

173 In the 1990s, Human Rights Watch documented the use of child soldiers by both the SPLA, headed by John Garang, and the breakaway SPLA-Nasir/United, headed by Riek Machar. Thousands of boys were encouraged to leave their homes for refugee camps in

to end child soldiering in South Sudan, UNICEF signed a memorandum of understanding with Salva Kiir, the then chief-of-staff of the rebel SPLA, in 2002. UNICEF later airlifted 3,551 children from the state of Northern Bahr el Ghazal to transit centres in the state of Lakes. In 2005, thousands of children were released, many from militias that had been absorbed into the SPLA.

Since South Sudan attained independence on 9 July 2011, it has been engaged in the difficult process of state-building. Before the current armed conflict started in December 2013, child soldiers were used both by NSAGs[174] and government forces in several conflicts of a smaller scale. Government commanders used child soldiers when it was conducive to their military goals. The armed conflict in South Sudan has killed thousands of civilians, forced some 2.2 million people to leave their homes, and plunged much of the country into a humanitarian crisis. Hundreds of children have been killed, thousands have fought in the conflict and hundreds of thousands have been displaced. The conflict has devastated the education sector: some 70 percent of the country's schools have been closed since 400,000 children have been forced out of schooling.

The Government of the Republic of South Sudan signed an Action Plan with the UN to end and prevent the recruitment and use of children by the SPLA on 13 March 2012. The government formally recommitted to the Action Plan on 24 June 2014, with an additional commitment to end all grave violations against children. It launched a national campaign, Children, Not Soldiers, on 29 October 2014. The SPLA-in-Opposition signed an Action Plan with the UN to end and prevent the recruitment and use of children in December 2015.

In spite of these agreements, the children of South Sudan continue to

---

Ethiopia, ostensibly for educational purposes, but they were also given military training. In 1991, there were an estimated 17,000 boys in these camps. Many of these boys, known as the 'Red Army', fought in the conflict. Human Rights Watch/Africa Human Rights Watch Children's Rights Project, Sudan: The Lost Boys, November 1994.

174 During the 2011–2013 insurgency; a group called the South Sudan Liberation Army/ Movement (SSLA/M), initially headed by Bapiny Monytuel, used children in their rebellion against the South Sudanese government. Some 200 children from this force were due to be released after Monytuel agreed to an amnesty deal in 2013. In addition, hundreds of child soldiers fought in the 2012–2013 rebellion headed by David YauYau in the Pibor area of Jonglei state. With the assistance of UNICEF and the government, YauYau in 2015 released 1,755 children from his forces. We Can Die Too: Recruitment and use of child soldiers in South Sudan, Human Rights Watch, December 2015, p. 18.

suffer the consequences of a brutal conflict. The peace agreement, signed in August 2015, calls for an end to all grave violations against children, the immediate and unconditional release of all children recruited by parties to the conflict and the screening of troops. The recruitment and use of children remains the most widely reported violation, and the UN estimates that the SPLA, SPLA-in-Opposition and other armed groups currently have several thousand children in their ranks. In 2015, 1,755 children were released from the South Sudan Democratic Movement/Army- Cobra Faction. The children received support from the UN and were reunified with their families. South Sudan's conflict has become increasingly fractured and despite the peace deal, it is most unlikely that violence and fighting between the various groups will stop. Therefore, the recruitment and use of child soldiers may also continue.

Syria

The armed conflict in the Syrian Arab Republic, once between the government and a limited number of anti-government armed groups, has morphed into multiple shifting conflicts involving countless actors and frontlines. A number of parties have been involved in the recruitment and use of children in Syria. The list includes the Syrian government, Free Syrian Army (FSA)-affiliated groups, Kurdish People Protection Units (YPG), Ahrar Al-Sham, Jabhat al-Nusra, and Islamic State in Iraq and al-Sham (ISIS).[175]The UN General Assembly has expressed concern at the continued deterioration of the humanitarian situation in the Syrian Arab Republic, in particular, sexual and gender-based violence, abduction, physical abuse, and the recruitment and use of children in the conflict.[176]

Syrian National Recruitment Law

Under Article 40 of the Constitution, conscription was made compulsory for all Syrians. In practice, it was applicable only to Syrian (and Palestinian) males who were above 19 years of age and were living in Syria. Under the Service of the Flag Law, Decree No. 115 of 5 October 1953, the minimum age for conscription was the "first day of January in the year in which a Syrian citizen reaches 19". The law reserved the right to lower the recruitment age to 18 in times of "war or emergency" from the "first day of January following

---

175 Report of the Secretary-General on Children and Armed Conflict in the Syrian Arab Republic to the UN Security Council, 2014.

176 UN General Assembly Resolution adopted on 9 December 2016, UN Doc. A/RES/71/130 of 19 December 2016.

the date on which the recruit reaches 18 years of age".[177] In 2005, military service was reduced from 30 to 24 months. In 2007, Decree No. 30 further amended the Flag Law and updated the conditions for the deferral of service and exemptions, including study and residency abroad. Those from families with only one son were also exempted. All Syrian males between the ages of 17 and 42 years required advance permission from the recruitment department of the Armed Forces to leave the country. Voluntary recruitment was open to men and women over 18. Article 6 of the Service of the Flag Law stipulated the procedures to be followed to prevent the direct participation in hostilities of members of the armed forces below 18 years of age. There was no known domestic legislation to criminalize the recruitment of under-18s, but Syria maintained that it closely monitored the ages of recruits. Syria held that all international instruments signed by the government, including the Optional Protocol to the CRC, were treated as domestic law, so that there was no need to enact a special law to incorporate such an instrument into domestic law. There were no reports that children were being recruited into government forces.[178]

The Human Rights Council has reported that government forces in Syria have committed gross violations of human rights and the war crimes of murder, hostage-taking, torture, rape and sexual violence, recruiting and using children in hostilities, and targeting civilians.[179]

Government-supported Armed Groups

In the ongoing conflict, the Syrian government is relying heavily on irregular and foreign forces, such as militias, Lebanese Shia Hezbollah fighters and Iranian fighters. Since 2015, the Syrian government has also received significant aerial support from Russia. President Assad has openly defended the

---

177 Initial Report by Syria to the UN Committee on the Rights of the Child on implementation of the Optional Protocol, UN Doc CRC/C/OPAC/SYR/1, 18 April 2007.

178 On acceding to the Optional Protocol to CRC in 2003, Syria supported the "straight-18" position, and stated that "the statutes in force and the legislation applicable to the Ministry of Defence of the Syrian Arab Republic do not permit any person under 18 ... to join the active armed forces or the reserve bodies or formations". Its initial report to the Committee on the Rights of the Child relating to the Optional Protocol was considered in October 2007. The Committee appreciated a number of Syria's legal commitments on child recruitment to date, but it urged Syria to enact legislation explicitly prohibiting the recruitment of children, whether by or against Syrian nationals.2008 report

179 Report of the independent international commission of inquiry on the Syrian Arab Republic, Human Rights Council, A/HCR/27/60 dated 13 August 2014.

involvement of Hezbollah, and Iranian and Russian fighters alongside Syrian government troops. There have been reports that a number of NSAGs in the region, notably Hizbollah in Lebanon and Hamas and Palestinian Islamic Jihad (PIJ) in the Occupied Palestinian Territory, have recruited individuals under the age of 18 years in their armed forces. Palestinian groups, including PIJ, Fatah and the Popular Front for the Liberation of Palestine-General Command (PFLP-GC), have also allegedly carried out military training inside Syria; but there is no information on whether it involved under-18s. Due to the low level of school registration and the limited amount of humanitarian assistance available to the refugee population, however, refugee children face a strong risk of being recruited by these NSAGs in the future.[180]

ISIS

The ISIS[181] is actively engaged in recruiting children, whom it has dubbed the "Ashbal al Khilafah" or "Cubs of the Caliphate". The ISIS sets itself apart from other NSAGs in the recruitment, training and use of children in armed conflict. Traditionally, armed groups do not advertise their recruitment of children and try to hide the practice. The ISIS has adopted a unique policy regarding its use of children and demonstrates an uncharacteristic transparency concerning the practice. The group sees children as its future, a perspective few terror organizations have adopted. Since Syria fell apart, the ISIS has assumed full control over schools and mosques. Though many of the original Syrian schoolteachers remain, they are forced to teach an ISIS-controlled curriculum to gender-segregated pupils.[182]Today, the ISIS has created a class of highly indoctrinated child warriors. The physical activity textbook is covered with images of soldiers training with weapons, and a textbook on Mohammed's teachings depicts gun-wielding soldiers serving under the ISIS

---

180 18 UN Committee on the Rights of the Child, Consideration of report submitted by Syria, Concluding observations, UN Doc. CRC/C/OPAC/SYR/CO/1, 5 October 2007.

181 Besides attracting more experienced and ideologically motivated foreign fighters since it proclaimed itself an Islamic caliphate, the ISIS has drawn an increasing number of Syrians to its ranks, particularly after forming alliances with local tribes in the ArRaqqah, Al Hasakah and Dayraz Zawr governorates.

182 ISIL had children go through training camps in Raqqa and elsewhere in which they were taught to decapitate blond-haired dolls and use guns... One mobile application provided for children taught the alphabet and another Islamic supplication (including instructions for taking up arms against western states). Olidort Jacob, Inside the Caliphate's Classroom: Textbooks, Guidance Literature, and Indoctrination Methods of the Islamic State, The Washington Institute for Near East Policy, August 2016, p. 9.

flag.[183]Parents continue to send their children to school and the failure to do so might place the entire family at risk. The ISIS has been punishing such families by taking their homes and refusing to provide food and protection. Through a socialization and selection process, the ISIS convinces children that entry into the Cubs of the Caliphate is a rare opportunity and something that is desirable for each child.[184]

After attending ISIS schools and acquiring military skills in their training camps, boys are subsequently used as soldiers, human shields, messengers, spies, guards and suicide bombers.[185] These roles are not always fixed and may change. Children are initially trained as spies, and taught to share information on family members, neighbours or friends who do not conform to the rules and practices of the 'caliphate'. If they succeed at this stage, they are assigned other roles that entail greater responsibility. Once they are on the frontline and engaging with the enemy, they are trained to spy on them as well. Children who show an aptitude for communicating the ISIS ideology are used to spread its message, gather support and recruit others.

Children are trained in military skills for combat on the frontline. Further, they are used to guard headquarters, manufacture explosives, function as snipers and man checkpoints. In Mosul, young boys have been used for patrolling and manning ISIS checkpoints. Children are also used to execute those who do not comply with the ISIS ideology.[186] Some children assist in executions by handing adult fighters knives, while others carry out executions themselves. Children are trained in how to commit suicide attacks, and are sometimes told to wear suicide vests while performing other jobs, such as guard duties, in case they come under attack. Children used specifically as

---

183 Casey Tolan, These Are the Textbooks Supposedly Used by the Islamic State. Fusion Media Network, LLC. 28 October 2015.

184 **How the Islamic State recruits and coerces children**, 24 August 2016, available at: http://theconversation.com/how-the-islamic-state-recruits-and-coerces-children-64285.

185 In an ISIS training camp in Al-Bab (Aleppo),children from the age of 14 to 15 years undergo the same training as adults and are offered financial rewards. At the camps, the recruited children receive weapons training and religious education. The existence of such camps seems to indicate that the ISIS systematically provides weapons training for children. In ArRaqqah, children from the age of 10 years are recruited and trained at ISIS camps.

186 Children are gathered to watch videos of mass executions of government soldiers. The effects of exposure to violence are heightened when they are forced to participate in such acts. Children learn to behead through practising on dolls. Though not the actual act of beheading, this mock drill aids in desensitization, facilitating the actual act. Children who become members of the ISIS may fulfil the role of the executioner.

suicide bombers wear vests or drive vehicles full of explosives into the area concerned and detonate them on arrival. Girls are given a domestic education, which focuses on how to look after the needs of the husband, making the ISIS ideology a vital part of bringing up children, and maintaining the house. The ISIS ideology has very specific rules for girls, who are known as the 'flowers and pearls' of the caliphate. Girls are to be fully veiled, remain hidden, and never leave the house, except in exceptional circumstances.[187]

Exposure to violence aims to prepare children for actual participation in violent acts such as execution.[188]In January 2017, the ISIS released a video showing children (Cubs of Caliphate) as young as ten beheading and shooting Kurdish prisoners. The young children, who seemed to be around 10 years old, were filmed wearing camouflage army-style uniforms while brutally killing their victims in Deirez-Zor, Syria. One extremely young boy was filmed shakily clutching a gun and shooting a man in the head, as another brandished a large knife before savagely cutting a man's throat. As a part of the video, the youngsters were also seen in rifle training and waving the group's distinctive flag. The video was released by the ISIS with an Arabic title that roughly translates to "Occasional in His Own Blood".[189]

The eighth issue of *Dabiq*, the ISIS' propaganda magazine, features an article titled "The Lions of Tomorrow". Although brief, it introduces the Cubs of the Caliphate and explains their importance to the Islamic State:

> The Islamic State has taken it upon itself to fulfil the Ummah's duty towards this generation in preparing it to face the crusaders and their allies in defence of Islam and to raise high the word of Allah in every land. It has established institutes for these *ashbal* (lion cubs) to train and hone their military skills, and to teach them the book of Allah and the Sunnah of His Messenger (*sallallahu 'alayhiwasallam*). It is these young lions to whom the Islamic State recently handed over two agents caught spying for Russian intelligence and an agent

---

187 Benotman Noman and Nikita Malik, The Children of Islamic State, Quilliam, March 2016, p. 41–45.

188 Anderson Kara, Cubs of the Caliphate: The Systematic Recruitment, Training, and Use of Children in the Islamic State, available at: www.drake.edu/media/departmentsoffices/international/nelson/2016.

189 Available at: https://www.thesun.co.uk/news/2564492/harrowing-isis-video-shows-children-as-young-as-10-beheading-and-shooting-kurdish-prisoners-in-syria/, accessed 10 March 2017.

caught spying for the Israeli Mossad, to be executed and displayed as an example to anyone else thinking of infiltrating the mujahidin.[190]

The ISIS' exploitation of children is on the rise, and they are being abducted and recruited at alarming rates. According to the Syrian Observatory for Human Rights, in 2015, the ISIS targeted schools and mosques to recruit 400 children. The UN Assistance Mission for Iraq estimated that in addition to those recruited, the ISIS had abducted 800–900 children between the ages of nine and 15 years. One expert estimated that there are at least 1,500 children in the ranks of the Caliphate. By using children as soldiers, suicide bombers and executioners, the ISIS has been gaining the psychological upper hand against its opponents. The ISIS videos have drawn global attention and are giving rise to increasing fear of the organization worldwide.[191]

The ISIS has not limited its recruitment or use of children to within its borders. A number of countries are experiencing increased levels of the recruitment of youth and their training in the ISIS ideology. Countries in the immediate vicinity of the ISIS are more vulnerable to the recruitment of children. The ISIS has violated IHL and IHRL and committed war crimes by recruiting and using children below the age of 15 years in armed conflict.[192]It is continuing to prime its children inside the Caliphate to become the jihadis of tomorrow, using the teachings of Mohammed to justify these actions.[193]

---

190 The Lions of Tomorrow, *Dabiq*: Shari'ah Alone Will Rule Africa, Issue 8 (2015): 20–21. Accessed at http://media.clarionproject.org/files/islamic-state/isis-isil-islamic-state-magazine-issue+8-sharia-alone-will-rule-africa.pdf.

191 Gorka Sebastian L., Katharine C. Gorka and Claire Herzog, Rising Threat: The Islamic State's Militarization of Children, Threat Knowledge Group, August 2016, p. 4.

192 Report of the independent international commission of inquiry on the Syrian Arab Republic, Human Rights Council, A/HCR/27/60 dated 13 August 2014, para 95.

193 The "Islam" that the Islamic State promotes in its literature blends the purism of Salafism with the empowerment of the Islamic State as the enforcer of Islam, with the justification that it is the only area in which this pure original Islam is applied and because, as caliphate, it has the authority to define what Islam is. By extension, as the IS view goes, anyone residing outside of IS territory or who refuses to defend its cause is not a true Muslim. Islamic concepts are reframed to include obedience to the Islamic State as a legally-binding obligation. For example, the group defines *hijra*(migration) as flight from a country of oppression to the Islamic State (rather than just flight from oppression). Inside the Caliphate's Classroom, Textbooks, Guidance Literature, and Indoctrination Methods of the Islamic State, The Washington Institute for Near East Policy, Policy Focus 147, August 2016.

Kurdish Armed Groups

The Kurdish People's Protection Units (YPG) have also consolidated their control over the de facto self-regulated Kurdish regions in the north, namely Afrin, Ayn al-Arab and Al-Jazeera. Instances of the recruitment of children under the age of 18 years by the YPG were documented in the Human Rights Council report (A/HRC/25/65). It has been reported that pursuant to their pledge of 5 July 14 to abolish such practices, the YPG have demobilized child soldiers from their ranks and undertaken to monitor adherence to their commitments.[194]

As the armed conflict in Syria has entered its fifth year, it has become multi-dimensional, engaging several areas of international law, including IHRL, IHL and ICL. The Independent International Commission of Inquiry on the Syrian Arab Republic, established by the UN Human Rights Council, stated in its eighth report that government forces continued to perpetrate massacres and conduct widespread attacks on civilians, systematically committing murder, torture, rape and enforced disappearance amounting to crimes against humanity, and also recruiting and using children in hostilities. The government was also accused of using chemical weapons. The Commission of Inquiry stated that non-state armed groups, including the ISIS, have committed massacres and war crimes, including murder, execution without due process, torture, enforced disappearance, rape and sexual violence, and the recruitment and use of children in hostilities.[195]

Yemen

Yemen is the poorest country in the Arabian Peninsula, with high levels of unemployment. In 2010, negotiations between the Yemeni government and the opposition on electoral and constitutional change failed. Protests followed in early 2011, resulting in a number of deaths and injuries. Following the killing of protestors by government forces, a number of officials resigned. The commander of the First Armoured Division (FAD) defected from the Yemeni army and ordered his soldiers to form a protective ring around "Change Square" to defend the protestors from future attacks from the state armed

---

194 Report of the independent international commission of inquiry on the Syrian Arab Republic, Human Rights Council, A/HCR/27/60 dated 13 August 2014, para 96(b).

195 Lattimer Mark, Shabnam Mojtahedi and Lee Anna Tucker, A Step towards Justice: Current accountability options for crimes under international law committed in Syria, Ceasefire Centre for Civilian Rights, UK, 2014, pp. 34.

forces and state-allied armed groups. In May 2011, state armed forces used live ammunition against peaceful protestors and subsequent increase in violence. It was reported that both government forces and anti-government protestors used tanks, mortar shells, machine guns and rocket-propelled grenades in their attacks on each other. On 3 June 2011, an explosion inside the mosque of the presidential palace killed 11 and seriously injured President Saleh. In addition to the 2011–2012 anti-government protests, Yemen has a history of instability and internal armed conflict.[196] In May 2012, during the military campaign against the *Ansar al-Sharia*,[197] the armed opposition group carried out a suicide attack which targeted a Yemeni military parade and killed nearly 100 people. In recent years, state armed forces and state-allied armed groups have been involved in numerous internal armed conflicts.

Article 149 of Yemen's Law No. 45 (2002) on child rights provides that persons under the age of 18 years cannot participate in armed conflict or be recruited. In spite of this prohibition, there have been consistent reports of the recruitment and use of children in hostilities by the state armed forces. In 2010, Human Rights Watch reported that children under 18 years of age had been recruited by the Yemeni army to fight in the 2009–2010 conflict against the *Al-Houthi* armed group. Since the outbreak of anti-government protests in January 2011 and the ensuing violence and civil unrest, there have been reports that the children in the ranks of the state armed forces were deployed to quell the violence and were used by the military as scouts, spies and human shields. The period after 2011 has reportedly seen widespread enlistment of children in the state armed forces, including the Republican Guard, Central Security Forces (paramilitary force under Ministry of Interior control) and FAD. In 2012, the Secretary-General for Children and Armed Conflict also reported the recruitment of children by Yemen's armed forces.[198]

---

196 Since 2004, the northernmost governorates of Yemen have experienced successive armed conflicts between an armed opposition group called the *Al-Houthi* and the state armed forces and state-allied tribal militias, causing thousands of deaths. Another conflict is ongoing in the south of Yemen, where the armed opposition group, *Ansar al-Sharia*, operates. This group reportedly has links with *al-Qaeda* in the Arab Peninsula and tried to impose a strict interpretation of Islamic law. By 2010, it had established a strong presence in the south, taking advantage of the absence of viable state institutions. It has been reported that the *Ansar al-Sharia* committed widespread and grave human rights abuses, including summary killings and amputations.

197 Al-Qaida in the Arabian Peninsula/Ansar al-Sharia.

198 The September 2011 and April 2012 reports on Yemen by the Office of the UN High Commissioner for Human Rights (OHCHR) both recorded that children had been directly involved in the violence, patrolling the streets in military uniform, serving at

In April 2012, the Ministry of Interior sent a letter to the heads of all security forces, instructing them to adhere to a minimum age of recruitment of 18 years, and to release any underage members. President Hadi also directed all military and security bodies not to recruit or use under-18s, pledged to stop recruiting and using child soldiers, and agreed to implement an action plan in accordance with Security Council Resolution 1612 (2005). In addition, on 3 December 2012, the Yemeni government endorsed the Paris Principles and Guidelines on Children Associated with Armed Forces or Armed Groups. However, as early as September 2012, it was reported that the enlistment of children by the state armed forces continued.

Today, several groups are fighting in Yemen. According to a UN report, the Houthi militants/ Ansar Allah; Al-Qaeda; government forces, including the Yemini Armed Forces, the First Armoured Division, the military police, the special security forces and Republic Guards; and pro-government militias, including the Salafists and Popular Army or Committees are attracting children to the battlefields.[199]

As of February 2017, UN agencies had documented nearly 1,500 cases of the recruitment of children by all parties to the conflict since March 2015. According to Amnesty International, the Huthis promise monetary incentives to the children's families to appease them: they pledge 20,000–30,000 Yemeni riyals (approximately USD 80-120) per child per month if he becomes a martyr at the front line. The Huthis also honour the families by printing memorial posters, to be put up locally as a tribute to their boys' contributions to the war efforts.[200]

---

government checkpoints whilst armed, or searching anti-government protestors. Children in armed conflict, Report of the Secretary-General, UN Doc A/66/782-S/2012/261, April 2012, paragraph 164; Report of the UN High Commissioner for Human Rights on the human rights situation in Yemen, UN Doc A/HRC/19/51, 13 February 2012, paragraph 43.

199 In addition to Yemen's official state armed forces, the government has historically relied on tribal militias for support in armed confrontation. These state-allied armed groups are commonly called the Popular Army. Whilst these militias are not formally under military command or legally connected to the Yemeni army, they have participated on the government's side in various internal armed conflicts. These tribal militias have been recruiting and using children in armed conflict.

200 Yemen: Huthi forces recruiting child soldiers for front-line combat, Amnesty International, 28 February 2017, available at:https://www.amnesty.org/en/latest/news/2017/02/yemen-huthi-forces-recruiting-child-soldiers-for-front-line-combat/.

The number of child soldiers in Yemen has grown alarmingly as the civil war drives both sides to seek further recruits. The humanitarian crisis has created all kinds of troubles for children. As the war drags on, children are being used to fuel the conflict. The need for money or intentional, deceptive persuasion and exploitation at the hands of warring rivals lures them into the battlefield. The war has disrupted education in the country. The parties to the conflict propagate their ideas regarding fighting among the children. They are wreaking havoc on the lives of children, who feel aimless, with schools no longer being their daily destination.[201]

In Yemen, the figure of 1,500 child soldiers may not be accurate. It could be just a fraction of the true number of child soldiers nationwide. Reports regarding child soldiers in Yemen reveal only the tip of the iceberg. Earlier, it was reported that a third of Yemen's fighters in the civil war were children. Not only do child soldiers battle on the bloody front line, they are also used to staff checkpoints, transport ammunitions or food for the fighters, or perform espionage and any other task associated with warfare.

The child soldiers of Yemen go to the battlefields with two things in mind: money and paradise. Several families know that their children have been fighting in some parts of the country. Some children look for income to provide for their families. Others believe that they will go to heaven if they get killed in battle. Some believe that fighting is a religious duty, and expect a sublime reward from God. However, in most cases, the pursuit of income is stronger than the pursuit of paradise. The people in Yemen have been on the brink of famine and work opportunities are extremely scarce.[202]

In 2014, the UN signed an action plan with the interim government of Yemen with the aim of curbing child recruitment in the military. The goal was to reintegrate conscripted children in society. Unfortunately, Yemen witnessed a military escalation and the collapse of peace talks in late 2014.

---

201 Khalid Al-Karimi, Poverty drives recruitment of child soldiers in Yemen, 6 March 2017, available at: https://www.alaraby.co.uk/english/comment/2017/3/6/poverty-drives-recruitment-of-child-soldiers-in-yemen.

202 In Yemen, when child soldiers join the war, the families remain waiting for one of two phone calls: One is the son's call, telling his parents he will send them his salary. The other is the call that tells them their son has "become a martyr". Not all families greet such news alike. Some wail nonstop, feeling the pain of a child lost. Other families express pride that their children are "martyrs". Both cases are heartbreaking. Khalid Al-Karimi, Poverty drives recruitment of child soldiers in Yemen, 6 March 2017, available at: https://www.alaraby.co.uk/english/comment/2017/3/6/poverty-drives-recruitment-of-child-soldiers-in-yemen.

The UN's action plan failed to take off. The UN has documented a fivefold increase in cases of the recruitment and use of children by armed groups, especially after the escalation of armed conflict on 26 March 2015. A shift was observed from largely voluntary enlistment to forced or involuntary recruitment, including through the provision of misleading information or incentives.[203]There is rampant poverty in Yemen and the country's ailing economy is continuing to deteriorate. Yemen's children are suffering and the end of this tragedy may yet be far. Desperate to survive against starvation or evade the feeling of humiliation when asking people for something to eat, they are being forced to opt for the front line. Child soldiering can die a death only if the civil war in Yemen comes to an end.[204]

In recent years, global attention has been focused on gaining a better understanding of the situation of child soldiers the world over. The above discussion on 14 nations where child soldiers have been recruited and used highlights the grave violations of international humanitarian and human rights law by the parties to conflict. The recruitment and use of children is, however, not limited to these territories. Protracted conflicts have had substantial consequences in terms of the recruitment of children—both by the state armed forces and NSAGs—in a few other states, like Sudan, Libya, Mali and the Philippines. Research has shown that children need not be 'combatants' to be perceived of as members of the armed forces or NSAGs. They may perform a variety of other tasks, both military and non-military, including scouting, spying, sabotage, training, drill and other preparations; acting as decoys, couriers, guards, porters and sexual slaves; and carrying out various domestic tasks and forced labour. While some children volunteer for recruitment, many others are conscripted or forcibly recruited; as the lines between compulsory, voluntary and forced recruitment are often blurred.[205]

---

203 Children and Armed Conflict, Report of the Secretary-General, UN Doc A/70/836-S/2016/360 dated 20 April 2016.

204 Khalid Al-Karimi, Poverty drives recruitment of child soldiers in Yemen, 6 March 2017, available at: https://www.alaraby.co.uk/english/comment/2017/3/6/poverty-drives-recruitment-of-child-soldiers-in-yemen.

205 Alfredson Lisa, Child soldiers, displacement and human security, *Disarmament Forum*, 2002 (3), pp. 17–28.

3 Grave Violations against Children in Armed Conflict

In 2005, the UN Security Council (in resolution 1612) condemned the recruitment and use of child soldiers by parties to armed conflict in violation of international obligations.[1] It also requested the Secretary General to report on the implementation of its resolutions and presidential statements, and include annexed lists of parties to armed conflict who are responsible for violations against children. In the implementation of the Children and Armed Conflict mandate, the Secretary-General identified six grave violations committed against children during armed conflict. The legal basis for these violations lies in relevant international law, which encompasses international humanitarian law (IHL), international human rights law (IHRL) and international criminal law (ICL).[2] The six grave violations are as follows:

---

[1] UN Security Council Resolution S/RES/1612 (2005) of 26 July 2005. This ground breaking resolution built on child protection efforts in the previous SC Resolutions 1261 (1999), 1314 (2000), 1379 (2001), 1460 (2003), and 1539 (2004), and set out important advancements for the protection of children at the ground level and for holding perpetrators of violations accountable. With the adoption and implementation of Resolution 1612, the children and armed conflict (CAC) agenda became a hallmark of the Security Council's thematic work.

[2] The key legal sources for the six grave violations are: the Four Geneva Conventions of 1949; two Additional Protocols to the Geneva Conventions, 1977; the Rome Statute of the International Criminal Court, 1998; customary IHL; the UN Convention on the Rights of the Child, 1989, and its Optional Protocols of 2000/2012; the Universal Declaration of Human Rights, 1948; the International Covenant on Civil and Political Rights, 1966; the International Covenant on Economic, Social and Cultural Rights, 1966; the ILO Convention 182, 1999; the Convention against Torture, 1984; and customary IHRL. The legal sources also include case laws of the International Criminal Tribunal for the former Yugoslavia (ICY), International Criminal Tribunal for Rwanda (ICTR), the Special Court for Sierra Leone (SCSL), the International Criminal Court, and the International Court of Justice.

> ➤ Recruiting and using child soldiers

> ➤ Killing or maiming children

> ➤ Sexual violence against children

> ➤ Attacks against schools or hospitals

> ➤ Abduction of children

> ➤ Denial of humanitarian access for children

These categories do not represent a comprehensive list of violations against children, but it has been determined that they constitute especially egregious violations and, as such, should receive priority attention. There are other ways in which children suffer during an armed conflict. They are forcibly displaced or have to seek refuge; they are held in detention, often with adults, and they are trafficked across borders for labour or commercial sex work and exploitation.

The Security Council also requested the Secretary General to establish a country-specific Monitoring and Reporting Mechanism (MRM) on grave violations against children. The Resolution 1612 established the Working Group on Children and Armed Conflict, which was the first of its kind. The Working Group is an official subsidiary body of the Security Council, consisting of all 15 members. It is empowered to take concrete actions towards halting violations and holding perpetrators accountable, and also to make recommendations for concrete actions to the Security Council.

I. Child Recruitment and Use

The term "recruitment" refers to compulsory, forced or voluntary conscription or enlistment of children under the age stipulated in international treaties into any kind of armed group(s). The term "use" refers to the use of children by armed forces or armed groups in any capacity, including, but not limited to, boys and girls used as fighters, cooks, porters, messengers, spies or for sexual purposes.[3] Girls are increasingly being recruited and used, with some estimates indicating that as many as 40 per cent of children associated with armed forces or armed groups are female. In addition to being used for

---

3   United Nations Children's Fund, The Paris Principles: Principles and Guidelines on Children Associated with Armed Forces or Armed Groups, UNICEF, New York, February 2007.

support functions and sexual purposes or to be forced into marriage, girls are also used in combat and to commit violent acts. For example, in Nigeria girls have been forced by Boko Haram to be suicide bombers, and used for the purpose of avoiding detection by security personnel.[4]

Recruiting or using children under the age of 15 as soldiers is prohibited under IHL. It is also prohibited by the Convention on the Rights of the Child (CRC) and the 1977 Additional Protocols to the Geneva Conventions. The rule that children must not be recruited into armed forces or armed groups and that they must not be allowed to take part in hostilities is considered customary international law, applying equally in situations of international and non-international armed conflict, and to both government armed forces and non-State armed groups. In 2004, the Special Court for Sierra Leone (SCSL) held in the *Hinga Norman* case that the recruitment and use of children in armed conflict is a war crime under customary international law. In addition, the statutes of the International Tribunals for the former Yugoslavia, Rwanda and Sierra Leone also declared that the recruitment and use of children under the age of 15 years in armed conflict is a war crime. Several decisions of the International Criminal Court go to show that individual commanders and political leaders may be held accountable for the recruitment and participation of children under the age of 15 in hostilities.

International human rights law has set the acceptable minimum age for direct participation in hostilities at 18 years. The Convention on the Rights of the Child's Optional Protocol on the Involvement of Children in Armed Conflict (2000) requires State parties to increase the minimum age for compulsory recruitment and for direct participation in hostilities to 18 years. Those countries that continue to permit the voluntary recruitment of children under the age of 18 must introduce strict safeguards. In addition, the Optional Protocol prohibits non-State armed groups under any circumstances from recruiting or using children under 18 years.

While not outright banning the recruitment of children under 18 in government armed forces, Additional Protocol I of the Geneva Conventions and the Convention on the Rights of the Child both require that when recruiting children between 15 and 18 years, priority should be given to the oldest. The International Labour Organization's Convention No. 182 declares

---

4   UN General Assembly, Annual report of the Special Representative of the Secretary-General for Children and Armed Conflict, A/HRC/34/44 dated 22 December 2016, para 13.

that recruiting children below the age of 18 is "one of the worst forms of child labour." The Paris Principles on Children Associated with Armed Forces or Armed Groups (2007) asks States to respect the international standards for recruitment and ensure that armed groups within their territory do not recruit children under the age of 18. The African Charter on the Rights and Welfare of the Child (1999) prohibits the "recruitment and direct participation in hostilities of any person under the age of 18 years."

When children associated with armed forces or armed groups are captured by opposing armed forces, the special protections afforded to them by IHL by virtue of their age remain applicable. In addition, the Optional Protocol insists that parties to a conflict pay particular attention to all children involved in hostilities during the disarmament, demobilization and reintegration process, including special programmes to provide for the "psychological recovery and social reintegration" of these children into society.

The unlawful or arbitrary detention of children is prohibited under IHL and IHRL. The arrest, detention or imprisonment of a child must be in conformity with national law, in line with international standards, and be used only as a measure of last resort and for the shortest appropriate period of time. When a child who has been recruited and used is alleged to have committed clearly defined crimes under international or domestic law, the specific circumstances and best interests of the child must be taken into account. Children (as well as all other detainees) must be treated humanely, including an absolute ban on torture and cruel, inhuman and degrading treatment. Further, special protections must be afforded to all children by virtue of their age.

II. Killing and Maiming of Children

If we look at the sufferings of children in armed conflict, nothing has changed in the last fifty years. No one can forget the gruesome image of the Vietnam War: A naked, burned nine-year-old girl (Phan Thi Kim Phuc) runs screaming down the road, chased by a cloud of Napalm. In a recent image of Aleppo, Syria (2016), a dazed and bloodied five-year-old boy (Omran Daqneesh) sits in the back of an ambulance, after surviving an airstrike from his own government. The increased use of explosive weapons and advanced technologies are responsible for killing and maiming thousands of children in at least 41 countries over the past two years. Research conducted into the use of explosive weapons in populated areas provides an indicator of the scale and scope of the impact of explosive weapons on children. An estimated 2,685 children were killed or maimed by explosive weapons in 898 incidents where the age of the casualties was reported. Nearly 84% of recorded child casualties occurred in populated areas; and on average 103 children were recorded killed or injured by explosive weapons every month. The conflict in Syria has claimed the lives of some 70,000 people, and an estimated 300,000 are believed to have been injured. While there is no exact figure for casualties among children, hospital reports show that an increasing number of children are being admitted with burns, gunshot wounds and injuries from explosions. Because children are smaller and their bodies more delicate, blasts from explosive weapons can result in more complex injuries to their organs and tissues.[5]

The right of civilians to not be arbitrarily deprived of life and the prohibition of killing or maiming civilians are principles firmly enshrined in IHL, IHRL and international jurisprudence. The prohibition of violence against civilians, including children, in particular murder, mutilation, cruel treatment and torture is a principle of customary international law, with universal applicability in all situations of armed conflict.[6] Common Article 3 of the Geneva Conventions is the most recognized source for this fundamental protection. It is universally applicable, allows no derogation and is binding on both the State armed forces and non-State armed groups. It prohibits violence against people, in particular murder of all kinds, mutilation, cruel treatment and torture.

---

5   Naziha, a 17-year-old mother, was hit by shrapnel while she was breastfeeding in her home. She was taken to hospital, but there was a delay in receiving medical care, and she is now paralyzed down one side of her body. She said: "One evening I was at my house with my husband and I was holding my daughter in my arms, breastfeeding. We heard a noise outside. Something hit the house, and I don't remember anything after that. Later I woke up at the hospital and I asked why I was there. They asked me if I remembered anything, but I didn't. They told me that I was hit by shrapnel. I know there was a delay treating me, but I don't remember it. All I know is that afterwards, I was disabled – I can't move my arm or my leg. Now I can't stand or sit without help. Many people have been injured and become disabled in Syria like this. This can't go on. Someone should put an end to it. People are losing their children, brothers, parents." Kimberly Brown, Explosive Weapons and Grave Violations Against Children, Position Paper, Save the Children Fund, London, 2013, p.11.

6   Common Article 3 to the four Geneva Conventions of 1949. Customary Rules 87, 89-92 and 135, Henckaerts, Doswald-Beck (eds.), *Customary International Humanitarian Law Vol. 1: Rules*, ICRC: Cambridge University Press, 2005. Article 147 of the Fourth Geneva Convention of 1949 lists "grave breaches" of the Conventions.

The two key principles of the law of armed conflict, distinction and proportionality, are enshrined in the Geneva Conventions and their Additional Protocols and are considered customary IHL. They apply to both the State and non-State armed groups in all situations of armed conflict.

The International Committee of the Red Cross has provided basic rules containing the crux of IHL. These rules are based on the principle of distinction that civilians, including children, should never be specifically targeted and that combatants must abide by certain limitations in choosing the means and methods of warfare. The rules provide that persons who do not take a direct part in hostilities are entitled to respect for their lives and their moral and physical integrity. They shall in all circumstances be protected and treated humanely without any adverse distinction. The principle of distinction is the cornerstone of IHL. It states that a distinction must always be made between combatants and civilians,[7] and between civilian objects[8] and military objectives. The principle of distinction prohibits all means and methods that cannot make a distinction between those who take part in hostilities, i.e., combatants, and those who do not and are therefore protected (AP I, Article 48).

International humanitarian law prohibits indiscriminate and disproportionate military attacks, as well as direct attacks against civilians. Such attacks may in some circumstances amount to grave breaches of IHL. The principle of proportionality prohibits military attacks if they result in civilian death or injury, or damage to civilian object that is excessive when

---

7   The term civilian means any person who is not a combatant or who does not belong to one of the categories of persons referred to in Article 4 A (1), (2), (3) and (6) of the Third Geneva Convention and in Article 43 of AP I. In case of doubt whether a person is a civilian, that person shall be considered to be a civilian. Civilians enjoy the protection unless and for such time as they take a direct part in hostilities. Under the customary IHL, a combatant is anyone who is the member of the armed forces, and a civilian is anyone who is not a member of the armed forces. The civilian population comprises all persons who are civilians.

8   The immunity from being object of attack extends to civilian objects. All objects that are not military objects are civilian ones. Article 52 (2) of AP I states that military objectives are limited to those objects which by their nature, location, purpose or use make an effective contribution to military action and whose total or partial destruction, capture or neutralization, offers a definite military of advantage. In case of doubt whether an object which is normally dedicated to civilian purposes, such as a place of worship, a house or other dwelling or a school, is being used to make an effective contribution to military action, it shall be presumed not to be so used. The dual use facilities such as power stations, electrical grid, railway communication system, which serves both civilian and military need, would be a legitimate military target. However, if foodstuff and water necessary for the survival of civilian populations is also used to feed the military, they must not be destroyed.

compared to the concrete and direct military advantage anticipated from the attack.[9]

The use of indiscriminate weapons, such as landmines, cluster munitions and chemical weapons, are contrary to the law of armed conflict and contravene several international treaties. Under Article 3 (a) of the Statute of the International Criminal Tribunal for the Former Yugoslavia (ICTY), the employment of "weapons calculated to cause unnecessary suffering" is regarded as a violation of the laws and customs of war, giving rise to individual criminal responsibility.[10] The use of projectiles and bullets manufactured from materials that are difficult to detect, or are undetectable by x-rays, such as glass or clear plastic, is prohibited since they unnecessarily inhibit the treatment of wounds.[11] Article 8 (2) (b) (xx) of the Rome Statute of the ICC states that "employing weapons, projectiles and material and methods of warfare which are of a nature to cause superfluous injury or unnecessary suffering or which are inherently indiscriminate in violation of the international law of the armed conflict" would be a war crime.

International human rights law (IHRL) stresses the paramount importance of the right to life, liberty and security of person. States have a responsibility to ensure these rights are respected, protected and fulfilled. Torture and cruel, inhuman or degrading treatment and mutilation are explicitly prohibited in international and non-international armed conflicts and by all parties by the Geneva Conventions and their Additional Protocols as well as under IHRL. On the contrary, parties to conflict are obliged to provide the wounded and sick with the medical care they require when circumstances allow. By virtue of their age, children also enjoy special protection under

9   Article 51.5 (b) of AP I accordingly states: "An attack which may be expected to cause incidental loss of civilian life, injury to civilians, damage to civilian objects, or a combination thereof, which would be excessive in relation to the concrete and direct military advantage anticipated," will be considered an indiscriminate attack. Article 57.2 (b) relating to precautions in attack states: "An attack shall be cancelled or suspended if it becomes apparent that the objective is not a military one or is subject to special protection or that the attack may be expected to cause incidental loss of civilian life, injury to civilians, damage to civilian objects, or a combination thereof, which would be excessive in relation to the concrete and direct military advantage anticipated."

10 Statute of the International Tribunal for the Prosecution of Persons responsible for Serious Violation of International Humanitarian Law Committed in the Territory of the Former Yugoslavia Since 1991 (ICTY), Report of the Secretary-General Pursuant to Paragraph 2 of Security Council Resolution 808 (1993), Vol. 32, *International Legal Materials (ILM)* 1159, 1192 (1993).

11 1980 Convention on prohibitions or restrictions on the use of certain conventional weapons which may be deemed to be excessively injurious or to have indiscriminate effects (CCW), Protocol I on Non-detectable Fragments.

the Geneva Conventions, which stipulates that all parties to a conflict must prioritize the welfare of vulnerable groups, including children, during hostilities. The CRC recognizes that every child has an inherent right to life and State parties must ensure to the maximum extent possible the survival and development of the child.[12] The international tribunals for Rwanda, the former Yugoslavia and Sierra Leone, and the International Criminal Court have successfully prosecuted commanders for murder, arbitrary killing, torture and other forms of ill-treatment against civilians, and have held commanders legally accountable for crimes committed by their soldiers.

Military actions targeting groups perpetrating extreme violence remains a matter of concern for the protection of children. Children caught in the middle of such operations have been killed and maimed and their homes and schools destroyed. The proliferation of airstrikes is of particular concern for the protection of children, as many airstrikes are of an indiscriminate nature. Non-State armed groups have adopted the tactics of placing children on the front line, either to engage in combat or as human shields. Children can also be victims of grave violations inside and around refugee camps or camps for internally displaced persons. Armed groups take advantage of the vulnerability and concentration of displaced populations in such camps to recruit children and commit other violations.

III. Sexual Violence against Children

The term "sexual violence" has been increasingly used in resolutions of the UN General Assembly[13] and of the Human Rights Council (HRC).[14] However,

---

12   The Convention on the Rights of Child, Articles 6 and 37.

13   The UN General Assembly Declaration on the Elimination of Violence Against Women, adopted by the UNGA in 1993, defines violence against women as "any act of gender based violence that results in, or is likely to result in, physical, sexual, or psychological harm or suffering to women, including threats of such acts, coercion or arbitrary deprivation of liberty, whether occurring in public or private life". It encompasses, but is not limited to, "physical, sexual and psychological violence occurring in the family, including battering, sexual abuse of female children in the household, dowry related violence, marital rape, female genital mutilation and other traditional practices harmful to women, non-spousal violence and violence related to exploitation; physical, sexual and psychological violence occurring within the general community, including rape, sexual abuse, sexual harassment and intimidation at work, in educational institutions and elsewhere; trafficking in women and forced prostitution; and physical, sexual and psychological violence perpetrated or condoned by the state, wherever it occurs". UN Doc. A/RES/48/104, 20 December 1993, Article 1 and 2.

14   Some examples are; 2010: HRC Resolution A/HRC/13/L.21 on the Rights of the Child:

the term has not been defined in the CRC, though the CRC includes "sexual abuse" in its definition of "violence" in Article 19 and specifically addresses protection from sexual exploitation and sexual abuse in Article 34.[15] The CRC Committee General Comment No. 13 sets forth a broad definition of violence against children, which includes sexual abuse and exploitation. It further defines sexual abuse and exploitation as including (i) The inducement or coercion of a child to engage in any unlawful or psychologically harmful sexual activity; (ii) The use of children in commercial sexual exploitation; (iii) The use of children in audio or visual images of child sexual abuse; and (d) Child prostitution, sexual slavery, sexual exploitation in travel and tourism, trafficking (within and between countries) and sale of children for sexual purposes and forced marriage. The sexual abuse of children, however, requires no element of exchange and can occur for the mere purpose of the sexual gratification of the person committing the act, whereas the sexual exploitation of children can be distinguished by an underlying notion of exchange.

It is estimated that there are 120,000 girl child soldiers worldwide and that in the last three decades girls have participated in armed conflicts in 58 countries, the proportion of girl combatants in African conflicts rising to about 30 to 40 per cent.[16] Recruitment makes girls vulnerable not only to the violence of war and psychological trauma, but also to sexual violence and abuse with a huge impact on their physical, mental and reproductive health. Sexual violence is increasingly becoming a characteristic of conflict and is often perpetrated against girls as well as boys in a rule of law vacuum.[17] In

---

The Fight Against Sexual Violence; 2011: UNGA Resolution 66/140 on the Girl Child mentions sexual violence against children; 2011: UNGA Resolution 66/141 on the Rights of the Child, Paragraph 23, mentions rape and other sexual violence against children.

15 The CRC refers to "all forms of sexual exploitation and sexual abuse" in Article 34, which elaborates on the requirement for State Parties to protect children from sexual exploitation and abuse as follows: "For these purposes, States Parties shall in particular take all appropriate national, bilateral and multilateral measures to prevent: (i) The inducement or coercion of a child to engage in any unlawful sexual activity; (ii) The exploitative use of children in prostitution or other unlawful sexual practices; (iii) The exploitative use of children in pornographic performances and materials."

16 D. Mazurana and K. Carlson, The Girl Child and Armed Conflict: Recognizing and Addressing Grave Violations of Girls' Human Rights, United Nations Division for the Advancement of Women in Collaboration with UNICEF, EGM/DVGC/2006/EP.12 (15-28 September 2006) p. 13.

17 Boys are also victims of sexual violence in conflict. For example, in Afghanistan the practice of Baccha Baazi (dancing boys), remains a widespread phenomenon. It is a form

some instances sexual violence is used as a tactic of war designed to humiliate a population or to force displacement. Some children experience sexual victimization which is not accompanied by physical force or restraint, but is nonetheless psychologically intrusive, exploitive and traumatic."[18] When girls who have been subjected to sexual violence return to their community, they may be accompanied by their children born as a result of sexual violence.[19] Upon returning, many face marginalization, discrimination and rejection by the family and community due to social and cultural norms related to sexual violence. These girl child soldiers remain at an even greater risk of rejection and abandonment.[20] Survivors of sexual violence endure psychological, physical, social, cultural, religious and economic repercussions in the aftermath of the assault and for the rest of their lives.[21]

Rape and other forms of sexual violence against children, both boys and girls, are serious violations of international human rights law and may amount to grave breaches of international humanitarian law. Acts of sexual violence may constitute a war crime, a crime against humanity or a constitutive act with respect to genocide. In 2009, the Security Council, in resolution 1882, added sexual violence against children as an additional trigger for listing parties to conflict in the Secretary-General's Annual Report on Children and Armed Conflict. The office of Children and Armed Conflict, together with partners prepared field guidance for subsequent implementation.[22] The sexual exploitation and abuse of children by UN peacekeepers is particularly

---

of sexual slavery and child prostitution in which boys are sold to wealthy or powerful men, including military and political leaders for entertainment and sexual activities.

18 The CRC Committee General Comment No. 13 on the Right of the Child to Freedom from All Forms of Violence, 2011.

19 In Sierra Leone, recruited young girls were used to fulfil the role of "wife" to rebel commanders; and as a consequence of related sexual activity many became pregnant and faced higher risks of exposure to sexually transmitted diseases. Denov, M., Girls in fighting forces: Moving beyond victimhood, summary of findings on girls in armed conflict from CIDA's child protection research fund, 2007. Available at: http://www.crin.org/docs/ CIDA_Beyond_forces.pdf, accessed 10 February 2017.

20 Bad Blood: Perceptions of children born of conflict-related sexual violence and women and girls associated with Boko Haram in northeast Nigeria, Research Summary, UNICEF Nigeria: International Alert, 2016.

21 Dallman Ashley, Prosecuting Conflict-Related Sexual Violence at the International Criminal Court, SIPRI Insight on Peace and Security, No. 2009/1, May 2009.

22 The Six Grave Violations Against Children during Armed Conflict: Legal Foundation, Working Paper No. 1, Office of the Special Representative of the Secretary General for Children in Armed Conflict, 2013.

disturbing because it is perpetrated against the very children that peacekeepers are supposed to protect. What is worse is that these peacekeepers who demand sexual favours in exchange for food are never prosecuted.[23]

Rape and other forms of sexual violence during armed conflict are prohibited under the 1949 Geneva Conventions and their Additional Protocols of 1977. Child-specific provisions of these treaties specifically forbid sexual violence against children. The obligation of humane treatment under Common Article 3 implicitly prohibits rape or any other sexual violence, be it against adults or children. Article 27 of the Fourth Geneva Convention explicitly prohibits such acts stating that: "Women [including girls] shall be especially protected against any attack on their honour, in particular against rape, enforced prostitution, or any form of indecent assault." In addition, a number of international treaties prohibit the sexual abuse and exploitation of adults and children. These include the 1984 Convention against Torture,[24] the 1949 Convention for the Suppression of the Traffic in Persons and of the Exploitation of the Prostitution of Others, and the 1993 Vienna Declaration of the World Conference on Human Rights.

The ICCPR and the 1979 Convention for the Elimination of all Forms of Discrimination Against Women (CEDAW) affirm a woman's right to liberty and security of person and to be free from discrimination. The CRC and its Optional Protocol on Trafficking and Exploitation unequivocally affirm that children must enjoy protection from torture, cruel, inhuman or degrading treatment, a protection broadly accepted as encompassing acts of rape and sexual violence. Regional human rights instruments such as the 1990 African Charter on the Rights and Welfare of the Child also explicitly forbid sexual violence against children.

---

23 Under Article 8, the Rome Statute allows the ICC to prosecute rape and sexual violence by combatants in the context of armed conflict as a war crime. The UN peacekeepers remain under the jurisdiction of their country specific penal codes and therefore their prosecution under the ICC may not be possible.

24 Article 1 of the 1984 UN Convention against Torture and Other Cruel, Inhuman or Degrading Treatment or Punishment states that "'torture' means any act by which severe pain or suffering, whether physical or mental, is intentionally inflicted on a person for such purposes as obtaining from him or a third person information or a confession, punishing him for an act he or a third person has committed or is suspected of having committed, or intimidating or coercing him or a third person, or for any reason based on discrimination of any kind, when such pain or suffering is inflicted by or at the instigation of or with the consent or acquiescence of a public official or other person acting in an official capacity."

International criminal law explicitly criminalizes rape and sexual violence during war and judicial recognition of its customary status in international law came in 1998 with a number of ground-breaking judgments by the International Tribunals for the Former Yugoslavia (ICTY) and Rwanda (ICTR). The statutes of the Special Court for Sierra Leone (SCSL), ICTY and ICTR all cite rape and sexual violence as war crimes and crimes against humanity. Sexual violence against civilians has been prosecuted by the ICTY and ICTR. This was the first time that an international tribunal convicted individuals solely on charges of sexual violence against women and girls.[25] In addition, the SCSL in *Prosecutor v. Alec Tamba Brima, Brazzy Camara and Borbor Kanu* (2007) established "forced marriage" as an offence under international criminal law when it found three militia leaders guilty of crimes against humanity for forcing girls into marriage. The Rome Statute of the ICC states that rape, sexual slavery, enforced prostitution, forced pregnancy, enforced sterilization or other forms of sexual violence of comparable gravity may constitute war crimes and crimes against humanity.[26]

In 2008, the Security Council, in its resolution 1820 on "Women, Peace and Security" recognized for the first time that "sexual violence, when used or commissioned as a tactic of war in order to deliberately target civilians or as a part of a widespread or systematic attack against civilian populations, can significantly exacerbate situations of armed conflict and may impede the restoration of international peace and security". In a report to the Security Council, the UN Secretary-General has stated, "Under international law, sexual violence is not synonymous with rape. The statutes and the case law of the ICTY, ICTR and SCSL, and the Elements of Crimes of the Rome Statute, define sexual violence as encompassing sexual slavery, enforced prostitution, forced pregnancy, enforced sterilization and any other form of sexual violence of comparable gravity, which may, depending on the circumstances, include

---

25 *Prosecutor v. Furundzija*, ICTY (1998): The ICTY Trial Chamber noted that prohibition of rape and serious sexual assault in armed conflict under customary international law has gradually crystallized. The Tribunal found the accused guilty of a violation of the laws and customs of war (outrages upon dignity, including rape). *Prosecutor v. Kunarac, Kovac and Vukovic*, ICTY (2000): The ICTY Trial Chamber found the accused guilty of crimes against humanity (rape) and violations of the law of customs of war (rape).

26 Article 7(1)(c), 7(1)(g), 8(2)(b), 8(2)(c), 8(2)(e) of the Rome Statute. Article 7 of the Rome Statute of the International Criminal Court includes among crimes against humanity "rape, sexual slavery, enforced prostitution, forced pregnancy, enforced sterilization, or any other form of sexual violence of comparable gravity" (when committed as part of a widespread or systematic attack directed against any civilian population, with knowledge of the attack).

situations of indecent assault, trafficking, inappropriate medical examinations and strip searches."[27]

Sexual violence against children encompasses sexual exploitation and sexual abuse of children and can be used as an umbrella term to refer to both acts of commission and omission and to physical as well as psychological violence. Children who experience sexual violence suffer from long-term psychological trauma and health consequences, including transmitted infections such as HIV/AIDS and early pregnancies. Their reintegration is a great challenge as communities often stigmatize girls who have been associated with armed groups and are suspected of having been raped. Young mothers of babies born of rape often stay with the armed group because of the family ties and dependency that evolve over time and to avoid social stigma. These girls and their children are particularly vulnerable to all forms of exploitation including prostitution and trafficking and need special protection.

International law protects children from abuse, including sexual abuse, and from discrimination based on gender. It also prohibits the recruitment and use of child soldiers, but does not distinguish between boys and girls and their different experiences of armed conflict. Girls are more vulnerable than boys to grave violations of their human rights through sexual violence, sexual exploitation, forced marriage, and increased exposure to sexually transmitted diseases.[28]

International law protects women from sexual violence or from discrimination based on gender, but does so without age distinction. There is no particular provision to protect girl child soldiers from sexual violence by members of their armed groups in international law. International criminal law criminalizes rape, sexual slavery, forced pregnancy and other forms of sexual violence as war crimes and crimes against humanity that can serve as a basis for the prosecution of the sexual violence suffered by girls.[29]

---

27 UN Secretary-General, Report on the Implementation of Security Council Resolutions 1820 (2008) and 1888 (2009), Doc. A/65/592 – S/2010/604, Paragraph 4. See also Security Council Resolutions on sexual violence in conflict 1820 (2008), 1888(2009), and 1325 (2000).

28 Stolen children: Abduction and recruitment in Northern Uganda, Human Rights Watch, 2003.

29 Mouthaan Solange, Barafooot, Pregnant and in the Kitchen: Am I a child soldier too? Women's Studies International Forum, Vol. 51, 2015, p. 91-100.

IV. Attacks on Schools and Hospitals

The term "attacks" includes the targeting of schools or medical facilities that cause the total or partial destruction of such facilities. Attacks against schools or hospitals are, in principle, contraventions of well-established international humanitarian law, including customary norms, and may constitute war crimes and crimes against humanity. Other than attacks, the normal operation of such facilities may be hampered by occupation, shelling, targeting for propaganda, or otherwise causing harm to such facilities or their personnel. A "school" denotes a recognizable education facility or learning site recognized and known by the community as a learning space and marked by visible boundaries.[30]

Around the world, schools are being transformed into a part of the battlefield. Parties to armed conflict have converted schools into bases by encircling playgrounds with barbed wire, and filling classrooms with cots for soldiers. They have established fortifications atop school buildings from which to survey the surrounding area, and they have positioned snipers in classroom windows.[31] Not only have they taken schools by force, but also established themselves inside institutions of higher education and put kindergartens and day-care centres to their use. The result is that students are either forced to stay at home and interrupt their education, or study alongside armed fighters while being potentially in the line of fire.

The devastating impact of armed conflict on education and healthcare facilities[32] can be seen in Afghanistan, the Central African Republic, Nigeria,

---

30 Office of the Special Representative of the Secretary-General for Children and Armed Conflict (OSRSG-CAAC), UNICEF, United Nations Department of Peacekeeping Operations (DPKO), Monitoring and Reporting Mechanism, Field Manual: Monitoring and Reporting Mechanism (MRM) on Grave Violations against Children in Situations of Armed Conflict, March 2012, p. 12; OSRSG-CAAC, Protect Schools and Hospitals: Guidance Note on Security Council Resolution 1998, May 2014.

31 The use of schools and universities as bases, barracks, firing positions, and armouries can transform these places of learning into military objectives. This can render them vulnerable to lawful attack under the law of armed conflict, in some circumstances even if students and teachers remain on site. Moreover, the presence of the fighting forces of parties to armed conflict in schools and universities often leads to students dropping out, reduced enrolment, lower rates of transition to higher levels of education, and overall poorer educational attainment. Girls are often disproportionately affected. Commentary on the Guidelines for Protecting Schools and Universities from Military Use during Armed Conflict, Global Coalition to protect Education from Attack, CARA, Human Rights Watch, Save the Children, UNICEF, UNESCO and UNHCR, 2014 .

32 In Afghanistan, the attack on the Medecins sans Frontiers hospital in Kunduz in October

the Syrian Arab Republic, South Sudan, Yemen, and the State of Palestine.[33] Schools have been bombed and children, students, teachers and auxiliary staff have been killed, maimed, abducted or otherwise subjected to inhuman treatment.[34] Three years of armed conflict in South Sudan has devastated the education sector, leading to the closure of 70 per cent of the schools in areas where most of the fighting has taken place; nearly 400,000 children have been forced out of schooling.[35] Non-state armed groups have destroyed 31 schools in India and prevented around two million children from going to school across the Kashmir valley.[36] In Syria, during the last five years of armed conflict, an estimated 2,400 schools have been damaged. One UN survey found that one-fifth of the schools in Damascus have been damaged or destroyed; in Idlib province, 60% have been damaged. In Nigeria, at least 70 teachers and 100 schoolchildren were killed or wounded between 2012 and 2013.[37] Even where schools are open, the average attendance is down to

---

2015 caused deaths and injuries of 49 medical staff. The hospital was the only fully functioning trauma care facility for the north-eastern region of Afghanistan and had provided lifesaving procedures to 5,000 people in the period running up to the attack. In Yemen, in Taiz, three health facilities were repeatedly hit in 23 separate incidents throughout 2015. Almost half of all medical facilities in the Syrian Arab Republic are closed or only partially functioning. In Aleppo, there have been a number of air strikes on hospitals and children living there are confronted with the almost impossible task of obtaining basic health care in order to survive.

33 Due to the continued, deliberate and indiscriminate attacks on schools by the warring parties, more than 3 million children inside the Syrian Arab Republic have ceased to attend classes on a regular basis. These attacks, many of which have killed teachers and students, have destroyed and damaged schools. Even where schools still operate, parents opt to keep children at home, fearing for their safety. There are continued reports of warring parties using schools for military purposes, including as depots, headquarters and barracks. Such use prevents students from attending and makes schools vulnerable to attack. UN Human Rights Council, Report of the Independent International Commission of Inquiry on the Syrian Arab Republic, A/HRC/31/68 dated 11 February 2016.

34 Global Coalition to Protect Education from Attack, Safe Schools Declaration, May 2015, p.1.

35 *We Can Die Too: Recruitment and Use of Child Soldiers in South Sudan*, Human Rights Watch, 2015, p. 15.

36 Pakistan based *Lashkar-e-Taiba* on September 27, 2016 issued a warning to Jammu and Kashmir education minister in India for trying to resume schools and colleges in the Valley. Lashkar spokesman Abdullah Ghaznavi quoted LeT operation chief Mehmood Shah and said: "Education Minister Naeem Akhtar should desist from trying to break the shutdown forcefully as Kashmiris are educated enough to decide what is good or bad for them." Terror groups destroy Kashmir schools in Taliban-type offensive, *The Times of India*, 27 October 2016.

37 Who will care for Us? Grave Violations Against Children in Northeast Nigeria, Watchlist on Children and Armed Conflict, September 2014, p.18-19.

approximately two days per week. Thousands of schools are being used as shelters by civilians; some of these are then being targeted by armed actors, as when, for example, a government jet dropped a 'barrel bomb' on a school that was sheltering 200–300 people, killing a dozen, including children.[38]

The ICRC has documented that in conflicts around the world, healthcare is frequently suspended, withdrawn or rendered impossible by violent events. Thousands of wounded and sick people can be denied effective healthcare when hospitals are damaged by explosive weapons. In a study of violent incidents affecting healthcare in 16 countries spread over two-and-a-half years, it found that the number of people killed or injured per event is greater when explosive weapons are used, as compared with other weapons and that explosive weapons resulted in more casualties and damage than any other weapons.[39] In Somalia, a nutrition centre run by the Red Crescent Society was hit by an air strike in December 2011, when the population was in dire need of food assistance.

Every individual's right to education is recognized in the International Covenant on Economic, Social and Cultural Rights, 1966. Children in particular are profoundly important beneficiaries of this right. In a conflict-ridden area, education is all the more vital for the social and general development of each community and for providing a basis for future development. Schools can provide a shelter for children where they can develop their social skills and learn useful things to contribute to their survival in their community. The Convention on the Rights of the Child sets out detailed obligations of States to ensure every child's right to education. However, the right to education means little if students cannot attend schools safely.

IHL recognizes the importance of providing education to children during armed conflict, offering specific protection to children, and acknowledging that educational facilities are ordinarily civilian objects not to be targeted unless they are turned into military objectives. It restricts the targeting of schools and universities, and the use of schools and universities in support of military effort, but does not prohibit such use in all circumstances and

---

38 See: UNICEF, *Syria Crisis Assessment*, UNICEF, February 2013; UN Human Rights Council, *Report of the Independent International Commission of Inquiry on the Syrian Arab Republic*, UN Human Rights Council, 2013, p 91; Save the Children, *Childhood Under Fire: The impact of two years of conflict in Syria*, Save the Children, 2013, p. 12.

39 *Health Care in Danger: A sixteen-country study*, Geneva: International Committee of the Red Cross (ICRC), 2011, p. 12.

allows for the targeting of schools and universities when they become military objectives.[40] In fact, intentionally direct attacks against them when they are not legitimate military objectives would constitute a war crime under the Rome Statute of the ICC.[41] Military objectives are defined as objects which by their nature, location, purpose or use make an effective contribution to military action and whose total or partial destruction, capture or neutralization, in the circumstances ruling at the time, offers a definite military advantage. In case of doubt whether a school or university is being used to make an effective contribution to military action, it shall be presumed not to be so used and thus to be a civilian object.[42]

IHL requires the parties to a conflict to take precautions against the effects of attack. To the extent that schools and universities are civilian objects, parties to an armed conflict shall, to the maximum extent feasible: (i) avoid locating military objectives within or near densely populated areas where schools and universities are likely to be located; (ii) endeavour to remove the civilian population, individual civilians and civilian objects under their control from the vicinity of military objectives; and (iii) take the other necessary precautions to protect those schools and universities under their control against the dangers resulting from military operations.[43] Locating military objectives (a weapons store, for example) near a school also increases the risk of its suffering incidental damage from an attack against the nearby military objectives that might be lawful under the law of armed conflict. Schools that can be characterized as being of great importance to the cultural heritage of a people are afforded additional protection by the 1954 Hague Convention for the Protection of Cultural Property and its 1999 Second Protocol. In particular, the use of such educational institutions for purposes which are likely to expose them to destruction or damage is prohibited, unless imperatively required by military necessity.[44]

---

40 AP I, Article 52 (1); this provision is also part of customary law for international and non-international armed conflicts. Jean-Marie Henckaerts and Louise Doswald-Beck, *Customary International Humanitarian Law: Rules*, Vol. 1, Rule 9 and 10, ICRC: Cambridge University Press, 2005.

41 Rome Statute, Article 8 (2) (b) (ii), Article 8 (2) (b) (ix), Article 8 (2) (c) (iv).

42 Additional Protocol I, Article 52 (2) and (3); This provision is also part of customary law for international and non-international armed conflicts. ICRC Customary IHL Study, Rule 8.

43 Additional Protocol I, Article 58 (a), (b), and (c).

44 The 1954 Hague Convention for the Protection of Cultural Property in the Event of Armed Conflict, Artilce 4(1), and ICRC Customary IHL Study, Rule 39.

Under the Fourth Geneva Convention, 1949, an occupying power is under an obligation to cooperate with the national and local authorities to facilitate the proper working of all institutions devoted to the care and education of children. Similarly, under Additional Protocol II, it is a "fundamental guarantee" that children shall receive an education in keeping with the wishes of their parents.[45]

The Security Council has expressed deep concern about the fact that the military use of schools in contravention of applicable international law may render schools legitimate targets of attack, thus endangering the safety of children. The member States are to take concrete measures to deter such use of schools by armed forces and armed groups.[46] In this regard, the Security Council has urged all parties to armed conflict to respect the civilian character of schools in accordance with IHL. In case of an attack on schools in contravention of IHL, the States have responsibilities under IHL to investigate and prosecute those responsible for the illegal acts.[47] The domestic laws of a few States as well as courts have also directed that schools and educational institutions should not be used for military purposes.[48]

The Security Council has adopted resolution 2286 (2016) demanding an end to impunity for those responsible for attacks against medical personnel and facilities. The Security Council has strongly condemned attacks and threats against the wounded and sick, medical personnel and humanitarian personnel exclusively engaged in medical duties, their means of transport and equipment, as well as hospitals and other medical facilities. The parties to armed conflict must comply with their obligations under international law, including international human rights law, and IHL, in particular their

---

45   The Fourth Geneva Convention, Article 50 and Additional Protocol II, Article 4(3)(a).

46   United Nations Security Council Resolution 2225, S/Res/2225 (2015), June 18, 2015, para. 26.

47   United Nations Security Council Resolution 2143, S/Res/2143 (2014), March 7, 2014, para. 18.

48   The Philippines law provides that public infrastructure such as schools shall not be utilized for military purposes such as command posts, barracks, detachments, and supply depots; An Act Providing for Stronger Deterrence and Special Protection against Child Abuse, Exploitation, and Discrimination, Providing Penalties for its Violation and Other Purposes, June 17, 1992, Article X(22)(e). The Supreme Court of India has ordered that: "There shall be a direction....to ensure that the security forces vacate all the educational institutions, school buildings and hostels." *Nandini Sundar v. The State of Chhattisgarh*, WP (Civil) No. 250 of 2007, Supreme Court order of 18 January 2011.

obligations under the Geneva Conventions of 1949 and their Additional Protocols of 1977 and 2005.

Hospitals and medical personnel are explicitly afforded special protection under international law. Customary international law declares that medical personnel and facilities, exclusively assigned as such, must be respected and protected in times of armed conflict. The Convention on the Rights of the Child recognizes the paramount importance of children's right to health. These rights are also reflected in international and regional legal instruments, including the Universal Declaration of Human Rights (1948) and the International Covenant on Economic, Social and Cultural Rights, which address the right of all persons to enjoy the highest attainable standard of physical and mental health. The targeting and destruction of hospitals obviously constitutes an obstacle to fulfilling these rights.

V. Abductions

The term "abduction" has been defined as an act of leading someone away by force or fraudulent persuasion.[49] During an armed conflict, particularly non-international, children are particularly vulnerable to abduction. In the last two decades, a number of incidences of abduction and hostage-taking have been reported from regions affected by non-international armed conflicts. Such abductions have been followed by other grave violations against children, such as recruitment, killing and maiming, sexual assault, trafficking, enslavement and forced pregnancy. The illicit transportation of children by State armed forces and non-State armed groups across borders for exploitation constitutes one of the worst forms of child trafficking.[50] In some instances, abducted children are detained arbitrarily by State armed forces or non-State armed groups. Parties to conflict also abduct children in systematic campaigns of violence and reprisal against civilian populations.

The Independent International Commission of Inquiry on the Syrian Arab Republic has brought out that in one incident in the Syrian Arab Republic, ISIL abducted approximately 150 young boys on their way home after school examinations in Aleppo. They were held in captivity for a few

---

49 *Black's Law Dictionary*, 2004, p. 4.

50 For instance Article 2-9 of the Convention Against Transnational Organised Crime's Protocol to Prevent, Suppress and Punish Trafficking in Persons, especially Women and Children (2003) expressly forbids all forms of human trafficking including for forced recruitment, prostitution and sexual slavery.

months, during which they were physically abused, indoctrinated and made to observe violent practices. In Nigeria, Boko Haram abducted hundreds of women and girls in major attacks in Chibok and across the country's northeastern region. Video statements released by Boko Haram indicated that the abductions were in retaliation against the Government for the detention of relatives and served as punishment for children attending western-style schools. In northeast Nigeria and neighbouring countries, a large number of children have been abducted and recruited by armed groups.

Abducting or seizing children against their will or the will of their guardians either temporarily or permanently and without due cause is illegal under international law. It may constitute a grave breach of the Geneva Conventions and in some circumstances amount to war crimes and crimes against humanity. The Geneva Conventions Common Article 3 prohibits the abduction of children. The forced displacement or deportation of a civilian population, both of which are expressly prohibited by the Geneva Conventions, may include instances of child abduction.[51] Abduction may amount to "enforced disappearance" and is thereby prohibited by several international legal instruments. Hostage-taking is forbidden by the International Convention against Taking of Hostages; Common Article 3 of the Four Geneva Conventions and other provisions of the Geneva Conventions of 1949.[52]

The arbitrary deprivation of liberty is prohibited under Rule 99 of Customary IHL, with universal application to all parties to conflict, government armed forces or non-state armed groups alike.[53] The concept that detention must not be arbitrary is part of both IHL and IHRL. Although there are differences between these branches of international law, both IHL and IHRL aim to prevent arbitrary detention by specifying the grounds for detention based on needs, in particular security needs, and by providing for certain conditions and procedures to prevent disappearance and to supervise the continued need for detention. The abduction of a child violates the rights of the child and family, as recognized by the UDHR, the Convention on

---

51 Article 49 and 147 of the Fourth Geneva, Article 85(4) of AP I, and Article 17 of AP II.

52 Article 34 and 147 the Fourth Geneva Convention; Articles 75(2) of AP I; Article 4(2) of AP II; Customary Rule 96 of ICRC; and Article 1 of the International Convention Against Taking of Hostages (1979).

53 Henckaerts Jean-Marie and Doswald-Beck Louise. 2005. *Customary International Humanitarian Law, Volume I, Rules*, ICRC: Cambridge University.

the Rights of the Child and the ICCPR.[54] The abduction of children is also prohibited under the regional human rights treaties.[55]

In its General Comment on Article 4 of the ICCPR (concerning states of emergency), the UN Human Rights Committee stated that States parties may "in no circumstances" invoke a state of emergency "as justification for acting in violation of humanitarian law or peremptory norms of international law, for instance….through arbitrary deprivations of liberty".[56] Human rights law establishes (i) an obligation to inform a person who is arrested of the reasons for arrest, (ii) an obligation to bring a person arrested on a criminal charge promptly before a judge, and (iii) an obligation to provide a person deprived of liberty with an opportunity to challenge the lawfulness of detention. The prohibition of arbitrary deprivation of liberty is established by State practice in the form of military manuals, national legislation and official statements. Most of these legislations apply the prohibition of unlawful deprivation of liberty to both international and non-international armed conflicts.[57]

The Security Council has explicitly expressed concern over abduction and hostage-taking in situations of conflict, giving particular attention to the abduction of women and girls by terrorist groups. In its resolution 2199 (2015), the Council condemned in the strongest terms abductions of women and children and expressed outrage at their exploitation and abuse by ISIL, the Nusrah Front and other individuals, groups, undertakings and entities associated with Al-Qaida. The Council has expressed grave concern over mass abductions of girls and urged all parties to conflict to release abducted children immediately, safely and unconditionally. It has also addressed issues relating to the hostage-taking of children more generally, including in its resolution 2143 (2014), in which it strongly condemned all violations of

---

54 Article 9, UDHR; Articles 8, 35 and 37, CRC; Articles 9 and 23 ICCPR.

55 For example under Articles 3 and 5 of the European Convention on Human Rights (1950); Article 6 and 7 of the American Convention on Human Rights (1969); Article 6 of the African Charter on Human and Peoples' Rights (1981); and Article 23 of the African Charter on the Rights and Welfare of the Child (1990). In its advisory opinions in the Habeas Corpus case and the Judicial Guarantees case in 1987, the Inter-American Court of Human Rights concluded that the writ of habeas corpus is among those judicial remedies that are "essential" for the protection of various rights whose derogation is prohibited under the American Convention on Human Rights and which is non-derogable in itself as a result.

56 UN Human Rights Committee, General Comment No. 29 on Article 4 of the ICCPR.

57 Henckaerts Jean-Marie and Doswald-Beck Louise. 2005. *Customary International Humanitarian Law, Volume I, Rules*, ICRC: Cambridge University, p. 347-48.

applicable international law involving the recruitment and use of children by parties to armed conflict, including abductions.

The abduction of children during armed conflict may amount to a serious violation of the rights contained in IHL and the CRC. The abduction of children as part of a pattern of disappearances, for participation in hostilities, for enslavement and for other forms of exploitation is prohibited under IHRL.[58] The ICC's Rome Statute states that "unlawful confinement" is a grave breach of the Geneva Conventions and may amount to a war crime. Perpetrators of hostage-taking or enforced disappearances are subject to criminal accountability before the ICC. In addition, the ICC has jurisdiction to hold to account those who enslave or deport children, or forcibly transfer them from one group to another.[59] The increase in the frequency and scale of abductions calls for greater protection measures for children. Children require safe release, family tracing, medical, psychological and legal assistance and facilitation of voluntary repatriation in the context of cross-border abductions.

VI. Denial of Humanitarian Access

According to the International Red Cross and Red Crescent Movement, "Measures are humanitarian if they meet the principles of neutrality, impartiality and independence. Aid measures that do not do this are not humanitarian, regardless of any well-meaning intentions and their effectiveness." Humanitarian aid addresses the victims of crises and disasters. It is aimed at saving lives and mitigating human suffering and is performed irrespective of the victims' ethnic, religious and political affiliations. The delivery of humanitarian aid and assistance during an armed conflict poses serious challenges to humanitarian organizations. The most compelling of these are insecurity and the risk posed by the constant bombardment. Explosive weapons are one of the key concerns, putting aid workers under threat and ruining the roads and buildings that act as the key infrastructure for delivering humanitarian aid. [60] For instance, the delivery of humanitarian

---

58 For example, abduction for the purpose of exploitation is child trafficking—prohibited under Article 3 of the CRC's Optional Protocol to the Convention on the Rights of the Child on the sale of children, child prostitution and child pornography (2000).

59 The Rome Statute of ICC, Articles 6(e), 7(1)(c)-(e), 7(1)(i), 8(2)(a) and 8(2)(c).

60 UN Relief and Works Agency (UNRWA), 'UNRWA Syria crisis situation update', UNRWA, 24 December 2012; available at: http://reliefweb.int/report/syrian-arab-republic/unrwa-syria-crisis-situation-update-24-december-2012.

assistance in Syria has been an ongoing challenge, as only a small group of international humanitarian organizations have been able to access the country. A few aid workers have been killed by explosive weapons while trying to extend assistance to civilians caught in the conflict. In February 2012 the ICRC called for a ceasefire so that humanitarian organizations could deliver much-needed aid. In the Israeli military offensive on Gaza in 2008-09, humanitarian operations were suspended because of the widespread use of explosive weapons.

Humanitarian aid workers also come under attack from members of non-State armed groups. In February 2017, suspected ISIL fighters killed at least six Afghan employees of the International Committee of the Red Cross (ICRC) who were carrying supplies to areas hit by deadly snowstorms. The majority of incidents of attacks on aid workers in recent years has taken place in six countries: Afghanistan, Pakistan, Somalia, Sudan, South Sudan and Syria.

Under international law, states bear the primary responsibility for ensuring the basic needs of their affected populations. This is a consequence of the principle of sovereignty and has been confirmed in international practice. For example, the UN General Assembly Resolution 46/182 of 1991 (Guiding Principles on Humanitarian Assistance) confirms that "each State has the responsibility first and foremost to take care of the victims of natural disasters and other emergencies occurring on its territory". Hence, the affected State has the primary role in the initiation, organization, coordination, and implementation of humanitarian assistance within its territory.

The denial of humanitarian access to children and attacks against humanitarian workers assisting children are prohibited under the Fourth Geneva Convention and its Additional Protocols.[61] Article 54 of AP I provides that starvation of civilians, including children, as a method of warfare is prohibited. Paragraph 2 of Article 54 states:

> It is prohibited to attack, destroy, remove or render useless objects indispensable to the survival of the civilian population, such as foodstuffs, agricultural areas for the production of foodstuffs, crops, livestock, drinking water installations and supplies and irrigation works, for the specific purpose of denying them for their sustenance

---

61 Articles 23 and 142 Fourth Geneva Convention; Articles 54 and 70 AP I; and Articles 14 and 18 AP II.

value to the civilian population or to the adverse Party, whatever the motive, whether in order to starve out civilians, to cause them to move away, or for any other motive.

Article 70 of AP dealing with relief action states: "If the civilian population of any territory under the control of a Party to the conflict (other than occupied territory), is not adequately provided with the supplies,[62] relief actions which are humanitarian and impartial in character and conducted without any adverse distinction shall be undertaken." Further, "Offers of such relief shall not be regarded as interference in the armed conflict or as unfriendly acts. In the distribution of relief consignments, priority shall be given to those persons, such as children, expectant mothers, maternity cases and nursing mothers, who, under the Fourth Convention or AP I, are to be accorded privileged treatment or special protection."

Article 14 of AP II, applicable in non-international armed conflict provides that the starvation of civilians as a method of combat is prohibited. It is therefore prohibited to attack, destroy, remove or render useless for that purpose, objects indispensable to the survival of the civilian population such as food-stuffs, agricultural areas for the production of foodstuffs, crops, livestock, drinking water installations and supplies and irrigation works. If the civilian population is suffering undue hardship owing to a lack of the supplies essential for its survival, such as foodstuffs and medical supplies, relief actions for the civilian population must be undertaken subject to the consent of the parties to the armed conflict.[63]

Under the Rome Statute a denial of access or attack may constitute a war crime and a crime against humanity.[64] Further, using starvation as a method of warfare or willfully impeding relief supplies may amount to a war crime or even genocide.[65] Intentional attacks against a peacekeeping or humanitarian

---

62 According to Article 69 of AP I, in addition to the duties specified in Article 55 of the Fourth Geneva Convention concerning food and medical supplies, the Occupying Power shall, to the fullest extent of the means available to it and without any adverse distinction, also ensure the provision of clothing, bedding, means of shelter, other supplies essential to the survival of the civilian population of the occupied territory and objects necessary for religious worship. Relief actions for the benefit of the civilian population of occupied territories are governed by Articles 59, 60, 61, 62, 108, 109, 110 and 111 of the Fourth Geneva Convention, and by Article 71 of AP I, and shall be implemented without delay.

63 Article 18, AP II.

64 The Rome Statute of ICC, Articles 8(2)(b) (iii), (xxv); 8(2)(e) (iii), (iv) and Article 7(b).

65 Articles 8(2)(b) (xxv) and 6(c), Rome Statute.

assistance mission acting in accordance with the UN Charter constitute a war crime.[66] Moreover, it is a principle of customary international law that parties to conflict must allow and facilitate aid to any civilian population in need, subject to their control.[67] The provision of such relief must be impartial in character and conducted without any adverse distinction, for example, based on race, age or ethnicity. Consent to provide relief to a civilian population, including children, must not be refused by a party to conflict on arbitrary grounds, and each party must refrain from deliberately impeding the delivery of relief supplies to civilians in need in areas under its control. The Security Council, the General Assembly and the Human Rights Council have repeatedly condemned such impediment. Denying humanitarian access to children may violate several basic human rights, including the right to survival and the right to be free from hunger, fundamental rights enjoyed by all people.[68] The denial of humanitarian access attracts criminal accountability, even in times of armed conflict. To cite an example, the SCSL declared it a war crime and in 2009 handed down the first ever convictions by an international tribunal to three militia leaders for targeting humanitarian workers and peacekeepers in deliberate attacks.[69]

In relief operations, children are entitled to special attention and must be provided with the care and aid they require. The Convention on the Rights of the Child has several provisions that necessitate the facilitation of humanitarian relief to children in need, including ensuring that children seeking refugee status "receive appropriate protection and humanitarian assistance".[70] The 2004 Guiding Principles on Internal Displacement, a non-binding document, states that the primary duty and responsibility for providing humanitarian assistance to internally displaced persons lies with national authorities. The national authorities must facilitate the free passage of humanitarian assistance and grant persons engaged in the provision of such assistance rapid and unimpeded access to the internally displaced.[71] IHL demands that humanitarian personnel have adequate access to refugee

---

66   Article 8(2)(b) (iii) and (xxv) Rome Statute.

67   Customary Rule 55; Henckaerts Jean-Marie and Doswald-Beck Louise. 2005. *Customary International Humanitarian Law, Volume I, Rules*, ICRC: Cambridge University.

68   Articles 11 and 12, ICESCR; Article 6, Convention on the Rights of Child.

69   *Prosecutor v. Sesay, Kallon and Gbao (RUF Case)*, February 2009; Article 4 (b) of the Statute of the SCSL.

70   Articles 22(1), 24 and 27, Convention on the Rights of Child.

71   Principles 25 and 30, Guiding Principles on Internal Displacement, 2004.

and displaced populations, including children. Additionally, regional human rights instruments and numerous Security Council resolutions direct parties to conflict to provide relief personnel access to refugee and displaced populations and ensure that their basic human needs are adequately met. Humanitarian personnel, their equipment and the buildings or other objects they utilize are afforded specific protection under the Geneva Conventions and their Additional Protocols.[72] Parties to conflict must ensure the freedom of movement of authorized humanitarian personnel, subject only to imperative military necessity. Medical transports and facilities are specifically provided with further protections, which are recognized as customary international law.

Under the law of occupation, there is a well-defined obligation for the Occupying Power to ensure that the basic needs of the population under its control are fulfilled. Article 55(1) of the Fourth Geneva Convention provides that the Occupying Power has the duty to ensure the provision of food and medical supplies for the civilian population. Article 69(1) of the Additional Protocol I further stipulates that the Occupying Power must ensure without adverse distinction the provision of clothing, bedding, means of shelter, and other supplies essential to the survival of the civilian population, as well as objects necessary for religious worship. However, if the Occupying Power is not in a position to fulfil its duty, it must agree to relief schemes on behalf of this population. This obligation is unconditional under Article 59 (1) of the Fourth Geneva Convention. The Occupying Power must either ensure that the civilian population receives essential supplies or agree to relief actions.[73]

The United Nations is the largest supplier and operator of humanitarian relief operations. The 1994 Convention on the Safety of United Nations and Associated Personnel was enacted to reinforce the sanctity of its relief personnel. The Security Council has repeatedly condemned attacks against UN humanitarian relief workers as clear violations of IHL and adopted resolutions after specific instances of aid workers being targeted or harmed in armed conflicts.

Experience in Somalia, Bosnia, Kosovo and Afghanistan has shown that linking military aims and humanitarian aid is very problematic, especially

---

72 Articles 70(4) and 71(2), AP I; and Article 18(2), AP II.

73 Schwendimann felix, The Legal Framework of Humanitarian Access in Armed Conflict, *International Review of the Red Cross*, Vol. 93, No. 884, December 2011, p. 993-1008.

when it comes to armed conflicts. The Security Council has a well- defined role in protecting humanitarian workers. It has called on parties to comply with international legal obligations and condemned them when they have failed to do so, imposing targeted measures on grave violators. It could make sure that the lines between political, military and humanitarian objectives are not blurred in peace negotiations and peacekeeping mandates. It could also use a variety of tools to ensure accountability for those who violate international norms.

4   Child Soldiers and International Law

The protection of children in armed conflict is increasingly becoming a cause for concern in international law. The 1907 Hague Convention Respecting the Laws and Customs of War on Land incorporated the principle of respect for family life, but did not specify whether children with or separated from their families were entitled to additional levels of protection. The League of Nations, in 1924, adopted the Declaration of the Rights of the Child, establishing the first global charter focusing on children's rights. This Declaration owed its origin to the concern for children affected by armed conflicts in the Balkans and provided that in times of distress, children should be the first to receive relief. However, it did not include any specific provision for the protection of children during an armed conflict. It was geared towards the economic, psychological and social needs of children and paved the way for many future international efforts to protect the rights of the child.

Despite the fact that a large number of children participated in the Second World War, the Geneva Conventions of 1949 failed to include any specific provision relating to child soldiers. Only the Fourth Geneva Convention contains a few provisions that could be considered as providing protection to children. Perhaps the issue of child soldiering was not considered important at that time. It is the two Additional Protocols to the Geneva Convention, which came in 1977, that form the basis of protection of child soldiers. The Geneva Conventions and their Additional Protocols form part of international humanitarian law (IHL), which is applicable only during armed conflict. International human rights law (IHRL) and international criminal law (ICL) prohibit child soldiering. The Rome Statute of the International Criminal Court (ICC) and the Optional Protocol to the Convention on the Rights of the Child on the Involvement of Children in Armed Conflicts (OP-CRC), both of which entered into force in 2002, significantly strengthen protections for children in armed conflict.

However, in spite of the stronger laws and advocacy that have resulted in UN Security Council resolutions, international agreements, domestic legislation, the establishment of country specific ad hoc tribunals, and the international criminal court, both national armies and rebel groups continue to recruit and use children in armed conflicts. This chapter focuses on the issue of child soldiers under IHL and IHRL, while the next chapter covers ICL relating to child soldiers.

International Humanitarian Law

International Humanitarian Law (IHL) is a set of rules which seek, for humanitarian reasons, to limit the effects of armed conflict. The four Geneva Conventions, which have been universally ratified, constitute the core treaties of IHL. The Conventions are supplemented by Additional Protocols I and II relating to the protection of victims of international and non-international armed conflict respectively.[1] IHL protects children in three ways: (i) it accords children special protection as a particularly vulnerable category of persons; (ii) it questions the use of children in military operations; and (ii) has a few provisions on taking into consideration children's immaturity if they commit offences during armed conflicts.

The Fourth Geneva Convention

The 1949 Fourth Geneva Convention relating to the Protection of Civilian Persons in Time of War was the first treaty that exclusively sought to provide protection for civilians during armed conflict. However, it is mainly concerned with the treatment of civilians who are in the hands of an opposing party or who are victims of war, rather than with regulating the conduct of parties to a conflict in order to protect civilians. It contains few provisions which could be regarded as providing protection to children. Articles 17, 23, 24 and 26 of the Convention provide for measures aimed at protecting children as a particularly vulnerable category of civilians. The terms 'children', 'protected persons' and 'protected persons over 18 years of age' are distinguished

---

1   Other international treaties prohibit the use of certain weapons and military tactics and protect certain categories of persons and objects from the effects of hostilities. These treaties include the 2014 Arms Trade Treaty. In addition, the 1998 Statute of the International Criminal Court established the Court's jurisdiction in respect of war crimes, thus strengthening State's obligation to prevent serious violations of IHL.

in the Convention. For the purpose of the Fourth Convention, 'child' or 'children' denotes a person under 15 years of age. The Convention creates a number of categories of children according to age. These are children, young children, children under seven years, children under 12 years, children under 15 years, children and young people, and protected persons under 18 years of age.[2] In Article 38, which applies to protected persons in the national territory of belligerents, children under 15 years of age are included amongst those persons who should enjoy preferential treatment to the same extent as nationals of the State concerned. The term, 'protected persons under 18 years of age' appears only once in Article 68 which states, "In any case, the death penalty may not be pronounced on a protected person who was under eighteen years of age at the time of the offence." Under the Convention, the Occupying Power is obligated to work with local authorities to facilitate the availability of institutions devoted to the care and education of children, the identification of and registration of parentage, and the education and care of orphaned or displaced children.

The provisions for the protection of children are only applicable in international armed conflict. Article 2 states that "the present Convention shall apply to all cases of declared war or of any other armed conflict which may arise between two or more of the High Contracting Parties." Although Article 3 contains some basic provisions for armed conflict not of an international character, it does not have any specific provision relating to child soldiers. The provisions of this Convention are applicable to every international armed conflict not only because almost every state is a party to the Geneva Conventions, but also because these conventions are now considered to be customary international law.

---

2 Article 14, concerning safety zones, indicates that such zones may protect in particular children under 15 years of age. Children are also mentioned in Article 17, which provides for the evacuation of civilians from besieged areas. Article 23, which deals with the free passage of relief consignments intended for the weakest categories of the population, explicitly refers to children under 15 years among the potential beneficiaries. Article 24 is entirely devoted to children, particularly children under 15 who are orphaned or who are separated from their families as a result of the war, and to the identification of children under 12 years of age. Article 50 deals with children in occupied territories and to the institutions devoted to their care. It provides: "The Occupying Power shall not hinder the application of any preferential measures in regard to food, medical care and protection against the effects of war, which may have been adopted prior to the occupation in favour of children under 15 years, expectant mothers, and mothers of children under seven years." In occupied territory, Article 51 prohibits compelling children under 18 years of age to work.

The Additional Protocols

The Additional Protocol I (AP I) has widened the protection[3] afforded to children in international armed conflicts, stating that they shall be the object of special respect and be protected from any form of indecent assault. It stipulates that children under the age of 15 may not be enrolled in the armed forces or take part directly in hostilities. As for persons between 15 and 18 years of age, it provides that recruitment priority should be given to those who are oldest. Article 77 of AP I dealing with the protection of child soldiers is as follows:

1. Children shall be the object of special respect and shall be protected against any form of indecent assault. The Parties to the conflict shall provide them with the care and aid they require, whether because of their age or for any other reason.

2. The Parties to the conflict shall take all feasible measures in order that children who have not attained the age of 15 years do not take a direct part in hostilities and, in particular, they shall refrain from recruiting them into their armed forces. In recruiting among those persons who have attained the age of 15 years but who have not attained the age of 18 years, the Parties to the conflict shall endeavour to give priority to those who are oldest.

3. If, in exceptional cases, despite the provisions of paragraph 2, children who have not attained the age of 15 years take a direct part in hostilities and fall into the power of an adverse Party, they shall continue to benefit from the special protection accorded by this Article, whether or not they are prisoners of war.

---

3   After several years of preparation and drafting, Geneva Additional Protocols I and II were formally adopted by the Swiss-convened Diplomatic Conference on the Reaffirmation and Development of IHL Applicable in Armed Conflicts in June 1977. As the Protocols Additional to the Geneva Conventions of 12 August 1949, they were intended to serve as supplements to the Geneva Conventions, and covered both international and non-international armed conflicts. Additional Protocol I (AP I) is extensive, consisting of 102 articles. It addresses protection for victims of not only international armed conflict, but also the armed conflicts in which peoples are fighting against colonial domination and alien occupation and against racist regimes in the exercise of their right of self-determination. Additional Protocol II (AP II) is a response to the need for establishing or clarifying the protection of victims in non-international armed conflicts, but is a much smaller document and only consists of 28 articles, making it quite limited in scope.

4. If arrested, detained or interned for reasons related to the armed conflict, children shall be held in quarters separate from the quarters of adults, except where families are accommodated as family units as provided in Article 75, paragraph 5.

5. The death penalty for an offence related to armed conflict shall not be executed on persons who had not attained the age of 18 years at the time the offence was committed.

This Protocol was derived from the Fourth Convention and other rules of international law which governed the protection of fundamental human rights in times of armed conflict, particularly the 1966 International Covenant on Civil and Political Rights and the Declaration of the Rights of the Child, which was adopted in 1959 by the UN General Assembly. Article 77 is not subject to any restrictions as regards its scope of application. It therefore applies to all children who are in the territory of States at war, whether or not they are affected by the conflict.[4] The term "children" used in paragraph 1 of Article 77 has not been defined in AP I. The ICRC, during the discussions on drafting of AP I, decided not to place specific age limits in paragraphs 1 and 4 as there was no precise definition of the term "children" at that time. The aim of the first paragraph is to assert that children are entitled to special respect and must be protected against any form of indecent assault. The second sentence places an obligation on Parties to a conflict to provide children with the care and aid they require.

The second paragraph has direct implications for the armed forces and is related to other provisions of the Protocol, including those dealing with combatants and prisoners of war, and protection of persons who have taken part in hostilities. It is primarily concerned with the nationals of the recruiting State, though it does not exclude nationals of other States. In other words, this article applies to a State's nationals, and to some extent protects them from their own authorities. According to the ICRC, it is conceivable on the basis of Article 77(2) of AP I for a father to oppose the recruitment of his son under the age of 15 or to request that in the event of his son's voluntary enrolment, he should not be accepted.

---

4   Sandoz Yves, Christophe Swinarski and Bruno Zimmermann. 1987. *Commentary on the Additional Protocols of 8 June 1977 to the Geneva Conventions of 12 August 1949*, Geneva: ICRC (henceforth: ICRC Commentary) p. 899.

According to the ICRC, the participation of children and adolescents in combat is an inhumane practice that should be ended. However, it has been observed that in occupied territories and in wars of national liberation, it would not be realistic to totally prohibit the voluntary participation of children under 15 years of age. Accordingly, paragraph 77(2) provides guidelines for "exceptional cases" where children under 15 years of age are likely to participate in hostilities. In such situations, the authorities employing them should be conscious of the heavy responsibility they are assuming and should give such children appropriate instructions on handling weapons, the conduct of combatants and respect for the laws and customs of war.[5]

Article 77(2) is related to Articles 51 and 147 of the Fourth Convention and to Article 23 of the Hague Regulations of 1907, which prohibit certain means of injuring the enemy. As regards the interpretation of "taking a direct part in hostilities", the ICRC Commentary indicates that "the intention of the drafters of the article was clearly to keep children under 15 outside armed conflict, and consequently they should not be required to perform such services....as gathering and transmission of military information, transportation of arms and munitions, provision of supplies, etc."[6] This raises the threshold to be applied while considering which activity is prohibited, affording children an increased scope of protection.

The Hostages Trial (*The United States of America v. Wilhelm List*) established the rule that: "A civilian who aids, abets or participates in fighting is liable to punishment as a war criminal under the law of wars. Fighting is legitimate only for the combatant personnel of a country. It is only this group that is entitled to treatment as prisoners of war and incurs no liability beyond detention after capture or surrender."[7]

Article 77 paragraph 3 does not do away with the obligation to refrain from recruiting children younger than 15 years of age; voluntary enrolment is not explicitly mentioned in AP I. Today, the minimum age for recruitment

---

5   ICRC Commentary p. 900-901.

6   The ICRC's commentary states that "taking direct part in hostilities" means "acts of war which by their nature or purpose are likely to cause actual harm to the personnel and equipment of the enemy armed forces." Such participation includes hostile acts without a weapon. ICRC Commentary page 901.

7   The Hostages Trial (*The United States of America v. Wilhelm List*) was held from 8 July 1947 until 19 February 1948 and was seventh of the 12 trials of war crimes the US authorities held in their occupation zone after the end of World War II.

in the armed forces in a majority of the States is 18 years. Only a few States recruit at the age of 16.In paragraph 4, relating to the arrest or detention of children, however, no age limit has been specified. According to the ICRC, it is reasonable to assume that children under 15 years of age must be detained in quarters separate from those of adults, except where families are accommodated as family units.[8]The provision contained in Article 77 paragraph 5 is similar to Article 68 (4) of the Fourth Geneva Convention, which provides that, in any case, the death penalty may not be pronounced by the courts of the Occupying Power on a protected person who is under eighteen years of age. Article 6 of the International Covenant on Civil and Political Rights (1966) also provides that the death sentence cannot be imposed for crimes committed by persons below 18 years of age.

According to Waschefort (2015), the aim of Article 77 is twofold. It prohibits the 'use' and 'recruitment' of children as soldiers. Both the use and prohibition of recruitment are subject to their own limitations. Article 77 does not absolutely ban the recruitment and use of children in armed conflict. The provision is relatively weak in its protection of children. For instance under Article 77, paragraph 2, it is not unlawful for a State to recruit and use children between 15 and 18 years of age; it is merely the State's recruitment practice that violates AP I.[9]

Article 78 of API addresses the evacuation of children from war-torn countries, providing that children are not to be evacuated, unless there are compelling reasons. Prior to any evacuation, parental consent is to be sought, if the parents can be found, and everything is to be done to ensure that children are reunited with their parents when the danger has passed. In addition, a child's education is to continue if he or she is evacuated. Possibly, this provision aims to avert the risk of children falling into the hands of non-state actors and being recruited by them.

The Second Additional Protocol (AP II) is applicable in non-international armed conflict and has been a matter of internal concern to the state within which the conflict takes place. Article 4, paragraph 3 of AP II provides that children shall be provided with the care and aid they require, and in particular:

---

8   ICRC Commentary p. 3197. The provision is similar to Article 82 of the Fourth Geneva Convention.

9   Waschefort Gus. 2015. *International Law and Child Soldiers*, Oregon: Oxford and Portland, pp.60-71.

(c) Children who have not attained the age of 15 years shall neither be recruited in the armed forces or groups nor allowed to take part in hostilities;

(d) The special protection provided by this Article to children who have not attained the age of 15 years shall remain applicable to them if they take a direct part in hostilities despite the provisions of sub-paragraph (c) and are captured;

Article 4 paragraph (c) of AP II, which states that "Children....shall neither be recruited in the armed forces or groups, nor allowed to take part in hostilities" does not leave any scope for making exceptions to the prohibition of recruitment of children below 15 years of age. Not only can a child not be recruited, or enlist himself, but furthermore he will not be allowed to take part in hostilities, i.e., to participate in military operations such as gathering information, transmitting orders, transporting ammunition and foodstuffs, or acts of sabotage. The aim of paragraph 4 (d) is to guarantee children special protection in the demanding situations of conflict. Therefore, children will continue to enjoy their privileged rights in case the age limit of 15 years laid down in subparagraph (c) is not respected. Unlike AP I, the Second Protocol offers increased protection for children who fall within its scope, and does not permit exceptions to the proscribed conduct, but extends the recruitment restrictions to groups other than the armed forces of the state.

Therefore AP II is an advancement over all previous IHL treaties in that it does not allow states any scope to manoeuvre away from the prohibition of recruitment of all of minors under the age of 15 minors, whether for direct or indirect participation. All forms of participation in hostilities are proscribed by omitting the distinction between direct and indirect participation. In certain ways, AP II can be perceived as being more forceful than AP I in terms of child protection. However, these apparently stronger measures apply only to non-international armed conflicts. Taken together, both the Protocols display positive advancements in the law for child soldiers in both international and non-international armed conflicts.[10]

A few commentators are of the opinion that AP I and II have not yet acquired the status of customary law, as they do not enjoy universal ratification as the four Geneva Conventions do. However, the Appeals Chamber of the

---

10 Fox Mary-Jane, Child Soldiers and International Law: Patchwork Gains and Conceptual Debates, *Human Rights Review*, October-December 2005, pp. 27-48.

Special Court for Sierra Leone concluded that "many of the provisions of AP II, including the fundamental guarantees, were widely accepted as customary international law by 1996."[11]

International Human Rights Law

The Convention on the Rights of Child

International Human Rights Law (IHRL) primarily seeks to regulate the way in which States treat people who are in their jurisdiction. While IHRL is not specifically designed to protect people during times of armed conflict, its provisions remain applicable at such times. Some human rights treaties or certain of their provisions can be exceptionally suspended or restricted by governments in times of a public emergency that are seen as a threat to the life of a nation. However, certain human rights treaties, such as the UN Convention on the Rights of the Child (CRC), 1989, do not allow derogation of rights, regardless of the situation in the country.[12] The CRC remains the most universally accepted human rights instrument in history, generating an unprecedented degree of formal commitments by states. All member states of the UN, with the exception of the United States have ratified the CRC. Some judicial authorities are of the view that the CRC became international customary law almost at the time of its entry into force.[13]

The CRC defines children as all human beings under the age of 18 years.[14]It contains a comprehensive set of economic, social and cultural rights, as well as civil and political rights, which are considered to be universal, indivisible and interdependent. There is to be no hierarchy in their implementation. Four general principles underpin the CRC: non-discrimination (Article 2); the best interests of the child (Article 3); the right to life, survival and development (Article 6); and the right of children to have their views heard and given due weight in all decisions affecting them (Article 12). These principles are to be taken into account in implementing

---

11 *Prosecutor v. Norman,* Case No. SCSL-2004-14-AR72(E), Judgment, 31 May 2004.

12 With 196 State Parties, the Convention has been almost universally ratified (only the United States is not a party to the Convention) and remains the most widely ratified international human rights treaty to date.

13 *Prosecutor v. Norman,* Case Number SCSL-2004-14-AR72(E), Judgment, 31 May 2004.

14 Article 1 of the CRC states, "For the purposes of the present Convention, a child means every human being below the age of eighteen years unless under the law applicable to the child, majority is attained earlier." No minimum age is defined.

all provisions of the Convention. Although there are several articles in the CRC that *ipso facto* preclude the possibility of recruitment of child soldiers, Article 38 is specifically related to the prohibition of child soldiers.

Article 38

1. States Parties undertake to respect and to ensure respect for rules of international humanitarian law applicable to them in armed conflicts, which are relevant to the child.

2. States Parties shall take all feasible measures to ensure that persons who have not attained the age of 15 years do not take a direct part in hostilities.

3. States Parties shall refrain from recruiting any person who has not attained the age of 15 years into their armed forces. In recruiting among those persons who have attained the age of 15 years but who have not attained the age of 18 years, States Parties shall endeavour to give priority to those who are oldest.

4. In accordance with their obligations under international humanitarian law to protect the civilian population in armed conflicts, States Parties shall take all feasible measures to ensure protection and care of children who are affected by an armed conflict.

During the drafting of Article 38, there was a strong move not only to ensure that its provisions did not in any way undermine the existing standards in IHL, but also to go beyond the existing standards so that children were protected up to the age of 18, in order to secure consistency with the rest of the Convention.

Paragraph 2 is an advancement over both AP I and II, since States Parties are not just obligated to take all feasible measures in regard to their own recruits, but to anyone at all who has not attained the age of 15. This would include non-state recruitment. It is also not restricted to any particular type of conflict. Paragraph 3 is almost identical to Article 77(2) of AP I, though it does not specifically .mention the term IHL. Like Article 77(2), it provides cautions against recruiting minors under the age of 15, with the proviso that if it becomes necessary to recruit minors under 18, the oldest are to be recruited first.

The main material difference between the two is that in AP I, the prohibition of the 'use' of children is separated from the prohibition of 'recruitment' by the words 'in particular'. This means that there is a greater obligation to prohibit 'recruitment' than 'use'. The CRC uses the world 'hostilities' in defining the prohibition of the use of child soldiers. Due to the different natures of the IHRL and IHL legal regimes, the CRC places an obligation on the state party to take all feasible measures to prevent children under 15 from participating directly in hostilities.

The Committee on the Rights of the Child has emphasized since 1992 that it is of the opinion that the Convention requires protection of all children under 18 from direct or indirect involvement in hostilities and that no one under the age of 18 should be recruited into armed forces. This has been reflected in comments to many States, severely condemning any recruitment of child soldiers. A few comments of the Committee are:

The United Kingdom

The Committee is deeply concerned that about one third of the annual intake of recruits into the armed forces is below the age of 18 years, that the armed services target young people and that those recruited are required to serve for a minimum period of four years, increasing to six years in the case of very young recruits." (United Kingdom CRC/C/15/ Add.188, para. 53).

Algeria

While noting with appreciation that the minimum age of compulsory recruitment is 19 years, the Committee notes with concern that the minimum age of voluntary recruitment, both in regular armed forces and in unregulated paramilitary forces, is unclear. The alleged cases of persons under 18 years of age being used by Government-allied paramilitary forces and armed political groups are cause for serious concern." (Algeria CRC/C/15/Add.269, para. 70)

Russian Federation

"The Committee is also concerned at the regulation 'On enrolling under-age citizens of the Russian Federation as wards of military units and providing them with essential allowances', which permits boys between the ages of 14 and 16 to be voluntarily recruited and attached to military units." (Russian Federation CRC/C/RUS/ CO/3, para. 70)

Liberia

"The Committee expresses its extremely deep consternation at the very high numbers of children who have been forcibly recruited into armed forces and armed groups, by all parties involved in the conflict, including children as young as nine years old. The Committee is also concerned that these children have been forced to carry goods and weapons, guard the checkpoints and often fight in the frontline, while girls have been raped, forced to become servants of the soldiers as well as become combatants...."[15] (Liberia CRC/C/15/Add.236, para. 58)

The Committee on the Rights of the Child has expressed concern at the wide scope of the UK's Declaration and called upon the government to review it. It has emphasized that States should take measures to secure the rights of all children within their jurisdiction in times of armed conflict and that the principles of the Convention are not subject to derogation in times of armed conflict. In particular, it has stressed that in the light of the definition of the child and the principle of the best interests of the child, no child under the age of 18 should be allowed to be involved in hostilities, either directly or indirectly, and that no child under 18 should be recruited into armed forces, either through conscription or voluntary enlistment.

As the disarmament, demobilization and rehabilitation of children is an indirect measure to prevent children from participating in armed conflict, Article 39 of the CRC is concerned with the post-conflict care of children, obligating States to assist in the physical and psychological recovery and reintegration of children who are victims of armed conflict. Article 40 protects the rights of children in conflict with the law with respect to due process and takes into account the need for rehabilitative, rather than punitive measures.[16]

---

15 The Committee has been of the view that recruitment does not necessarily mean that children are deployed as soldiers. The study on the *Impact of Armed Conflict on Children* notes that children are also forced to serve in supporting roles, as cooks, porters, messengers and spies. Most are adolescents, though many child soldiers are 10 years old or younger: "While the majorities are boys, girls also are recruited. The children most likely to become soldiers are those from impoverished and marginalized backgrounds and those who have become separated from their families." UN, Report of the Independent Expert of the Secretary-General, Ms. Graca Machel, 'Impact of Armed Conflict on Children', A/51/306, 26 August 1996, paragraphs 34 and 35).

16 There are four main supporting juvenile justice documents: UN Standard Minimum Rules for the Administration of Juvenile Justice (Beijing Rules) 1985; UN Rules for the

Despite the fact that the only a few provisions of the CRC relate specifically to armed conflict, all of its provisions apply to children during conflict and internal disturbances and there are no provisions allowing derogation of these rights in times of national emergency. However, the enforcement of the Convention is limited in times of conflict. The greatest weakness of the CRC is the fact that as a human rights document, it is limited to addressing States, and thus not to any other parties, such as non-State armed groups, to a conflict. Textually the CRC does not create an obligation on a State Party to the Convention to prohibit non-State entities from recruiting children.[17] This shortcoming was recognized quickly, and by 1992 the UN Committee on the Rights of the Child recommended the idea of extending Article 38(2) and drafting a protocol to the CRC.

Optional Protocol to the CRC

The Optional Protocol to the Convention on the Rights of the Child on the Involvement of Children in Armed Conflict (OP-CRC), which entered into force on 12 February 2002, is a milestone in the campaign, strengthening the legal protection of children and helping to prevent their use in armed conflict.[18] The OP-CRC, ratified by 166 States[19] and signed by an additional

---

Protection of Juveniles Deprived of their Liberty (Havana Rules) 1990; UN Guidelines for the Prevention of Juvenile Delinquency (Riyadh Guidelines) 1990; and the Vienna Guidelines for Action on Children in the Criminal Justice System (Vienna Guidelines) 1997. Both during and in the aftermath of conflict, children under 18 who directly participated in the conflict can find themselves subject to charges in criminal or military courts. The standards mentioned above are important in ensuring that children charged with committing crimes in the context of armed conflict are treated in a manner that respects their human rights (for example, that they have access to legal representation, they are provided a fair trial, they are only deprived of liberty as a last resort, they are detained separately from adults and they are treated humanely while detained) and promotes their rehabilitation and reintegration.

17 Waschefort Gus. 2015. *International Law and Child Soldiers*, Oregon: Oxford and Portland, p. 90-91.

18 Before the OP-CRC was adopted by the General Assembly, three other instruments relating to child soldiers were adopted and entered into force. All three support, and in one case strengthen, the standards set by the OP-CRC. These are: (1) The African Charter on the Rights and Welfare of the Child, which entered into force in November 1999, was the first regional treaty to establish 18 as the minimum age for all recruitment and participation in hostilities; (2) Convention No. 182 of the International Labour Organization concerning the Prohibition and Immediate Action for the Elimination of the Worst Forms of Child Labour was adopted in June 1999 and entered into force in November 2000; and (3) The Rome Statute establishing the International Criminal Court.

19 The United States has ratified the OP-CRC without being a party to the CRC. Attached

13 States, is a landmark instrument representing universal opposition to the harmful impact of armed conflict on children. The Protocol raises the minimum age for direct participation in hostilities to 18 years from the previous minimum age of 15 years specified in the CRC and other legal instruments. It prohibits the compulsory recruitment by government forces of anyone under the age of 18, and calls on State Parties to raise the minimum age for voluntary recruitment above 15, and to implement strict safeguards when the voluntary recruitment of children under 18 years is permitted. In the case of non-State armed groups, the treaty prohibits all recruitment – voluntary and compulsory – under the age of 18.

The OP-CRC amends the CRC by making 18 the minimum age for conscription. This change is significant because it marks a shift in international opinion regarding the age at which it is acceptable to conscript children.

The first three articles of the OP-CRC are concerned with direct participation in hostilities, compulsory recruitment, and voluntary recruitment, respectively. Article 1 stipulates that States Parties "shall take all feasible measures to ensure that members of their armed forces who have not attained the age of 18 years do not take a direct part in hostilities." This article only deals with 'use', and not 'recruitment'. The qualifiers 'all feasible measures' and 'direct part in hostilities' have been retained, but the age threshold has been lifted to 18 years.[20]

Direct participation may be interpreted as encompassing not only active participation in combat, but also military activities and direct support functions such as scouting, spying, sabotage and acting as decoys, couriers, porters, cooks or assistants at military checkpoints. It might also include the use of girls for sexual purposes or in forced marriages. This broader definition

---

to their Article 3 declaration, the US has added a section entitled 'Understanding', where it is stated that "The United States understand that the United States assumes no obligations under the Convention on the Rights of Child by becoming a party to the protocol. Declaration of the USA upon ratification dated 23 December 2002.

20 One of the key issues during the negotiations on the drafting of the OP-CRC concerned the age limit for participation in hostilities. The majority of delegations expressed their support for a clearly designated limit of 18 years for participation as well as all forms of recruitment. This would be consistent with the general age of majority specified in the CRC as well as most national legislation. Compromise language was eventually agreed upon in the final text, limiting the application of the OP-CRC to children's "direct part in hostilities." This compromise accommodated the interests and concerns of delegations whose national laws and practices permitted recruitment of children under 18 years of age. United Nations, E/CN.4/2000/74, 27 March 2000, paragraphs 57-59.

of child soldiering, though not legal, is reflected in the definition of a "child soldier" contained in the Cape Town Principles, which are used to prevent the use of child soldiers and for disarmament, demobilization and reintegration.

The OP-CRC is weak in its language regarding the obligations of States. It requires, for example, that States take "all feasible measures" to ensure that children are not recruited for direct involvement in hostilities. The fact remains that the question of what is "feasible" in any particular context is controversial, and some States have taken advantage of the Protocol's vagueness to make declarations interpreting the word "feasible" in ways that weaken their obligations under the OP-CRC. For example, the UK and the US have made the following declarations on their understanding of Article 1 of the OP-CRC.

The UK

The United Kingdom of Great Britain and Northern Ireland will take all feasible measures to ensure that members of its armed forces who have not attained the age of 18 years do not take a direct part in hostilities. The United Kingdom understands that Article 1 of the OP-CRC would not exclude the deployment of members of its armed forces under the age of 18 to take a direct part in hostilities where: (a) there is a genuine military need to deploy their unit or ship to an area in which hostilities are taking place; and (b) by reason of the nature and urgency of the situation: (i) it is not practicable to withdraw such persons before deployment; or (ii) to do so would undermine the operational effectiveness of their ship or unit, and thereby put at risk the successful completion of the military mission and/or the safety of other personnel.

The USA

The US understands that, with respect to Article 1 of the OP-CRC: (A) the term "feasible measures" means those measures that are practical or practically possible, taking into account all the circumstances ruling at the time, including humanitarian and military considerations; (B) the phrase "direct part in hostilities" (i) means immediate and actual action on the battlefield likely to cause harm to the enemy because there is a direct causal relationship between the activity engaged in and the harm done to the enemy;

and (ii) does not mean indirect participation in hostilities, such as gathering and transmitting military information, transporting weapons, munitions, or other supplies, or forward deployment; and (C) any decision by any military commander, military personnel, or other person responsible for planning, authorizing, or executing military action, including the assignment of military personnel, shall only be judged on the basis of all the relevant circumstances and on the basis of that person's assessment of the information reasonably available to the person at the time the person planned, authorized, or executed the action under review, and shall not be judged on the basis of information that comes to light after the action under review was taken. **No Basis for Jurisdiction by any International Tribunal:** The US understands that nothing in the OP-CRC establishes a basis for jurisdiction by any international tribunal, including the International Criminal Court.

According to Waschfort, the above declarations highlight the margin of appreciation afforded to State Parties by utilizing the subjective obligations that is created by the language 'all feasible means' and high threshold of participation in hostilities, i.e., 'direct part in hostilities'.[21]

The OP-CRC makes two important distinctions with respect to recruitment by States Parties versus non-State armed groups or entities; and compulsory versus voluntary recruitment. Article 2 requires States Parties to ensure that persons who are under 18 are not compulsorily recruited into the armed forces. Article 3 calls upon States Parties to raise the minimum age for the voluntary recruitment of persons into their armed forces from that set out in the CRC. The second paragraph of this article authorizes a States Party to determine the minimum age at which it will permit voluntary recruitment into its armed forces. Where a State Party permits voluntary recruitment under the age of 18, it must comply with the following minimum safeguards as set forth in Article 3, paragraph 3(a): (i) recruitment must be genuinely voluntary; (ii) recruitment must be conducted with the informed consent of the person's parents or legal guardians; (iii) recruits must be fully informed of military duties; and (iv) recruits must provide reliable proof of age prior to acceptance into national military service.

---

21 Waschefort Gus. 2015. *International Law and Child Soldiers*, Oregon: Oxford and Portland, p. 93.

As part of the ratification or accession process, Article 3(2) of the OP-CRC requires States to submit a "binding declaration" whose purpose is to establish the minimum age for voluntary recruitment into the State's national armed forces. A State may strengthen its declaration at any time by notifying the Secretary-General of the United Nations. Some examples of the binding declaration on voluntary recruitment submitted by a few states is as follows:

Bangladesh

In accordance with Article 3 (2) of the OP-CRC, the Government of Bangladesh declares that the minimum age at which it permits voluntary recruitment into its national Armed Forces is 16 years for non-commissioned soldiers and 17 years for commissioned officers, with informed consent of parents or legal guardian, without any exception. The Government has adopted certain safeguards to ensure that such recruitment is not forced or coerced. Before a recruit presents himself he has to submit a written declaration from his parents or legal guardians consenting to his recruitment. If the parent or legal guardian is illiterate the declaration is verified and counter-signed by the Chairman of the Union Parishad. The recruit is required to present birth certificate, matriculation certificate and full school records. Officers and other ranks without exception are required to undergo two years of compulsory training. This ensures that they are not assigned to combat units before the age of 18.

Canada

Pursuant to Article 3 (2) of the OP-CRC, Canada hereby declares: (1) The Canadian Armed Forces permit voluntary recruitment at the minimum age of 16 years. (2) The Canadian Armed Forces have adopted the following safeguards to ensure that recruitment of personnel under the age of 18 years is not forced or coerced: (a) All recruitment of personnel in the Canadian Forces is voluntary. Canada does not practice conscription or any form of forced or obligatory service. In this regard, recruitment campaigns of the Canadian Forces are informational in nature. If an individual wishes to enter the Canadian Forces, he or she fills in an application. If the Canadian Forces offer a particular position to the candidate, the latter is not obliged to accept the position. (b)Recruitment of personnel under the age of 18 is done with the informed and written consent of the person's parents or legal guardians. The National Defence Act, Article 20 paragraph 3, states that a person under the age of 18 years shall not be enrolled without the consent of one of the parents or the guardian of that person. (c) Personnel under the age of 18 are fully informed of the duties involved in military service. The Canadian Forces provide, among other things, a series of informational brochures and films on the duties involved in military service to those who wish to enter the Canadian forces; and (d) personnel under the age of 18 must provide reliable proof of age prior to acceptance into national military service. An applicant must provide a legally recognized document, that is, an original or a certified copy of their birth certificate or baptismal certificate, to prove his or her age.

India

Pursuant to Article 3 (2) of the OP-CRC, the Government of India declares that: (i) The minimum age for recruitment of prospective recruits into Armed Forces of India (Army, Air Force and Navy) is 16 years. After enrollment and requisite training period, the attested Armed Forces personnel is sent to the operational area only after he attains 18 years of age; (ii) Recruitment into the Armed Forces of India is purely voluntary and conducted through open rally system/ open competitive examinations. There is no forced or coerced recruitment into the Armed Forces.

The UK

In accordance with Article 3 (2) of the OP-CRC: The minimum age at which individuals may join the UK Armed Forces is 16 years. This minimum broadly reflects the minimum statutory school leaving age in the UK, that is, the age at which young persons may first be permitted to cease full-time education and enter the full-time employment market. Parental consent is required in all cases of recruitment under the age of 18 years. The UK maintains the following safeguards in respect of voluntary recruitment into the armed forces: 1. The United Kingdom Armed Forces are manned solely by volunteers; there is no compulsory recruitment. 2. A declaration of age, backed by an authoritative, objective proof is an integral and early requirement in the recruitment process.

These procedures include the involvement of the parent(s) or legal guardian(s) of the potential recruits.

The USA

The Government of the USA declares, pursuant to Article 3 (2) of the OP-CRC that - (A) the minimum age at which the US permits voluntary recruitment into the Armed Forces of the US is 17 years of age; (B) The US has established safeguards to ensure that such recruitment is not forced or coerced, including a requirement in section 505 (a) of title 10, United States Code, that no person under 18 years of age may be originally enlisted in the Armed Forces of the US without the written consent of the person's parent or guardian, if the parent or guardian is entitled to the person's custody and control; (C) Each person recruited into the Armed Forces of the US receives a comprehensive briefing and must sign an enlistment contract that, taken together, specify the duties involved in military service; and (D) All persons recruited into the Armed Forces of the United States must provide reliable proof of age before their entry into military service.

Vietnam

To defend the Homeland is the sacred duty and right of all citizens. Citizens have the obligation to fulfil military service and participate in building the all-people national defence. Under the law of the Socialist Republic of Vietnam, only male citizens at the age of 18 and over shall be recruited into military service. Those who are under the age of 18 shall not be directly involved in military battles unless there is an urgent need for safeguarding national independence, sovereignty, unity and territorial integrity.

The requirement to raise the minimum age for voluntary recruitment included in Article 3 allows for an exception. Schools operated by or under the control of the armed forces of the States Parties are not required to raise the age for voluntary recruitment [Article 3(5)].[22] The below-18 age minimum set for voluntary recruitment and the exemption made for military schools were included at the behest of delegations who argued that in many countries

---

22   Article 3, paragraph 5 states that the requirement to raise the age in paragraph 1 of the article (i.e., 18 years) does not apply to schools operated by or under the control of the armed forces of the States Parties, in keeping with articles 28 and 29 of the Convention on the Rights of the Child.

the function of military service is not limited to defence. These schools also provide young people an opportunity to acquire knowledge and skills, and access to education that may be useful to them in the future.

The fourth and fifth articles of the OP-CRC pertain to non-State armed groups and establish a framework for holding non-State armed groups accountable for child soldiering. Article 4(1) of the OP-CRC prohibits armed groups from recruiting children under 18 years of age either forcibly or voluntarily and from using them in hostilities. The clause preventing child recruitment and use by armed groups is an important feature of the OP-CRC, given that most armed conflicts today are internal or non-international and that the majority of children used in armed conflicts are recruited – often forcibly – by non-State armed groups. Article 4(1) does not require armed groups to be actively engaged in an armed conflict for its provisions to apply. It also prohibits the recruitment of children under 18 prior to the outbreak of hostilities. The text of Article 4(1) reflects the traditional view that only States have obligations under international human rights law and can become parties to treaties, whereas the behaviour of non-State entities is to be regulated by domestic law.

The OP-CRC uses 'should not, under any circumstances' instead of 'must not' or 'shall not' while outlining the prohibitions against the recruitment or use of persons under 18 years by armed groups, reflecting the strong views of the international community without conferring any legal status on such armed groups. Further, Article 4(3) ensures that the application of article 4 would not confer legal status on an armed group. In addition to prohibiting all recruitment of children by non-State armed groups, Article 4(2) imposes a duty on all States Parties to regulate the behaviour of armed groups, including by prohibiting and criminalizing the recruitment and use of children under 18 years. This regulation of activities might include the adoption of domestic legislation. The OP-CRC provision on non-State armed groups does not create an international obligation on non-State parties; the duty lies with the State Parties to enforce this standard on non-State parties by enforcing a penal legislation.[23]

The OP-CRC also addresses post-conflict issues, including the demobilization of child soldiers. Article 6 provides that persons "recruited

---

23 For instance, in February 2006 the Sri Lankan Penal Code was amended to make "engaging/recruiting children for use in armed conflict" a crime punishable by 20 years' imprisonment.

or used in hostilities" are to be demobilized and accorded "all appropriate assistance for their physical and psychological recovery and their social reintegration." The language of Article 6 makes it abundantly clear that children voluntarily or forcibly recruited into armed groups and non-State forces are to be included in demobilization and reintegration efforts.

The CRC and its Optional Protocol were important and much-needed steps in creating an awareness of and codifying the special needs of armed minors in situations of peace and conflict. Of these, the OP-CRC is the main international legal instrument to specifically address the use of children as soldiers. Though it does not specifically define child soldiers, it establishes the parameters within which children can or cannot be used in government or non-government armed forces.

The proponents of the OP-CRC have articulated five strengths of the Optional Protocol; it has (i) established an international standard for the employment of children in conflict; (ii) codified a legal norm by which states can be held accountable; (iii) set a minimum age requirement that makes it more difficult for governments and non-state actors to fabricate; (iv) encouraged States to implement existing national laws and policies or enact domestic standards; and (v) raised public awareness regarding the use of child soldiers.[24] Notwithstanding all this, the OP-CRC suffers from vagueness. For instance, Article 1 stipulates that States "shall take all feasible measures to ensure that members of their armed forces who have not attained the age of 18 years do not take a direct part in hostilities."

The OP-CRC and the CRC Committee

The CRC has a unique institutional power to interpret humanitarian law — perhaps greater than that of the Human Rights Committee, whose constitutive treaty, the International Covenant on Civil and Political Rights, does not refer explicitly to IHL. The CRC Committee, constituted under Article 43 of the CRC, has played a significant role in the processes leading tothe drafting of the CRC Protocol.[25]Until 2014, the CRC Committee was

---

24 Rachel Stohl, Children in Armed Conflict: Assessing the Optional Protocol, *Journal of Conflict, Security and Development*, Vol. 2, No. 2, 2002, p. 135-140.

25 The CRC Committee on October 9, 1992 undertook "Children in Armed Conflicts" as the subject for its first general discussion and recommended the adoption of an optional protocol raising the minimum age for recruitment into the armed forces to 18 years. The Committee also proposed a study on children affected by armed conflicts. Pursuant to the

not vested with the power to accept individual complaints or inter-State complaints, or to initiate an enquiry into an alleged violation of the provisions of the OP-CRC.[26] Thus the Committee had no means of compelling a State to initiate action in case of violations. The complaint procedure is the heart of the human rights protection system as it develops public confidence and enhances the development of human rights jurisprudence. This shortcoming was overcome with the adoption of the Third Optional Protocol to the CRC (OP3-CRC) in 2014.

The Third Optional Protocol to the CRC

The Third Optional Protocol to the CRC (OP3-CRC) established an international complaints procedure for violations of the child rights contained in the CRC and its two Protocols. It entered into force in April 2014, allowing children from States that have ratified to bring complaints about violations of their rights directly to the UN Committee on the Rights of the Child if they have not found a solution at national level. [27] The OP3-CRC provides two new ways for children to challenge violations of their rights by States: (i) A

---

recommendation of the Committee, the U.N. General Assembly, in 1993, requested that the Secretary-General appoint an expert (MsGracaMachel) to study the impact of armed conflict on children. See: UN, Report of the Independent Expert of the Secretary-General, Ms. GracaMachel, 'Impact of Armed Conflict on Children', A/51/306, 26 August 1996.

26 The Committee in its concluding observation on the initial report of the UK (under CRC) has recommended that the state party provide training on the OP-CRC to all members of its armed forces, including those involved in international operations. Further, training on the provisions of the OP-CRC be provided to all relevant professionals, including those working with asylum-seekers and refugee children, migration authorities, police, lawyers, judges, including military judges, medical professionals, social workers and journalists. The Committee also asked the UK to consider reviewing its position and raise the minimum age for recruitment into the armed forces to 18 years in order to promote the protection of children through an overall higher legal standard; in recruiting among those persons who have not yet attained the age of 18, priority to be given to those who are the oldest. The Committee on the Rights of Child: CRC/C/OPAC/GBR/CO/1, dated 17 October 2008. In its response to Cambodia's report, the Committee first noted the legacy of twenty years of armed conflict and went on to recommend "that the State party take effective measures for the identification, demobilization and psychological rehabilitation and reintegration in society of child soldiers and to undertake awareness-raising campaigns for army officials to prevent the further recruitment of child soldiers." CRC Committee: Concluding Observations: Cambodia: CRC/C/15/Add.128, 28 June 2000.

27 The Optional Protocol to the Convention on the Rights of the Child on a Communications Procedure was adopted and opened for signature, ratification and accession by General Assembly resolution A/RES/66/138 of 19 December 2011, and entered into force on 14 April 2014. As on 31 December 2016, it has been ratified by 29 states and signed by 22 states.

communication procedure, which enables children to bring complaints about violations of their rights to the UN Committee on the Rights of the Child, if they have not been fully resolved in national courts, and (ii) An inquiry procedure for grave and systematic violations of child rights.

Under Article 6 of the OP3-CRC, communications may be submitted by or on behalf of an individual or group of individuals, within the jurisdiction of a State Party, claiming to be victims of a violation by that State party of any of the rights set forth in any of the following instruments to which that State is a party: (i) The CRC (ii) The OP-CRC on the sale of children, child prostitution and child pornography, and (iii) The OP-CRC on the involvement of children in armed conflict. Article 13 of the OP3-CRC empowers the Committee to call for a report from a State Party, if it receives reliable information indicating grave or systematic violations of the rights set forth in the Convention or in the Optional Protocols. The Committee may designate its members to conduct an urgent inquiry and if required, make a visit with the consent of the State Party concerned. The Committee may invite the State Party to inform it of the measures taken in response to the inquiry.

International Labour Organization (ILO) Convention 182

Tens of millions of children around the globe work in the most abhorrent conditions that rob them of their childhood, their health, and sometimes even their lives. They do so because their survival and that of their families depend on it, and in many cases because unscrupulous adults take advantage of their vulnerability. In June 1999, the ILO adopted Convention No. 182 Concerning the Prohibition and Immediate Elimination of the Worst Forms of Child Labour. The Convention, which came into force on 19 November 2000, set the goal of eradicating the worst forms of child labour. It requires ratifying States to take immediate and effective measures to prohibit and eliminate the worst forms of child labour as a matter of urgency.

Article 2 of the Convention defines a child as a person under the age of 18 years. It defines "the worst forms of child labour" as "all forms of slavery or practices similar to slavery, such as the sale and trafficking of children, debt bondage and serfdom and forced or compulsory labour, including forced or compulsory recruitment of children for use in armed conflict."[28]Article 3 of

---

28 Article 3 (a), ILO Convention No. 182 Concerning the Prohibition and Immediate Elimination of the Worst Forms of Child Labour, 2000.

the Convention includes the followings as "the worst form of child labour": (i) The use, procuring or offering of a child for prostitution, for the production of pornography or for pornographic performances; (ii) The use, procuring or offering of a child for illicit activities, in particular for the production and trafficking of drugs as defined in the relevant international treaties; and (iii) Work which, by its nature or the circumstances in which it is carried out, is likely to harm the health, safety or morals of children.[29]

The State Parties are required to ensure that existing legislation is reviewed by the competent body of the government to determine whether it unequivocally prohibits the worst forms of child labour for all children under the age of 18, including forced or compulsory recruitment of children in armed conflict. Recommendation 190 accompanying Convention 182 encourages States to make such recruitment a criminal offence.[30]By 31 October 2017, 181 countries have ratified this Convention. The wide acceptance of the Convention could be considered as a strong indication that the prohibition of the forcible recruitment of children under the age of 18 has become customary international law.

The Arms Trade Treaty

The proliferation of automatic weapons and lightweight arms as a result of international arms trade has increased the utility of the child soldier. Children aged 10 and younger can use assault weapons just as effectively as adults because weapons have become light and simple enough for them to use.[31]Thus, when an armed conflict is prolonged, the State armed forces and non-State groups are more likely to use children to replenish their ranks.. Consider the following facts about small arms and children in conflict zones:[32]

---

29 Article 3 (b)-(d), ILO Convention No. 182 Concerning the Prohibition and Immediate Elimination of the Worst Forms of Child Labour, 2000.

30 FonsekaBhawani, The Protection of Child Soldiers in International Law, *Asia-Pacific Journal of Human Rights and the Law*, Vol. 2, No. 2, 2001, p. 69-89.

31 In Sierra Leone during the decade-long civil war, the use of child soldiers has been facilitated by improvements in military technology. Guns, such as the Soviet-made AK-47 or the American M-16, are becoming increasingly simple to use and can be stripped and reassembled by children as young as 10. These rifles are inexpensive and easily available, obtained in some parts of Africa for less than US$ 6 each. UNICEF, The State of the World's Children 1996.

32 Vandergrift Kathy and David Lochhead, Small Arms, Children, and Armed Conflict: A Framework for Effective Action, 2004.

> ➢ There are more than 600 million small arms in the world today. Eight million new weapons are produced each year.

> ➢ At least 16 billion units of ammunitions are produced annually, more than two bullets for every man, woman, and child on the planet.

> ➢ More injuries, displacements, rapes, kidnapping, and acts of torture involve the use or threatened use of small arms than any other type of weapon.

> ➢ Lightweight, easy-to-use, low-cost small arms have enabled the use of child soldiers in more than 30 armed conflicts in the world.

> ➢ The availability and misuse of small arms constitute an important factor in preventing the delivery of assistance to children in need. Most child deaths in conflict zones are from preventable diseases due to the lack of access to assistance.

> ➢ Easy access to small arms increases the severity of conflicts that involve young people and fuels the continuation and escalation of armed conflict.

On 2 April 2013 the UN General Assembly adopted the Arms Trade Treaty (ATT), which entered into force on 24 December 2014. It has been ratified by 92 States and 42 have signed it so far. The ATT is the first treaty to attempt to regulate the global transfer of conventional arms (and ammunitions). It represents a milestone in the quest to prevent the illicit and irresponsible transfer of arms to countries where they can be used for the commission of serious human rights and humanitarian law violations. It is believed that if effectively implemented, the ATT could prevent the flow of arms to armed actors who unlawfully recruit children or use them to participate in hostilities.[33]

The link between child soldiers and the transfer of arms, particularly small arms and light weapons, has been well established. Ms Graca Machel, the UN Secretary-General's expert on children and armed conflict, found that the proliferation of inexpensive and lightweight weapons was contributing to the unlawful recruitment of children and their use in hostilities.[34] The UN

---

33 The Arms Trade Treaty and its implication for preventing child soldiers - a preliminary assessment Child Soldiers International, 7 May 2013.

34 The Impact of Armed Conflict on Children, Report of the expert of the Secretary-General,

Secretary-General and his Special Representative for Children and Armed Conflict (SRSG) have consistently pointed to the correlation between the easy availability of small arms and human rights abuses against children, including their recruitment and use as soldiers. They have repeatedly called for bans on the export or supply of small arms and military assistance to the parties concerned.

The ATT in Article 1, sets as its object the establishment of international standards for the regulation of international trade in conventional arms and to prevent the illicit trade of these arms and their diversion. The categories of conventional arms are spelled out in Article 2. Of particular relevance for the prevention of the recruitment and use of child soldiers, are "small arms and light weapons". Categories of ammunitions (Article 3) and parts and components (Article 4) are also listed out.

Under the treaty, the States Parties to the ATT shall prohibit any transfer of conventional arms (or ammunitions or parts) when such transfer would: (i) violate obligations set out in UN Security Council resolutions under Chapter VII of the UN Charter, in particular in relation to arms embargoes; (ii) violate other international agreements to which they are party, particularly related to transfer of or illicit trafficking in conventional arms; and (iii) be used in the commission of genocide, crimes against humanity, grave breaches of the 1949 Geneva Conventions, attacks directed against civilians or civilian objects, or other war crimes (Article 6). The third category of prohibitions was the focus of much of the negotiations. The language adopted requires knowledge at the time of the authorization that the arms would be used to commit such crimes. Further, while not providing an exhaustive list of war crimes, it refers to war crimes as defined in international agreements to which the State is a party.

Given the well-established link between the transfer of arms and child recruitment, the transfer of arms to parties which unlawfully recruit or use children in hostilities would, in most cases, fall within the scope of those transfers prohibited by Article 6 of the ATT.[35] This is particularly relevant

---

Ms Graca Machel, submitted pursuant to General Assembly resolution 48/157 (Machel Report), UN Doc. A/51/306, 26 August 1996.

35 For instance, during Sri Lanka's 25-year civil war, both the Tamil Tiger rebels and a pro-government paramilitary group recruited child soldiers; the Tigers alone recruited over 5,700 children during the final years of the war. Both parties continued to receive weapons from external sources despite the use of child soldiers and other serious human

given that children are recruited and used by both State forces and armed opposition groups in most contemporary armed conflicts. The unlawful recruitment of children or their use in hostilities constitutes a serious violation of international human rights and humanitarian law.

The UN Security Council resolutions on children and armed conflict have regularly condemned violations of international law related to the recruitment and use of child soldiers. Hence, beyond prohibiting the transfer of arms to parties which recruit or use child soldiers when this falls under Article 6, the ATT will require States Parties to assess whether any arms transfer could be used to commit or facilitate the unlawful recruitment of children or their use in hostilities. This is particularly so, given the express requirement to take into account the risk that such arms transfer may facilitate violence against children. Child recruitment is often accompanied by the use or threat of armed violence. It is strongly believed that the adoption of the ATT represents a significant step in the efforts to regulate international arms trade and hence, in the use of children in armed conflict.[36]

Customary IHL

The ICRC Customary Rules of IHL provide that children must not be recruited into armed forces or armed groups and they must not be allowed to take part in hostilities.[37] State practice establishes these rules as a norm of customary international law applicable in both international and non-international armed conflicts. Article 22 (2) of the African Charter on the Rights and Welfare of the Child also prohibits the recruitment of children and their participation in armed conflicts. The recruitment of children is prohibited in several military manuals, including those which are applicable in

---

rights abuses. An effective Arms Trade Treaty could stop such practices of child soldier recruitment in future.

36 Statement by Bishop Elias Taban, Head of the Sudan Evangelical Alliance: "I have spent over 40 years of my life at war. I became a child soldier at the age of 12, and I know firsthand that the weapons that can do the most harm – small arms such as AK47s and handguns – are often considered the least. Sudan has become a dumping ground for small arms. Much of the tragic loss of life we witness isn't just caused by large military-weapons, but arms that any man, woman, or child can carry. The Arms Trade Treaty would slow the flow of these weapons onto black and grey markets and would help keep them out of the hands of war lords, terrorists, drug dealers, and thugs."

37 Rules 136 and 137, Henckaerts Jean-Marie and Louise Doswald-Beck, *Customary International Humanitarian Law*, Volume I: Rules, ICRC: Cambridge University Press, 2005.

non-international armed conflicts. It is also prohibited under the legislation of many States. Alleged practices of recruiting children, for example, in Burundi, the Democratic Republic of the Congo, Liberia, Myanmar and Uganda, have generally been condemned by States and international organizations. In a resolution adopted in 1996 on the plight of African children in situations of armed conflict, the OAU Council of Ministers exhorted all African countries, in particular the warring parties in those countries embroiled in civil wars, to refrain from recruiting children.[38] The UN Secretary-General has announced a minimum age requirement for soldiers involved in UN peacekeeping missions and has asked States to send in their national contingents of soldiers preferably not younger than 21 years of age, and in no case less than 18.

Extraterritorial Obligation to Prevent the Use of Child Soldiers

International law has been defined as the body of rules and principles of action that are binding upon civilized states in their relations with others.[39] Traditionally, states are only responsible for obligations in the conventions that they have signed. They can voluntarily take on obligations, but can only be held to the obligations they have signed on to. Most treaties obligate states to take action in support of, or refrain from taking action against, people within their territory or jurisdiction. This is based on the traditional notion of state sovereignty, whereby states are only responsible for people within their jurisdiction.

However, states also have "extraterritorial obligations" to persons outside of their territory or jurisdiction. These extraterritorial obligations are emerging as the world is becoming more globalized and there is a growing perception that one country's action may have impacts on another country. Extraterritorial obligations would be applicable to the prevention of the recruitment and the use of child soldiers. For example, if a state A is providing financial aid to another state or a non-state actor B, and the aid is being utilized to arm child soldiers, A has the extraterritorial obligation to 'influence' B to stop the recruitment and the use of child soldiers. The use of the term 'influence' refers to a state's ability to affect the actions of non-state actors or another state, primarily through incentives or threats. If a state has influence

---

38 OAU Council of Ministers, Resolution Number 1659 (LXIV) of 1996.

39 The Vienna Convention on the Law of Treaties, Article 2(1)(a) defines a treaty as an international agreement concluded between States in written form and governed by international law whether embodied in a single instrument or in two or more related instruments.

over another state or actor who may violate IHL/IHRL, the influential state has an obligation to prevent that state or actor from taking illegal actions.[40] The OP-CRC regarding child soldiers create an extraterritorial obligation for states. States have an obligation to uphold the right of all children to not be conscripted. Under this obligation, states should take no action that would lead to another state's or non-state actor's use or recruitment of child soldiers.

Promoting respect for human rights is a core purpose of the United Nations. The Security Council and the General Assembly have issued a number of resolutions on the legal obligation of States to ensure respect for IHL in conflicts to which they are not a party. The Secretary General, in a report submitted to the Security Council has affirmed: "Under the Fourth Geneva Convention, each State Party undertakes a series of unilateral engagements, *vis-a-vis* itself and at the same time *vis-a-vis* the others, of legal obligations to protect those civilians who are found in occupied territories following the outbreak of hostilities." Further, "The Security Council should consider making a solemn appeal to all the State Parties to the Fourth Geneva Convention that have diplomatic relations with Israel, drawing their attention to their obligation under Article 1 of the Convention to ensure respect for the present Convention in all circumstances" and urging them to use all the means at their disposal to persuade the Government of Israel to change its position as regards the applicability of the Convention.[41]

Under international law there are three main actions that states must undertake to uphold the human rights of people in their jurisdiction: the obligation to respect, to protect, and to fulfil each right. Article 1 common to the four Geneva Conventions of 1949 and AP I of 1997 provides: "The High Contracting Parties undertake to respect and to ensure respect for the present Convention /Protocol in all circumstances." Similarly, Article 2 of the CRC holds that states have an obligation to "respect and ensure the rights set forth in the present Convention to each child......" Article 38 of the CRC provides that "States Parties undertake to respect and to ensure respect for rues of IHL applicable to them in armed conflict which are relevant to the child." The Preamble to the 1976 International Covenant on Civil and Political Rights (ICCPR) also provides that State Parties must promote universal respect for, and observance of, human rights and freedoms.

---

40 Hakimi Monica, State Bystander Responsibility, *European Journal of International Law*, Vol. 21, 2010, p. 341-385.

41 Report Submitted to the Security Council by the Secretary-General in Accordance with Resolution 605 (1987), UN Doc. S/19443, 21 January 1988, paragraphs 24–27.

The prominent position of this obligation "to respect and to ensure respect" at the beginning of each treaty increases its importance. The State Parties are required not merely to undertake to respect the Convention/ Protocol, but also to ensure respect for it. The duty to protect provides that a state must try to avoid violations of the rights set forth in a treaty by other individuals or entities.

Table 1: The Status of Ratification of Treaties Relevant to Child Soldiers

S. No.	Instrument	Entry into Force	State Parties*
1.	Fourth Geneva Convention	21 October 1950	196
2.	Additional Protocol I	7 December 1978	174
3.	Additional Protocol II	7 December 1978	164
4.	Convention on the Rights of Child (CRC)	2 September 1990	196
5.	OP-CRC (children in armed conflict)	12 July 2002	166
6.	OP3-CRC (complaint procedure)	14 April 2014	29
7.	ILO Convention No. 182	19 November 2000	181
8.	Rome Statute of ICC	17 July 1998	124
9.	Armed Trade Treaty, 2014	24 December 2014	92

*As on 31 October 2017.

It is evident from Table 1 that the Geneva Conventions and the CRC have universal ratification and have gained the status of customary international law. The Additional Protocols I and II, the OP-CRC and the ILO Convention 182 have near universal ratification, while the Rome Statute has been ratified by 124 States. The Arms Trade Treaty, which is of recent origin, has also been ratified by a large number of states. For ensuring their obligations under a treaty, the states must disseminate it to different actors in society including the civilian population. They should also take adequate measures to translate the legal obligation into actual respect and compliance by the society. In fact, IHL and IHRL must be seen by the states as a social contract to protect human life and dignity even in times of armed conflict, where acts of violence are lawfully justified. The obligation to respect also binds organized armed groups, in accordance with Common Article 3 to the Geneva Conventions. In fact, compliance with IHL is the primary responsibility of the parties to a conflict.

The interests protected by the Fourth Geneva Conventions, CRC and OP-CRC are of such fundamental importance to the human person that every state party has a legal interest in their observance. The words 'in all circumstances' indicate that the obligations to respect and to ensure respect apply both during armed conflict and in peacetime, depending on the obligation in question. A military, economic, geographical or other factual inequality of the parties to the conflict does not affect their obligations under the Conventions; the Conventions must be observed regardless of actual capacity. Further, according to the ICRC study on customary international humanitarian law, the obligation to respect and ensure respect is not limited to the Geneva Conventions but to the entire body of IHL binding upon a particular State. The International Court of Justice (ICJ) has also asserted the imperative nature of the obligation to ensure respect for IHL. In the *Nicaragua* case, the ICJ considered that even though the US was not a party to the NIAC, it had an obligation to ensure respect for the Geneva Conventions in all circumstances. It further added that this obligation did "not derive only from the Conventions themselves, but from the general principles of humanitarian law".[42]

Since the CRC entered into force in 1990, international attention has increasingly been focused on the plight, problems and protection of children. The OP-CRC was a significant milestone in the international community's attempt to elaborate norms to deal with the participation of children in armed conflicts. The OP-CRC amended the CRC's minimum age for recruitment in the armed forces from 15 to18. It obligated states parties to ensure that persons who have not attained the age of 18 years are not compulsorily recruited in their armed forces. Recognizing that children are an easy target for non-state armed groups, the Protocol extended the prohibition to such groups. On becoming a party to the OP-CRC, a state must set forth a binding declaration establishing its minimum voluntary recruitment age and safeguards adopted to comply with the Protocol. State parties that permit

---

42 *Case Concerning Military and Paramilitary Activities in and Against Nrcaragua* (*Nicaragua v. USA*) International Court of Justice, 27 June 1986.

voluntary recruitment of individuals under the age of 18 into their national armed forces must maintain safeguards to ensure, as a minimum, that such recruitment is genuinely voluntary and is carried out with the informed consent of the person's parents or legal guardians. Such recruits must also be fully informed of the duties involved in military service and must provide reliable proof of age prior to acceptance into national military service.

The 1999 ILO Convention defines a child as a person under the age of 18 years and recognizes that forced labour is a modern variant of slavery. It defines the worst forms of child labour as including all forms of slavery and forced or compulsory recruitment of children for use in armed conflict. It encourages States to make the recruitment of child soldiers a criminal offence. Regrettably, it only seeks to protect children who are forcibly recruited and does not extend protection to those who are voluntarily recruited. The rules of IHL recognize the vulnerability of children in armed conflict and aim to protect children in armed conflict. However, the special protection afforded to children under IHL does not adequately recognize their involvement in armed conflict. The Arms Trade Treaty of 2014 has a great potential in preventing the unlawful recruitment of children or their use in armed conflict. The widespread acceptance of the international norm prohibiting the recruitment and use of child soldiers shows the customary nature of the prohibition and the universal need to uphold the obligation to prevent the use of child soldiers.[43]

---

43 The Special Court for Sierra Leone (SCSL) has held in the *Norman* case that the widespread recognition and acceptance of the norm prohibiting child recruitment in AP II and the CRC provides compelling evidence that the conventional norm entered customary international law. Special Court for Sierra Leone, *Prosecutor against Sam Hinga Norman*, Case No. SCSL-2004-14-AR72(E), Decision on preliminary motion based on lack of jurisdiction (child recruitment) (appeals chamber), 31 May 2004, page 7396, paragraph 20.

5   Prosecution under International Criminal Law

Earlier international courts, such as the International Military Tribunals of Nuremberg and Tokyo and the United Nations Tribunals for the former Yugoslavia and for Rwanda, referred to crimes against children mainly as part of atrocities against civilians or against certain ethnic or religious groups. Crimes against children have been receiving more focused attention only in the recent past. This chapter analyses the extent to which international and "mixed" or "hybrid" criminal courts, in particular the Special Court for Sierra Leone (SCSL) and the International Criminal Court (ICC) have focused on crimes against children and dealt with children as victims. It highlights the major role played by the SCSL and then by the ICC in criminalizing as war crimes the conscription or enlistment of children and their use in active participation in hostilities. The SCSL was the first to hand down convictions for these crimes. The first two cases before the ICC also concerned the unlawful recruitment of children or their use in hostilities.

Special Court for Sierra Leone

The Sierra Leonean civil war began in March 1991 when the Revolutionary United Front (RUF) forces, taking advantage of local discontent and regional instability, attempted to overthrow the government and exercise control over the country's economic resource—the diamond mines.[1] During the conflict, the government was overtaken several times by intra-governmental factions. The RUF forces took full advantage of the regime changes, advanced on

---

1   On March 23, 1991, about 100 fighters calling themselves the Revolutionary United Front (RUF) crossed the border from Liberia into Sierra Leone. The RUF was led by Foday Sankoh and allegedly acted in concert with Charles Taylor, then warlord and later president of Liberia. It is believed that Taylor backed the RUF financially to gain access to Sierra Leone's diamond reserves and destabilize the country.

government forces and eventually gained substantial control over the diamond mines. The Government, in its turn, engaged private security firms and the Nigerian-led Economic Community of West African States Monitoring Group (ECOMOG) to protect itself from the RUF. In a decade of conflict, it is estimated that as many as 75,000 civilians were killed and 500,000 were displaced.[2]

The RUF rebels intentionally targeted children during their raids. Young boys and girls were forcefully recruited into their ranks. Young girls were often raped and forced to become "wives" or sexual slaves, while boys were forced to commit violent acts. During the civil war, an estimated 5000 juvenile soldiers committed widespread and systematic atrocities in defiance of international conventions. The RUF forces, comprising 30 percent juvenile soldiers, implemented a brutal war operation referred to by RUF commanders as "Operation No Living Thing". During the operation, the rebel forces ripped through Freetown, raping thousands of women, killing innocent civilians, and destroying the capital city. The juvenile soldiers earned a reputation throughout the region as fearless and blood-thirsty killers, and were considered the cruelest combatants of the war.[3]

The use of child soldiers was not confined to the RUF alone. The Armed Forces Revolutionary Council (AFRC) and the Civil Defence Forces (CDF) also made use of them. It is estimated that up to 7,000 children fought in this war.[4] Many of these children were forcibly conscripted. In the most common scenario, combatants stormed into a home, killed one family member, and forced a young male to kill another relative. The combatants were often drugged on a regular basis, particularly before going into battle,

---

2   Whilst the majority of crimes were committed by the Revolutionary United Front (RUF) and the Armed Forces Revolutionary Council (AFRC), government forces and the Civil Defense Forces (CDF) also committed serious crimes.

3   Large numbers of children were coerced to participate in the war, often facing death for non-compliance. Some juvenile soldiers, however, acted voluntarily, serving as commanders and foot soldiers during executions and mutilations. Thousands of innocent Sierra Leoneans suffered amputation and mutilation at the hands of rebel forces. The RUF's most notorious act of terror was chopping off the hands of those said to have cast votes in 1996 for pro-government candidate Ahmed Tejan Kabah. The Sierra Leonean Government, in response, adopted similarly gruesome war tactics.

4   The total number of children who have been officially disarmed in Sierra Leone is 6,904. UN High Commissioner for Human Rights, Report of the United Nations High Commissioner for Human Rights on the Human Rights Situation in Sierra Leone, UN Doc. A/57/284, 7 August 2002.

with a substance locally known as "brownbrown" that is thought to be a combination of heroin and cocaine or gunpowder. The goal was to eradicate thesense of family or community and to supplant it with allegiance to the faction and commanders, who became surrogate parents or community elders. Some of the notorious atrocities committed by the warring factions were the amputation of hands, feet, arms and legs, other forms of mutilation, including the cutting off of noses, ears, and lips, and even acts of cannibalism, particularly by the Kamajors.[5]

In July 1999, US diplomats brokered the Lome Peace Accord, which offered amnesty to all combatants and endowed the RUF regime with inclusion in the new government in exchange for disarmament and demobilization. However, the UN Secretary-General's Special Representative insisted that international crimes of genocide, crimes against humanity, war crimes, and other serious violations of IHL would not be protected by the amnesty proviso. To implement the Accord, the UN pledged nearly 6,000 peacekeeping troops to the region. However, the war continued to rage as RUF forces refused to adhere to the Accord and in May 2000 took 5,000 UN peacekeepers as hostage. The conflict ultimately ceased when the UN, Britain, and the US dispatched to Sierra Leone the world's largest peacekeeping mission.[6]

The UN and the Government of Sierra Leone jointly established the Special Court on 14 August 2000.[7] The Court had a hybrid judicial system administered concurrently by the UN and the Sierra Leone Government.[8]It was composed of a trial chamber, an appellate chamber, the prosecutor's office, and the registry, and had jurisdiction over persons alleged to bear the greatest responsibility "for serious violations of IHL and Sierra Leonean law

---

5   Perrielo Tom and Marieke Wierda, Special Court of Sierra Leone under Scrutiny, Prosecution Case Studies Series, The International Centre for Transitional Justice (ICTJ), March 2006.

6   The conflict was officially declared over in 2002, after the 'symbolic' burning of arms.

7   The Court was formally established and became operational in April 2002 after the Sierra Leone Parliament enacted the Special Court Agreement, 2002 (Ratification) Act.

8   The Special Court was the first 'hybrid' international criminal court to be established – 'hybrid' in the sense that it involved a mixture of international and domestic law and personnel. As such, it was a departure from the model of the ad hoc tribunals for the former Yugoslavia and Rwanda (ICTY and ICTR) on the one hand, and the International Criminal Court (ICC) on the other, and was welcomed by many as a potentially more effective and efficient form of international criminal justice.

committed in the territory of Sierra Leone since 30 November 1996."[9] In 2001 the UN Security Council called upon all members to: "…put an end to impunity, prosecute those responsible for genocide, crimes against humanity, war crimes, and other egregious crime perpetrated against children and ensure the post-conflict truth-and-reconciliation processes address serious abuses involving children."[10]

The statute of the SCSL conferred *ratione materiae* jurisdiction for crimes against humanity, war crimes, and other serious violations of IHL. It also included certain Sierra Leonean crimes committed on national territory. These concerned the abuse of children under 14 years of age and the offence of arson. Articles 3 to 6 of the statute are as follows.

Article 3: Crimes against humanity

The Special Court shall have the power to prosecute persons who committed the following crimes as part of a widespread or systematic attack against any civilian population: (a) Murder; (b) Extermination; (c) Enslavement; (g) Deportation; (e) Imprisonment; (f) Torture; (g) Rape, sexual slavery, enforced prostitution, forced pregnancy and any other form of sexual violence; (h) Persecution on political, racial, ethnic or religious grounds; and (i) Other inhumane acts.

Article 3: Violations of Article 3 common to the Geneva Conventions and AP II

The Special Court shall have the power to prosecute persons who committed or ordered the commission of serious violations of article 3 common to the Geneva Conventions of 12 August 1949 for the Protection of War Victims, and of Additional Protocol II thereto of 8 June 1977. These violations shall include: (a) Violence to life, health and physical or mental well-being of persons, in particular murder as well as cruel treatment such as torture, mutilation or any form of corporal punishment; (b) Collective punishments; (c) Taking of hostages; (d) Acts of terrorism; (e) Outrages upon personal dignity, in particular humiliating and degrading treatment, rape,

---

9   Article 1, Statute of the Special Court Agreement, 2002; 30 November 1996 was considered as an appropriate starting date for the temporal jurisdiction of the Court because it marked the commencement of a new phase in the conflict as the date in which the Abidjan Peace Accord was signed wherein all warring factions had agreed to end their hostilities.

10   UN Doc. S/RES/1379 of 2001.

enforced prostitution and any form of indecent assault; (f) Pillage; (g) The passing of sentences and the carrying out of executions without previous judgement pronounced by a regularly constituted court, affording all the judicial guarantees which are recognized as indispensable by civilized peoples; and (h) Threats to commit any of the foregoing acts.

Article 4: Other serious violations of IHL

The Special Court shall have the power to prosecute persons who committed the following serious violations of IHL: (a) Intentionally directing attacks against the civilian population as such or against individual civilians not taking direct part in hostilities; (b) Intentionally directing attacks against personnel, installations, material, units or vehicles involved in a humanitarian assistance or peacekeeping mission in accordance with the Charter of the United Nations, as long as they are entitled to the protection given to civilians or civilian objects under the international law of armed conflict; (c) Conscripting or enlisting children under the age of 15 years into armed forces or groups or using them to participate actively in hostilities.

Article 5: Crimes under Sierra Leonean law

The Special Court shall have the power to prosecute persons who have committed the following crimes under Sierra Leonean law: (a) Offences relating to the abuse of girls under the Prevention of Cruelty to Children Act, 1926: (i) Abusing a girl under 13 years of age, contrary to section 6; (ii) Abusing a girl between 13 and 14 years of age, contrary to section 7; (iii) Abduction of a girl for immoral purposes, contrary to section 12. (b) Offences relating to the wanton destruction of property under the Malicious Damage Act, 1861: (i) Setting fire to dwelling houses, any person being therein, contrary to section 2; (ii) Setting fire to public buildings, contrary to sections 5 and 6; (iii) Setting fire to other buildings, contrary to section 6.

Articles 3 and 4 were drawn from common Article 3 of the Geneva Conventions of 1949 and AP II, both of which apply to non-international armed conflicts. Article 3 provided jurisdiction to prosecute violations of common Article 3 of the Geneva Conventions and of AP II. Article 4(c) gave the court jurisdiction to prosecute persons responsible for 'conscripting or enlisting children under the age of 15 years into armed forces or groups or using them to participate actively in hostilities.' This provision was taken directly from Article 8(e)(vii) of the Rome Statute of the ICC which in turn has its roots in AP II. The SCSL focused on prosecuting the top echelon responsible for the atrocities, in particular, those leaders who had threatened the establishment of and implementation of the peace process in Sierra Leone.

The official age of majority in Sierra Leone is 21 years. Section 4 of the Interpretation Act, 1967, defines a child as a person that has not attained the age of 21 years. Prior to and during the period of the conflict, there was no specific legislation setting out a minimum age for voluntary recruitment into the national armed forces. However, section 16(2) of the Sierra Leone Military Forces Act, 1961, prohibits forcible recruitment of children under the age of 17-and-a-half years. Recruitment of such persons was permitted only with the consent of the parent or guardian of the child.[11]

Given its relatively narrow jurisdictional mandate and time frame, the SCSL focused on a limited number of cases. Four trials were conducted against ten accused.[12]The leaders of the RUF, AFRC and the CDF were jointly and

---

11   Apart from the CRC and OP-CRC, the African Charter on the Rights and Welfare of the Child (ACRWC) which is an African regional human rights instrument also prohibits the recruitment and use of children to participate directly in hostilities. Adopted in 1990, the ACRWC defines a child as a person below the age of 18 years. Article 22(1) of the ACRWC obligates state parties to take cognizance of and respect the rules of IHL applicable to children in armed conflicts. Under article 22(2), states parties are to take 'all necessary measures' to ensure that children do not take 'a direct part in hostilities' and to further refrain from recruiting them. Sierra Leone has ratified the ACRWC and as a member of the African Union (AU), it was under an obligation to respect its commitments under the ACRWC by promoting the rights and welfare of its children and to protect them from involvement in armed conflict as a common standard agreed upon by state parties to the ACRWC.

12   In March 2003 the Prosecutor brought the first of 13 indictments against leaders of the RUF, the AFRC, and the CDF, and the then Liberian President Charles Taylor. Ten persons were brought to trial. Two others died and the third fled Sierra Leone shortly before he was indicted. One person died during the course of his trial, and proceedings against him were terminated. The first convictions for recruiting and using child soldiers by SCSL were in 2007. Alex Tamba Brima, Ibrahim Bazzy Kamara and Santigie Borbor Kanu, former leaders of the AFRC, were found guilty of enlisting children under the age of 15 years into armed forces or groups or using them to participate actively in hostilities (Judgment, SCSL-04-14-T, 2 August 2007; Judgment, SCSL-04-16-T, 20 June 2007). Subsequently, Issa Hassan Sesay and Morris Kallon, of the RUF, were found guilty of this crime (Judgment, SCSL-04-15-T, 25 February 2009). Nine persons were convicted and sentenced to terms of imprisonment ranging from 15 to 52 years.

severally charged with the recruitment of children under the age of 15 years or using children to 'participate actively in hostilities'. In the fourth case, the SCSL convicted Charles Taylor, former President of Liberia, for aiding and abetting and planning crimes against humanity and war crimes during the armed conflict in Sierra Leone.[13] He was subsequently sentenced to 50 years in prison.[14] Taylor's trial was high-profile given his status as a former head of state who had been indicted by the SCSL while he was still president.[15] Taylor was accused of receiving "blood diamonds" from rebels in Sierra Leone in exchange for arms and ammunition.[16]

---

13 *Prosecutor v. Taylor*, Case No SCSL-03-01-I, Amended Indictment, 17 March 2006. Count 1: acts of terrorism; Count 2: murder; Count 3: violence to life, health and physical or mental well-being of persons, in particular murder; Count 4: rape; Count 5: sexual slavery and any other form of sexual violence; Count 6: outrages upon personal dignity; Count 7: violence to life, health and physical or mental well-being of persons, in particular cruel treatment; Count 8: other inhumane acts; Count 9: child soldiers; Count 10: enslavement; Count 11: pillage.

14 In a highly controversial decision, the Security Council, relying on its Chapter VII enforcement powers, adopted Resolution 1688 on 16 June 2006, authorizing Taylor's transfer to The Hague. The President of the SCSL thereafter issued an order giving judicial imprimatur to the decision. Taylor was tried at The Hague and was transferred to a prison in the UK in October 2013 to serve the remainder of his sentence – the result of an agreement between the SCSL and the UK government. By the rules of the UK judicial system, Mr. Taylor, 65, has 43 years left to serve and will only be eligible for early release after serving two-thirds of his sentence, at which point he will be more than 90 years old. Jalloh, Charles C., Special Court for Sierra Leone: Achieving Justice? *Mich. J. Int'l L.*, Vol. 32, 2011, p. 395-460.

15 *Prosecutor v. Taylor*, Case No SCSL-03-01-T, Trial Chamber II, judgment dated 18 May 2012. It was one of the longest trial judgments ever issued by an international criminal tribunal (2,532 pages). Sentencing judgment dated 30 May 2012.

16 In the Revolutionary United Front (RUF) Cases, the Trial Chamber ordered joint trials January 2004. The Prosecutor obtained an amended indictment in August of 2006, alleging eight counts of crimes against humanity, eight counts of war crimes, and two counts of other serious violations of international humanitarian law. The charges included murder, rape, sexual slavery, other inhumane acts, violence to life, terrorizing the civil population, collective punishments, mutilation, pillage, use of child soldiers, and attacks on UN peacekeeping personnel. The charges in the Armed Forces Revolutionary Council (AFRC) cases were on 14 counts, including the war crimes and crimes against humanity of murder, extermination, rape, acts of terrorism, collective punishments, unlawful killings, sexual violence, use of child soldiers, enslavement, and other inhumane acts. In the Civil Defence Forces (CDF) cases, the crimes included the commission of war crimes, crimes against humanity, and other serious violations of IHL. The eight counts included murder, acts of terrorism, collective punishments, pillage, looting and burning, terrorizing the civilian population, and causing physical violence and mental suffering. Charges were not included for sex related crimes. In the fourth case, Charles Taylor, former President of Liberia was charged with eleven counts of war crimes, crimes against humanity, and

SCSL: Jurisprudence on the Use of Child Soldiers

Two aspects of the use of child soldiers were considered by the Trial Chamber: (i) the recruitment of 'children below the age of 15 years into armed forces or groups' and (ii) the use of child soldiers to 'actively participate in hostilities.' On the first issue,[17] the Trial Chambers stated that there were two forms which were conscription and enlistment. Trial Chamber I (TCI) in *Prosecutor v Issa Hassan Sesay* was of the view that conscription involves an element of force on the part of the perpetrator either by abduction or forced military training of individuals. Trial Chamber II (TC II) also defined conscription in similar terms in *Prosecutor v Alex Tamba Brima* by stating that it involves compulsion which in some instances included the force of law. With regard to child soldiers, TC I pointed out that conscription should be interpreted as including acts of coercion such as abduction and forced recruitment which is carried out by armed groups against children for the purpose of using them to 'participate actively in hostilities'. The Chambers were of the opinion that enlistment on the other hand lacked the element of coercion and involves 'accepting or enrolling' persons who present themselves voluntarily for recruitment.[18]

According to one of the judges, the crime of "conscripting or enlisting children or using them to participate actively in hostilities," may be committed in three different ways: (i) by conscripting children (which implies compulsion, albeit in some cases through force of law); (ii) by enlisting them (which merely means accepting and enrolling them when they volunteer), or (iii) by using them to participate actively in hostilities (i.e., taking the more serious step, having conscripted or enlisted them, of putting their lives

---

other serious violations of IHL. These include: murder; acts of terrorism; the use of child soldiers; pillage; violence to life, health, and physical or mental wellbeing of persons, in particular cruel treatment, sexual slavery, and other forms of sexual violence, rape; and outrages against personal dignity. He was not accused of carrying out these crimes himself; rather, he was charged with assisting and encouraging, acting in concert with, directing, controlling and/or being the superior of the RUF, AFRC), the joint RUF-AFRC junta and/ or Liberian fighters.

17 Children can be recruited through abduction, coercion, manipulation, propaganda or conscription, or by exploiting their hope to escape impoverished circumstances. In some cases children believe they will be protected by armed groups. They also are sometimes motivated or convinced by others of the need to fight to defend their communities or redress inequalities, or in response to discrimination.

18 *The Prosecutor v Alex Tamba Brima, Kamara and Kanu,* Trial Chamber II, SCSL-04-16-T, 20 June 2007.

directly at risk of combat)."[19] The Chambers, however, noted that attributing voluntary consent to enlist into an armed group to a child below the age of 15 years 'particularly in a conflict setting' is of 'questionable merit' and therefore consent in such instance can never be a valid defence.[20]

Regarding culpability for using children to 'actively participate in hostilities,' the Trial Chambers applied the 'risk standards' in order to determine activities that would make a child soldier 'a legitimate target'. These activities were limited to combat or military activities directly related to combat. The Chambers excluded certain activities which though not related to combat equally endangered the lives of child soldiers.

The Trial Chamber I, in *Prosecutor v Issa Hassan Sesay,*while defining 'active participation in hostilities' stated that it involved acts of war such as killing and raping of civilians and burning of houses. The Chamber added that it included not only combat operations but also military activities linked to combat such as acting as spies, decoys or manning military checkpoints. TC II, on the other hand, in *Prosecutor v Alex Tamba Brima*, defined 'active participation in hostilities' as encompassing activities that put children's lives 'directly at risk in combat'. The Trial Chambers also listed activities that amounted to 'active participation in hostilities' for which the accused persons could be held criminally liable. These activities included using children in combat, guarding military camps, mines, acting as spies or bodyguards, informants, decoys, manning checkpoints and acting as human shields. In *Prosecutor v. Charles Ghankay Taylor*, the Trial Chamber II held that using a child to amputate limbs or flog civilians would constitute active participation, as would their capture of girls for sexual purposes, looting and burning. The very carrying of arms and ammunition would seem to suffice as well. The Chamber held that merely sending trained child soldiers to a fighting area sufficiently places the children at risk and amounted to participating actively in hostilities.[21]

---

19 Judge Robertson in his separate opinion appended to the Appeals Chamber Judgment in the case of T, *Prosecutor v. Sam Hinga Norman*, Case No. SCSL-2004-14-AR72(E). ·

20 *Prosecutor v Norman, Fofana & Allieu Kondewa*, Indictment, SCSL-2004-14-PT (11-21) 5 February 2004. Also see *Prosecutor v Issa Hassan Sesay et al*, Trial Chamber I, SCSL-04-15-T, 2 March 2009, para 187.

21 SCSL, *Prosecutor v. Charles Ghankay Taylor*, SCSL-03-01-T, judgment (Trial Chamber II), 18 May 2012, p. 535, para. 1476.

Charges relating to crimes against girls and women were included in most of the indictments issued by the SCSL, and several persons have been convicted for sexual slavery, held as a crime against humanity. In the detailed charges against individuals girls were specifically mentioned as a distinct victim group.[22] The SCSL convicted individuals for acts of "forced marriage", which constitutes a crime against humanity. Although not explicitly included in the Statute of SCSL, forced marriage was deemed to be covered under the residual category of "other inhumane acts" constituting crimes against humanity.[23]

There is no doubt that the SCSL has made a significant contribution to the development of IHL by bringing in new jurisprudence in the area of the recruitment and use of child soldiers.[24] However, if a stringent interpretation of 'active participation in hostilities' is adopted without taking into consideration all relevant factors, suitable protection would not be offered to many child soldiers. This may create a loophole which would enable perpetrators to utilize child soldiers in support functions and other capacities falling outside the standard threshold in an attempt to escape criminal liability in the future. Setting a rigid standard to determine what amounts to 'active participation in hostilities' as the SCSL did without taking into consideration the entire context of the conflict defeats the whole essence of the prohibition against the recruitment and use of child soldiers.[25]

The SCSL was succeeded on 1 January 2014 by the Residual Special Court for Sierra Leone (RSCSL),[26] which will deal with matters arising from

---

22 For instance see indictments for *Issa Hassan Sesay, Morris Kallon* and *Augustine Gbao*, 2004-15-PT, 2 August 2006; *Alex Tamba Brimba, Brima Bazzy Kamara, Santigie*, and *Borbor Kanu*, 2004-16-PT, 18 February 2005; *Charles Ghankay Taylor*, SCSL, 2003-01-I, 7 March 2003; *Johnny Paul Koroma*, SCSL, 2003-03-I, 7 March 2003.

23 Aptel Cecile, Children and Accountability for International crimes: The Contribution of International Court, Innocenti Working Paper, UNICEF, August 2010.

24 The first conviction in the SCSL (and first ever conviction for crimes of child recruitment) was the Judgment of 20 June 2007, in which Trial Chamber II of the SCSL in the case of Brima, Kamara and Kanu, (AFRU case), found that the accused were individually criminally responsible for conscripting children under the age of 15 years into an armed group and/or using them to participate actively in hostilities.

25 Sonsiama Doris AM, A Critical Analysis of the Jurisprudence of the Special Court for Sierra Leone on the Use of Child Soldiers, unpublished LL M dissertation, Makerere University, 2011, p. 65.

26 Article 1.1 of the Statute of RSCSL provides that the Residual Court will maintain, preserve and manage its archives, including the archives of the Special Court; provide for

the ongoing legal obligations of the tribunal which could include the review of applications by convicts for early release or the judicial review of their convictions.[27] Judges may also be called on to preside over any contempt of court proceedings.[28]

The International Criminal Court

The International Criminal Court (ICC), created under the Rome Statute of 17 July 1998, is the most significant international organization to be created since the UN.[29] The ICC Statute has paved the way for the prosecution of international as well as non-international criminal atrocities. Genocide, crimes against humanity and war crimes are enumerated in Articles 6, 7, 8 of the Statute. Certain crimes committed against children fall under the jurisdiction of the ICC. The inclusion of the crime of child recruitment in the Rome Statute was a turning point in the history of international criminal justice.[30] It enables the prosecution and punishment of perpetrators who recruit or use children in hostilities.

---

witness and victim protection and support; respond to requests for access to evidence by national prosecution authorities; supervise enforcement of sentences; review convictions and acquittals; conduct contempt of court proceedings; provide defence counsel and legal aid for the conduct of proceedings before the Residual Special Court; respond to requests from national authorities with respect to claims for compensation; and prevent double jeopardy.

27 The Residual Special Court was established pursuant to an agreement signed between the United Nations and the Government of Sierra Leone on 11 August 2010. It was ratified by Parliament on 15 December 2011 and signed into law on 1 February 2012. The agreement stipulates that the RSCSL shall have its principal seat in Freetown, but shall carry out its functions at an interim seat in The Netherlands with a sub-office in Freetown for witness and victim protection and support. The RSCSL, like the SCSL, is funded by voluntary contributions from the international community, but the agreement permits it to seek alternative means of funding. The RSCSL has an oversight committee to assist in obtaining adequate funds and to provide advice and policy direction on non-judicial aspects of the Court.

28 For more details visit: http://www.rscsl.org/.

29 The UN General Assembly (UNGA), in 1995, constituted an ad-hoc committee for the establishment of a permanent international criminal court. This ad-hoc committee, which later was called the Preparatory Commission (PrepCom), prepared a draft statute, which finally was discussed and adopted in 1998, in the Plenipotentiaries Conference convened by the UNGA in Rome, Italy. See: UN Doc A/RES/52/160 of 1998. The Rome Statute was adopted on 17 July 1998, with 120 votes in favour, 7 against and 2 abstentions.

30 Frostad Magne, Child Soldiers: Recruitment, Use and Punishment, *International Family Law, Policy and Practice*, Vol. 1.1, Winter 2013, p. 71-89.

The Rome Statute Article 8 (2) (b) (xxvi) states: "Conscripting or enlisting children under the age of 15 years[31] into national armed forces or using them to participate actively in hostilities," in international armed conflict would be a war crime.[32]Article 8 (2) (e) (vii), lays down a similar provision in relation to non-international armed conflicts: "Conscripting or enlisting children under the age of 15 years into armed forces or groups or using them to participate actively in hostilities."[33]The Rome Statute adopts the phrase "conscripting or enlisting" for child recruitment, suggesting that forcible recruitment and recruitment of volunteers are both prohibited. Consistent with this definition, the ICC has jurisdiction over the war crime of conscripting or enlisting children under 15 into national armed forces or armed groups and of using children as active participants in hostilities. Thus, during an armed conflict any recruitment, both involuntary and voluntary, of children under 15 by any armed force or group is prohibited. Additionally, the Rome Statute contains an expansive definition of "participation in hostilities." It states that the "use of children in a direct support function such as acting as bearers to take supplies to the front line, or activities at the front line itself, would be included within the terminology."The offence does not require any element of force and the consent of the child is no defence. The prohibition in Article 8 covers three types of offences: enlistment, conscription and use.[34]The offences are of a continuous nature and end only when the child either leaves the force or group, or turns 15.[35]

---

31 Unfortunately, the Rome Statute has set the minimum age for recruitment at 15 years. Further, the protection is provided only to children who "participate actively in hostilities" and leaves children who take indirect participation beyond the realm of Article 8(2) (b) (xxvi) and Article 8 (2) (e) (vii). Perhaps, such formulation came from the need for consensus. Efforts to be made by the international organizations and NGOs, such as Human Rights Watch, UNICEF and ICRC to raise this minimum age to 18 years.

32 The Elements of Crimes provide that "the perpetrator conscripted or enlisted one or more persons into the national armed forces or used one or more persons to participate actively in hostilities." As a consequence, a child's consent to enlist is only of interest in relation to sentencing or reparations. The Elements of Crimes, Official Records of the Assembly of States Parties to the Rome Statute of the International Criminal Court, First session, New York, 3-10 September 2002 (United Nations publication, Sales No. E.03.V.2 and corrigendum), part II.B.

33 Rome Statute of the International Criminal Court, UN Doc. A/CONF.183/9 (1998), Article 8 (2) (b) (xxvi); and Article 8 (2) (e) (vii).

34 ICC, *Prosecutor v. Thomas LubangaDyilo*, ICC-01/04-01/06-2842, judgment (Trial Chamber I), 14 March 2012, pp. 262-263, pp. 276-277, paragraph 609.

35 ICC, *Prosecutor v. Thomas Lubanga Dyilo*, ICC-01/04-01/06-2842, judgment (Trial Chamber I), 14 March 2012, pp. 262-263, p. 282, para. 618, and SCSL, *Prosecutor v.*

The elements of the crime provide the following guidance in relation to Article 8(2)(b)(xxvi): (i) Such person or persons were under the age of 15 years; (ii) The perpetrator knew or should have known that such person or persons were under the age of 15 years; (iii) The conduct took place in the context of and was associated with an international armed conflict; and (iv) The perpetrator was aware of factual circumstances that established the existence of an armed conflict. The Elements for Article 8(2)(e)(vii) are almost identical, with the difference that 'armed conflict not of an international character' is used instead of 'international armed conflict', and 'armed groups' replace 'national armed forces'.

War crimes in the ICC Statute include "violations of the laws and customs applicable in international armed conflict, within the established framework of international law," including "committing rape, sexual slavery, enforced prostitution, forced pregnancy, enforced sterilization, or any other form of sexual violence also constituting a grave breach of the Geneva Conventions."[36] The inclusion of the phrase "or any other form of sexual violence" gives the provision an open-ended character, though this proviso is itself qualified by the fact that such violence must amount to a grave breach. Further, according to the Rome Statute, the trafficking of children is expressly included in the definition of "enslavement", which is a crime against humanity;[37] and it is a war crime to direct attacks against buildings dedicated to education[38].

The Crime of Genocide: Forcible Transfer of Children

Article 6 of the Rome Statute defines the crime of genocide as an act "committed with the intent to destroy, in whole or in part, a national, ethnical, racial or religious group, as such". The components of genocide are: (a) killing members of the group; (b) causing serious bodily or mental harm to the members of the group; (c) deliberately inflicting on the group conditions

---

Charles Ghankay Taylor, SCSL-03-01-T, judgment (Trial Chamber II), 18 May 2012, p. 165, para. 443.

36 The Rome Statute, Article 8 (b)(xxii).

37 The Rome Statue, Article 7 (1) (c).

38 The Rome Statute, Articles 8(2)(b)(ix) and 8(2)(e)(iv). Children associated with armed groups are exposed to consequences which destroy the valuable childhood of a person's life, and deprives them of key services such as education and healthcare. Elisabeth Schauer, *The Psychological Impact of Child Soldiering*, Report of Ms Elisabeth Schauer following the 6 February 2009 "Instructions to the Court's expert on child soldiers and trauma" ICC-01/04-01/06-1729-Anx1, 25 February 2009) p. 3.

of life calculated to bring about its physical destruction in whole or in part; (d) imposing measures intended to prevent births within the group; and (e) forcibly transferring children of the group to another group. The elements of the crime of genocide are: (i) the group (national, ethnical, etc.); (ii) the intention (to destroy in whole or in part), (iii) the context (in an emerging pattern of similar conduct directed against that group or that the conduct itself effects destruction); and (iv) the conduct (killing, rape, etc).

Thus, Article 6 of the Rome Statute terms the forcible transfer of children an act of genocide. "The forcible transfer of children is not restricted to physical force, but may include threat of force or coercion, such as that caused by fear of violence, duress, detention, psychological oppression or abuse of power, against such person or persons or another person, or by taking advantage of a coercive environment. The elements of the crime establish that a child, for the purposes of Article 6(e), is a person under the age of 18 years.

Rome Statute: Protective Measures

In order to support children and provide for their safety during court proceedings, the ICC has put several protective measures in place. These include the adoption of closed sessions and the establishment of a victim and witness protection unit that takes into account the special needs of children who have experienced trauma or sexual violence. The Statute of the ICC and its Rules of Procedure and Evidence state that the Court shall take appropriate measures to protect the safety, physical and psychological wellbeing, dignity and privacy of child victims and witnesses during investigation and prosecution. These include:

> To assist traumatized children in giving their testimony (for example, in the presence of a psychologist or a family member) –Rule 88(2), Rules of Procedure and Evidence

> To allow applications for child victims to participate in proceedings – Rule 89(3), Rules of Procedure and Evidence[39]

> To ensure that the questioning of a child is carried out in a way that reduces the chances of further traumatizing the child – Rule 112(4),

---

39   In order to ensure that victims receive support in the application process to request participation or reparations before the ICC, there is a Victims Participation and Reparations Section(VPRS) within the Registry.

Rules of Procedure and Evidence

> ➤ To address the need for staff with expertise in supporting children who are victims or witnesses of violence – Article 42(9), Rome Statute

> ➤ To appoint child supporters to protect and assist children through all stages of the proceedings – Rule 17(3), Rules of Procedure and Evidence

> ➤ To set up a Victims and Witnesses Unit (VWU)which provides protective measures and security arrangements, counselling and other appropriate assistance for witnesses, victims who appear before the Court, and others who are at risk on account of testimony given by such witnesses – Article 43(6), Rome Statute. The main purpose of the VWU is to prevent the re-victimization of victims and witnesses as a result of their participation in proceedings before the ICC.

These provisions facilitate the participation of victims in ICC proceedings, provide support and protection to victims and witnesses, and facilitate victims' access to reparations. It is necessary to adopt a child rights approach throughout all the ICC organs. Such an approach would require a paradigm shift from child protection approaches in which children are perceived and treated as "objects" in need of assistance rather than as rights holders entitled to non-negotiable rights to protection.[40]

Child Soldier Protection under Human Rights Laws

During the Rome Conference, UNICEF called upon the States to use the CRC as the guiding reference and framework for the work of the ICC whenever the situation of children is at stake.[41] The State authorities, while trying a child soldier must remember their obligation under CRC Article 40 (1) to reintegrate the child into society.[42] Article 40 provides that a child accused of a crime should be treated in a manner consistent with the promotion of the child's sense of dignity and worth, which reinforces the child's respect for the human rights and fundamental freedoms of others and

---

40 CRC Committee, General comment No. 13 (2011): The right of the child to freedom from all forms of violence, CRC/C/GC/13, 18 April 2011, para. 59.

41 UNICEF and the Establishment of the International Criminal Court, 17 March 1998, ICC Preparatory Works, p. 1-2, available at <http://www.legal-tools.org/en/doc/f0fa26/>

42 Committee on the rights of the child, General Comment No. 10 (2007): Children's rights in juvenile justice, UN Doc. CRC/C/GC/10, 25 April 2007, paragraph 29.

which takes into account the child's age and the desirability of promoting the child's reintegration and the child's assuming a constructive role in society. Article 37 (a) of the CRC prohibits the death penalty for offences committed by a person below the age of 18 years. The Committee on the Rights of the Child has recommended that the States Parties must abolish all forms of life imprisonment for offences committed by persons under the age of 18; further, in case a child is awarded life imprisonment, periodic review of the punishment must be undertaken.[43]

Article 38(1) of the CRC states that parties to the Convention will respect the rules of IHL that are applicable to them in armed conflict which are relevant to children. Under international criminal law, the protection afforded to persons detained varies according to the individual's status as either a prisoner of war or civilian internee. This classification stems from the distinction drawn during armed conflict between combatants and civilians. A child soldier is considered a combatant under the Geneva Conventions if he or she falls into one of the following categories: (i) Member of a state's armed forces, including militias and volunteer corps that are part of it; (ii) Member of a state's militia or volunteer corps if the organization has a military hierarchy, a distinctive emblem, carries arms openly and respects the laws and customs of war; (iii) Member of an armed force that pledges allegiance to an authority that the Detaining Power does not recognize; and (iv) Inhabitant of a non-occupied territory that spontaneously resists an invasion by enemy forces.[44] If a child combatant does not fall into one of the above categories, he or she has civilian status. If the civilian status of a child soldier can be proven, he or she will be afforded greater protection under IHL than if he or she is deemed a combatant. If child is a combatant, he or she is protected by prisoner of war status during detention. Additional Protocol I, Article 77 affords a child special protection: "Children shall be the object of special respect and shall be protected against any form of indecent assault." Further, "The Parties to the conflict shall provide them with the care and aid they require whether because of their age or for any other reason."[45]

---

43 The CRC Article 37(a) and Committee on the rights of the child, General Comment No. 10 (2007): Children's rights in juvenile justice, UN Doc. CRC/C/GC/10, 25 April 2007, paragraph 77.

44 The Third Geneva Convention of 1949 relative to the Protection of Prisoners of War, Article 4 (A).

45 Grover Leena, Trial of the Child Soldier: Protecting the Rights of the Accused, *Heidelberg Journal of International Law*, Vol. 65, 2005, pp. 217-238.

Some authors are of the view that the ICC as an international organization is not bound by IHRL treaties, which are signed and ratified by states and refer specifically to state responsibility. Since the ICC is not a party to IHRL treaties, it is not formally bound by their provisions or the case law of human rights courts. However, Cryer expresses a contrary opinion. According to him, international criminal law developed in response to mass abuses of IHL and IHRL.[46]Article 36 of the Rome Statute accordingly states that ICC judges "shall" either have established competence in criminal law and procedure or international law, such as IHL and law of human rights. The requirement to have judges specialized in these two areas of law illustrates that IHL and IHRL are linked with the Rome Statute of the ICC. Article 21(3) of the Rome Statute also requires that the application and interpretation of the law be made pursuant to internationally recognized human rights.

To date, there have been three cases before the ICC in which charges of the enlistment, conscription and use of children have been framed against the accused persons. Only one case has been decided. The case details are as follows.

I. *The Prosecutor v. Thomas Lubanga*

Thomas Lubanga Dyilo was one of many African warlords who played a key role in the endless conflicts in the eastern part of the Democratic Republic of Congo (DRC).[47]Lubanga was one of the founders of the Union of Congolese Patriots (UPC) and commander-in-chief of their military wing, the Patriotic Force for the Liberation of Congo (FPLC). The UPC/FPLC was described as an army of children and it was estimated that nearly 40% of the UPC cadre were under the age of 18, with some as young as seven. It was reported that the UPC/FPLC utilized child soldiers wearing school uniforms, forcibly recruiting the entire 5th grade of a school in one town and surrounding a neighbourhood and abducting the children in another.

Under Lubanga's leadership, the UPC massacred, tortured, mutilated

---

46 Robert Cryer. 2007. *An Introduction to International Criminal Law and Procedure*, Cambridge University Press, p. 353-354.

47 The Democratic Republic of Congo ratified the Rome Statute, the founding treaty of the ICC, on April 11, 2002. This allowed the court jurisdiction over war crimes, crimes against humanity, and genocide committed by Congolese nationals or on Congolese territory after July 1, 2002, the date that the Rome Statute entered into force in the DRC. The ICC only has jurisdiction in cases where the national government proves unwilling or unable to investigate and prosecute the relevant crimes.

and raped civilians in northeast DRC. The violence was so extreme that on 30 May 2003, the Security Council adopted Resolution 1484, authorizing the deployment of an emergency force to Bunia. In late February 2005, Lubanga's forces were involved in the murder of nine Bangladeshi UN Peacekeepers near the town of Kafe. The DRC referred the situation to the ICC in March 2004 under Article 14 of the Rome Statute. In June 2004, the ICC prosecutor opened an investigation of grave crimes allegedly committed in the DRC. Lubanga was arrested in March 2005 by the DRC for alleged violations of the DRC military criminal code, including murder, genocide, crimes against humanity and illegal detention. On 16 March 2006, Lubanga was transferred to The Hague for trial by the ICC.[48] He was charged and eventually found guilty as a co-perpetrator of enlisting and conscripting children under the age of 15 years into the FPLC and using them to participate actively in hostilities from September 2002 to August 2003.[49]

Age of the Child Soldiers

The applicable war crime for non-international armed conflict, Article 8 (2) (e)(vii), covers the recruitment ('conscripting or enlisting') of children under fifteen 'into armed forces or groups', i.e., it extends to any armed group within the meaning of IHL.[50] There was strong evidence that children under 15 had

---

48 Following initial investigation into crimes allegedly committed in the Ituri District since 1 July 2002, the Prosecution filed an application for the issuance of a warrant of arrest for Thomas Lubanga Dyilo on 13 January 2006. On 10 February 2006, Pre-Trial Chamber I issued a warrant of arrest under seal for Lubanga. On 17 March 2006, the Congolese authorities surrendered Mr Lubanga Dyilo, who was then detained at the Kinshasa Penitentiary and Re-education Centre, to the Court. He was then transferred to the Court's Detention Centre in The Hague. The warrant was unsealed on 17 March 2006. On 20 March 2006, Mr Lubanga Dyilo made his first appearance before the Court. At this hearing, the Chamber verified Thomas Lubanga Dyilo's identity and ensured that he had been informed of the crimes which he was alleged to have committed and of his rights before the Court.

49 *Prosecutor v. Thomas Lubanga Dyilo*, Judgment, ICC-01/04-01/06 (Trial Chamber I), 14 March 2012; Decision on Sentence, ICC-01/04-01/06 (Trial Chamber I), 10 July 2012, paragraphs 38-39.

50 'Recruitment' is a superior term encompassing both 'conscription' and 'enlistment'. It is used in the primary prohibitions of Article 77 (2) of AP I (international armed conflicts) and of Article 4 (3)(c) of AP II (non-international armed conflicts). During the negotiations leading to the Rome Conference the crime's definition changed repeatedly, but the term 'recruiting' was dominant until the Conference. It was later replaced by 'conscripting or enlisting'. This was primarily done to meet the concerns of the United States. For more details see: Herman Hebel and Darryl Robinson, 'Crimes within the Jurisdiction of the Court', in Roy S. Lee (ed.). 1999. *The International Criminal Court: The Making of the*

served in the UPC/FPLC during the period of armed conflict. Witnesses testified before the Trial Chamber of the ICC how the child soldiers would play childhood games, and how the female child soldiers would braid grass as if they were braiding the hair of a doll. In fact, the lack of adult attitudes and demands were some of the perceived advantages of using child soldiers.

However, determining the age of the child soldiers in the UPC/FPLC proved challenging for the Trial Chamber.[51] The Court considered witnesses from international and non-governmental organizations, both prosecution and defence witnesses, and also video evidence. The Office of the Prosecutor (OTP) had relied on medical examinations to prove the age of the children under consideration. Medical specialists later testified in Court that based on X-ray images, some recruits may have been as young as ten or eleven years old at the time when they were allegedly FPLC fighters. Others, however, were probably not as young, pointing out that the poor quality of the X-ray images created a margin of error.[52]

While agreeing with the defence that it was difficult to distinguish between a twelve- or thirteen-year-old and a fifteen- or sixteen year old, the court found that photographs and video extracts depicted children who were clearly under the age of 15. Even a defence witness declined to testify that the UPC did not utilize child soldiers, stating that one could not deny that some might have got through the net. The Trial Chamber considered two main clinical methods for forensic age estimation and ruled: "These examinations were not meant to determine a person's age with precision; furthermore, the model is based on European and American populations rather than those from Sub-Saharan Africa, and the methodology has not been updated for 50 years. Therefore, it is suggested this approach will only provide an approximate answer, particularly given it is not an exact science."

Finally, the Trial Chamber held that even allowing for a wide margin of

---

Rome Statute; Issues, Negotiations, Results, The Hague: Kluwer Law International.

51 The civil administration in the DRC was non-existence at the relevant time. Therefore, civil status documents confirming the age of child soldiers, which were recruited by the FPLC, were extremely hard to obtain by the prosecution. The investigators did not contact village chiefs or former schoolteachers to verify the age of specific victims because it was deemed to be too dangerous for the children and their families.

52 Kurth Michael E., The *Lubanga* Case of the International Criminal Court: A Critical Analysis of the Trial Chamber's Findings on Issues of Active Use, Age, and Gravity, *Goettingen Journal of International Law*, Vol. 5, No. 2, 2013, p. 443.

error in assessing an individual's age, it is feasible for non expert witnesses to differentiate between a child who is undoubtedly less than 15 years old and a child who is undoubtedly over 15. The Trial Chamber, after examining a video, was convinced that numerous children below the age of 15 years were recruited and used by the UPC/FPLC. Furthermore, the sheer volume of credible evidence relating to the presence of children below the age of 15 within the ranks of the UPC/FPLC demonstrated conclusively that a significant number were part of the UPC/FPLC army.[53]

The Trial Chamber confirmed the pre-trial chamber's finding that enlistment entails accepting and enrolling individuals who volunteer to join the armed forces while conscription implies some form of compulsion. Though the defence of consent was never raised by Lubanga's counsel, the Trial Chamber discussed the matter and concluded that children under the age of 15 are eventually unable to give genuine and informed consent. The Judges ruled that the Rome Statute criminalizes any form of enrolment of children under 15 years of age by whatever means due to the fact that this category of victims does not possess the intellectual capacity to give genuine consent.

Activities Lubanga's Child Soldiers Performed

Having established that Lubanga and the UPC/FPLC utilized children under the age of 15, willing and unwilling, the Court next considered whether the activities the children performed constituted 'active participation in hostilities'. The trial chamber found that Lubanga recruited and utilized child soldiers as young as eight for a variety of functions including fighting in battles, serving as body guards and military guards, escorting high ranking UPC/FPLC officials and performing domestic work. Under Lubanga's leadership, the UPC/FPLC even formed a special unit of small children, or "kadogos", with a strength of less than 45 members.

---

53 A number of witnesses stated the children under consideration were visibly under 15 years of age by comparing them to other juveniles, describing their general behavior or their state of physical development. In one case, some children were said to have weighed less than their weapons and could barely carry the AK-47s they were given. One former member of the FPLC testified that some of the young boys would cry for their mothers when they were hungry and would play children's games during the day while they had their weapons next to them. *Prosecutor v. Thomas Lubanga Dyilo,* Transcript of 25 March 2009, ICC-01/04-01/T-154-Red2-ENG, 41.

Active Participation

The Trial Chamber observed that the term 'active participation' was not defined in the Rome Statute, the Rules or the Elements of Crimes. The prosecution and the legal representative for the victims adopted the meaning used by the pre-trial chamber in Lubanga that "active participation in hostilities means not only direct participation in hostilities but covers active participation in combat-related activities such as scouting, spying, sabotage, and acting as decoys, couriers or being posted at military checkpoints. The defence argued that active participation in hostilities equates to acts of war, which by their nature or purpose are likely to cause actual harm to the personnel and equipment of the enemy armed forces. The Trial Chamber also considered the Statute of the Special Court for Sierra Leone (SCSL), the first international tribunal which had dealt with the offences relating to child soldiers.

In terms of offences committed by child soldiers, the Statute of the SCSL is identical to the Rome Statute. In examining the issue of active participation in hostilities, the SCSL had observed that an armed force requires logistical support to maintain its operations. Any labour or support that gives effect to, or helps maintain operations in a conflict constitutes active participation. Hence carrying loads for the fighting faction, finding and/or acquiring food, ammunition or equipment, acting as decoys, carrying messages, making trails or finding routes, manning checkpoints or acting as human shields constitute active participation as much as combat or actual fighting does.

However, to constitute active participation, the support roles would need to put the child soldiers' lives "directly at risk in combat". The pretrial chamber in Lubanga elaborated, explaining that activities like serving as a bodyguard would need to have a direct impact on the level of logistic resources and on the organization of operations required by the other party to the conflict. Thus, children who were engaged in activities clearly unrelated to hostilities would not be considered as having actively participated in hostilities.

Both the pretrial and trial chambers in Lubanga relied on a draft version of the Rome Statute, which, in a footnote stated that the words "using" and "participate" have been adopted in order to cover both direct participation in combat and active participation in military activities linked to combat such as scouting, spying, sabotage and acting as decoys or couriers. It would not cover activities clearly unrelated to hostilities such as delivering food to an airbase or being used as domestic staff in an officer's married accommodation. However, a direct support function such as acting as bearers to take supplies to the front line, or activities at the front line itself, would be included within the terminology.

The Trial Chamber did not provide a comprehensive legal definition of 'active use', but rather made a case-by-case analysis of the specific evidence presented. It held that many of the activities under consideration, such as children acting as bodyguards for commanders of the FPLC or guarding military facilities in the Ituri district, could eventually be qualified as active use under Article 8 (2) (e) (vii) of the Rome Statute.

Conviction and Sentence

On 14 March 2012, the Trial Chamber convicted Lubanga Dyilo of committing, as co-perpetrator, war crimes consisting of enlisting and conscripting children under the age of 15 years into the FPLC and using them to participate actively in hostilities in the context of an armed conflict not of an international character from 1 September 2002 to 13 August 2003. On 10 July 2012, the Trial Chamber sentenced him to a total period of 14 years of imprisonment. The time he spent in the ICC's custody was to be deducted from this total sentence.

The Appeals Chamber

The Appeals Chamber confirmed both the conviction and the sentence on 1 December 2014. While confirming, the Appeals Chamber explained that the standard of review for both the verdict and sentence is deferential with respect to the Trial Chamber's assessment of the facts and determination of the sentence. The Appeals Chamber only intervenes if the Trial Chamber's findings were unreasonable. With regard to the assessment and determination of the age of the child soldiers, the Appeals Chamber deferred to the Trial Chamber's conclusions. In the view of the Appeals Chamber, the Trial Chamber's conclusions were not unreasonable. The Appeals Chamber rejected every ground of appeal raised by the defence, and confirmed the Trial Chamber's verdict and decision establishing the sentence of 14 years.

On 3 March 2015, the Appeals Chamber delivered its judgment on the appeals against the Trial Chamber's decision establishing the principles and procedures to be applied to reparations in the Lubanga case. The Appeals

Chamber amended the Trial Chamber's order for reparations and instructed the Trust Fund for Victims[54] to present a draft implementation plan for collective reparations to the newly constituted Trial Chamber I within six months. The Appeals Chamber established the necessary minimum elements required for a reparations order, and the principles governing the reparations for victims, including the fact that all victims are to be treated fairly and equally as regards reparations, irrespective of whether they participated in the trial proceedings. The Appeals Chamber confirmed the Trial Chamber's finding that reparations programmes should include measures to reintegrate former child soldiers in order to eradicate the victimization, discrimination and stigmatization of these young people.[55] It also highlighted that a gender-inclusive approach should guide the design of the principles and procedures to be applied to the reparations.

The Plight of the Girl Child Soldier

Though there was widespread evidence of the sexual abuse of girls by their commanders, the ICC ignored the role gender played in defining the experiences of girl soldiers. The domestic work done by many girl soldiers was not considered to be dangerous enough to fall under the category of

---

54 The establishment of the ICC on 1 July 2002 also resulted in the creation of the Trust Fund for Victims (TFV) by the States parties to the Rome Statute. The Fund's mission is to support and implement programmes that address harm resulting from genocide, crimes against humanity and war crimes. The TFV is funded by voluntary contributions from States, international organizations and other donors. The money collected allows the Fund to fulfil its two mandates, namely the mandate of general assistance to victims in situations where the ICC is active, and the mandate to contribute to the implementation of orders for reparations to victims in particular cases before the Court. As part of its mandate, in preparing a reparations plan in a particular case, the Fund takes into account the amount it has available. It can, based on a plan adopted by the judges, request further contributions from States and other donors if need be. The Fund will assess the damage suffered by the victims affected directly or indirectly by the crimes committed by Mr Lubanga. In accordance with the order of the Appeals Chamber, it will prepare a plan of collective reparations, taking into account the possibility of providing medical services (including psychological support) as well as assistance for general rehabilitation, housing, education and training. The cost of these collective reparations programs will be evaluated and submitted to the judges of Trial Chamber I.

55 The Appeals Chamber also found that the Trial Chamber erred in not making Mr Lubanga personally liable for the collective reparations due to his current state of indigence. The Appeals Chamber held that reparations orders must establish and inform the convicted person of his personal liability with respect to the reparations awarded, and that if the Trust Fund for Victims advances its resources in order to enable the implementation of the order, it will be able to claim the advanced resources from Mr Lubanga at a later date.

'active use'. During the trial several witnesses testified that sexual abuse of child soldiers took place on a regular basis. 48 Girl soldiers were held as sex slaves by different commanders, who called them their 'wives'. The majority of the Trial Chamber considered these acts to be irrelevant to the charge of child soldiering. The OTP could also have charged Lubanga with rape, sexual slavery, etc. in accordance with Article 8 (2) (e) (vi) of the Rome Statute, but it did not.[56]

The Appeals Chamber's decision that the widespread and systematic rape and sexual violence against girl soldiers did not amount to the active use of children in hostilities was disappointing. This was perhaps due to the narrow definition that was adopted by the majority in defining the tasks which constitute 'active participation'. This excluded female interests from being represented in international law.[57] Keeping this in view, the ICC must establish a reparative regime that can adequately address sexual violence that most children, particularly girl child soldiers encounter during an armed conflict.

The first judgment of the ICC in the Lubanga case was a milestone in the progressive development of international criminal law. Determining what constitutes 'active participation' has been a grey area since Article 77(2) of AP I used the phrase 'direct part in hostilities' to create a distinction between two different types of participation in international conflicts—indirect and direct. This gap in IHL, which fails to protect children from non-traditional combat roles, is mirrored in the CRC and its Optional Protocol. The Rome Statute was the first treaty to move away from this direct versus indirect classification, instead invoking 'active' as the benchmark for prohibited participation. The question of what constitutes 'active' has proved challenging for the

---

56 The Judges did not considered themselves competent to close this gap on their own initiative because Article 74 (2) *Rome Statute* does not allow the Trial Chamber to rule beyond what is brought before the Court by the OTP. However, Judge Odio Benito in her dissenting opinion disagreed with these findings. She was of the view that the ICC under an obligation to produce a general definition of the crime of child soldiering and not limit itself to the scope of the charges brought before it. Separate and Dissenting Opinion of Judge Odio Benito, *Prosecutor v. Lubanga*, Judgment, *supra* notes 2 & 34, 2-3, para. 6. Also see: Kurth Michael E., The *Lubanga* Case of the International Criminal Court: A Critical Analysis of the Trial Chamber's Findings on Issues of Active Use, Age, and Gravity, *Goettingen Journal of International Law*, Vol. 5, No. 2, 2013, p. 440.

57 Hamid Noor, The untold story of the girl soldiers of the Congo: the International Criminal Court case of Lubanga, available at: https://cdn.auckland.ac.nz/assets/humanrights/Research/Noor-Hami-final.pdf .

international judiciary, as they initially chose to create lists of acts that fall within the scope of the prohibition. This approach is ineffective in giving effect to the terms of the Rome Statute. Instead a case-by-case assessment, as followed in *Lubanga*, would be more effective in determining the issue of active participation in future.

II. *The Prosecutor v. Bosco Ntaganda*

Bosco Ntaganda, former Deputy Chief of the PFLC, the armed wing of the UPC, was known as the "Terminator" or "Warrior" among his troops for his tendency to lead from the front and directly participate in military operations. He served in a number of rebel groups throughout eastern Congo for over a decade. In April 2012, Ntaganda and a group of Congolese soldiers mutinied to form the M23, a rebel group alleged to have committed horrific human rights violations, including summary executions, mass rape, and forced recruitment of child soldiers. Ntaganda was accused of 13 counts of war crimes including rape, sexual slavery, enlistment and conscription of child soldiers under the age of fifteen years and using them to participate actively in hostilities. He was also accused of five crimes against humanity allegedly committed in Ituri (DRC).[58]

The Pre-Trial Chamber found substantial grounds to believe that Ntaganda bears individual criminal responsibility pursuant to different modes of liability for different crimes. Ntaganda was charged with direct perpetration and indirect perpetration under article 25(3)(a) of the Rome Statute and with ordering and inducing the commission of a crime under article 25(3)(b). Ntaganda was also charged with the commission or attempted commission of crimes under article 25(3)(d). Under article 28(a) of the Statute, Ntaganda was charged as a military commander for crimes committed by his subordinates. The charges against Ntaganda pertain exclusively to his involvement in the war in Ituri between 2002 and 2003.

---

58 Ntaganda is charged with the war crimes of murder and attempted murder; attacking civilians; rape; sexual slavery of civilians; pillaging; displacement of civilians; attacking protected objects; destroying the enemy's property; rape and sexual slavery of child soldiers; and enlisting and conscripting child soldiers under the age of fifteen years and using them to participate actively in hostilities. Ntaganda is also charged with the crimes against humanity of murder and attempted murder; rape; sexual slavery; persecution; and forcible transfer of population.

The ICC issued its first arrest warrant against Ntaganda in 2006, charging him with enlisting, conscripting, and using child soldiers in the war in Ituri. Notwithstanding this pending warrant, the Congolese government permitted Ntaganda to serve and eventually become a general in the Congolese army in 2009. Though the Congolese government assisted in the arrest and transfer to The Hague of other Congolese officials accused of war crimes, it maintained that arresting Ntaganda would threaten the fragile peace in the country. In July 2012, the ICC issued a second arrest warrant, expanding the charges to include other grave crimes committed by the UPC during the war in Ituri, including murder, persecution, and rape based on ethnic grounds. Ntaganda is the first accused to surrender voluntarily to the ICC. He showed up at the US embassy in Kigali, Rwanda, and asked to be transferred to The Hague.

On 9 June 2014, Pre-Trial Chamber II unanimously confirmed the charges against Ntaganda and committed him for trial. The prosecution used video evidence to show that Ntaganda commanded a group that raped women and pillaged Ituri villages using forcibly recruited and trained child soldiers. The Chamber rejected the defence's argument that the charges violated IHL which is "not intended to protect combatants from crimes committed by combatants within the same group". The Chamber was of the opinion that child soldiers do not necessarily lose their special protections under IHL solely by virtue of their membership in an armed group, especially considering the coercion often underlying such membership. Under Article 8(2)(e)(vii) of the Rome Statute, which prohibits children under the age of 15 from participating in hostilities, children lose the protection afforded to them by IHL only during direct/active participation in hostilities, but the sexual character of the crimes, which involved elements of force/coercion or the exercise of rights of ownership, logically precluded active participation in hostilities.

On 2 September 2015, the trial in the case opened before Trial Chamber VI. On 3 January 2017, the Chamber found that it had jurisdiction over the alleged war crimes of rape and sexual slavery of child soldiers and rejected the defence's challenge thereto. The Chamber concluded that there is never a justification to engage in sexual violence against any person and such conduct [rape and sexual slavery] is prohibited at all times, both in times of peace and during armed conflicts, and against all persons, irrespective of any legal status.

The case against Bosco Ntaganda is an integral component of a larger effort to ensure justice for the victims of longstanding and systematic violence throughout the DRC. It is the first time that the ICC has held that sexual violence against child soldiers by their own commanders could constitute war crimes.[59]

III. *The Prosecutor v. Dominic Ongwen*

Dominic Ongwen was allegedly responsible for seven counts of crimes committed on or about 20 May 2004 at the Lukodi IDP Camp in the Gulu District of Uganda. The charges against him were three counts of crimes against humanity: murder, enslavement, inhumane acts of inflicting serious bodily injury and suffering; and four counts of war crimes: murder, cruel treatment of civilians, intentionally directing an attack against a civilian population, and pillaging.

In issuing the warrant of arrest, the Pre-Trial Chamber II found that there were reasonable grounds to believe that during the period from 1 July 2002 to an unspecified date in 2004, the Lord's Resistance Army (LRA), an armed group, allegedly carried out an insurgency attempt against the Government of Uganda and the Ugandan Army, also known as the Uganda People's Defence Force (UPDF), and local defence units (LDUs). There were reasonable grounds to believe that the LRA had directed attacks against both the UPDF and LDUs, and that, in pursuing its goals, it had engaged in a cycle of violence and established a pattern of "brutalization of civilians". The violent acts included murder, abduction, sexual enslavement, mutilation, and mass burning of houses and looting of camp settlements. Civilians, including children, were believed to have been abducted and forcibly "recruited" as fighters, porters and sex slaves and to contribute to attacks against the Ugandan army and civilian communities. Ongwen's warrant of arrest was issued on 8 July 2005 and unsealed on 13 October 2005.[60]

On 21 December 2015, the prosecutor charged Ongwen with crimes in addition to those set out in the warrant of arrest: a total of seventy counts.[61] The expanded charges against Ongwen included sexual and gender-based crimes – forced marriage, rape, torture, sexual slavery, and enslavement –

---

59 *The Prosecutor v. Bosco Ntaganda*, ICC-01/04-02/06; for more details see: https://www. icc-cpi.int/drc/ntaganda.

60 *ICC, The Prosecutor v. Dominic Ongwen*ICC-02/04-01/15.

61 The additional charges related to attacks on the Pajule IDP camp, the Odek IDP camp and the Abok IDP camp. The counts brought against the suspect in the context of these attacks include attacks against the civilian population, murder, attempted murder, torture, cruel treatment, other inhumane acts, enslavement, outrages upon personal dignity, pillaging, destruction of property, and persecution.

committed from 2002 to 2005and the conscription and use of children under the age of 15 to participate actively in hostilities from 2002 to 2005 in Sinia Brigade.

Ongwen is a former child soldier from northern Uganda. He was abducted and conscripted into the LRA at the age of nine. It is claimed that he was brutalized. He came of age in the LRA, rose through the ranks and became a Brigadier Commander. Ongwen escaped in January 2015. Later, he surrendered to the US Special Forces and was promptly transferred to the ICC.

In March 2016, an ICC Pre-Trial Chamber confirmed the charges against Ongwen. He is the only LRA accused in custody. The rest are dead or at large. The charges against Ongwen are many in number and horrific in content. Some of these are crimes that he himself suffered: unlawful recruitment of children into armed groups and cruel treatment (both war crimes), and enslavement (crime against humanity). The trial in the case began on 6 December 2016.

On 7 March 2014, the ICC found Katanga guilty of the crime against humanity of murder and the war crimes of wilful killing, intentional attacks against the civilian population, pillaging and destruction of property. However, he was acquitted of charges of sexual slavery and rape as well as of using child soldiers. In 2012 the judges changed the mode of liability against Katanga to being liable as an accessory to the conflict rather than the principal perpetrator as it was felt that the prosecution had not proved its original charge. The majority of the ICC judges found that while there were children in Katanga's militia, there was insufficient evidence to prove beyond reasonable doubt that Katanga was responsible for this crime. On 23 May 2014, the ICC sentenced Katanga to 12 years in prison. While there were some negative reactions in the international community to the acquittal over sexual violence, there was a more muted response to the acquittal over the use of child soldiers.[62]

ICC: Preliminary Examination

The Office of the Prosecutor (OTP) has received a number of communications pursuant to Article 15 in relation to the situation in Afghanistan, Colombia

---

62 *The Prosecutor v. Katanga and Ngudjolo* Confirmation of Charges ICC-01.04-01/07, 2008.

and Nigeria.[63] The acts allegedly committed by members of the Taliban and affiliated armed groups in Afghanistan includethe following war crimes in the context of a non-international armed conflict: murder, intentionally directing attacks against the civilian population, intentionally directing attacks against humanitarian personnel, intentionally directing attacks against protected objects, conscripting or enlisting children under the age of 15 years or using them to participate actively in hostilities, and killing or wounding treacherously a combatant adversary. These war crimes were committed on a large scale and as part of a plan or policy.

There is a reasonable basis to believe that war crimes under Article 8 of the Rome Statute have been committed in the context of the non-international armed conflict in Colombia, including, murder, attacks against civilians, torture and cruel treatment, outrages upon personal dignity, taking of hostages, rape and other forms of sexual violence, and conscripting, enlisting and using children to participate actively in hostilities.

In line with its policy on sexual and gender-based crimes, the OTP is conducting further analysis into the Boko Haram's attacks against women and girls, including (a) abductions, (b) forced marriages, rapes, sexual slavery and sexual violence, (c) use of women and girls for operational tasks such as suicide attacks and (d) murders, with a view to assessing whether such conduct was targeted at females because of their sex and/or socially constructed gender roles, and therefore could qualify as gender-based crimes. The Office has paid specific attention to crimes committed against children, including conscripting and enlisting children under the age of 15 years into armed groups and using them to participate actively in hostilities. The Office has also identified incidents where the victims of alleged crimes (such as murder, sexual and gender-based crimes and abductions) committed by the Boko Haram included children,.

Prosecution of Child Soldier under International Criminal Law

The Statute of the Special Court of Sierra Leone (SCSL) gave the Prosecutor authority to indict children for crimes they committed between the ages of 15 and 18. Article 7 of the Statute dealing with jurisdiction over persons of 15 years of age provided: "The Special Court shall have no jurisdiction over any person who was under the age of 15 at the time of the alleged commission of

---

63 ICC Report on Preliminary Examination Activities 2016, 14 November 2016.

the crime. Should any person who was at the time of the alleged commission of the crime between 15 and 18 years of age come before the Court, he or she shall be treated with dignity and a sense of worth, taking into account his or her young age and the desirability of promoting his or her rehabilitation, reintegration into and assumption of a constructive role in society, in accordance with international human rights standards, in particular the rights of the child." Further, "In the disposition of a case against a juvenile offender, the Special Court shall order any of the following: care guidance and supervision orders, community service orders, counselling, foster care, correctional, educational and vocational training programmes, approved schools and, as appropriate, any programmes of disarmament, demobilization and reintegration or programmes of child protection agencies."

The age of criminal responsibility in the Statute is complicated. It provides three categories of perpetrators: (i) No jurisdiction over children below 15 years of age at the time of commission of crime; (ii) Ordinary jurisdiction over persons aged 18 years or older at the time of commission of the crime; and (iii) Specific limited jurisdiction in relation to offenders aged 15 to 18 years.[64] The approach taken by the drafters of the Statute to cover persons aged between 15 and 18 is desirable for a number of reasons. First, it sets 15 years as the clear demarcation between 'child' and 'adult' that is missing in the Rome Statute, where a child is less than 15, but a legally responsible adult is over 18. Second, should a child ever have been the subject of a trial by the SCSL, any 'punishment' would have been construed in terms of rehabilitation and reintegration.[65] The prosecutor at the SCSL had clarified that his office would not indict a person for crimes committed when he was a child. Aware of the clear legal standard highlighted in IHL, the intent in choosing not to prosecute was to rehabilitate and reintegrate this lost generation back into society. Article 19(1) of the SCSL supported this trend by prohibiting the imprisonment of juvenile offenders.[66]

---

64 Waschefort Gus. 2015. *International Law and Child Soldiers*, Oregon: Oxford and Portland, p. 138.

65 McBride Julie. 2014. *The War Crime of Child Soldier Recruitment*, TMC Asser Press, p. xii.

66 Article 19 (1) of the SCSL Statute dealing with 'Penalties' provides: "The Trial Chamber shall impose upon a convicted person, other than a juvenile offender, imprisonment for a specified number of years. In determining the terms of imprisonment, the Trial Chamber shall, as appropriate, have recourse to the practice regarding prison sentences in the International Criminal Tribunal for Rwanda and the national courts of Sierra Leone."

The Rome Statute of the ICC prohibits the prosecution of child soldiers. Article 26 of the Statute provides that the Court shall have no jurisdiction over any person who was under the age of 18 at the time of the alleged commission of a crime. Even if a person has crossed the age of 18 at the time of trial, he or she cannot be held fully responsible for a crime if committed before attaining the age of 18.[67]A number of child rights advocates, including UNICEF, supported this provision of the ICC and shared the view that international judicial mechanisms are not well suited for prosecuting children who have allegedly committed crimes under international law. Such mechanisms should focus primarily on prosecuting the political and military leaders who are responsible for planning and ordering the commission of such crimes. Article 37 of the CRC requires State Parties to ensure that capital punishment or life imprisonment without the possibility of release is not imposed for offences committed by persons under 18 years of age.

Domestic Trial of Child Soldiers

The international human rights treaty system does not prohibit the prosecution of children by a State.[68] Many domestic jurisdictions allow the prosecution of children who commit crimes, with the age threshold for criminal responsibility goes down to as young as six years.[69] The Amnesty International has held that in some cases, child soldiers must be held accountable for their actions, but any criminal action against them must respect international fair trial standards.[70] The United Nations, in 1990, issued the Standard Minimum Rules for the Administration of Juvenile Justice and Guidelines for the Prevention of Juvenile Delinquency. These

---

67 *United States of America v. Omar Ahmed Khadr*, Amicus Brief filed by Sarah H. Paoletti on behalf of Canadian parliamentarians and law professors, international law scholars with specific expertise in the area of IHL, ICL and IHRL and foreign legal associations, 18 January 2008, p. 21.

68 IHRL does not specify a minimum age at which a child can be held criminally responsible for his or her actions. The CRC Article 40(3)(a) only provides that States must fix a specific age below which children cannot be held legally responsible. If a child is to be prosecuted in a domestic court for the alleged commission of a crime under national or international law, a number of judicial safeguards should be put in place. Common Article 3 to the Geneva Conventions describes the fundamental guarantees for persons *hors de combat*, including detainees, applicable in all situations of armed conflict. It fails, however, to specify the exact rights to which an accused is entitled.

69 Leveau, Fanny, Liability of Child Soldiers Under International Criminal Law, *Osgoode Hall Review of Law and Policy*, Vol. 4, No. 1, 2014, p. 53.

70 Child Soldiers: Criminals or Victims? Part II, Amnesty International, 22 December 2000.

standards and guidelines represent rules that are applicable to child soldiers, because such children need the greatest guarantees in respect of their human rights. Though not legally binding, these standards are designed to serve as a convenient standard of reference.

The International Covenant on Civil and Political Rights (ICCPR), applicable in both times of peace and armed conflict, outlines in greater detail the minimum requirements of due process in human rights law. In the determination of any criminal charge, everyone shall be entitled to the following minimum guarantees: (i) To be informed promptly and in detail in a language which he understands of the nature and cause of the charge against him; (ii) To have adequate time and facilities for the preparation of his defence and to communicate with a counsel of his own choosing; (iii) To be tried without undue delay; (iv) Not to be compelled to testify against himself or to confess guilt; (v) In the case of juvenile persons, the procedure shall take account of their age and the desirability of promoting their rehabilitation; (vi) Everyone convicted of a crime shall have the right to his conviction and sentence being reviewed by a higher tribunal according to law.[71]

In the last two decades, there have been a few cases where child soldiers have been prosecuted for war crimes in Africa. In 2000, a few trials were held in the Democratic Republic of Congo (DRC) and a 14-year-old child soldier was executed, eight child soldiers were sentenced to death and a number of children were exonerated.[72] In 2001, there were more trials against child soldiers in the DRC, following which four boys of age between 14 and 16 were sentenced to death. However, due to the intervention of the Human Rights Watch they were not executed.[73] In Rwanda, children were charged with committing genocide, an international crime implemented domestically.[74] In

---

71   Article 14, The International Covenant on the Civil and Political Rights (ICCPR), 1976.

72   Katherine Fallah, Perpetrators and Victims: Prosecuting Children for the Commission of International Crimes, *African Journal of International and Comparative Law*, Vol. 14, No. 1, p. 98-99.

73   Ibid, p. 141-142.

74   Two institutions allowed prosecution of child soldiers: the domestic courts and *gacaca* proceedings. *Gacaca* proceedings are a traditional method of dispute resolution adapted to promote accountability for offenses related to genocide. *Gacaca* proceedings are different from the Rwandan conventional courts because their focus is on both retribution and reconciliation. Because of this, *gacaca* proceedings offer a more diversified array of punishment ranging from imprisonment to community service. *Gacaca* proceedings also recognize that minors should be treated differently from adults. Minors under 14 years cannot face prosecution but can be placed in special solidarity camps, whereas minors

Uganda, two former child soldiers were accused of treason. These charges were later withdrawn, following a protest by the Human Rights Watch, on the basis that Uganda was under the international obligation to rehabilitate child soldiers.[75] More recently, a Canadian Citizen Omar Khadr was tried by the United States; his case is discussed in greater detail.

The Case of Omar Khadr

Omar Khadr, a Canadian citizen, was born in 1986. It is alleged that his father was a high-ranking member of the Egyptian Islamic Jihad, a senior Al-Qaeda operative and a close associate of Osama bin Laden. It is also alleged that from 1996 until 2001, Khadr travelled throughout Afghanistan with his father, meeting senior Al-Qaeda members and visiting Al-Qaeda training camps and guest houses. Khadr is said to have received training in the use of arms and explosives and, on completion of his training, joined a team of Al-Qaeda operatives constructing and planting landmines targeted against US and coalition forces.

Khadr was 15 years old when he allegedly threw a grenade that killed Sergeant Christopher Speer of the US military during a firefight between US Special Forces and a group of Al-Qaeda operatives. Khadr was the only survivor among the group of militants. He sustained three bullet injuries, but an American medic managed to save his life. Khadr was later transferred to a hospital at the Bagram Air Base. In 2002, after his treatment, Khadr was transferred to Guantanamo Bay, Cuba. He had just turned 16 and was one of the youngest prisoners ever held at Guantanamo. The Canadian government initially opposed Khadr's transfer to Guantanamo and urged the US to take into account his juvenile status. The US ignored Canada's request. In early 2003 and again in 2004, Canadian intelligence officials were allowed to interrogate Khadr at Guantanamo Bay, on condition that they shared the information with the Americans, who were preparing to prosecute him.

Khadr was kept in confinement until November 2005 and was later charged under the newly created system of Guantanamo Military Commissions with conspiracy, murder by an unprivileged belligerent, and

---

between fourteen and eighteen must benefit from reduced punishment. Leveau Fanny, *Liability of Child Soldiers Under International Criminal Law*, *Osgoode Hall Review of Law and Policy*, Vol. 4, No. 1, 2014, p. 56.

75 Uganda: Letter to Minister of Justice, Human Rights Watch, 19 February 2003.

attempted murder by an unprivileged belligerent.[76]The commissions were based on the well-known system of military courts-martial. However, human rights and legal groups — even the United States Supreme Court — criticized the commissions for the lack of due process and for criminalizing conduct retroactively. The commissions made no distinction between youths and adults, and their rules allowed for indefinite detention even after acquittal. These commissions were later struck down as being unconstitutional.

After the Military Commission Act was signed, new charges were framed against Khadr. These included murder in violation of the law of war, attempted murder in violation of the law of war, conspiracy, and providing material support for terrorism and spying. In October 2010, he entered a guilty plea under the US law. According to the plea agreement, Khadr pleaded guilty to five counts of war crimes and was sentenced to eight years in prison with the possibility of parole. This sentence was in addition to the eight years that Khadr had already served at Guantánamo Bay. In September 2012, Khadr was transferred to Canada under terms of the International Transfer of Offenders Act. Canadian prison authorities classified Khadr as a maximum-security prisoner, despite the fact he had been considered a minimum-security inmate at Guantanamo and one who had never caused any problems. On 7 May 2015, Khadr was released on bail on conditions including that he would wear an electronic tracking bracelet and would reside with his lawyer.

Khadr's case is controversial in many respects and his prosecution has been widely criticized. The US government had given him the status of "unlawful enemy combatant". This was a new terminology used in an armed conflict and was and coined by the US. Since the US had signed and ratified the OP to the CRC on the Involvement of Children in Armed Conflict and the ILO Convention No. 182 concerning the elimination of the worst from of child labour, it was under obligation to rehabilitate a former child soldier. Several international law experts were of the opinion that Omar Khadr should not have been prosecuted. In prosecuting Omar Khadr, the US did not respect its international obligations in terms of respecting juvenile justice standards. Omar Khadr was the first child to stand trial for a war crime since the Nuremburg trials.

---

76 *The United States v Omar Khadr*, Case No 05-0008, United States Military Commission,

David Crane has aptly expressed his opinion on the prosecution of the child soldier: "Omar Khadr, a young Canadian, could have been a child in Sierra Leone. But he was in Afghanistan, in similar circumstances, not of his making or under his control, in an environment from which, as a child, there was no escape. Legally, morally, and politically the international community, including the US, has separated out children from the horrors of combat, to protect and nurture, to rehabilitate and support, and not to punish. No children found in combat should be held liable for their acts."[77]

International law protects children not only against recruitment and use in hostilities but also against any form of cruel, inhumane and degrading treatment. The recruitment and use of children in armed forces or groups blatantly violates the rights of children to be treated with dignity and to enjoy their childhood. Using children to participate in hostilities constitutes an affront to the principles of civilized nations irrespective of the nature of the child's involvement. The Special Court of Sierra Leone (SCSL) was the first international tribunal specifically mandated to address the crime of child recruitment and thus provides a unique reference point for examining the crime in international criminal justice. All the accused before the SCSL were charged with the crime of child recruitment. The SCSL sent a clear message to the world that a person who recruits child soldiers into a conflict is a war criminal, but the children recruited and forced to commit unspeakable acts are not. It was a pioneering step in the evolution of international war crimes tribunals.

The ICC Trial Chamber in the *Lubanga case* concluded that 'conscription', 'enlistment' and 'use' are three separate offences. Thus, the Chamber held that a child might be enlisted or conscripted, irrespective of whether she or he is later used to participate in hostilities. It rejected the defence's submission that enlistment and conscription were necessary for the purpose of using a child to participate actively in hostilities. The highest level of protection for children is the interpretation that children under the age of 15 cannot legally give consent to join an armed group. The ICC has been successful in prosecuting those responsible for the recruitment of children in armed conflict and subjecting them to cruel and inhuman treatment. The Statute of the SCSL and the Rome Statute have taken divergent paths on the

---

77 Crane David M., Prosecuting Children in Times of Conflict: The West African Experience, *Human Rights Brief*, Vol. 15, No.3, 2008, p. 15.

issue of prosecuting child soldiers, with the Rome Statute choosing to restrict jurisdiction to those over the age of 18. Even with the establishment of the ICC, the Special Court is a model that can work in the future, if required, to combat impunity in troubled areas of the world.

6   Looking Ahead

Child soldiers continue to be used in ongoing armed conflicts throughout the world. They are being exploited by leaders of all hues, from political leaders and commanders of state militaries to leaders of armed groups and criminal gangs. These leaders are ruthless and amoral. They know that the benefits of using child soldiers far outweigh the costs. They have been responsible for shockingly high levels of brutality and disregard for human life and dignity.

Although the number of governments that openly deploy under-18s directly in hostilities is relatively few, a significant number are complicit in allowing children to be used by government-related paramilitaries, militias, and civilian defence organizations or by armed opposition groups that they illicitly support.[1] While most states follow the Zero-under-18 Campaign',[2] the NSAGs have not paid due attention to the concerns of the United Nations, NGOs or the media about the use of child soldiers in hostilities.

The figure of 300,000 child soldiers has been used for years, though many armed conflicts have begun, ceased, or been renewed since it was

---

1   Release and reintegration of child soldiers: One part of a bigger puzzle, Paper presented by the Coalition to Stop the Use of Child Soldiers at the International Interdisciplinary Conference on Rehabilitation and Reintegration of War-Affected Children, 22-23 October 2009 – Brussels, Belgium.

2   Zero under 18 is the campaign aimed at achieving universal ratification of the Optional Protocol to CRC on the Involvement of Children in Armed Conflict in order to establish a moral consensus, that: (i) No child should participate in hostilities, (ii) No child should be forced to serve in armed forces and armed groups, and (iii) Every former child soldier will be assisted in starting a new life free from violence. The campaign was launched by the Office of the Special Representative of the Secretary-General for Children and Armed Conflict in cooperation with UNICEF and the Office of the High Commissioner for Human Rights in May 2010.

introduced. However, it really does not matter whether the figure has come down to 250,000 or gone up to 350,000; what is important is that the recruitment and use of child soldiers constitutes one of the most egregious violations of children's rights. In reality though, the recruitment and use of children in armed conflicts is growing because children provide a quick and easy way of replenishing the ranks in NSAGs,[3]which have now begun to use children primarily for psychological effect. Children are being used as a propaganda tool, killing prisoners on camera with knives and pistols, and not only for engaging opponents on the battlefield.

The Child Soldiers International, in its recent report,[4]has brought to light the fact that a number of States have failed to take measures to prevent the recruitment and use of children by the armed forces or NSAGs. States have responsibilities towards children who are at risk of recruitment and use as child soldiers. The Optional Protocol to the CRC requires States to take measures to implement its provisions beyond their own borders, through cooperation and assistance. In this regard, States must ensure that their trade in or transfer of arms or other forms of military assistance does not contribute to the violation of the norms contained in the Arms Trade Treaty of 2014. The relationship between the proliferation of small arms and increase in children's involvement in armed conflict is well established.[5]In this era of globalization States should be liable for actions that adversely affect people outside their territories, They have obligations under the Optional Protocol and other international treaties to prevent the transfer of arms in situations where human rights and IHL abuses occur.

In the last two decades, the United Nations and its organs have taken certain effective steps to end the recruitment and the use of child soldiers. The UN Security Council has established an innovative framework to address

---

3   Burkhart III, John A., Watch Out for the Children: Army Policy and Child Soldiers, Thesis, Naval Postgraduate School California, June 2016, p. 8.

4   Louder Than Words: An agenda for Action to end state use of child soldiers, Child Soldier International, 2012, p. 162.

5   In 2002, there were approximately 639 million small arms in circulation worldwide; that equates to about 1 weapon for every 10 people on the planet. This number of small arms has increased over the years. This was perpetuated by the fact that an AK-47 could be purchased for as little as Rs 500 (or US $ 8) in different countries, throughout the world. A number of developed countries have also transferred weapons to the NSAGs to fight the regime which they consider oppressing. In addition to the abundance of available weapons, weapon systems have been simplified in their use; therefore, with only limited training, children can be taught all they need to know in order to kill.

the issue of child soldiers and grave violations against them. In 1999, the Security Council unanimously adopted its first resolution on children affected by armed conflict. Since then it has adopted several additional resolutions on the issue. These resolutions relate not only to parties to a conflict, but involve a broad range of actors who are responsible for enhancing the protection framework for children affected by armed conflict. These actors include other UN bodies, member States, corporate actors, international and regional organizations, and financial institutions.

The Security Council has welcomed annexes to the Secretary-General's report that enumerate parties that recruit and use children and established a working group that meets on a bimonthly basis to review issues relating to children and armed conflict. While the Security Council resolution 1379 (2003) asked for the "shame" listing of parties that recruit and use children in conflict, resolution 1882, passed in August 2009, further requested the listing of parties that commit sexual violence against children and those who kill and maim children with impunity. Significantly, resolution 1882 also establishes a vital link between the Security Council's Children and Armed Conflict (CAAC) Agenda and its Sanctions Committees, a major step towards concrete action against perpetrators. The Security Council has focused on six grave violations against children in armed conflict. These are killing and maiming, sexual violence, recruitment and use, denial of humanitarian access, abduction, and attacks on schools and hospitals. Each of these violations against children during armed conflict may constitute: (i) Grave breaches of the Geneva Conventions and their Additional Protocols; (ii) Violations of customary norms of international law; (iii) Violations of obligations contained in the CRC and other international and regional human rights treaties; and (iv) War crimes or crimes against humanity under the Rome Statute.

The international community has shifted its focus to criminalizing the recruitment of children in armed conflict. The conviction of Thomas Lubango Dyilo by the International Criminal Court is the best example of this. It may make other NSAG leaders consider the consequences before recruiting and using child soldiers or committing other gross violations of their rights. However, much more has to be achieved. As visible in Syria, most future conflicts are likely to be protracted, and fought by armed groups for personal gain in cities. The lines between gangsters, warlords, insurgents, paramilitary forces, and drug traffickers are becoming blurred. All of these will increasingly operate in urban environments and make use of children.

The criminal responsibility of acts carried out by child soldiers lies with the indirect perpetrator, i.e., the recruiter or the conscripting agent and the adult exercising effective control over these children. The recent trend of the use of children as suicide bombers by the ISIS is just one indicator that a strong message is required to be conveyed to perpetrators by the world community.[6]The ISIS has exposed young children to violence and indoctrinated them in the name of God to create perfect fighters who would love to fight and die for the sake of building an Islamic State.

According to Machel (2000), child soldiers are exposed to extreme violence and suffering, and become desensitized to the horror around them.[7]They are used not only as combatants, but also as cooks, porters, messengers, spies and for sexual purposes. Nearly all girls abducted by NSAGs are forced into sexual slavery and subjected to physical and emotional violence. These children are deprived of their rights to education, care and the protection of their families. They need to be disarmed and reintegrated into the society. Over the past 25 years, disarmament, demobilization and reintegration (DDR) programmes have been introduced in more than 30 countries and are frequently mandated by UN Security Council resolutions.

Engagement with child soldiers has been a challenging for both military and law enforcement agencies. Members of State armed forces and UN peacekeeping forces are often faced with a moral dilemma while contemplating the use of force against child soldiers: under what conditions would it be permissible for them to use force?

This chapter analyses the issues of targeting child soldiers and disarmament, demobilization and reintegration of child soldiers before discussing the measures that may be taken for the eradication of child soldiering from the world.

---

6   A growing body of evidence makes clear that the Islamic State (IS) is actively exploiting children on the battlefield in order to gain the upper hand against stronger and better armed adversaries. Recently on 20 August 2016, 54 people were killed and 66 injured at a wedding in Turkey, and the alleged perpetrator was a 12 to 14-year-old boy wearing a suicide vest. Five days later, the IS released a video of five young boys dressed in desert camouflage executing at point-blank range five Kurdish fighters. Gorka Sebastian L., Gorka Katharine C., and Claire Herzog, The Islamic State's Militarization of Children: Special Report, Threat Knowledge Group, September 2016, pp. 13.

7   Machel, G., International Conference on War Affected Children: The Impact of Armed Conflict on Children: A Critical Review of Progress Made and Obstacles Encountered in Increasing Protection for War-Affected Children, 2000, Winnipeg, Canada.

A. Targeting Child Soldiers

I killed two informers in Medellin. They were aged 38 and 42. I wasn't afraid to kill them because I had already been in combat. Our collaborators had seen them talking to para-militaries. I had their address, and went to their house. There were two of us, but I was the one who had to do the killing. It was a test for me. I was thirteen. It was the same year that I joined the FARC-EP. After doing it, I felt really big, like a real killer. But sometimes when I thought about it, I felt sad and I wanted to cry.[8]

*   *   *   *

I found interaction with child soldiers problematic, both morally and practically. On the one hand, I realized they were children and that their wrongdoings were not really their own fault. On the other hand, their very ignorance of normal morality made them particularly dangerous. Most of the rebels I encountered were too young to remember life before the civil war and their commanders were quick to exploit this. When the bullets started flying, I am afraid their age became irrelevant.[9]

*   *   *   *

For soldiers with any sense of honour at all, fighting children offers a no-win situation. To be defeated by children would almost certainly bring death, derision and disgrace, while to win would carry the taint of having killed mere children.[10]

These three statements depict the reality of child soldiering today. Children have emerged as a low-cost way for NSAGs to mobilize their armed forces. Armed with the smaller, lighter, and more powerful weapons available today, children can constitute a lethal force. Many children are forcibly recruited after being orphaned or cut off from their families. Often drugged, they are beaten and threatened with death unless they fight and commit atrocities such as killing people from their own villages.

---

8 A 13-year-old former Colombian child soldier.

9 Maj Phil Ashby, QGM, Royal Marines.

10 Lt Gen Romeo Dallaire (Retd), former force commander of the United Nations Assistance Mission for Rwanda (UNAMIR).

They serve as decoys, mine cleaners, spies, and early-warning systems, at the cost of losing their lives, to protect adult troops. Even certain States have been known to have deployed persons below 18 years of age in armed conflict.

In international law, very little has been written about the controversial issue of the targeting of child soldiers in an armed conflict. International lawyers have conveniently avoided commenting on the rules of engagement (ROE) with child soldiers. For any professional force, child soldiers present a complicated question, which is more difficult than the issue of civilian casualties. Children are traditionally considered outside the scope of armed conflict.[11] For any civilized military, killing civilians in an armed conflict is not the goal. A child is considered a privileged civilian. When soldiers are faced with the problem of having to choose between firing on 12-year-olds or holding back and facing the potential threat of being shot, their effectiveness is severely diminished. On the one hand, engagement with children provokes the provision of safety and care, while on the other hand, child soldiers pose a life threat, as every other armed opponent. Confrontation with child soldiers is likely to lead to a sense of shame and guilt and subsequent mental health problems. This can be demoralizing for professional troops and can affect unit cohesion. The NATO forces operating in Bosnia and in West Africa faced serious problems of clinical depression and post-traumatic stress disorder among soldiers who had faced child soldiers.[12]

---

11   In an armed conflict children are victims who enjoy special protection (under article 77 of Additional Protocol I), even if engaged in the direct use of armed force (under article 77 (3) Additional Protocol I and article 4 (3) of Additional Protocol II), and consequently raise moral dilemmas every time that opponent armed forces exercise the legitimate right of self-defence.

12   During the deployment of Dutch units in Bosnia in 1995 a Dutch non-commissioned officer (NCO) made a transit tour to another compound in a Mercedes Benz all terrain vehicle. During one of the stops at a roadblock, which was controlled by Serbian forces, he was forced to come out of his vehicle in order to being interrogated. One of the soldiers at this roadblock was a child warrior, not older than 15 years. This child warrior cocked his rifle with the loop against the head of the Dutch NCO. The interrogation was carried out by other Serbian soldiers and the NCO never saw the child warrior again. After redeployment to the Netherlands he resumed his duties in military barracks. Before he retired at the age of 50 he deployed in two other operations. After his retirement the NCO developed a chronic Post Traumatic Stress Disorder (PTSD), which devastated his sleep and made him hyper aroused at daytime. Due to this hyper arousal, he got very easily upset. His family motivated him to seek treatment for his complaints at the Central Military Hospital in Utrecht. During the therapeutic sessions of the cognitive behavioural therapy, it appeared that the image of the child warrior, cocking his rifle against the head of the NCO was the worst experience. The very image was so powerful because of the huge contrast between his

The question of whether or when to engage with a child soldier on the battlefield is a morally compelling issue. Just war theory and the principle of non-combatant immunity draw distinctions within a population—certain individuals are to be protected from the horrors of war. This protection afforded to non-combatants is quite specific in international law. Child soldiers are not non-combatants, but they are distinct from adult troops because they are minors, who are mostly recruited by force and may lack the capability to make moral judgements.[13]

The issue of targeting child soldiers raises two distinct legal questions: first, whether child soldiers are combatants like any other combatants, and second, if so whether the means used to target them should follow the same rules as for adult combatants. Since children have special rights under IHL and human rights treaties, every action of troops against them remains open to external monitoring and scrutiny.

In order to devise an effective ROE for engagement with child soldiers in any military operation, it is necessary to understand the advantages of child soldiering and the general characteristics of child soldiers.[14]Children are valuable to NSAGs because they are easy to train, require minimal resources and are mostly given short-term training.[15] Violence is often used as a method

---

own powerful military role, fully supported by the international community and morally justified and the child warrior, seemingly powerless but fully controlling the situation without any moral limitations. Part of the cognitive behavioural therapy is the effective questioning of the assumptions in this image, like 'were you so powerful as you thought you were' and 'was the child soldier so powerless as you thought he was?' Child Soldiers as the Opposing Force, Final Report of the HFM-159/RTO Task Group, The Research and Technology Organization of NATO, AC/323(HFM-159)TP/222, January 2011, p. 2.6.

13 Emily Kalah Gade, The Child Soldier: The Question of Self-defence, *The Journal of Military Ethics*, Vol. 10, No. 4, December 2011.

14 The specific ROE provide the circumstances under which soldiers may use lethal force or open fire. Depending on where a military unit is deployed, they fall under a theater-specific ROE, or the military's standing rules of engagement (SROE). These SROE and theater-specific ROE must be evaluated and analyzed, prior to deployment, and can be adjusted depending on where the mission is located, who is participating in the mission, or if a unit is operating as part of a larger multinational coalition. Burkhart III, John A., Watch Out for the Children: Army Policy and Child Soldiers, Thesis, Naval Postgraduate School California, June 2016, p. 13.

15 It takes a year to train before you [professional soldiers] can go to the front to fight. With us, it was a week. All you have to know is to point the gun away from you and know the commands to crawl and know when to attack in ambushes. That was it. After a week, we were on the front lines. For more details on life of child soldiers see: Beah Ismael (2007), *A Long Way Gone: Memoire of a Child Soldier*, New York: Sarah Crichton Books.

to produce good and fast results. Seen as instruments, they are toughened by other children under the supervision of senior juveniles. Children eat less, drink less, are not paid, serve as pack animals, are able to cook, can collect wood without drawing attention, normally have no next of kin to worry about them and consequently are replaceable and disposable. They may not need uniforms, and are able to carry out logistic activities without leaving a military trace because of which they are considered perfect couriers. Girl soldiers, who are great fighters and the best logisticians, can also serve as instruments of sexual satisfaction for senior members of the forces. Children have a good visual memory and can easily identify weapons, numbers, types of vehicles, colours, locations, faces, inscriptions, and marks. In operational engagements, children have proved to be remarkable frontline fighters. They move fast, shoot accurately, and are merciless.[16]

According to Singer (2006), child soldiers are not merely children, they can be ruthless killers capable of the most brutish and violent actions. Children take risks that an adult professional soldier may avoid. In addition, they lack of regard for the rules of engagement and indulge in massive violations of IHL, including the routine killing and mutilation of civilians.[17]The key characteristics of child soldiers are:

> They may show little or no fear, a disregard for life and for the basic rules/laws of war.

> They can be daring and tenacious in combat, particularly when under the influence of drugs or when compelled by political or religious zeal.[18]

> They are unable to fully comprehend the risks and consequences of their behaviour and have a so-called "underdeveloped death

---

16 Tenente-coronel Francisco Jose Bernardino da Silva Leandro, Generic guidelines for the use of force against "Child Soldiers" in Peace Operations, Revista Militar No. 2523 - Abril de 2012, pp. 371 - 386.

17 Every soldier retains the fundamental right of self-defence and has the right to the use of force to protect himself against an imminent attack or a direct armed attack. It is not a soldier's fault that an armed youngster points a deadly weapon at them. I don't think any sane person wants to harm or kill a child, but I don't think any sane soldier would allow a person to shoot them or one of their mates. Without thinking twice, without hesitation, you eliminate the threat as quickly as possible. Rene Provost, 12 January 2016, available at: http://www.ejiltalk.org/targeting-child-soldiers/.

18 Kaplan, Eben. 2005. *Child Soldiers around the World*, Washington, DC: Council on Foreign Relations.

concept". This might turn them into fierce fighters who could be even deadlier than adult combatants.[19]

> Child soldiers show more aggression than adult combatants as they perceive violence as something positive and fascinating.[20]

> Child soldiers positively enhance the fighting capacity of NSAGs.[21]

Child soldiers may kill prisoners, their own wounded, and civilians. They know no other world than their world of violence. It is precisely the immaturity of children that makes it possible to exploit them. This exploitation takes place in situations in which the rules of law and the rules of IHL have disappeared.[22]

Before soldiers are deployed in any armed conflict, it should be made clear to them that a child soldier is an effective combatant whose bullets can be as lethal as the bullets of any other armed opponent. This insight might prevent the shame and guilt that soldiers feel when they have to fight against child soldiers. The ROE[23] should be checked on their relevance to

---

19 Singer, Peter. 2006. *Children at war*, Berkeley, CA: University of California Press.

20 The morning after the lieutenant's speech, we proceeded to practice killing the prisoners the way lieutenant had done. There were five prisoners and many eager participants. Five of us were chosen for the killing exhibition. The five men were lined up in front of us on the training ground with their hands tied. We were supposed to slice their throat and the corporal's command. The person whose prisoner died quickest would win the contest. We had our bayonets out and supposed to look in the faces of the prisoners as we took them out of this world. I didn't feel anything for him and just waited for corporal's order. The corporal gave a signal with pistol shot and I grabbed the man's head and slit his throat in one fluid motion. His Adam's apple made way for the sharp knife, and I turned bayonet on its zigzag edge as I brought it out... his eyes rolled up and they looked me straight.... the prisoner leaned his weight on me as he gave out his last breath. I dropped him on ground and wiped my bayonet on him. I reported to the corporal, who was holding a timer....I was proclaimed the winner. We celebrated that day's achievement with more drugs. Beah Ismael. 2007. *A Long Way Gone: Memoire of a Child Soldier*, New York: Sarah Crichton Books, p. 124-25. Also see: Wessells, Michael. 2006, *Child soldiers: From Violence to Protection*, Cambridge, MA: Harvard University Press.

21 Haerroos and Bohmelt, The Impact of Child Soldiers on Rebel Groups' Fighting Capacities, available at: http://www.polver.uni-konstanz.de/en/holzinger/team/roos-van-der-haer/publications/, accessed 10 April 2017.

22 Singer, P.W. 2006. *Children at War*, University of California Press, Berkeley, Los Angeles.

23 No ROE should limit a combatant's right to use force, up to and including deadly force, to protect him or herself – or other force personnel – from immediate threat of serious injury or death. They must be reminded that the use of authorized force should never be more than what is necessary, reasonable and proportional, based on the prevailing circumstances.

confrontations with child soldiers as regards fighting, arresting and disarming them. When forced into close engagement, forces should prioritize the targeting and elimination of any adult leaders. Wherever possible, military commanders should explore the options of using non-lethal weapons in situations involving child soldiers. These may not only be more effective and humane in dealing with child soldiers, but could also avoid public outrage against the military forces.[24] Psychological operations should be integrated into the overall efforts to convince child soldiers to stop fighting and leave their units to facilitate the process of their rehabilitation and reintegration into society. The following points must be kept in mind by military personnel likely to encounter child soldiers.

> Child soldiers react very differently from adult soldiers. They must therefore be treated differently. Identifying child soldiers can be an issue. They do not conform to stereotype.

> Professional soldiers are trained to adhere to and uphold the basic laws of war. Child soldiers in rebel forces are not. This potentially places the professionals at increased risk.

> Force needs to be met with force, despite the age of the attackers. However, it must be remembered that there are alternatives to lethal force.

> Serious consideration should be given to the subject of dealing with female child combatants as separate from that of child soldiers as a whole. Specialized training of personnel may be required to deal with them effectively.

> IHL lags behind the changes in modern warfare. It is not flexible enough to address the threat of child soldiers realistically. However, troops must all be trained in the basic principles of IHL.

> A distinction should be made between theoretical and practical applications of law.

Whitman Shelly, Tanya Zayed and Carl Conradi. 2013. *Child Soldiers: A Handbook for Security Sector Actors*, The Romeo Dallaire Child Soldiers Initiative, Canada, p. 63-66.

24 In responding to any child soldier engagements, public relations officers should call attention to minimize the killing of child soldiers, such as the use of non-lethal weapons, psychological operations, and firing for shock effect. At the same time, they must make it clear that child soldiers are just as lethal with an assault rifle as an adult.

> ROE concerning child soldiers must be issued in advance and role playing must form a part of the preparation for any operation that may involve engagement with child soldiers.

> The directive must provide clear guidance on the rights and responsibilities of professional soldiers when interacting with child soldiers.

> There must be a directive requiring the live capture of child soldiers where feasible, keeping in mind the associated risk to military personnel and civilians.

UN Peacekeeping Operations: In contrast to a child soldier, professional military combatants are taught to uphold the rules of IHL, with severe consequences for those who fail to do so. Engagement with child soldiers may disrupt the paradigms of professional soldiering and the cultural values peacekeepers hold on children. Child soldiers exhibiting a threatening posture towards peacekeeping forces are a legitimate target to detain, to keep in custody to disarm,[25] to neutralize, to separate from adult dominance, and as a last resort to use lethal fire with non-lethal intent.[26] The main aim should be to disrupt the use of children in armed conflicts by engaging the leadership who exercise complete power over the child soldiers and those who effectively control the recruitment activities. Enlisted children are victims to be protected from their recruiters and are to be returned to their youth as soon as possible. Peacekeepers bear special responsibilities in this context. Military

---

25 Article 37, the Convention on the Rights of Children, 1989, provides: (a) No child shall be subjected to torture or other cruel, inhuman or degrading treatment or punishment. Neither capital punishment nor life imprisonment without possibility of release shall be imposed for offences committed by persons below eighteen years of age; (b) No child shall be deprived of his or her liberty unlawfully or arbitrarily. The arrest, detention or imprisonment of a child shall be in conformity with the law and shall be used only as a measure of last resort and for the shortest appropriate period of time; (c) Every child deprived of liberty shall be treated with humanity and respect for the inherent dignity of the human person, and in a manner which takes into account the needs of persons of his or her age. In particular, every child deprived of liberty shall be separated from adults unless it is considered in the child's best interest not to do so and shall have the right to maintain contact with his or her family through correspondence and visits, save in exceptional circumstances.

26 Combatants who confront child soldiers in an opposing force can lawfully defend themselves, using the minimum necessary force. They may also use the amount of force needed to further their military aim - but their actions must carefully balance military considerations against the need to respect human life and well-being (the proportionality principle).

commanders of peacekeeping forces play a fundamental role in dealing with children associated with armed groups, especially through their leadership, their will to enforce accountability and support integration. Individual peacekeepers must understand that they are there to protect youth, and not to destroy it. In confrontations with child soldiers, regular forces are at a high risk of losing international support in the wake of media reports from the viewpoint of the child soldiers.

Most militaries in the world have updated their military doctrines, policies, and training manuals to take into consideration the current operational environment, however, the same cannot be said of the interaction with child soldiers. In most countries ROE concerning child soldiers are either weak or non-existent. It is necessary for military and paramilitary forces to develop standard ROE and standard operating procedures (SOPs) that can guide their members during engagements with child soldiers.

B: From Soldiers to Citizens

Disarmament, Demobilization, and Reintegration

Since 1989, when the issue of child soldiers first became a feature of IHL, significant measures have been taken to end the involvement of children in armed conflict.[27] Article 6 of the Optional Protocol to the CRC requires State parties to take all feasible measures to ensure that children who are illegally recruited or used in hostilities are demobilized or otherwise released and receive

---

27 The phenomenon of child soldiering has received an increasing amount of attention as a result of three internationally significant events. First, the signing of the international Convention of the Rights of the Child in 1989 which has been ratified universally (except the USA), put the rights of children on the international agenda of the United Nations (UN). Second, the end of the Cold War in 1989 brought about an increase of UN peacekeeping missions along with disarmament, demobilization and reintegration programs (DDR) over the course of the following three decades. The combination of global attention on children's rights and to international intervention in civil conflicts led to the third event, which was the 1996 publication of the UN report by Graca Machel titled *The Impact of Armed Conflict on Children*. The report estimated that there were approximately 300 000 child soldiers worldwide. These three events brought the issue of child soldiering to the forefront, and as a result both the international community and academics have been interested in understanding who child soldiers are, what they do and how they are demobilized and reintegrated into civilian life. Rivard Lysanne, Child Soldiers and Disarmament, Demobilization and Reintegration Programs: The Universalism of Children's Rights vs. Cultural Relativism Debate, *The Journal of Humanitarian Assistance, available at:* https://sites.tufts.edu/jha/archives/772, accessed 19 April 2017.

appropriate support for their reintegration.[28] Disarmament, Demobilization and Reintegration (DDR) is a process that is designed to contribute to, and support wider national and international post-conflict peace-building efforts aimed at restoring stability, security, development and peace.[29]

The aim of DDR of children associated with armed forces and groups is to ensure their effective and sustainable reintegration into the society. A fundamental principle of children's DDR is that their release and reintegration should not depend on any formal peace process or be contingent on the establishment of formal DDR programmes, but rather should be prioritized at all times including when hostilities are ongoing. The elements of the DDR process work together and support each other; demobilization is a tool to achieve reintegration, which in turn prevents re-recruitment of child soldiers.

Guiding Principles of DDR

In the last two decades, a framework of international law and policy has been established to protect children from military exploitation. Article 39 of the CRC calls on States Parties to take appropriate measures to promote the physical and psychological recovery and social reintegration of child victims of armed conflict. Under ILO Convention No. 182, States Parties are to take immediate and effective measures to secure the prohibition and elimination of the worst forms of child labour, which includes the forced or compulsory recruitment of children for use in armed conflict (a child being defined as a person under the age of 18). The 1977 Additional Protocol I and Protocol II call for the protection of children in armed conflict, forbid the recruitment and use of children under the age of 16 in conflict, and provide for the special

---

28 Article 6 (3) of the OP to CRC on the Involvement of Children in Armed Conflict provides: "States Parties shall take all feasible measures to ensure that persons within their jurisdiction recruited or used in hostilities contrary to this Protocol are demobilized or otherwise released from service. States Parties shall, when necessary, accord to these persons all appropriate assistance for their physical and psychological recovery and their social reintegration."

29 DDR technically involves disarmament, which is the collection, documentation and control/disposal of weapons from ex-combatants and, sometimes, the civilian population; demobilization, which focuses on the formal and controlled discharge of active combatants from armed forces/groups; and reintegration which is focused on helping ex-combatants return to their communities, acquire civilian status and gain sustainable employment and income. DDR in Peace Operations: A Retrospective Department of Peacekeeping Operations, Office of the Rule of Law and Security Institutions DDR Section, United Nations, 2014, p. 2-4.

treatment of children under detention and their reintegration into society.

The CRC Committee's General Comment No. 6 on "Treatment of unaccompanied and separated children outside their country of origin" states: "Child soldiers should be considered primarily as victims of armed conflict. Former child soldiers, who often find themselves unaccompanied or separated at the cessation of the conflict or following defection, shall be given all the necessary support services to enable reintegration into normal life, including necessary psychosocial counselling. Such children shall be identified and demobilized on a priority basis during any identification and separation operation. Child soldiers, in particular, those who are unaccompanied or separated, should not normally be interned, but rather, benefit from special protection and assistance measures, in particular as regards their demobilization and rehabilitation."[30]

As outlined in the international treaties and other documents, the following guiding principles remain applicable at all stages of DDR: (i) **The child's right to life, survival and development**: The right to life, survival and development is not limited to ensuring a child's physical well-being, but includes the need to ensure full and harmonious development, including at the spiritual, moral and social levels, where education plays a key role; (ii) **Non-discrimination**: States shall ensure respect for the rights of all children within their jurisdiction — including non-national children; regardless of race, sex, age, religion, ethnicity, opinions, disability or any other status of the child, the child's parents or legal guardians; (iii) **Child participation**: Children should be allowed to express their opinions freely, and those opinions should be "given due weight in accordance with the age and maturity of the child". Children should be consulted at all stages of the demobilization and reintegration process, and actions that affect them should be in their best interests and keeping in view their needs and concerns. In particular, children should participate in making decisions concerning family reunification, and career and educational opportunities; and (iv) **The child's best interests**: Actions that affect the child should be based on an assessment of whether those actions are in the child's best interests. A child should participate in determining what is in his/her best interests. .

---

30 The Committee on the Rights of the Child, General Comment No. 6, 2005, CRC/GC/2005/6, paragrahs 56 to 59.

DDR Programme

DDR is an important component of any peace-building effort. Disarmament involves collecting, documenting, gaining control and disposing of small arms, ammunition and explosive weapons from combatants and civilians. Demobilization refers to ending the combatant's association with armed forces or groups. It is the formal and controlled absolution of active combatants from armed forces and groups followed by short-term assistance. Reintegration is defined as the process through which ex-combatants acquire civilian status and gain sustainable employment and income.[31]

Disarmament and Demobilization:

In the first stage of this process, children are disarmed, preferably by a military authority. The eligibility of a child soldier for disarmament should never be based on the handing in of a weapon or proof of familiarity with weaponry, because not all children associated with NSAGs would have used weapons or been combatants. The children should enter the demobilization and reintegration process irrespective of whether they present themselves at the assembly points with weapons or ammunitions. They should be given the option of receiving a document certifying the surrender of their weapons if there is a procedure requiring them to do so, and if this is in their best interests.

The help-aid agencies must work together to give priority to physically removing children from contact with adult combatants and a security system should be established to prevent adults' access to them.[32]The transition from

---

31 In most cases reintegration helps in (i) to downsize army or militia groups by redirecting the human and material resources to post-conflict reconstruction; (ii) to build confidence, to bring stability and security by providing former child soldiers with an alternative to armed conflict; (iii) to assist combatants in assuming productive roles in civil society and the work force; and (iv) in the long-term, to address the root causes of the armed conflict and to facilitate sustainable development. Krech, R. 2003. *The Reintegration of Former Child Combatants: A Case Study of NGO Programming in Sierra Leone.* Toronto: Ontario Institute for Studies in Education of the University of Toronto.

32 In order to protect child soldiers' rights and to meet their special needs, the World Banks has set certain guidelines for DDR programmes. The guidelines direct that child soldiers must be separated from military authority and protected through the establishment of special reception centres during demobilization, as long as their stay prior to being reunited with their families and communities is as short as possible. Child protection personnel, usually directed by UNICEF, first separate the children from the adults at disarmament and demobilization sites.

military to civilian life may be difficult for children, because in spite of the difficulties they encountered, they may have found a defined responsible role, purpose and power in the NSAG. The objective of the separation is to break up the relationship of authority and the links of control between the child soldiers and their commanders and to ensure that they are offered the reintegration packages developed for children.[33] At this stage, child soldiers can suffer from a great variety of illnesses; however, some of the pressing medical issues they generally face are malnutrition, open or infected wounds, STDs and for some, drug addiction. Once their condition has stabilized, children can be slowly introduced to the final stage i.e. reintegration.

Reintegration

The right of child soldiers to receive support for reintegration into society is enshrined in Article 39 of the CRC: "State Parties shall take all appropriate measures to promote ... social reintegration of a child victim of ... armed conflicts".[34]Reintegration is a social and economic process with an open time-frame, taking place primarily in communities at the local level. It is part of the general development of a country and a national responsibility, and often necessitates long-term external assistance.[35]Child-centered reintegration is multilayered, comprising family reunification; mobilizing and enabling care systems in the community; medical screening and healthcare, including reproductive health services; schooling and/or vocational training; psychosocial support; and social, cultural and economic support. The process of reintegration must be meaningful and sustainable.

The physical end of conflict does not necessarily end the ordeals of children for whom experiencing violence has been the norm. These children

---

33 Williamson, J., The Disarmament, Demobilization and Reintegration of Child Soldiers: Social and Psychological Transformation in Sierra Leone, *Intervention*, Vol. 4(3), 2006, p. 185-205.

34 The Paris Principles describe child reintegration as "the process through which children transition into civil society and enter meaningful roles and identities as civilians who are accepted by their families and communities in a context of local and national reconciliation." According to the Principles sustainable reintegration is achieved "when the political, legal, economic and social conditions needed for children to maintain life, livelihood and dignity have been secured. This process aims to ensure that children can access their rights, including formal and non-formal education, family unity, dignified livelihoods and safety from harm." *The Principles and Guidelines on Children Associated with Armed Forces or Armed Groups (Paris Principles)*, February 2007.

35 IDDRS (2006). *Integrated DDR Standards*. New York: United Nations.

may bear scars of conflict and effective reintegration is vital so that they can contribute to a peaceful society. Former child soldiers experience trauma and stigma that can make it difficult for them to go back to their communities to begin or resume their education. Girls face greater difficulties in being accepted back into their families and communities as they are often stigmatized and may be accompanied by children.

An inclusive approach helps the sustainable reintegration of former child soldiers and other child victims of conflict. It prevents stigmatization and avoids the impression that joining NSAGs brings rewards. Reintegration efforts can take the form of assistance for children to join schools or vocational training institutions, health care systems, youth groups, apprenticeships or other work opportunities, etc. Reintegration efforts originally intended for demobilized children, such as accelerated learning programmes, to help children in reintegration into the community in broader terms. Cultural, religious and traditional rituals, such as traditional healing, cleansing and forgiveness rituals, can also play an important role in the protection and reintegration of children into their communities. Care should be taken, however, to ensure that religious beliefs serve the best interests of the child, especially in places where religious or cultural values may have played an important role in recruitment. The UN's Integrated DDR Standards recommend that the reintegration process should extend over a period of five years or more in order to give children a viable long-term alternative to military life.[36]

Neglected Needs of Girl Child Soldiers

Gender is perceived differently within the NSAGs as compared to the civilian society. For instance, girls may be perceived as having crossed the gender divide by playing combative roles, which are traditionally considered a male preserve. In certain communities, such girls are said to have lost their femininity. As a result, former girl child soldiers may be considered unsuitable for many traditional roles that a girl is expected to perform in a society. After the ceasefire in Nepal in 2006, many girl soldiers were forced to very low positions in the traditional Nepalese society. Girl soldiers in Colombia, who fought as equals to their male counterparts, faced similar challenges.

---

36 UN Integrated DDR Standards, Section 5.30: Children and DDR, Sub-section 3.4: Reintegration.

Girl child soldiers are often rejected, excluded and harassed upon returning to their families and communities. They may be considered to be dangerous killers, or stigmatized as HIV carriers. If they escaped from captivity, their families may fear retaliation from the armed group. The girls who face the greatest difficulty are those who were sexually abused as child soldiers, and return home pregnant or with 'fatherless' children. These girls have been identified as an extremely vulnerable group with regard to psychosocial reintegration. In many post conflict settings worldwide, they have often been excluded from DDR programmes offered to former combatants.[37] It is estimated that approximately 40 per cent of the child soldiers in the Democratic Republic of Congo were girls. However, the numbers of girls in the reintegration programmes was extremely low. Unfortunately, DDR programmes lack a gender sensitive approach and are ill-equipped to address the complex social, psychological, and medical needs of girl child soldiers. Some self-demobilized girls in the DRC were traced and included in the programme, but most former girl soldiers remain without any support.[38]Besides, many girl child soldiers choose to stay in NSAGs as they know that reintegration into the community would be extremely difficult. DDR programmes must, therefore, employ community-based strategies to help in the reintegration of girls, in particular unwed mothers. .

Successful DDR

Some points which may be kept in mind while implementing DDR are as follows.

> Each post-conflict situation presents its own unique profile with specific challenges. A thorough research in the socio-political and cultural context of an armed conflict must be undertaken by the aid organizations before initiating a DDR programme.[39]

> Demobilization and reintegration programmes must be tailored to

---

37 Shanahan Fiona, Cultural Responses to the Reintegration of Formerly Abducted Girl Soldiers in NorthernUganda, *Psychology & Society*, Vol. 1 (1), p. 14 28.

38 NduwimanaDonatien, Reintegration of Child Soldiers in Eastern Democratic Republic of Congo: Challenges and Prospects, International Peace Support Training Centre, Occasional Paper, Series 4, No. 2, 2013, p. 8.

39 The post-conflict success models of DDR exported from one country may be inappropriate for the ongoing conflict in other places. Pauletto Elettra and Preeti Patel, Challenging Child Soldier DDR Processes and Policies in the Eastern Democratic Republic of Congo, *Journal of Peace, Conflict and Development*, issue 16, November 2010, p. 48.

the needs of the societies in which they are implemented rather than being based on a 'one size fits all' blueprint.[40]

➢ Leaders of NSGAs should be informed about the rule of law and child protection, including the prohibition of child recruitment and its harmful consequences, so that they release child soldiers without threatening them or making unrealistic promises, and do not re-recruit them.[41]

➢ Children should be informed about their rights and the DDR process in terms that they can understand, so that they can become positively engaged in the process.

➢ Members of NSAGs and actors in the demobilization exercise must not make promises to children about DDR that cannot be kept.[42]

➢ Families, communities and the civil society in general should be informed about children's rights, the demobilization process, the living conditions of children associated with armed forces and groups, and the difficulties they face, so that they can play a protective and supportive role in the children's reintegration. Community sensitization activities help to ensure that the communities' expectations are realistic before a former child soldier returns.

---

40 Porto J. Gomes, Imogen Parsons and Chris Alden, From Soldiers to Citizens: The Social, Economic and Political Reintegration of UNITA Ex-Combatants, ISS Monograph series, No. 130, March 2007, pp. 171.

41 The role of the international community is thus instrumental in applying political pressure to continue to bring perpetrators of recruitment of children to trial. It has been reported that Lubanga's trial at the International Criminal Court was the main reason for Nepalese rebels to release 3,000 child soldiers at once. Pauletto Elettra and Preeti Patel, Challenging Child Soldier DDR Processes and Policies in the Eastern Democratic Republic of Congo, *Journal of Peace, Conflict and Development*, issue 16, November 2010, p. 51.

42 In a study undertaken on reintegration of child soldiers in Liberia, majority of the participants expressed dissatisfaction with their reintegration. Their dissatisfaction centered around two sub-themes: broken promises and obstacles. Several of the participants reported that they were dissatisfied with their reintegration because they did not receive the reintegration assistance they were promised. A few of the participants admitted that they initially received some of the reintegration benefits such as the first two stipends totaling approximately US$ 300 and some vocational skills training; however, they gradually became disappointed after the rest of the reintegration assistance (shelter, tools, stipend, counseling, medical care, etc.) were unfulfilled. Brownell Gracie E., The Reintegration Experiences of Ex-Child Soldiers in Liberia, Unpublished Thesis, The University of Texas at Arlington, December 2013.

> International and national DDR staff should be aware of children, especially girls, in armed groups and forces, understand what steps to take to obtain their immediate release and know how to assist them after release.

> The socio-cultural perceptions of girls in general, and former girl soldiers in particular, requires further investigation to understand how negative perceptions about girl soldiers hamper their reintegration and how to address the stigmatization of girl soldiers.[43]

> The volatile, non-permissive environments in which DDR programmes operate often require great flexibility and improvisation on the side of the programmers.

By definition, achieving the goal of DDR is a long-term exercise that must be closely coordinated with other peace-building, reconstruction and reconciliation processes. The rights of former child soldiers, or indeed any child, cannot be fully realized in a context characterized by on-going insecurity, poverty, discrimination and injustice. The UN's Integrated DDR Standards recommend that child reintegration should extend over a period of five years or more in order to give children a viable long-term alternative to military life.

UNICEF has an important role to play in the protection of children particularly in times of conflict. Within the framework of DRR, it has the responsibility of monitoring the implementation of the CRC, which is the standard against which UNICEF measures the success or failure of efforts to serve the best interest of children. UNICEF advocates for parental education and psycho-social counselling initiatives in all of its country programmes in order to assist child development and build capacities that will facilitate re-attachment to families and communities. It has been an active partner, providing financial and technical support to NGOs like Save the Children and governments to implement DDR programmes with a particular focus on child soldiers.[44]

---

43 Tonheim, M and Odden G, Former Girl Soldiers in Congo: The Bumpy Road Towards Reintegration, 2013.

44 Legrand, J. C., Lessons Learned from UN ICEF Field Programs For the Prevention of Recruitment, Demobilization, and Reintegration of Child Soldiers, 1999.

A large number of children have been released through DDR programmes in conflict-affected countries including Afghanistan, Angola, Burundi, the Central African Republic, Colombia, the DRC, Liberia, Sierra Leone and Sudan. Angola's demobilization exercise, which lasted from 1995 to 1997, was one of the most extensive in the history of the United Nations. It was perhaps the first time that children were specifically included in a peace process. Elsewhere, for example in Nepal and Sri Lanka, large-scale recruitment of children effectively ceased with the end of hostilities, although the DDR programme was not fully successful due to various internal political reasons.[45]While DDR programmes and funding for them are generally short-term, successful reintegration is a long-term exercise which needs to be linked to longer-term recovery and reconstruction programmes. The root causes of recruitment in each given context must be addressed and a greater emphasis placed on prevention in order to break cycles of recruitment and re-recruitment of child soldiers.

The United Nations Mission in Sierra Leone (UNAMSIL) was successful in disarming more than 75,000 combatants, including 6,845 child soldiers (506 girls). The success of the DDR programme prompted the World Bank office in Sierra Leone to observe that officials from neighbouring countries and even the Great Lakes region were visiting Sierra Leone because it "is considered as the best practice example throughout the world of a successful DDR programme". The World Bank and UNDP, along with the Government of Sierra Leone, worked closely with UNAMSIL in planning, funding and implementing DDR.[46]

---

45 In Sri Lanka, the continued efforts since the late 1990s to bring an end to recruitment and use of underage children by the Liberation Tigers of Tamil Eelam (LTTE) resulted in a series of commitments by the LTTE and led to the release of hundreds of children over the years and also reduced the rates of child recruitment. However, as of the end of January 2009, there were over 1,400 children in the LTTE ranks (due to underreporting it is likely that the actual figure was significantly higher). During the final months of the conflict between January and May 2009, there was a renewed and massive wave of forced recruitment of children by the LTTE. The new recruits received minimal training and many are believed to have been among the thousands of casualties in the final weeks of the war. Also see:Bleie Tone and Ramesh Shrestha, DDR in Nepal: Stakeholder Politics and the Implications for Reintegration as a Process of Disengagement, Centre for Peace Studies – University of Troms, 2012, pp. 56.

46 United Nations Mission in Sierra Leone (UNAMSIL), Fact Sheet 1, Disarmament, Demobilization and Reintegration, December 2005.

Changing Nature of DDR

Over the years, the scale, complexity and scope of DDR programmes have grown and the number of people counted as 'combatants' eligible for DDR benefits has increased. During the First Global DDR Summit held in Colombia in 2013, the involvement of municipal and regional authorities was discussed by the launch of the African Union's DDR capacity building programme (AU DDRCP). In 2015 a joint UN Department of Peacekeeping Operations (UNDPKO) and UN University policy research platform, called 'Building New DDR Solutions' which focuses on the strategic challenges that DDR programmes face in dealing, for example, with radicalization and violent extremism was discussed. In response to the shifting anatomy of armed conflict, the DDR concept has increasingly been reconfigured to deal with (i) armed groups while conflict is ongoing and without a negotiated peace accord being in place, and (ii) situations of armed conflict that involve hybrid forms of violence as well as a range of armed actors that control or influence significantly, populations and territories, without being part of peace negotiations or under direct state control. These second generation DDR programmes include initiatives that aim specifically at disarming and dismantling militias (DDM), transforming and providing exit options for at-risk youth and gangs, and developing alternative approaches to disarmament and control of unregulated weapons, such as the 'flexible sequencing' of DDR in which reintegration precedes demobilization and disarmament (RDD).[47] The 'second generation' DDR engages a much broader range of templates for violence reduction than traditional DDR.

The key to a successful DDR process remains family and community acceptance and reconciliation and psycho-social support that is reflective of local social and cultural practices. Sensitization and awareness campaigns are important in helping local communities better understand the conditions in which child soldiers lived. The major challenges to an effective DDR programme could be corruption, disruption by armed groups, insufficient funding of education and other skill-oriented training schemes for ex-child soldiers. This may de-motivate the children especially when they know that they would return home to depend on families affected by conflict and/

---

47 FranziskaSeethaler, Assessing the Impact of DDR Programmes: Possibilities and Challenges, United Nations University Office in New York, Policy Brief - March 2016; Munive, J. and Stepputat, F., Rethinking Disarmament, Demobilization and Reintegration Program, Stability: International Journal of Security and Development, Vol. 4(1), 2015, available at: http://www.stabilityjournal.org/articles/10.5334/sta.go/, accessed 17 April 2017.

or displacement and unable to meet their expenses. The lack of long- term planning has been partly responsible for the failure of the reintegration of former child soldiers in the DRC and some other places.

C: The ICRC and Child Soldiers

The International Committee of the Red Cross (ICRC)[48], an independent, neutral and impartial international organization, helps children in general. According to the ICRC, children who have been recruited by armed forces or armed groups and are accused of having committed domestic or international crimes during armed conflicts should be treated first and foremost as victims.[49] As far as child soldiers are concerned, the ICRC works at each of the following stages: (i) before and during the conflict, to prevent the recruitment of children into armed forces or groups and to protect child soldiers in detention; (ii) after the conflict, to support the rehabilitation of former child soldiers; and (iii) at any time, to reunite children with their families.

The ICRC is the guardian of IHL and has a responsibility to promote and help develop it. It spreads knowledge of IHL and human rights laws, encourages States to comply with their treaty obligations. Specifically, the ICRC helps to prevent the enlistment of child soldiers in two ways: through its standard-setting activities and through its operations in the field. It reminds States and armed groups of their obligations under IHL. The organization's Advisory Service provides necessary assistance to States to draw up national laws to implement humanitarian law and supports them in enforcing the CRC and its Optional Protocol. In the training of armed forces in IHL, the ICRC pays special attention to emphasizing obligations relating to child protection and welfare. Both Geneva Conventions and their Additional Protocols prohibit the imposition of the death penalty for children younger than 18 at the time the offence is committed.

Children separated from parents, refugees and internally displace persons (IDPs) are more vulnerable than those living with their families under normal

---

48 According to the ICRC mission statement, the overall humanitarian mission of the institution, as an "impartial, neutral and independent organization" rooted in IHL, is "to protect the lives and dignity of victims of armed conflict and other situations of violence and to provide them with assistance". The ICRC is part of the International Red Cross and Red Crescent Movement.

49 Children and Detention, International Committee of the Red Cross, Geneva, November 2014, p. 7.

circumstances, and hence, more at risk of being recruited into armed forces or groups. The ICRC endeavours to ensure that family members are kept together and, when they are separated by conflict, tries to reunite them. It works to ensure the protection of children separated from their parents or care-givers by identifying them and placing them in the temporary custody of an adult or an institution where they will be cared for. It searches for and, if possible, restores contact between children and their relatives until they can be reunited. In 2016, the ICRC reunited 2000 children and their families, almost half of them being demobilized child soldiers. At the end of 2016, some 8,000 cases were still pending, including about 600 demobilized children.[50] The ICRC also tries to monitor the situation of demobilized children after they have been reunited with their families.[51]

The Council of Delegates of the International Red Cross and Red Crescent Movement (representing the ICRC, the International Federation of Red Cross and Red Crescent Societies and the National Red Cross and Red Crescent Societies) has undertaken to promote the principle of non-recruitment and non-participation in armed conflict of persons under the age of 18 years and to take action to protect and assist child victims of conflict. It has also committed itself to work for the welfare and the well-being of children affected by armed conflict.

According to the ICRC, former child soldiers must be reintroduced into the educational system and helped to find employment through vocational training or income-generating projects. This is crucial for preventing their becoming marginalized, which often leads to their being recruited again.[52]The first priority is to try to reunite children with their families and home communities. Many such communities might be living in poverty, thus the reintegration of such children may require financial support from international organizations. Former child soldiers may project an image of violence and fear which can make it impossible for the family and community to accept them. In such cases, appropriate measures must be taken, which

---

50 Text of speech delivered in Paris on 6 February 2007 by Alain A., head of protection activities at the ICRC, on the occasion of the conference "Free Children From War" organized by UNICEF and the French Ministry of Foreign Affairs. Available at: https://www.icrc.org/eng/resources/documents/statement/children-statement-060207.htm, accessed 10 April 2017.

51 Annual Report 2015, ICRC, Geneva.

52 Children in War, International Committee of the Red Cross, Geneva, November 2009, p.11.

may include medical and psychological care.

The ICRC holds that the States that are not party to the conflict also share responsibility for securing respect for IHL. The same is true of the media, international NGOs, the UN system, as well as international courts and other international institutions and mechanisms. The ICRC regularly makes approaches to armed groups and to government authorities and forces on the basis of its contacts with the families of children who are separated or recruited, information obtained in other ways and its own monitoring exercises. Due to its neutrality and impartiality, it often has access to armed groups with whom few or no other actors have contact. The ICRC constantly reminds armed forces and groups of their obligations and of the ban on the recruitment of child soldiers. It not only stresses that it is illegal to recruit child soldiers, but emphasizes that children associated with such forces/ groups retain certain rights and are entitled to protection. This includes the right not to be ill-treated or sexually abused and to receive the requisite food and care.[53]

D: Children, Not Soldiers Campaign

Most states now restrict military enlistment to persons who have attained the age of eighteen. However, some of them directly or indirectly encourage the recruitment of children through their support of proxy armed groups.[54]Others while not formally recruiting children in their armed forces, use them in military-related activities. For instance, in Colombia, Israel and Syria, children are not formally recruited, but have been reportedly used for military purposes including intelligence gathering and as human shields. In order to

---

53 Text of speech delivered in Paris on 6 February 2007 by Alain A., head of protection activities at the ICRC, on the occasion of the conference "Free Children From War" organized by UNICEF and the French Ministry of Foreign Affairs. Available at: https:// www.icrc.org/eng/resources/documents/statement/children-statement-060207.htm, accessed 10 April 2017.

54 Beyond their armed forces, states also bear responsibility for the actions of NSAGs allied to them. These groups can include irregular paramilitaries and "self-defence" militias. They may also include armed groups operating in other countries to which a state provides support. Such groups play a significant role in contemporary armed conflicts and it is common for them to have children in their ranks, often in significant numbers.It has been reported that 10 states were associated in such practices between January 2010 and June 2012. These are Chad, Cote d'Ivoire, the Democratic Republic of the Congo, Libya, Myanmar, Somalia, South Sudan, Sudan, United Kingdom and Yemen. *Louder Than Words: An agenda for Action to end state use of child soldiers*, Child Soldier International, 2012, p.11-12.

prevent the recruitment of children under the age of 18, it is necessary that the Optional Protocol to CRC be universally adopted.

In March 2014, the "Children, Not Soldiers" campaign was launched jointly by the Special Representative of the Secretary General for Children and Armed Conflict and UNICEF, with the aim of ending the recruitment and use of children by armed forces by 2016.[55]An action plan was negotiated between the governments of Afghanistan, Chad, the DRC, Myanmar, Somalia, South Sudan, Sudan, and Yemen and the UN to identify the key actions that the governments would take to prevent and stop the recruitment and use of children by the State forces.

As a result of the campaign, the governments of seven States have signed action plans to achieve the target.[56]The campaign was successful to a large measure in its first year. Chad completed all the reforms and measures included in its action plan and was taken off the UN Secretary-General's list of child recruiters. Over 400 children were released from the national army in Myanmar. There was only one case of child recruitment by the national army in the DRC in 2014 and the child was released. In Afghanistan, the recruitment of children declined in 2014, and only 5 cases were recorded by the UN. The Government of Sudan is currently negotiating an action plan to end and prevent child recruitment. However, because of the deterioration

---

55 The "Children, Not Soldiers" campaign opened the door to constructive dialogue with governments and other parties to conflict on protecting children and women, as well as to press them toward compliance with international child rights standards. In order to achieve the goals of the campaign and strengthen child protection in diverse country contexts a broad inter-agency partnership is essential, including the Office of the Special Representative of the Secretary-General for Children and Armed Conflict, UNICEF, the Department of Peacekeeping Operations (DPKO), the Department of Political Affairs (DPA), Office of the United Nations High Commissioner for Human Rights and the International Labour Organization, in close collaboration with relevant Member States, other United Nations agencies and NGOs, as well as communities, families and children, themselves.

56 These Action Plans vary between countries, but according to the UN website, common steps include: (i) Criminalizing the recruitment and use of children by armed forces; (ii) Issuing a military order to stop and prevent child recruitment; (iii) Investigating and prosecuting those who recruit and use children; (iv) Appointing child protection specialists in security forces; (v) Releasing all children identified in the ranks of security forces; (vi) Providing regular, unimpeded access to military camps and bases so child protection actors can verify that no children are in the ranks; (vii) Providing reintegration programmes for children; (viii) Strengthening birth registration systems and integrating age-verification mechanisms in recruitment procedures; and (ix) Implementing national campaigns to raise awareness and to prevent the recruitment of children.

in the situation in South Sudan and Yemen, these governments were unable to implement their action plans. Though the focus of the campaign has been on government forces, 16 NSAGs in the CAR, Darfur, Mali, South Sudan and Syria have also committed to take measures regarding violations against children and launched internal sensitization campaigns on the protection of children, particularly in relation to the prohibition of their recruitment and use.

Despite the fact that considerable progress has been made towards ending the recruitment and use of children in conflict in the last 30 years,[57] tens of thousands of boys and girls under the age of 18 are still being recruited and used in conflicts worldwide. In South Sudan alone, 16,000 children have been recruited and used by the armed forces and groups since the start of the conflict in 2013. In Yemen, all parties to the armed conflict have engaged in the widespread recruitment of children. The situation is worst in Syria, where the IS has been actively involved in large-scale radicalization and use of children in armed conflict.

A large number of children alleged to be associated with armed groups are being arrested and detained, deprived of their liberty and treated as security threats. This can have a profoundly negative impact on their long-term physical, emotional and cognitive development. International humanitarian law requires that children deprived of liberty must be afforded special protection and treatment in keeping with their age. In particular, they must be held separate from adults, except in those cases when an entire family is detained as a unit.

The Optional Protocol to the CRC on the involvement of Children in Armed Conflict requires States to ensure that children under 18 are not compulsorily recruited into their armed forces. It also forbids anyone under 18 to participate in hostilities. States are required to take all feasible measures to prevent the recruitment and use of children under the age of 18 by NSAGs. Only 166 countries have ratified the Protocol. On 25 September 2015, countries have adopted a set of goals (Sustainable Development Goals) to end poverty, protect the planet and ensure prosperity for all as part of a new development agenda. They also agreed to end the recruitment and use of child soldiers and fulfil the provisions of the Optional Protocol to the CRC. Specifically, Target 8.7 compels the States to take immediate and effective

---

57 The report by Graca Machel, "Impact of armed conflict on children" was published on 26 August 1996, highlighting for the first time the plight of children in armed conflict.

measures to "secure the prohibition and elimination of the worst forms of child labour, including the recruitment and use of child soldiers, and by 2025 end child labour in all its forms".

Various nations have taken their own actions to prevent the recruitment and use of child soldiers. For instance, Australia, Belgium, Germany and Sri Lanka[58] among others, have introduced domestic laws that make anyone involved in recruiting or using child soldiers under 15 criminally liable. However, two permanent members of the Security Council, the UK and the USA seem to hold a different opinion. The US has been financially assisting and supporting countries involved in the recruitment and the use of child soldiers, while in the UK a person can enrol in the military forces at the age of 16.[59]

The US Child Soldiers Prevention Act, 2008 prohibits military assistance to governments that recruit or use child soldiers, or support militias or paramilitaries that use child soldiers. The only way to circumvent this restriction is for the President to waive this ban on the ground of national interest. In the last seven years, the US President has granted waivers to a number of countries where the recruitment and use of child soldiers has been reported.[60] For example, Syrian rebel groups, supported by the US and other

---

58 Sri Lanka abides by the articles of the Convention on the Rights of the Child. Accordingly, all recruitment to the Sri Lankan Armed Forces is voluntary and between the ages of 18 and 22 at the time of enlistment. The Penal Code (Amendment) Act No 16 of 2006 relating to the prohibition on the recruitment of children as combatants was enacted in Parliament on 1 January 2006. Under this Act, engaging or recruiting children for use in armed conflict is now recognized as an offence. Any person convicted of this offence shall be liable to imprisonment of either description for a term not exceeding 30 years and to a fine.

59 The UK and Belarus are the only countries in Europe which still allow recruitment from age 16. The army in the UK accepts applications from children aged 15 years and 7 months.

60 For instance, Iraq appeared on the US Child Soldiers Prevention Act list for the first time in 2016, and immediately received a full waiver, allowing the authorization of an estimated $150 million in foreign military financing (FMF). FMF enables recipients to purchase US defence articles, services, and training, and is used primarily to fund arms transfers. The US has provided full or partial waivers for Somalia for each of the last four years. Between fiscal year 2011 and fiscal year 2015, the US authorized nearly $20 million in direct commercial arms sales to Somalia. In Financial Year (FY) 2015, it authorized nearly $13 million in "Section 1206" assistance, which is used to train and equip forces for counter-terrorism operations. South Sudan received a full waiver in 2012 and 2013, and partial waivers in 2014, 2015, and 2016. The assistance authorized through the waivers included over $20 million in arms sales in FY 2013. Until the Houthi overthrow of the Yemeni government,

western countries, have been found to have used children in various roles, most notably as snipers and suicide bombers.[61]

The US armed services regularly target children under 17 for military recruitment in violation of the terms of the Optional Protocol to the CRC. The US also fails to accord basic protections to former child soldiers from other countries. Omar Khadr, for example, was in the custody of the Department of Defence since he was 15 years old. The US detained the alleged child soldier at Guantánamo for a period of prolonged pretrial detention without charge; denied him access to legal counsel for over two years; reportedly subjected him to torture and other cruel, inhuman and degrading treatment; and denied him independent psychological assessment and treatment.[62] If the US President is to assert leadership on human rights issues, it is necessary that the US join the rest of the world in ratifying the CRC.

The British armed forces recruited 2,250 persons under the age of 18 in the year 2015-2016. Of these, nearly 1,800 were enlisted for the army to make up for shortfalls in the infantry.[63] In a recent article, researchers have debated whether enlisting persons below the age of 18 in the armed forces in counterproductive. According to the report, while there is no evidence that early enlistment brings benefits that later enlistment cannot, there is evidence

---

the US provided full waivers for Yemen for five consecutive years (2010-2014). As a result, more than $236 million in military assistance (primarily foreign military financing, excess defense articles, and counter-terrorism assistance) and more than $84 million in arms sales was authorized since FY2011. Filip Andrada, Humanity First – Children Not Soldiers, 20 October 2016. Available at: http://www.hscentre.org/policy-unit/humanity-first-children-soldiers/, accessed 12 April 2017.

61 Lawrence Fraser, Addressing the Issue of Child Soldiers, The Organization for World Peace, 17 January 2017, available at: https://theowp.org/reports/addressing-the-issue-of-child-soldiers/, accessed 10 March 2017.

62 Soldiers of Misfortune, US Violation of the Optional Protocol on the Involvement of Children in Armed Conflict, American Civil Liberty Union, pp. 48.

63 The British Army's recruitment policies state that it uses recruitment of minors as *an opportunity to mitigate Standard Entry [adult] shortfalls, particularly for the Infantry*. The Infantry has the highest fatality and injury rate of any major branch of the armed forces, with infantrymen in Afghanistan seven times more likely to be killed than personnel in the rest of the British armed forces. Army policy also imposes a longer minimum service period on those who enlist under age 18 than on adult recruits. British Army Increases Recruitment of Children, 25 November 2016, available at: http://vfpuk.org/2016/british-army-increases-recruitment-of-children/. Also see: Ministry of Defence, *UK armed forces biannual diversity statistics 2016*, 1 October 2016.

that the policy carries substantial risks of detriment to young people.[64] Recruiting children aged 16 and 17 into the army places them at greater risk of death, injury and long-term mental health problems than those recruited as adults. Child recruits are more vulnerable to mental health problems such as alcohol abuse, suicide, self-harm, post-traumatic stress disorder than adult recruits.[65]In recent years, former child soldiers and those affected by conflict have shared their stories publicly.[66]

The rules of IHL recognize the vulnerability of children in armed conflict and establish a series of rules aiming to protect children in armed conflict. However, the special protection afforded to children under IHL does not adequately recognize their involvement in armed conflict. The Arms Trade Treaty of 2014, however, has a strong potential to prevent the unlawful recruitment of children or their use in armed conflict. The widespread acceptance of an international norm prohibiting the recruitment and use of child soldiers shows the customary nature of the prohibition and the universal need to uphold the obligation to prevent the use of child soldiers.[67]

A number of NGOs have played prominent roles in the prevention and protection of child soldiers throughout the world. The leading organizations are Amnesty International, Human Rights Watch, Defence for Children International, International Save the Children Alliance, Jesuit Refugee Service,

---

64 Gee David and Taylor Rachel, Is it Counterproductive to Enlist Minors into the Army? *The RUSI Journal*, Vol. 161, No. 6, 2016, p. 39.

65 Rhianna Louise, Christina Hunter and Sally Zlotowitz, The Recruitment of Children by the UK Armed Forces: A Critique from Health Professionals, Medact, London, 2016, pp. 20; Hill Amelia, Under-18s in army 'face greater injury, death and mental health risks', 18 October 2016, available at; https://www.theguardian.com/uk-news/2016/oct/18/under-18s-in-army-face-greater-injury-death-and-mental-health-risks, accessed 19 April 2017.

66 For example, Romeo Dallaire penned *They Fought Like Soldiers, They Die Like Children* and Emmanuel Jal wrote *War Child: A Child Soldier's Story* about his experience in Sudan and South Sudan; Hamse Warfa wrote *America Here I Come: A Somali Refugee's Quest for Hope* about his upbringing in Somalia; and Ishmael Beah authored *A Long Way Gone: Memoirs of a Boy Soldier* about his childhood during the Sierra Leone Civil War. The film "A Good Lie" portrayed the true story of four orphaned Sudanese children and their journey through the Second Sudanese Civil War to the United States.

67 The Special Court for Sierra Leone (SCSL) has held in the *Norman* case that the widespread recognition and acceptance of the norm prohibiting child recruitment in AP II and the CRC provides compelling evidence that the conventional norm entered customary international law. Special Court for Sierra Leone, *Prosecutor against Sam Hinga Norman*, Case No. SCSL-2004-14-AR72(E), Decision on preliminary motion based on lack of jurisdiction (child recruitment) (appeals chamber), 31 May 2004, page 7396, paragraph 20.

the Quaker United Nations Office in Geneva, International Federation Terre des Hommes, and World Vision International. In 1998, these organizations formed the "Coalition to Stop the Use of Child Soldiers". Over the years, a global network of interested NGOs, aid agencies, research institutes, and other linked coalitions was built to fight against the use of child soldiers. This resulted in a series of regional agreements being adopted for the protection of child soldiers. [68]

Recommendations

The following recommendations addressed to the United Nations, the international community and the governments of States may serve as future guidelines to protect children in situations of armed conflict.

The United Nations

The United Nations should strive for universal ratification of the Optional Protocol to the CRC on the Involvement of Children in Armed Conflict. The UN agencies must ensure the involvement of families and communities in the DDR process of former child soldiers. Gender sensitive rehabilitation and reintegration initiatives must be developed for girls affected by sexual exploitation and violence and these should be implemented by well-trained staff. UNICEF must provide sufficient economic support for the gender-specific, community-based, socio-economic rehabilitation and reintegration of children, which should include formal or informal education and vocational training. The UN must ensure that members of the peacekeeping forces guilty of any of the six grave offences against children are prosecuted by the national courts and the trial proceedings are made available for public scrutiny. Specific prohibitions should be established in international law to prevent the sale or transfer of arms and other forms of military assistance to States in which children are known to be, or may potentially be, unlawfully recruited or used in hostilities by the State armed forces.

---

68 These include the 1996 OAU Resolution on the Plight of African Children in Situation of Armed Conflicts; the 1997 Capetown Principles; the 1998 European Parliament Resolution on Child Soldiers; the 1999 Declaration by the Nordic Foreign Ministers Against the Use of Child Soldiers; the 1999 Berlin Declaration on the Use of Children as Soldiers; the 1999 Montevideo Declaration on the Use of Children as Soldiers; the 1999 Maputo Declaration on the Use of Children as Soldiers; the 2000 Organization of American States (OAS) Resolution on Children and Armed Conflict; and the 2001 Amman Declaration on the Use of Children as Soldiers.

International Community and NGOs

International NGOs should ensure effective monitoring and reporting of the recruitment and use of children in hostilities, and safeguard the rights of child victims and witnesses of such use by armed forces and NSAGs. NSAGs may consider that they are not amenable to any international legal standards relating to child soldiers as they are not signatories to these treaties. However, they must be reminded by the NGOs that they could be prosecuted as war criminals under the emerging international criminal law regime and sanctions could be used against them and their business interests.[69] To help girls used in conflict, the international community needs to respond not only to the direct challenge of preventing the use of children in conflict, but also to the pervasive problem of gender-based violence. There is a need for greater involvement of women to end the use of child soldiers. NGOs and donors should provide consistent and long-term funding for reintegration programmes for children affected by armed conflict, including healthcare, psychosocial support, education and vocational training.

The States

All States must criminalize the recruitment and use of children and spell out the consequences for offenders. Ideally there should be a blanket prohibition on both "direct" and "indirect" participation in order to protect children not only from deployment as combatants or in other frontline roles, but also from the dangers that can result from indirect participation. Investigations and prosecutions of child recruiters should be prioritized.[70]

---

69 The Security Council in 2005 established the mechanism to monitor and report on six 'grave violations' committed by states and NSAGs on children, one of them being 'recruiting and using child soldiers'. One of the consequences for NSAGs of committing these violations is to be listed in an Annex of the Report of the Secretary-General on children and armed conflict, which can lead to sanctions being imposed against such groups.90 In that context, the age limit of recruitment of children is set at 18 years old, as in the Optional Protocol to the Convention of the Rights of the Child, and not 15 years old, which is the standard required in Additional Protocols I and II.

70 In Sri Lanka, a former member of the Liberation Tigers of Tamil Eelam (LTTE) was y sentenced to life imprisonment for recruitment of child soldiers to fight during the civil war. In 2008, complaints were lodged with police against the former LTTE cadre K. Dasan for abducting children on several occasions for recruitment as child soldiers to fight the Sri Lankan armed forces. Dasan had also forcibly recruited his own daughter in the final phase of the war in 2009. At that time, police failed to arrest him as he was with the LTTE. Following his return to his home in Kilinochchi, the police had taken him into custody on a complaint made by his family and produced him in court for trial. The police produced

One of the most important tools for preventing child recruitment is universal birth registration, which makes it possible to assess the age of potential recruits. The States must provide facilities for birth registration at shelters for refugees IDPs. States that lack efficient political and administration structures should team up with NGOs and international organizations to gain expertise and technical assistance for specialist services to help former child soldiers.

The relationship between the proliferation of small arms and children's involvement in armed conflict is well established and obligations exist under the Optional Protocol to the CRC and other international treaties to prevent the transfer of arms to situations where human rights abuses occur. The States must ensure that their trade in or transfer of arms or other forms of military assistance does not contribute to the violation of human rights.

All persons associated with recruitment processes in the military and paramilitary forces should be fully aware of their obligations under international and domestic law, including in relation to the minimum age at which compulsory and voluntary recruitment is permitted. Age criteria and age verification procedures for recruitment should be included in basic training for military/ paramilitary recruiting authorities and be reflected in military instructions and guidelines. These instructions should specify the disciplinary sanctions applicable to those who fail to uphold them. Military recruiters should know what documentation constitutes proof of age and should be personally responsible for verifying the reliability of the identification document. A copy of the document should be placed on the file of every candidate for recruitment.

International standards on the administration of juvenile justice, as well as the protections contained in the CRC, must be applied to all children, without exception, including children detained under national security legislations. Member States need to uphold international standards on juvenile justice, with detention used only as a last resort and a guarantee that detained juveniles would be separated from detained adults. Child-friendly legal provisions and alternatives to detention must be introduced into the justice system to ensure the physical and psychological well-being of children exposed to armed conflict.

---

him in court to face trial. On 26 July 2017, the Vavuniya High Court found him guilty and sentenced him to life imprisonment under the Prevention of Terrorism Act (PTA). See: http://www.colombopage.com/archive_17B/Jul26_1501089741CH.php

Education is essential to prevent the recruitment and use of children in hostilities. The military use of schools in conflict affected countries must be stopped. Governments must implement the UNICEF Guidelines on Protecting Schools and Universities from Military Use during Armed Conflict and to endorse the Safe Schools Declaration. In areas where abduction or forced recruitment of children takes place, increased security at and near schools is needed to ensure that children can pursue their education in safety.

Protecting children in countries affected by armed conflict requires extensive work and a comprehensive approach. In the last 20 years, nearly 125,000 child soldiers have been released and reintegrated due to the efforts of the UN agencies, the international community and the States themselves. In order to achieve the complete eradication of child soldiers by 2021---the twenty-fifth anniversary of Graca Machel's ground breaking report, which helped to lay the foundation to address the issue of the impact of armed conflict on children—a broad inter-agency partnership is needed. The international community must take a positive stand to end the use of child soldiers and to hold to account those who brutalize children.

APPENDICES

A. The 1997 Cape Town Principles

Adopted at the symposium[1] on the Prevention of Recruitment of Children into the Armed Forces and on demobilization and Social Reintegration of Child Soldiers in Africa, 30 April 1997, Cape Town, South Africa

Definitions

"Child soldier" in this document means any person under 18 years of age who is part of any kind of regular or irregular armed force or armed group in any capacity, including but not limited to cooks, porters, messengers, and those accompanying such groups, other than purely as family members. It includes girls recruited for sexual purposes and forced marriage. It does not, therefore, only refer to a child who is carrying or has carried arms.

"Recruitment" encompasses compulsory, forced and voluntary recruitment into any kind of regular or irregular armed force or armed group.

"Demobilization" means the formal and controlled discharge of child soldiers from the army or from an armed group.

The term "psycho-social" underlines the close relationship between the psychological and social effects of armed conflict, the one type of effect continually influencing the other. By "psychological effects" is meant those experiences which affect emotions, behaviour, thoughts, memory and learning ability and how a situation may be perceived and understood. By "social effects" is meant how the diverse experiences of war alter people's relationships to each other, in that such experiences change people, but also through death, separation, estrangement and other losses. "Social" may be extended to include an economic dimension, many individuals and families

---

1   The purpose of the symposium was to bring together experts and partners to develop strategies for preventing recruitment of children --- in particular, for establishing 18 as the minimum age of recruitment --- and for demobilizing child soldiers and helping them reintegrate into society. The Cape Town Principles and Best Practices are the result of that symposium held during 27-30 April 1997. They recommend actions to be taken by governments and communities in affected countries to end this violation of children's rights.

becoming destitute through the material and economic devastation of war, thus losing their social status and place in their familiar social network.

Prevention of Child Recruitment

1.   A minimum age of 18 should be established for any person participation in hostilities and for recruitment in all forms into any armed forces or armed groups.

2.   Governments should adopt and ratify an Optional Protocol to the Convention on the Rights of the Child raising the minimum ages from 15 to 18.

3.   Governments should ratify and implement pertinent regional and international treaties and incorporate them into national law, namely:

    a.   The African Charter on the Rights and Welfare of the Child which upon entry into force will establish 18 as the minimum age for recruitment and participation;

    b.   The two Additional Protocols to the 1949 Geneva Conventions and the Convention on the Rights of the Child, which currently establish 15 as the minimum age for recruitment and participation.

4. Governments should adopt national legislation on voluntary and compulsory recruitment with a minimum age of 18 years and should establish proper recruitment procedures and the means to enforce them. Those responsible for illegally recruiting children should be brought to justice. These recruitment procedures must include:

    a.   Requirement of proof of age;

    b.   Safeguards against violations;

    c.   Dissemination of the standards to the military, especially the recruiters;

    d.   Publicization of the standards and safeguards to the civilian population, especially children at risk of recruitment and their families and those organizations working with them;

    e.   Where the government establishes, condones or arms

militias or other armed groups, including private security forces, it must also regulate recruitment into them.

5.   A permanent International Criminal Court should be established whose jurisdiction would cover, inter alia, the illegal recruitment of children.

6.   Written agreements between or with all parties to the conflict which include a commitment on the minimum age of recruitment should be concluded. The SPLM/Operation Lifeline Sudan Agreement on Ground Rules (July 1995) is a useful example.

7.   Monitoring, documentation and advocacy are fundamental to eliminating child recruitment and to informing programmes to this end. Community efforts to prevent recruitment should be developed and supported.

   a.   Local human rights organisations, the media, former child soldiers, and teachers, health workers, church leaders and other community leaders can play an important advocacy role.

   b.   Establish a dialogue between government and communities in which children are regarded as adults before the age of 18 about the importance of the 18-year limit for recruitment.

   c.   Provide children with alternative models to the glorification of war, including in the media;

   d.   Government representatives, military personnel and former opposition leaders can be instrumental in advocating, negotiating and providing technical assistance to their counterparts in other countries in relation to the prevention of recruitment of child soldiers, as well as their demobilization and reintegration.

8.   Programmes to prevent recruitment of children should be developed in response to the expressed needs and aspirations of the children.

9.   In programmes for children, particular attention should be paid to those most at risk of recruitment: children in conflict zones, children (especially adolescents) separated from or without families, including

children in institutions; other marginalized groups (e.g. street children, certain minorities, refugees and the internally displaced); economically and socially deprived children.

a.   Risk mapping can be helpful to identify the groups at risk in particular situations, including such issues as areas of concentration of fighting, the age and type of children being militarized and the main agents of militarization;

b.   Promote respect for international humanitarian law;

c.   To reduce volunteerism into opposing armed forces, avoid harassment of or attacks on children, their homes and families;

d.   Monitor recruitment practices and put pressure on recruiters to abide by the standards and to avoid forced recruitment.

10.   All efforts should be made to keep or reunite children with their families or to place them within a family structure. This can be done for example through warnings (e.g. by radio or posters) of the need to avoid separation, or through attaching identification to young children, except where this would expose them to additional risk. For further ideas, see "Unaccompanied Minors: Priority Action Handbook for UNICEF/UNHCR Field Staff".

11.   Ensure birth registration, including for refugees and internally displaced children, and the provision of identity documents to all children, particularly those most at risk of recruitment.

12.   Access to education, including secondary education and vocational training, should be promoted for all children, including refugee and internally displaced children. Adequate economic provision or opportunities also need to be considered for children or their families.

13.   Special protection measures are needed to prevent recruitment of children in camps for refugees and internally displaced persons.

a.   Refugee camps should be established at a reasonable distance from the border, wherever possible;

b.   The civilian nature and humanitarian character of camps for refugees and internally displaced persons should be ensured. Where this is a problem, specific educational and vocational programmes for children, including adolescents, are even more critical;

c.   Host governments, if necessary with the assistance of the international community, should prevent the infiltration of armed elements into camps for refugees and internally displaced persons, and provide physical protection to persons in such camps.

14.   The international community should recognize that children who leave their country of origin to avoid illegal recruitment or participation in hostilities are in need of international protection. Children who are not nationals of the country in which they are fighting are also in need of international protection.

15.   Controls should be imposed on the manufacture and transfer of arms, especially small arms. No arms should be supplied to parties to an armed conflict who are recruiting children or allowing them to take part in hostilities.

Demobilization

16.   All persons under the age of 18 should be demobilized from any kind of regular or irregular armed force or armed group. Direct and free access to all child soldiers should be granted to relevant authorities or organizations in charge of collecting information concerning their demobilization and of implementing specific programmes.

17.   Children should be given priority in any demobilization process.

18.   In anticipation of peace negotiations or as soon as they begin, preparations should be made to respond to children who will be demobilized.

a.   Prepare initial situation analysis/needs assessment of children and their communities;

b.   Ensure coordination between all parties to avoid duplication and gaps;

c. Where there is access to governmental and other local structures, incorporate and (where necessary) strengthen existing capacities to respond;

d. Ensure training of staff who will be involved in the process;

e. Organize logistical and technical support in collaboration with agencies responsible for the formal demobilization process;

f. Ensure that the demobilization package is of a long-term, sustaining nature rather than in the form of an immediate "reward", taking into account the implications of the nature of the package for future recruitment of children.

19. The issue of demobilization of children should be included in the peace process from the beginning.

20. Where children have participated in armed conflict, peace agreements and related documents should acknowledge this fact.

21. The demobilization process should be designed as the first step in the social reintegration process.

22. The demobilization process should be as short as possible and take into account the human dignity of the child and the need for confidentiality.

a. Ensure adequate time and appropriate personnel to make children feel secure and comfortable so that they are able to receive information, including about their rights, and to share concerns;

b. Wherever possible, staff dealing with the children should be nationals;

c. Special measures must be taken to ensure the protection of children who are in demobilization centres for extended periods of time;

d. Children should be interviewed individually and away from their superiors and peers;

e. It is not appropriate to raise sensitive issues in the initial interview. If they are raised subsequently, it must be done only when in the best interest of the child and by a competent person;

f.   Confidentiality must be respected;

g.   All children should be informed throughout the process of the reasons why the information is being collected and that confidentiality will be respected. Children should be further informed about what will happen to them at each step of the process;

h.   Wherever possible, communication and information should be in the mother tongue of the children;

i.   Particular attention should be paid to the special needs of girls and special responses should be developed to this end.

23.   Family tracing, contacts and reunification should be established as soon as possible.

24.   Priority should be given to health assessment and treatment.

a.   As soon as possible during the demobilization process, all children should undergo assessment of their physical health and receive treatment as necessary;

b.   Particular responses should be developed for girls;

c.   Particular responses are needed for children with special needs, e.g. children with disabilities, child soldiers with children of their own, children with substance abuse problems and sexually-transmitted diseases (HIV/AIDS, etc,);

d.   Ensure linkages between the demobilization process and existing programmes which are competent to deal with the health needs of children.

25.   Monitoring and documentation of child involvement, as well as advocacy for demobilization and release of children, should be undertaken throughout the armed conflict. Community efforts to this end should be supported.

26.   Children who leave any armed forces or groups during on-going hostilities have special needs for protection which must be addressed. During on-going hostilities there is rarely any formal demobilization. However, children may leave the army, for example by escaping or as a result of being captured or wounded. This may compromise their security, protection and access to services. Despite difficulties in identifying such children, there must be recognition of their special needs for protection:

a.   Efforts should be made for an early start to programmes and family tracing for unaccompanied children;

b.   Efforts should be made to ensure that re-recruitment does not occur. The likelihood of re-recruitment can be reduced if: (i) children are returned to their care-givers as soon as possible; (ii) children are informed of their rights not to be recruited; and (iii) where children have been formally demobilized, others are informed of this fact;

c.   Any assembly areas must be sufficiently far from the conflict zones to ensure security. Particular problems may include: (i) some children may not be able to go home; (ii) some areas may be inaccessible for tracing; (iii) families of some children may be in camps for refugees or internally displaced persons; and (iv) the risk of the children being placed in institutions.

27.   Illegally recruited children who leave the armed forces or armed groups at any time should not be considered as deserters. Child soldiers retain their rights as children.

28.   Special assistance and protection measures must be taken on behalf of children and those recruited as children. See for example "Basic Rights Recognized For the Angolan Under-aged Soldiers".

29.   Ensure to the extent possible that demobilized children return to their communities under conditions of safety.

30.   Ensure that demobilized children are not discriminated against in services and benefits for demobilized soldiers.

31.   Ensure that the rights of children involved in the demobilization process are respected by the media, researchers and others. With specific regard to journalists, a code of conduct should be developed in order to prevent the exploitation of child soldiers by the media. Such a code should take account of inter alia the manner in which sensitive issues are raised, the child's right to anonymity and the frequency of contacts with the media.

Return to family and Community Life

32.   Family reunification is the principal factor in effective social reintegration.

  a. For family reunification to be successful, special attention must be paid to re-establishing the emotional link between the child and the family prior to and following return;

  b. Where children have not been reunited with their family, their need to establish and maintain stable emotional relationships must be recognized;

  c. Institutionalization should only be used as a last resort, for the shortest possible time, and efforts to find family-based solutions should continue.

33.   Programmes should be developed with the communities, built on existing resources, taking account of the context and community priorities, values and traditions.

  a. Programmes responding to the needs of the children should be developed. They should seek to enhance the self-esteem of children, promote their capacity to protect their own integrity and to construct a positive life. Activities must take into account the age and stage of development of the child and accommodate the particular requirements of girls and children with special needs;

  b. Programmes can only develop through relationships of trust and confidence, require time and a commitment of resources, and will necessitate a close and on-going cooperation between all actors involved;

c.   The impact of the conflict on children and their families must be assessed in order to develop effective programming. This should be undertaken through interviews and discussions with the children concerned, the families and the community as well as, where appropriate, the government. The information should be gathered as early as possible to enable preparation and planning;

d.   Policies and strategies to address the situation of demobilized child soldiers should be developed and implemented on the basis of such assessments.

34.   The capacity of the family and community to care for and protect the child should be developed and supported.

a.   Identify and support traditional resources and practices in the community which can support the psycho-social integration of children affected by war;

b.   Assess and understand the socio-economic context with specific reference to poverty, and food and nutritional security;

c.   Identify and build on the traditional ways of generating income, traditional apprenticeships, credit and money-making schemes;

d.   Initiate dialogue with communities to understand their main concerns for their children and their perception of their own roles and responsibilities with regard to the children.

35.   Programmes targeted at former child soldiers should be integrated into programmes for the benefit of all war-affected children.

a.   Whilst stressing that it is essential to normalize the life of child soldiers, it is important to recognize that all children in a community will have been affected to some degree by the conflict. Programmes for former child soldiers should therefore be integrated into efforts to address the situation of all children affected by the conflict, while ensuring the continuing implementation of specific rights and benefits of demobilized children;

b.   The existing health, education and social services within the communities should be supported.

36.   Provision should be made for educational activities which reflect: the loss of educational opportunities as a consequence of participation; the age and stage of development of the children; and their potential for promoting development of self-esteem.

37.   Provision should be made for relevant vocational training and opportunities or (self-) employment, including for children with disabilities. Upon completion of vocational skills training, trainees should be provided with the relevant tools and, where possible, with start-up loans to promote self-reliance.

38.   Recreational activities are essential for psycho-social well-being. Recreational activities should be included in all reintegration programmes for war-affected children. These contribute to the children's psycho-social well-being, facilitate the reconciliation process and form part of their rights as children.

39.   Programme development and implementation should incorporate the participation of the children and, with due regard for the context of reintegration, reflect their needs and concerns.

40.   Psycho-social programmes should assist children to develop and build those capacities that will facilitate a re-attachment to families and communities.

41.   Monitoring and follow-up of the children should take place to ensure reintegration and receipt of rights and benefits. Use community resources for this, e.g. catechists, teachers or others, depending on the situation.

42.   In order to be successful, reintegration of the child within the community should be carried out in the framework of efforts towards national reconciliation.

43.   Programmes to prevent recruitment of child soldiers and to demobilize and reintegrate them should be jointly and constantly monitored and evaluated with communities

Cape Town, 30 April 1997.

B. The 2007 Paris Commitments to Protect Children from Unlawful Recruitment or Use by Armed Forces or Armed Groups

We,

Ministers and representatives of countries having gathered in Paris on 5 and 6 February 2007 to strongly reaffirm our collective concern at the plight of children affected by armed conflict, our recognition of the physical, developmental, emotional, mental, social and spiritual harm to children resulting from the violation of their rights during armed conflict, and our commitment to identifying and implementing lasting solutions to the problem of unlawful recruitment or use of children in armed conflict;

Recalling all the international instruments relevant to the prevention of recruitment or use of children in armed conflict, their protection and reintegration, and to the fight against impunity for violators of children's rights, as well as relevant regional instruments, as listed in the Annexe hereto, and in particular calling upon all States which have not done so yet to consider ratifying as a matter of priority the Convention on the Rights of the Child and the Optional Protocols thereto;

Recalling UN Security Council resolutions 1261 (1999), 1314 (2000), 1379 (2001), 1460 (2003), 1539 (2004) and 1612 (2005) which have repeatedly condemned and called for an end to the unlawful recruitment and use of children by parties to armed conflict contrary to international law, and led to the establishment of a Monitoring and Reporting mechanism and of a Working Group to address violations of children's rights committed in times of armed conflict;

Recalling the 1997 Cape Town principles ("Cape Town principles and best practices on the prevention of recruitment of children into the armed forces and on demobilization and social reintegration of child soldiers in Africa"), that have been helpful to guide decisions and actions taken to prevent the unlawful recruitment of children under 18 years of age into armed forces or groups, stop their use, secure their release, provide protection and support their reintegration or integration into family, community and civilian life;

Deeply concerned those girls continue to be largely invisible in programming and diplomatic initiatives regarding the unlawful recruitment and use of children by armed forces or groups and committed to reversing and redressing this imbalance;

Deeply concerned that the Millennium Development Goals of universal primary education and the development of decent and productive work for youth will not be reached as long as children continue to be unlawfully recruited or used in armed conflicts;

Recognizing that States bear the primary responsibility for providing security to and ensuring the protection of all children within their jurisdiction, that children's reintegration into civilian life is the ultimate goal of the process of securing their release from armed forces or groups, and that planning for reintegration should inform all stages of the process and should commence at the earliest possible stage;

We commit ourselves:

1. To spare no effort to end the unlawful recruitment or use of children by armed forces or groups in all regions of the world, i.e. through the ratification and implementation of all relevant international instruments and through international cooperation.

2. To make every effort to uphold and apply the Paris principles ("The Principles and Guidelines on Children Associated with Armed Forces or Armed Groups") wherever possible in our political, diplomatic, humanitarian, technical assistance and funding roles and consistent with our international obligations.

In particular we commit ourselves:

3. To ensure that conscription and enlistment procedures for recruitment into armed forces are established and that they comply with applicable international law, including the Optional Protocol to the Convention on the Rights of the Child on the involvement of children in armed conflict, and to establish mechanisms to ensure that age of entry requirements are fully respected and that responsibility for establishing the age of the recruit rests with the recruiting party.

4. To take all feasible measures, including legal and administrative measures, to prevent armed groups within the jurisdiction of our State

that are distinct from our armed forces from recruiting or using-children under 18 years of age in hostilities.

5. To adhere to the principle that the release of all children recruited or used unlawfully by armed forces or groups shall be sought un-conditionally at all times, including during armed conflict, and that actions to secure the release, protection and reintegration of such children should not be dependent on a cease-fire or peace agreement or on any release or demobilization process for adults.

6. To fight against impunity, and to effectively investigate and pros-ecute those persons who have unlawfully recruited children under 18 years of age into armed forces or groups, or used them to participate actively in hostilities, bearing in mind that peace or other agreements aiming to bring about an end to hostilities should not include am-nesty provisions for perpetrators of crimes under international law, including those committed against children.

7. To use all available means to support monitoring and reporting ef-forts at the national, regional and international levels on violations of child rights during armed conflict, including in relation to the unlawful recruitment or use of children, and in particular to support the monitoring and reporting mechanism established by Security Council resolutions 1539 and 1612.

8. To fully cooperate with the implementation of targeted measures taken by Security Council against parties to an armed conflict which unlawfully recruit or use children, such as, but not limited to, a ban on arms and equipment transfers or military assistance to these par-ties.

9. To take all necessary measures, including the elaboration of rules of engagement and standard operating procedures, and the training of all relevant personnel therein, to ensure that children recruited or used by enemy armed forces or groups who are deprived of their liberty are treated in accordance with international humanitarian law and human rights law, with special consideration for their status as children.

10. To ensure that all children under 18 years of age who are detained on criminal charges are treated in accordance with relevant international law and standards, including those provisions which are specifically

applicable to children; and that children who have been unlawfully recruited or used by armed forces are not considered as deserters under applicable domestic law.

11. To ensure that children under 18 years of age who are or who have been unlawfully recruited or used by armed forces or groups and are accused of crimes against international law are considered primarily as victims of violations against international law and not only as alleged perpetrators. They should be treated in accordance with international standards for juvenile justice, such as in a framework of restorative justice and social rehabilitation.

12. In line with the Convention on the Rights of the Child and other international standards for juvenile justice, to seek alternatives to judicial proceedings wherever appropriate and desirable, and to ensure that, where truth-seeking and reconciliation mechanisms are established, the involvement of children is supported and promoted, that measures are taken to protect the rights of children throughout the process, and in particular that children's participation is voluntary.

13. To ensure that children who are released from or have left armed forces or groups are not used for political purposes by any party, including political propaganda.

14. To ensure that children who cross international borders are treated in accordance with IHL and humanitarian and refugee law, and in particular, that children who flee to another country to escape unlawful recruitment or use by armed forces or armed groups can effectively exercise their right to seek asylum, that asylum procedures are age and gender-sensitive and that the refugee definition is interpreted in an age and gender-sensitive manner taking into account the particular forms of persecution experienced by girls and boys, including unlawful recruitment or use in armed conflict, and that no child is returned in any manner to the borders of a State where there is real risk of torture or cruel inhuman or degrading treatment or punishment or when that child is recognized as a Convention refugee according to the 1951 Refugee Convention, or of unlawful recruitment, re-recruitment or use by armed forces or groups, assessed on a case by case basis.

15. To ensure that children who are not in their state of nationality, including those recognized as refugees and granted asylum are fully

entitled to the enjoyment of their human rights on an equal basis with other children.

16. To advocate and seek for the inclusion in peace and ceasefire agreements by parties to armed conflicts that have unlawfully recruited or used children of minimum standards regarding the cessation of all recruitments, the registration, the release and the treatment thereafter of children, including provisions to meet the specific needs of girls and their children for protection and assistance.

17. To ensure that any programmes or actions conducted or funded to prevent unlawful recruitment or use of children and to support children unlawfully recruited or used by armed forces or groups are based on humanitarian principles, meet applicable minimum standards, and develop systems for accountability, including the adoption of a code of conduct on the protection of children and on sexual exploitation and abuse.

18. To ensure that armed forces or groups having unlawfully recruited or used children are not allowed to secure advantages during peace negotiations and security sector reforms, such as using the number of children in their ranks to increase their share of troop size in a power sharing agreement.

19. To ensure that any funding for child protection is made available as early as possible, including in the absence of any formal peace process and formal disarmament, demobilization and reintegration (DDR) planning, and to also ensure that funding remains available for the time required and for activities in communities benefiting a wide range of children affected by armed conflict in order to achieve full and effective integration or reintegration into civilian life.

20. In that context, we, Ministers and representatives of countries having gathered in Paris on 5 and 6 February 2007, welcome the update of the 1997 Cape Town principles, which will be a useful guide in our common efforts to respond to the plight of children affected by armed conflicts.

Annexure: The documents annexed to the Paris Commitment are:

(A)   International instruments: (i) The 1989 Convention on the Rights of the Child; (ii) The 2000 Optional Protocol to the Convention on the Rights of the Child on the involvement of children in armed conflict; (iii) The four Geneva Conventions of 1949 and their Additional Protocols of 1977; (iv) The 1951 Refugee Convention and its 1967 Protocol; (v) The 1999 ILO Worst Forms of Child Labour Convention 182; and (vi) The Rome Statute of the International Criminal Court.

(B)   Regional instruments and initiatives: (i) The 1999 African Charter on the Rights and Welfare of the Child, and the revised Arab Charter on Human Rights, which prohibits the exploitation of children in armed conflict; (ii) The Association of South East Asian Nations (ASEAN) Declaration on the Commitments for Children in ASEAN 2001; (iii) The adoption of "Guidelines on Children and Armed Conflict" by the European Union in 2003 and the Implementation Strategy for the Guidelines agreed in January 2006; (iv) Resolution 1904 of the Organisation of American States in 2002; and (v) The Cape Town Principles and best practices on the prevention of recruitment into the armed forces and on demobilization and social reintegration of child soldiers in Africa in 1997.

C. The Paris Principles

Principles and Guidelines on Children Associated with Armed Forces or Armed Groups

1. Introduction

1.0   Hundreds of thousands of children are associated with armed forces and armed groups in conflicts around the world. Girls and boys are used in a variety of ways from support roles, such as cooking or portering, to active fighting, laying mines or spying and girls are frequently used for sexual purposes. This recruitment and use of children violates their rights and causes them physical, developmental, emotional, mental, and spiritual harm.

1.1 The recruitment and use of children by armed forces and armed groups has been a focus of international attention and has been widely condemned, yet children continue to be involved in adult wars and to become disabled or die in such conflicts. While the release and reintegration into civilian life of many of these children has been supported through interventions and programmes designed to assist them, others have returned home on their own, often to face an uncertain future and a further fight for acceptance from their family and community. Girls in particular are likely to be stigmatized and even rejected by their community if it is known that they have been used by an armed force or armed group and the rejection of their children may be even more severe. Other children are encouraged by their families and communities to participate in armed conflict, despite the danger and harm this involves. Despite their experiences, such children are resilient and can contribute constructively to reconstruction and reconciliation efforts if given appropriate help, support and encouragement.

Background to the principles

1.2 Almost a decade after they were agreed, UNICEF initiated a global review of the "Cape Town Principles and Best Practices on the Prevention of Recruitment of Children into the Armed Forces and on Demobilization and Social Reintegration of Child Soldiers in Africa" ("the Cape Town Principles"). Adopted in 1997, the Cape Town Principles were the result of a symposium organised by UNICEF and the NGO Working Group on the

Convention on the Rights on the Child to develop strategies for preventing recruitment of children, demobilising child soldiers and helping them to reintegrate into society. The Principles have obtained recognition well beyond this original group to become a key instrument to inform the development of international norms as well as shifts in policy at the national, regional and international levels.

1.3 The accumulated knowledge gained from wide ranging and diverse experience in this field since 1997 has led to a more community-based and inclusive approach. There is a growing awareness of the multiple dimensions of the use of children by armed forces or armed groups and the complexities of dealing with the problem and addressing root causes. Together with changes such as the inclusion of recruitment of children under 15 years as a war crime in the International Criminal Court Statute and the development of jurisprudence in this area, these factors prompted recognition of the need to update the Principles and to increase their endorsement beyond actors who specialize in children's rights.

1.4 An extensive review process was undertaken by UNICEF together with partners involving seven regional reviews, some including regional or sub-regional workshops, carried out in 2005 and 2006. This led to agreement on the need for two documents; the first a short and concise document – The Paris Commitments to Protect Children Unlawfully Recruited or Used by Armed Forces or Armed Groups (The Paris Commitments) and this second, complementary document

The Principles and Guidelines on Children Associated with Armed Forces or Armed Groups (The Paris Principles), which provide more detailed guidance for those who are implementing programmes. Drafting of the documents was carried out in consultation with a reference group representing a wide range of actors. Revisions were made to incorporate recommendations made during a meeting held in New York in October 2006 which brought together implementing organisations, experts and other interested parties from across the globe. Broad political endorsement from States for the Paris Commitments and Paris Principles at a ministerial meeting held in Paris in February 2007

Based on international law and standards and on the 1997 Cape Town Principles, the Paris Principles incorporates knowledge and lessons learned and in particular emphasize the informal ways in which boys and girls both become associated with and leave armed forces or armed groups. Taking a child rights-based approach to the problem of children associated with armed forces or armed groups, the Principles underscore the humanitarian imperative to seek the unconditional release of children from armed forces or armed groups at all times, even in the midst of conflict and for the duration of the conflict. The Principles recognize that, in situations of armed conflict, States and armed groups are the primary actors responsible for the protection of civilians in their effective control and that if they are unable or unwilling to meet all of their humanitarian responsibilities directly they are charged with enabling the provision of humanitarian action by impartial actors.

The Principles are based on the certain lessons drawn from global experience in implementing programmatic interventions to prevent recruitment, protect children, support their release from armed forces or armed groups and reintegrate them into civilian life. The lessons are: (i) The precise nature of the problem and the solution will vary according to the context. A situation analysis, including a gender analysis, should inform and guide all interventions; (ii) Any solution should address the needs of all children affected by armed conflict and incorporate activities to develop and support local capacity to provide a protective environment for children; (iii) The protective environment should incorporate measures to prevent discrimination against girls whose use in armed conflicts is pervasive yet often unrecognized and to promote their equal status in society; (iv) A long term commitment by all actors to prevent the unlawful recruitment or use of children, promote their release from armed forces or armed groups, protect them and support their reintegration is essential; and (v) The family including the extended family and clan and the community should be actively incorporated in the development and implementation of interventions and activities, and they in turn should participate in finding solutions.

For solutions to be sustainable, child protection needs to span humanitarian and development programmes, requiring a strategic, child-centred coordination between civil society, humanitarian/emergency, peacekeeping and development and reconstruction actors. In order to address the underlying causes of child recruitment, to address the fluid nature of most armed conflicts and to address the need to take action for children while conflict is still active, the preparation of an appropriate strategic response, supported by adequate funding, is required urgently as soon as children's unlawful recruitment or use by armed forces or armed groups is identified as a possibility and for the immediate, medium and long term. From the earliest possible stages, development actors should also involve themselves in strategies for the prevention of unlawful recruitment and the reintegration of children into civilian life.

The Paris Principles are designed to guide interventions for the protection and well-being of such children and to assist in making policy and programming decisions. The principles aim to guide interventions with the following objectives: (i) To prevent unlawful recruitment or use of children; (ii) To facilitate the release of children associated with armed forces and armed groups; (iii) To facilitate the reintegration of all children associated with armed forces and armed groups; and (iv) To ensure the most protective environment for all children. While it is recognized that no one set of 'best practice' applies in all contexts, these Principles are designed to provide a framework and bring together ideas and approaches which have been used successfully across the globe.

The Paris Principles, as well as the Paris Commitments, are also designed to assist States and donors in meeting their obligations and taking funding decisions. Effort has been made to ensure that the Principles are consistent with relevant international law, notably legislation related to the minimum age of recruitment. While recognizing that States have different obligations under international law, a majority of child protection actors will continue advocating for States to strive to raise the minimum age of recruitment or use to 18 in all circumstances.

D. The UN Convention on the Rights of Child, 1989

The Convention on the Rights of the Child (CRC) was adopted by the UN General Assembly on 20 November 1989, and it entered into force on 2 September 1990.

Article 1

For the purposes of the present Convention, a child means every human being below the age of 18 years unless, under the law applicable to the child, majority is attained earlier.

Article 38

1. States Parties undertake to respect and to ensure respect for rules of international humanitarian law applicable to them in armed conflicts which are relevant to the child.

2. States Parties shall take all feasible measures to ensure that persons who have not attained the age of 15 years do not take a direct part in hostilities.

3. States Parties shall refrain from recruiting any person who has not attained the age of 15 years into their armed forces. In recruiting among those persons who have attained the age of 15 years but who have not attained the age of 18 years, States Parties shall endeavour to give priority to those who are oldest.

4. In accordance with their obligations under international humanitarian law to protect the civilian population in armed conflicts, States Parties shall take all feasible measures to ensure protection and care of children who are affected by an armed conflict.

Article 39

States Parties shall take all appropriate measures to promote physical and psychological recovery and social reintegration of a child victim of: any form of neglect, exploitation, or abuse; torture or any other form of cruel, inhuman or degrading treatment or punishment; or armed conflicts. Such recovery and reintegration shall take place in an environment which fosters the health, self-respect and dignity of the child.

E. Optional Protocol to the Convention on the Rights of the Child on the Involvement of Children in Armed Conflict

(Entry into force 12 February 2002)

The States Parties to the present Protocol,

Encouraged by the overwhelming support for the Convention on the Rights of the Child, demonstrating the widespread commitment that exists to strive for the promotion and protection of the rights of the child,

Reaffirming that the rights of children require special protection, and calling for continuous improvement of the situation of children without distinction, as well as for their development and education in conditions of peace and security,

Disturbed by the harmful and widespread impact of armed conflict on children and the long-term consequences it has for durable peace, security and development,

Condemning the targeting of children in situations of armed conflict and direct attacks on objects protected under international law, including places that generally have a significant presence of children, such as schools and hospitals,

Noting the adoption of the Rome Statute of the International Criminal Court, in particular, the inclusion therein as a war crime, of conscripting or enlisting children under the age of 15 years or using them to participate actively in hostilities in both international and non-international armed conflict,

Considering therefore that to strengthen further the implementation of rights recognized in the Convention on the Rights of the Child there is a need to increase the protection of children from involvement in armed conflict,

Noting that article 1 of the Convention on the Rights of the Child specifies that, for the purposes of that Convention, a child means every human being below the age of 18 years unless, under the law applicable to the child, majority is attained earlier,

Convinced that an optional protocol to the Convention that raises the age of possible recruitment of persons into armed forces and their participation in hostilities will contribute effectively to the implementation of the principle that the best interests of the child are to be a primary consideration in all actions concerning children,

Noting that the twenty-sixth International Conference of the Red Cross and Red Crescent in December 1995 recommended, inter alia, that parties to conflict take every feasible step to ensure that children below the age of 18 years do not take part in hostilities,

Welcoming the unanimous adoption, in June 1999, of International Labour Organization Convention No. 182 on the Prohibition and Immediate Action for the Elimination of the Worst Forms of Child Labour; which prohibits, inter alia, forced or compulsory recruitment of children for use in armed conflict,

Condemning with the gravest concern the recruitment, training and use within and across national borders of children in hostilities by armed groups distinct from the armed forces of a State, and recognizing the responsibility of those who recruit, train and use children in this regard,

Recalling the obligation of each party to an armed conflict to abide by the provisions of international humanitarian law,

Stressing that the present Protocol is without prejudice to the purposes and principles contained in the Charter of the United Nations, including Article 51, and relevant norms of humanitarian law,

Bearing in mind that conditions of peace and security based on full respect of the purposes and principles contained in the Charter and observance of applicable human rights instruments are indispensable for the full protection of children, in particular during armed conflict and foreign occupation,

Recognizing the special needs of those children who are particularly vulnerable to recruitment or use in hostilities contrary to the present Protocol owing to their economic or social status or gender,

Mindful of the necessity of taking into consideration the economic, social and political root causes of the involvement of children in armed conflict,

Convinced of the need to strengthen international cooperation in the implementation of the present Protocol, as well as the physical and psychosocial rehabilitation and social reintegration of children who are victims of armed conflict,

Encouraging the participation of the community and, in particular, children and child victims in the dissemination of informational and educational programmes concerning the implementation of the Protocol,

Have agreed as follows:

Article 1

States Parties shall take all feasible measures to ensure that members of their armed forces who have not attained the age of 18 years do not take a direct part in hostilities.

Article 2

States Parties shall ensure that persons who have not attained the age of 18 years are not compulsorily recruited into their armed forces.

Article 3

1. States Parties shall raise the minimum age for the voluntary recruitment of persons into their national armed forces from that set out in article 38, paragraph 3, of the Convention on the Rights of the Child, taking account of the principles contained in that article and recognizing that under the Convention persons under the age of 18 years are entitled to special protection.

2. Each State Party shall deposit a binding declaration upon ratification of or accession to the present Protocol that sets forth the minimum age at which it will permit voluntary recruitment into its national armed forces and a description of the safeguards it has adopted to ensure that such recruitment is not forced or coerced.

3. States Parties that permit voluntary recruitment into their national armed forces under the age of 18 years shall maintain safeguards to ensure, as a minimum, that:

(a) Such recruitment is genuinely voluntary;

(b) Such recruitment is carried out with the informed consent of the person's parents or legal guardians;

(c) Such persons are fully informed of the duties involved in such military service;

(d) Such persons provide reliable proof of age prior to acceptance into national military service.

4. Each State Party may strengthen its declaration at any time by notification to that effect addressed to the Secretary-General of the United Nations, who shall inform all States Parties. Such notification shall take effect on the date on which it is received by the Secretary-General.

5. The requirement to raise the age in paragraph 1 of the present article does not apply to schools operated by or under the control of the armed forces of the States Parties, in keeping with articles 28 and 29 of the Convention on the Rights of the Child.

Article 4

1. Armed groups that are distinct from the armed forces of a State should not, under any circumstances, recruit or use in hostilities persons under the age of 18 years.

2. States Parties shall take all feasible measures to prevent such recruitment and use, including the adoption of legal measures necessary to prohibit and criminalize such practices.

3. The application of the present article shall not affect the legal status of any party to an armed conflict.

Article 5

Nothing in the present Protocol shall be construed as precluding provisions in the law of a State Party or in international instruments and international humanitarian law that are more conducive to the realization of the rights of the child.

Article 6

1. Each State Party shall take all necessary legal, administrative and other measures to ensure the effective implementation and enforcement of the provisions of the present Protocol within its jurisdiction.

2. States Parties undertake to make the principles and provisions of the present Protocol widely known and promoted by appropriate means, to adults and children alike.

3. States Parties shall take all feasible measures to ensure that persons within their jurisdiction recruited or used in hostilities contrary to the present Protocol are demobilized or otherwise released from service. States Parties shall, when necessary, accord to such persons all appropriate assistance for their physical and psychological recovery and their social reintegration.

Article 7

1. States Parties shall cooperate in the implementation of the present Protocol, including in the prevention of any activity contrary thereto and in the rehabilitation and social reintegration of persons who are victims of acts contrary thereto, including through technical cooperation and financial assistance. Such assistance and cooperation will be undertaken in consultation with the States Parties concerned and the relevant international organizations.

2. States Parties in a position to do so shall provide such assistance through existing multilateral, bilateral or other programmes or, inter alia, through a voluntary fund established in accordance with the rules of the General Assembly.

Article 8

1. Each State Party shall, within two years following the entry into force of the present Protocol for that State Party, submit a report to the Committee on the Rights of the Child providing comprehensive information on the measures it has taken to implement the provisions of the Protocol, including the measures taken to implement the provisions on participation and recruitment.

2. Following the submission of the comprehensive report, each State Party shall include in the reports it submits to the Committee on the Rights of the Child, in accordance with article 44 of the Convention, any further information with respect to the implementation of the Protocol. Other States Parties to the Protocol shall submit a report every five years.

3. The Committee on the Rights of the Child may request from States Parties further information relevant to the implementation of the present Protocol.

Article 9

1. The present Protocol is open for signature by any State that is a party to the Convention or has signed it.

2. The present Protocol is subject to ratification and is open to accession by any State. Instruments of ratification or accession shall be deposited with the Secretary-General of the United Nations.

3. The Secretary-General, in his capacity as depositary of the Convention and the Protocol, shall inform all States Parties to the Convention and all States that have signed the Convention of each instrument of declaration pursuant to article 3.

Article 10

1. The present Protocol shall enter into force three months after the deposit of the tenth instrument of ratification or accession.

2. For each State ratifying the present Protocol or acceding to it after its entry into force, the Protocol shall enter into force one month after the date of the deposit of its own instrument of ratification or accession.

Article 11

1. Any State Party may denounce the present Protocol at any time by written notification to the Secretary- General of the United Nations, who shall thereafter inform the other States Parties to the Convention and all States that have signed the Convention. The denunciation shall take effect one year after the date of receipt of the notification by the Secretary-General. If, however, on the expiry of that year the denouncing State Party is engaged in armed conflict, the denunciation shall not take effect before the end of the armed conflict.

2. Such a denunciation shall not have the effect of releasing the State Party from its obligations under the present Protocol in regard to any act that occurs prior to the date on which the denunciation becomes effective. Nor shall such a denunciation prejudice in any way the continued consideration of any matter that is already under consideration by the Committee on the Rights of the Child prior to the date on which the denunciation becomes effective.

Article 12

1. Any State Party may propose an amendment and file it with the Secretary-General of the United Nations. The Secretary-General shall thereupon communicate the proposed amendment to States Parties with a request that they indicate whether they favour a conference of States Parties for the purpose of considering and voting upon the proposals. In the event that, within four months from the date of such communication, at least one third of the States Parties favour such a conference, the Secretary-General shall convene the conference under the auspices of the United Nations. Any amendment adopted by a majority of States Parties present and voting at the conference shall be submitted to the General Assembly of the United Nations for approval.

2. An amendment adopted in accordance with paragraph 1 of the present article shall enter into force when it has been approved by the General Assembly and accepted by a two-thirds majority of States Parties.

3. When an amendment enters into force, it shall be binding on those States Parties that have accepted it, other States Parties still being bound by the provisions of the present Protocol and any earlier amendments they have accepted.

Article 13

1. The present Protocol, of which the Arabic, Chinese, English, French, Russian and Spanish texts are equally authentic, shall be deposited in the archives of the United Nations.

2. The Secretary-General of the United Nations shall transmit certified copies of the present Protocol to all States Parties to the Convention and all States that have signed the Convention.

F. Rome Statute of the International Criminal Court

The Rome Statute establishes a permanent criminal court to try persons charged with committing war crimes, crimes against humanity, and genocide. In its definition of war crimes the statute includes "conscripting or enlisting children under the age of fifteen years into national armed forces or using them to participate actively in hostilities" (Article 8(2)(b)(xxvi)) in international armed conflict; and in the case of an internal armed conflict, "conscripting or enlisting children under the age of fifteen years into armed forces or groups or using them to participate actively in hostilities" (Article 8(2)(e)(vii)). The statute also defines sexual slavery as a war crime (Article 8(2)(b)(xxii) and Article 8(2)(e)(vii)) and a crime against humanity (Article 7(1)(g)). The treaty came into force and the court came into being on 1 July 2002.

G. The 1977 Additional Protocol I to the four Geneva Conventions of 1949

Article 77(2) of Additional Protocol I: applicable to international armed conflicts, states: "The Parties to the conflict shall take all feasible measures in order that children who have not attained the age of 15 years do not take a direct part in hostilities and, in particular, they shall refrain from recruiting them into their armed forces. In recruiting among those persons who have attained the age of 15 years but who have not attained the age of 18 years the Parties to the conflict shall endeavour to give priority to those who are oldest."

H. The 1977 Additional Protocol II to the four Geneva Conventions of 1949

Article 4(3)(c) of the Additional Protocol II: applicable to non-international armed conflicts, states: "Children who have not attained the age of 15 years shall neither be recruited in the armed forces or groups nor allowed to take part in hostilities".

I. Customary International Humanitarian Law

State practices have established the customary rule as a norm of customary international law applicable in both international and non-international armed conflicts. Contained in Article 136 and 137, they provide that "Children must not be recruited into armed forces or armed groups;" and "Children must not be allowed to take part in hostilities."[2]

Regional Standards

J. African Charter on the Rights and Welfare of the Child

The Charter is the only regional treaty which addresses the issue of child soldiers. It was adopted by the Organization of African Unity (now the African Union) and came into force in November 1999. It defines a child as anyone below 18 years of age without exception. It also states that: "States Parties to the present Charter shall take all necessary measures to ensure that no child shall take a direct part in hostilities and refrain in particular, from recruiting any child" (Article 22.2).

K. The Security Council Resolution

Since 1998, the Security Council has adopted numerous resolutions for the protection of children and prevention of their recruitment and use in armed conflict.[3] The first two resolutions, 1261 of 1999 [4] and 1314 of 2000,[5]

---

2   Jean-Marie Henckaerts and Louise Doswald-Beck, *Customary International Humanitarian Law*, Vol. I, UK: Cambridge University Press, 2005.

3   These resolutions are: S/RES/1261 (1999), S/RES/1314 (2000), S/RES/1379 (2001), S/RES/1460 (2003), S/RES/1539 (2004), S/RES/1612 (2005), S/RES/1882 (2009), S/RES/1998 (2011), S/RES/2225 (2015), S/RES/2272 (2016) and S/RES/2286(2016).

4   On 25 August 1999, the Security Council adopted Resolution 1261 on Children and armed conflict, building on the Geneva Convention (1949) and the Additional Protocols (1977), the Convention on the Rights of the Child (1989), International Labor Organization Convention 182 (1999), and the Rome Statute of the International Criminal Court (1998).

5   In August 2000, the Security Council adopted Resolution 1314 on Children and armed conflict, welcoming the adoption by the General Assembly on May 25 2000 of the Optional Protocol to the Convention on the Rights of the Child on the Involvement of

identified areas of concern, such as the protection of children from sexual abuse, and the linkage between small arms proliferation and armed conflict. The Council urged the states to end of the recruitment and use of children in armed conflict in violation of international humanitarian law, through political and other efforts including promotion of alternatives for children to their participation in armed conflict. Recognizing the serious impact of the proliferation of arms on the security of civilians, particularly children, the Council stressed the importance of all Members to restrict arms transfers which could provoke or prolong armed conflicts. The Council also urged the states and the UN system to facilitate, and accelerate, the disarmament, demobilization, rehabilitation and reintegration of children used as soldiers.

At this early stage, the resolutions contained essentially generic statements and had a limited impact. From 2001 onwards the resolutions included concrete provisions. One of the most grounds breaking and controversial was the request in resolution 1379 of November 2001 for the Secretary-General to attach to his report:

> *a list of parties to armed conflict that recruit or use children in violation of the international obligations applicable to them, in situations that are on the Security Council's agenda or that may be brought to the attention of the Security Council by the Secretary-General, in accordance with Article 99 of the Charter of the United Nations, which in his opinion may threaten the maintenance of international peace and security...*

Nevertheless, there was little evidence on the ground that these measures were successful in getting armed groups and governments to stop violations of international norms. In light of this, on January 30, 2003, the Security Council adopted Resolution 1460 on Children and armed conflict, reaffirming the previous resolutions on the same subject. The resolution emphasized the responsibility of States to end impunity and to prosecute those responsible for genocide, crimes against humanity, war crimes and other egregious crimes perpetrated against children, including the recruitment and use of children

---

Children in Armed Conflict. The resolution also refers to the Ottawa Convention on the Prohibition of the Use, Stockpiling, Production and Transfer of Antipersonnel Mines and their Destruction, as well as several regional initiatives on war affected children, including the West-African Conference on War-Affected Children held in Accra, Ghana, and the International Conference on War-affected Children held in Canada.

less than 15 years for military purposes.[6] The Secretary-General was asked to: (i) report on the progress made by parties in stopping the recruitment or use of children in armed conflict; (ii) develop specific proposals for monitoring and reporting on the application of international norms on children and armed conflict; and (iii) include protection of children in armed conflict as a specific aspect of all his country- specific reports.

A further decision in 2004, in resolution 1539, requested that the Secretary-General "devise urgently" an action plan for a comprehensive monitoring and reporting mechanism that could provide accurate and timely information on grave violations against children in war zones. The resolution asked for parties listed in the Secretary-General's reports to prepare concrete plans to stop the recruitment and use of children in armed conflict.

Action Plans were designed to end and prevent violations against children for which parties to conflict are listed. For example, an Action Plan to end the recruitment and use of child soldiers by Government security forces can include the following actions:

---

6   Security Council Resolution 1460 (2003) requires listed parties to enter into talks with the United Nations to agree clear and time bound action plans to end child recruitment and use. The concept of action plans is now also applied more broadly to other grave violations against children for which parties can be listed. A number of listed parties have signed action plans, including five government forces and 12 non-state armed groups. Of these, five have fully complied with the action plan and were subsequently de-listed.

L. Action Plan: How to End the Recruitment and use of Children in Armed Conflict

One: Issue military command orders prohibiting the recruitment and use of children

Two: Release all children identified in the ranks of security forces

Three: Ensure children's reintegration into civilian life

Four: Criminalize the recruitment and use of children

Five: Integrate age-verification mechanism in recruitment procedure

A major breakthrough came the following year in resolution 1612 with the establishment of a formal monitoring and reporting mechanism and a Security Council Working Group on Children and Armed Conflict.[7] The Council agreed to set up a mechanism to report on killings, abduction, abuse and sexual exploitation of children in armed conflict, the recruiting of child soldiers and attacks on schools and hospitals. The resolution was partly a response to the lack of accurate information and action plans requested in resolution 1539 and aimed at stopping the use of child soldiers and the exploitation of children in war zones by governments and insurgent armed groups. Negotiations, led by France and Benin, took months, with many states wary about targeting individual countries. The resolution also reaffirmed the Council's intention to consider imposing targeted sanctions, including arms embargoes, travel bans and financial restrictions, against parties that continued to violate international law relating to children in armed conflict.[8]

7   Resolution 1612 established the monitoring and reporting mechanism (MRM) on grave violations against children in armed conflict. The purpose of the MRM is to provide for the systematic gathering of accurate, timely and objective information on grave violations committed against children in armed conflict. Resolution 1612 also established the Security Council Working Group on Children and Armed Conflict which consists of the 15 Security Council members. The Working Group reviews reports of UN Secretary-General on children in armed conflict in specific country situations and makes recommendations to parties to conflict, Governments and donors, as well as UN actors on measures to promote the protection of war-affected children.   .

8   The implementation of Resolution 1612 began in earnest with the establishment of Country Task Forces on Monitoring and Reporting Mechanism. A first wave of Action Plans were signed and implemented in Cote d'Ivoire, Uganda, Sri Lanka and Nepal. In total, 18 Action Plans were signed under Radhika Coomaraswamy's tenure and 8 parties delisted, representing a mix of national security forces and non-State armed groups. In April 2006, Coomaraswamy became the second Special Representative of the Secretary-

Resolution 1882 was adopted on 4 August 2009. It expanded the criteria for identifying state and non-state parties that could be listed in the Secretary-General's annexes to include killing and maiming and rape and other sexual violence against children. The resolution also called on parties engaged in killing and maiming and sexual violence against children to prepare action plans outlining steps to stop these crimes. Resolution 1998 was adopted on 12 July 2011. It expanded the criteria for inclusion in the annexes to the report on children and armed conflict to parties that engage in recurrent attacks on schools and hospitals in armed conflicts, as well as recurrent attacks or threats of attacks against schoolchildren and educational and medical personnel. This resolution also asked the Working Group to consider within one year a broad range of options for increasing pressure on persistent perpetrators of violations and abuses committed against children in situations of armed conflict.

Resolution 2068 was adopted on 19 September 2012 by a vote of 11 in favour to none against with four abstentions (Azerbaijan, China, Pakistan and Russia). This was the first time a resolution on children and armed conflict was not adopted unanimously. This resolution has a strong focus on persistent perpetrators and justice and impunity, reiterating concern about persistent perpetrators and calling upon member states to bring to justice those responsible for such violations through national and international justice systems. It reiterated the Council's readiness to adopt targeted and graduated measures against persistent perpetrators. It furthermore reiterated its call to the Working Group on Children and Armed Conflict to consider a range of options for increasing pressure on persistent perpetrators. Significantly, it asked the Secretary-General to continue to submit annual reports to the Council, triggering an annual cycle of reports.

Resolution 2143 was adopted on 7 March 2014 with all 15 members voting in favour. While reiterating a number of key issues, the resolution contained some new elements, including references to the use of schools by armed forces, encouraging member states to establish a vetting mechanism to ensure those who have committed violations against children are not included in army ranks, recommendations for child protection training for peacekeepers and military personnel, support for the "Children, Not Soldiers" campaign and the role of child protection advisers in integrating child protection in

---

General for Children and Armed Conflict.

mission activities.[9] There have been significant improvements and a reduction in verified cases of recruitment and use of children by national security forces, especially in Afghanistan, the Democratic Republic of the Congo, Myanmar and Sudan.[10] The importance of security sector reform in mainstreaming child protection, including through age-assessment mechanisms, to prevent underage recruitment and establishment of child protection units in national security forces constituted new elements. The resolution focused also on the role regional organizations can play in child protection and the need to incorporate child protection provisions in peace agreements.

Security Council has taken further steps to address the protection of children in armed conflict. Resolution S/RES/2225 (2015) reiterated all previous forms of international law addressing children in armed conflict: Convention on the Rights of the Child and its Optional Protocol on the involvement of Children in armed conflict, the Geneva Conventions of 12th August 1949, and the Additional Protocols of 1977. Resolution 2225 added abductions as an additional violation to trigger inclusion of a party in the annexes of the Secretary-General's annual report.

Resolution 2272 adopted by the Security Council on 11 March 2016 expressed deep concern about the serious and continuous allegations and under-reporting of sexual exploitation and abuse by United Nations peacekeepers and non-United Nations forces, including military, civilian and police personnel, and stressed that sexual exploitation and abuse, among other crimes and forms of serious misconduct, by any such personnel was unacceptable. *The Council endorsed* the decision of the Secretary-General to repatriate a particular military or police unit of a contingent when there is credible evidence of widespread or systemic sexual exploitation and abuse by that unit. Resolution 2286 of 2016 recalled the obligation of states under international humanitarian law to distinguish between civilian populations

---

9   In 2014, the Special Representative launched the campaign "Children, Not Soldiers" with UNICEF to bring about a global consensus that child soldiers should not be used in conflict. The campaign was designed to generate momentum, political will and international support to turn the page once and for all on the recruitment of children by national security forces in conflict situations. At the time of the launch, the countries concerned by the campaign were: Afghanistan, Chad, the Democratic Republic of the Congo, Myanmar, Somalia, South Sudan, Sudan and Yemen. Representatives from each of these countries attended the launch event and expressed their full support to reach the objectives of "Children, Not Soldiers".

10   20 Years to better Protect Children affected by Conflict, Office of the Special Representative of the Secretary-General for Children and Armed Conflict, UN, December 2016.

and combatants, and the prohibition against indiscriminate attacks, and the obligations to do everything feasible to verify that the objectives to be attacked are neither civilians nor civilian objects and are not subject to special protection. The Resolution demanded all parties to armed conflicts fully comply with their obligations under international law, including international human rights law, as applicable, and international humanitarian law, in particular their obligations under the Geneva Conventions of 1949 and the obligations applicable to them under the Additional Protocols of 1977 and 2005, to ensure the respect and protection of all medical personnel and humanitarian personnel exclusively engaged in medical duties, their means of transport and equipment, as well as hospitals and other medical facilities.

General Assembly

The General Assembly in 1996 created the mandate of Special Representative for Children and Armed Conflict (CAAC).[11] The first report of the Special Representative of the Secretary-General for CAAC (A/53/482) highlighted that the development and proliferation of lightweight automatic weapons has made it possible for very young children to bear and use arms. Many more are being used in indirect ways that are more difficult to measure, such as cooks, messengers and porters. Children have also been used for mine clearance, spying and suicide bombing. In 1999, the first resolution on children and armed conflict placed the issue of children affected by war on the Security Council's agenda. The resolution identified and condemned 6 grave violations affecting children the most in times of conflict, and requested the Secretary-General to report on the issue.

Over the years, the General Assembly has adopted essential treaties and resolutions to create a normative framework to better protect children from the effects of war. The Convention on the Rights of the Child and its Optional Protocol on the involvement of children in armed conflict provide the foundation for the protection of children. The Convention on the Rights

---

11 In 1996, Graca Machel presented her report titled "*Impact of armed conflict on children*", to the General Assembly. She identified children as the primary victims of armed conflict and included a set of recommendations, including the nomination of a Special Representative of the Secretary-General on children and armed conflict to keep the protection of children very high on the international human rights, peace, security, and development agendas. The resulting creation of the Office of the Special Representative for Children and Armed Conflict (General Assembly resolution 51/77 of 12 December 1996) has driven greater awareness — and greater action on the protection of children caught in armed conflict world over.

of the Child has almost universal ratification and the Special Representative continues to advocate with Members States who have not yet done so to ratify the Optional Protocol. In addition, every year, the General Assembly adopts a resolution on the Rights of the Child, which addresses current issues and challenges. The Special Representative presents his/her report to the General Assembly annually with information on progress achieved, challenges and outlines ongoing cooperation to better address the plight of children affected by conflict. With the submission of the report, the Assembly is kept abreast of the most pressing and emerging issues. Effective advocacy and action by successive Special Representatives has resulted in the release of tens of thousands of children from the armed forces and NSAGs, and accountability for perpetrators has increased. There is also global consensus among Member States that children should not be recruited and used in conflict, and that they should be protected from all other grave violations.

M. The Kathmandu Declaration on the Use of Children as Soldiers

Some 150 delegates from 30 countries including representatives of Asia-Pacific governments, UN agencies and NGOs working on children's rights attended the 15-18 May 2010 conference in Kathmandu. The conference declaration asked Asia-Pacific states to ratify the Optional Protocol to the Convention on the Rights of the Child that prohibits involvement of anyone under 18 in armed conflict. It also urged that regional forums such as the Association of South East Asian Nations (ASEAN) and the South Asia Association for Regional Cooperation (SAARC), and organizations such as the Group of Eight (G-8) include the declaration on their agendas. It called on NGOs in the region to disseminate and work to implement the declaration, and to encourage further consultation on the issue. The declaration urged peaceful resolution of disputes.

N. Amman Declaration on the use of Children as Soldiers

Participants in the Amman Conference on the Use of Children as Soldiers, held in Amman, Jordan from 8-10 April 2001;

Deeply appreciating the call for a world free of child soldiers made by Her Majesty Queen Rania Al-Abdullah in her speech to the Conference;

Affirming that no child under 18 years should be the instrument or object of violence;

Appalled that more than 300,000 children (girls and boys) under 18 years of age are currently participating as soldiers in armed conflicts worldwide;

Recalling that all children are entitled to all the rights and freedoms in the Convention on the Rights of the Child without discrimination of any kind, irrespective of the child's or his or her parent's or legal guardian's race, colour, sex, language, religion, political or other opinion, national, ethnic or social origin, property, disability, birth or other status;

Welcoming the adoption by the UN General Assembly of the Optional Protocol to the Convention on the Rights of the Child on the involvement of children in armed conflict which prohibits the use of children under the age of 18 years in armed conflicts;

Acknowledging the causes leading to armed conflict and the participation of children, including foreign occupation and forced displacement; poverty, neglect, injustice and economic disparity; lack of access to education and other opportunities; a culture of militarization and violence, including through toys, computer games, violent films and cartoons, and media images; the proliferation of small arms; intolerance and discrimination;

Stressing the obligation of the States Parties to the four Geneva Conventions of 1949 and their Additional Protocols of 1977 to both respect and ensure respect for the provisions of these Conventions, in particular the situation of civilians in times of occupation according to the Fourth Geneva Convention;

Reaffirming the UN Charter commitment to save succeeding generations from the scourge of war and the need to seek peaceful alternatives, promote human security and involve children in building peace and reconciliation;

Noting the UN Security Council's call in Resolutions 1261 (28 August 1999) and 1314 (11 August 2000) for concerted international action to stop the use of children as soldiers, its strong condemnation of the targeting of children and places that have a significant presence of children, and willingness to take steps to minimize the potential harm to children when imposing sanctions;

Recalling Resolution on Child Care and Protection in the Islamic World of the Ninth Session of the Islamic Summit Conference in Doha, State of Qatar in November 2000 which called for the non-involvement of (refugee) children in any armed conflict and not to enlist them in the armed forces or for any other actions which might expose their personal safety and security to danger.

Welcoming the Resolution for a Framework on the Rights of the Child adopted by the Summit of the League of Arab States in Amman in March 2001;

Welcoming the adoption of the Statute of the International Criminal Court which makes the conscripting or enlisting of children under the age of 15 years or using them to participate actively in hostilities a war crime, both in international and internal armed conflict and whether by armed forces or armed groups;

Welcoming the inclusion of forced or compulsory recruitment for use in armed conflict as one of the worst forms of child labour in ILO Convention 182;

Welcoming the entry into force of the African Charter on the Rights and Welfare of the Child which prohibits all recruitment and direct participation in hostilities of children under 18 years;

Noting the UN Secretary-General's decision that UN peacekeepers should be at least 21 and in no case less than 18 years of age;

Welcoming the declarations on the use of children as soldiers from previous regional conferences in Maputo (April 1999), Montevideo (July 1999), Berlin (October 1999) and Kathmandu (May 2000);

Mindful of preparations for the UN General Assembly Special Session on Children in September 2001 which will further underscore the international community's resolve to protect children from all forms of exploitation, violence, discrimination and abuse;

Determined to put an end to the use of children under 18 years of age as soldiers:*

1.   Solemnly declare that the use in hostilities of any child under 18 years of age by any armed force or armed group is unacceptable;

2.   Urge all states to ratify or accede to the Optional Protocol to the Convention on the Rights of the Child on the involvement of children in armed conflict, without reservations and declaring at least 18 years as the minimum age for all forms of voluntary recruitment;

3.   Encourage states to use the forthcoming United Nations General Assembly Special Session on Children (September 2001) as an opportunity for signature or to announce their ratification or accession to the above Optional Protocol;

4.   Call upon all armed forces and armed groups to end the recruitment and use of children under 18 and to immediately demobilize or release into safety children already being used as soldiers;

5.   Call upon states who have not already done so to ratify the four Geneva Conventions of 1949, the two Additional Protocols of 1977, the 1951 Refugee Convention and its 1967 Protocol, the Rome Statute of the International Criminal Court, the Ottawa Landmines Treaty, the ILO Worst Forms of Child Labour Convention, 182;

6.   Call upon the states parties to the Fourth Geneva Convention to take all necessary measures to ensure full respect for its provisions, in particular in relation to the protection of children under occupation;

7.   Call upon all states to ensure the effective and universal implementation of these international standards and protection for children, including refugee and displaced girls and boys, in national legislation and practice, including through:

- Reviewing national legislation to ensure conformity with international standards;

- Criminalizing the use in hostilities and recruitment of children under 18 in their national laws;

- Strengthening the international human rights mechanisms, in particular the Committee on the Rights of the Child;

- Establishing or strengthening national mechanisms for the rights of the child;

- Ensuring compulsory and comprehensive birth registration;

6. Call upon all states to ensure the special protection of all children living under occupation, child detainees and child participants in armed conflict or civil strife, through the strict application of international human rights and humanitarian law, including international standards on juvenile justice and the use of lethal force;

7. Call upon all states and other relevant bodies to ensure the translation, raising of awareness and widespread dissemination of these standards at all levels of society and effective training of military and police personnel, peacekeepers and officials in child rights and protection, and to incorporate these into educational and military curricula;

8. Call upon all states, including those outside the region, not to supply small arms or light weapons to any government or armed group which recruits or uses children as soldiers, and to take steps to prevent individuals and companies from doing so;

9. Urge states to adopt legislation holding companies accountable for activities which directly or indirectly involve children in hostilities or military activity and call on companies to adopt and abide by codes of conduct to this effect;

10. Urge armed groups to make written commitments to abide by the Optional Protocol to the Convention on the Rights of the Child on involvement of children in armed conflict;

11. Call on religious scholars to conduct studies showing the positive role religion can play in combating child soldiering and its negative impact on children;

12. Call on religious and community leaders to promote a culture of peace, tolerance and understanding and raising awareness about the rights of the child;

13. Encourage states to enhance preventive measures for all children, especially those at risk, by addressing the causes of child soldiering, in particular poverty, discrimination, displacement, injustice and lack of education, including by:

- Creating educational and vocational opportunities

- Ensuring education for tolerance, non-discrimination and respect for others

- Empowering children to be actively engaged in community-building without resorting to violence

- Ending military training programmes for children, which encourage the militarization of society, aggressive attitudes and entrenchment of occupation;

- Strengthening the family as the main protective unit for the child;

6. Call on the national, regional and international media to promote positive images and attitudes instead of focussing on violence;

7. Call upon all states to ensure the special needs of former child soldiers are met through effective and appropriate programmes of rehabilitation and reintegration into society, taking account of the specific needs of particular groups of children, such as girls, refugees and disabled children;

8. Call upon all governments, including those outside the region, the UN system and international institutions to provide adequate assistance to ensure the implementation of the above aims, in particular by providing short-term and long- term resources to support alternative employment and demobilization, rehabilitation and reintegration for child soldiers;

9. Request the League of Arab States, the Organization of Islamic Conference, the Gulf Cooperation Council, the Arab Maghreb Union, the Organization of African Unity the Euro-Mediterranean Partnership and other regional bodies to endorse and work for the implementation of this Declaration;

10. Call on the Directorate of Childhood of the Arab League to promote this declaration, particularly to all participants of the meetings of the Technical Consultative Committee for the Arab Child;

11. Call upon all states, international organizations, NGOs and civil society, in particular those of the Middle East and North Africa region, to work for the implementation and monitoring of this Declaration, including through the participation of children themselves and the creation of national, regional and international networks;

12. Encourage His Majesty's Government of the Hashemite Kingdom of Jordan to present this Declaration to the Human Security Network Ministerial Meeting in Petra (May 2001); and

13. Express their warm appreciation to Her Majesty Queen Rania Al-Abdullah for her patronage of and participation in this conference and to His Majesty's Government of the Royal Hashemite Kingdom of Jordan and the Jordan Institute of Diplomacy for hosting this important event.

Adopted in Amman on 10 April 2001

*According to the 1977 Commentary on the Additional Protocols, recruitment covers any means (formal or *de facto*) by which a person becomes a member of the armed forces or an armed group, so it includes conscription (compulsory/ obligatory military service), voluntary enlistment, and forced recruitment. According to the UN Document A/CONF.183/2/Add.1, participation in hostilities covers both direct participation in combat and also active participation in military activities linked to combat such as scouting, spying, sabotage and the use of children as decoys, couriers or at military checkpoints and the use of children in a direct support function such as acting as bearers to take supplies to the front line, and all activities at the front line itself.

BIBLIOGRAPHY

Abani, Chris. 2007. *Song for Night*, New York: Akashic Books.

Abbott Amy, Child Soldiers - The Use of Children as Instruments of War, *Suffolk Transnational Law Review* , Vol. 23, No. 2, 2000, p. 499-538.

Achvarina Vera and Simon Reich, No Place to Hide: Refugees, Displaced Persons, and the Recruitment of Child Soldiers, *International Security*, Vol. 31(1), 2006, p. 127–164.

Ahmed Sibghatullah, Seeking to Dissuade: Does the International Legal Framework offer Enough Protection to Child Soldiers, Long Thesis, Central European University Budapest, 29 December 2011.

Alfredson Lisa, Child soldiers, displacement and human security, *Disarmament Forum*, 2002 (3), p. 17-28.

Alternative Report to the Committee on the Rights of Child on the Occasion of Pakistan's fifth periodic report on the Convention on the Rights of Child, Child Soldier International NGO Report, July 2015, p. 15.

Anderson Kara, "Cubs of the Caliphate", The Systematic Recruitment, Training, and Use of Children in the Islamic State. S-122 available at: www.drake.edu/media/departmentsoffices/international/nelson/2016.

Andvig Jens Christopher and Scott Gates, Recruiting Children for Armed Conflict, Ford Institute for Human Security, 2007, pp. 30.

Aptel Cecile, Children and Accountability for International crimes: The Contribution of International Court, Innocenti Working Paper, UNICEF, August 2010.

Babatunde Abosede Omowumi, Harnessing traditional practices for use in the reintegration of child soldiers in Africa: examples from Liberia and Burundi, *Intervention*, Volume 12, Number 3, 2014, p. 379-392.

Bakker Christine, Prosecuting International Crimes Against Children: The Legal Framework, Innocenti Working Paper, UNICEF, June 2010, p. 34.

Batchelder Elena, 'Child Soldiers: An Exception in International Law', The *Lubanga Trial*: Lessons Learned, Issues in International Criminal Justice, Vol. II, No. I, 2012, p. 62-72.

Beah Ismael. 2007. A Long Way Gone: Memoire of a Child Soldier, New York: Sarah Crichton Books.

Beber Bernd and Christopher Blattman, The Logic of Child Soldiering and Coercion, International Organization, 67, p. 65-104, July 2011.

Begley Tracey B., The Extraterritorial Obligation to Prevent the Use of Child Soldiers, *Am U Int'l Rev*, Vol. 27, No. 3, 2012, p. 613-640.

Benotman Noman and Nikita Malik, *The Children of Islamic State*, London: Quilliam, 2016, p. 100.

Bleie Tone and Ramesh Shrestha, DDR in Nepal: Stakeholder Politics and the Implications for Reintegration as a Process of Disengagement, Centre for Peace Studies – University of Troms, 2012, p. 56.

Bogen Katherine W., Rape and Sexual Violence: Questionable Inevitability and Moral Responsibility in Armed Conflict, *Scholarly Undergraduate Research Journal at Clark*: Vol. 2, Article 6, p. 15.

Boyden Jo and Joanna de Bery (eds.). 2004. *Children and Youth on the Front Line: Ethnography, Armed Conflict and Displacement*, New York: Berghan Books.

Briefing on accountability for child recruitment and use in Sri Lanka, Child Soldier International, February 2014.

Burkhat, John A., Watch out for the children: Army policy and child soldiers, Monterey, California: Naval Postgraduate School, June 2006, p. 66.

Burman Erica, Innocents Abroad: Western Fantasies of Childhood and the Iconography of Emergencies, *Disasters*, Vol. 18 (3), 1994, p. 238–253.

Cape Town Principles and Best Practices, Cape Town, South Africa, 27-30 April 1997..

Carpenter Charli, Protecting children born of sexual violence and exploitation in conflict zones: Existing practice and knowledge gaps, Findings from Consultations with Humanitarian Practitioners, December 2004 – March 2005, University of Pittsburg, Ford Institute for Human Security,

p. 23..

Caschetta A. J., Does Islam Have a Role in Suicide Bombing? *Middle East Quarterly*, Summer 2015, p. 1-19.

Chamberlain Cynthia, Children and the International Criminal Court: Analysis of the Rome Statute through a children's rights perspective, Unpublished Thesis, Leiden University, 2014.

Child Soldiers and other Children Associated with Armed Forces and Armed Groups, Geneva: ICRC, August 2012, p. 16.

Child Soldiers for Adult Wars: Exploitation in Nepal and Sri Lanka, International Labour Office, 2006, p. 56.

Child Soldiers: Global Report 2008, Coalition to Stop the Use of Child Soldiers.

Children and Armed Conflict: A Guide to International Humanitarian and Human Rights Law, International Bureau for Children's Right, p. 458.

Children and Detention, International Committee of the Red Cross, Geneva, November 2014.

Children and Justice During and in the Aftermath of Armed Conflict, Working Paper No. 3, United Nations Office of the Special Representative of the Secretary-General for Children in Armed Conflict, September 2011, p. 56.

Children in Rank, The Maoists' Use of Child Soldiers in Nepal, Vol. 19, No. 2(C), Human Rights Watch, February 2007, p. 76.

Children, Not Soldiers, A Programme Strategy to End the Recruitment and Use of Children by Government Security Forces, UNICEF, October 2014, p. 3.

Christoph Reuter. 2002. *My Life Is A Weapon: A Modern History of Suicide Bombing*, Princeton and Oxford: Princeton University Pres.

Conradi Carl, Mitigating Children's Involvement in Maritime Piracy, *Canadian Naval Review*, Vol. 60, No. 2, 2014, p. 16-20..

Crane David M., Prosecuting Children in Times of Conflict: The West African Experience, *Human Rights Brief*, Vol. 15, No.3, 2008, p. 11-17.

Cremer Hendrik, Shadow Report Child Soldiers 2013, German Coalition to Stop the Use of Child Soldiers.

Cuni Enarda and Lamce Juelda, The Right to Protect Children under International Law: The Case of Child Soldiers, *Academic Journal of Interdisciplinary Studies*, Vol. 2, No. 8, October 2013, p. 670-677.

Cynthia, Chamberlain Bolanos, Crimes under the jurisdiction of International Criminal Court and children, University of Leiden, 2014, p. 47.

Dallaire Romeo. 2011. *They Fight Like Soldiers: They Die Like Children*, London: Arrow Books, p. 307.

Dallman Ashley, Prosecuting Conflict-Related Sexual Violence at the International Criminal Court, SIPRI Insight on Peace and Security, No. 2009/1, May 2009, p.16.

Desierto Diane A., Leveraging International Economic Tools to Confront Child Soldiering, *International Law and Politics*, Vol. 43, 2011, p. 337-418.

Drumbl, Mark A. 2012. *Reimagining Child Soldiers in International Law and Policy*, Oxford: Oxford University Pres.

Drumbl, Mark A, The effects of the *Lubanga* Case on Understanding and Preventing Child Soldiering, *Yearbook of International Humanitarian Law*, Vol. 15, 2012, p. 87-116.

Drumbl Mark A., Child Pirates: Rehabilitation, Reintegration, and Accountability, *Case W. Res. J. Int'l L.*, Vol. 46, 2015, p. 235-278.

DDR in Peace Operations: A Retrospective Department of Peacekeeping Operations, Office of the Rule of Law and Security Institutions DDR Section, United Nations, 2014.

Eliminating the worst forms of child labour, A Practical Guide to ILO Convention No. 182, Handbook for Parliamentarians No. 3 -2002, ILO, p. 149.

Emilsen William W, Teenage Suicide Missions: The Role of Religion in the Recruitment of Young Suicide Bombers, *Forum on Public Policy*, 2008, p. 1-14.

Emily Kalah Gade, The Child Soldier: The Question of Self-defence, *The Journal of Military Ethics*, Vol. 10, No. 4, December 2011.

Field Sarah M., UN Security Council Resolutions Concerning Children Affected by Armed Conflict: In Whose 'Best Interest'? *International Journal of Children's Rights*, Vol. 21, 2013, p. 127-161.

Fisher Kirsten J. 2013. *Transitional Justice for Child Soldiers: Accountability and Social Reconstruction in post-conflict Context*, Palgrave/Springer.

Fonseka Bhawani, The Protection of Child Soldiers in International Law, *Asia-Pacific Journal of Human Rights and the Law*, Vol. 2, No. 2, 2001, p. 69-89.

Fox Mary-Jane, Child Soldiers and International Law: Patchwork Gains and Conceptual Debates, *Human Rights Review*, October-December 2005, p. 27-48.

Francis, David J, Paper Protection' Mechanisms: Child Soldiers and the International Protection of Children in Africa's Conflict Zones, *Journal of Modern African Studies*, Vol. 45 (2), 2007, p. 207–231.

Freedson Julia, Yvonne Kemper, and Singh S., Children in Armed Conflict Accountability Framework, Conflict Dynamics International, June 2015, p. 62.

Freeland, Steven, Child soldiers and international crimes: how should international law be applied? *New Zealand Journal of Public and International Law*, Vol. 3, Issue 2, November 2005, p. 303–328.

Frostad Magne, Child Soldiers: Recruitment, Use and Punishment, *International Family Law, Policy and Practice*, Vol. 1.1, Winter 2013, pp. 71-89.

Gee David and Taylor Rachel, Is it Counterproductive to Enlist Minors into the Army? *The RUSI Journal*, Vol. 161, No. 6, 2016, p. 36-48.

Gichoya Florence, Girls as the New Weapons of terror in West Africa, *Africa Policy Institute (API) Research Note*, issue No. 8, March 2016, pp. 1-4.

Godoy Magdalena, Sexual Violence in Armed Conflict under International Law: The interplay between IHL, Human Rights Law and International Criminal Law, Unpublished Thesis, University of Pretoria, 2016, p. 172.

Gogg Charu Lata, Child recruitment in South Asian Conflict: A Comparative Analysis of Sri Lanka, Nepal and Bangladesh; Chatham House: The Royal Institute of International Affairs, 2006, pp. 52.

Gopal Srinivas and Jayashree G., Twenty-First Century Terrorism in Pakistan, *CLAWS Journal*, Summer 2013, p. 253-261.

Gorka Sebastian L., Gorka Katharine C., and Claire Herzog, The Islamic State's Militarization of Children: Special Report, Threat Knowledge Group, September 2016, p. 13.

Grey rosemary, Protecting Child Soldiers from Sexual Violence by Members of the Same Military Force: A re-conceptualization of IHL, International Crime Database (ICD) Brief No. 10, April 2015, p. 13.

Grimland Meytal, Alan Apter and Ad kerkhof, The Phenomenon of Suicide Bombing, *Crisis*, Vol. 27, No. 3, 2006, p. 107-118.

Grossman, Nienke, The Rehabilitation or Revenge: Prosecuting Child Soldiers for Human Rights Violations, *Georgetown Journal of International Law*, Vol. 38, No. 2, 2007, p. 323-62.

Happold, Matthew, Child Soldiers in International Law: The Legal Regulation of Children's Participation in Hostilities, *Netherlands International Law Review*, Vol. 47, No. 1, 2000, p. 27-52.

Hart Jason, "The Politics of Child Soldiers", *Brown Journal of World Affairs*, Vol. III, Issue I, Fall/Winter 2006, p. 217-226.

Harvey Rachel, Children and Armed Conflict: A Guide to International Humanitarian and Human Rights Law, International Bureau for Children's Right, p. 92.

Harvey Rachel, Child soldiers in the UK: Analysis of recruitment and deployment practices of under-18s and the CRC, June 2002, p. 37.

Hedkvist Elin, Girls and Boys at War: Prohibition in International Law against the Use of Child Soldiers, Fall 2009, University of Orebro: School of Law, Psychology and Social Work, p. 53.

Honwana, Alcinda. 2006. *Child Soldiers in Africa*, Philadelphia: University of Pennsylvania Pres.

Horgan John G, Max Taylor, Mia Bloom, and Charlie Winter, From Cubs to Lions: A Six Stage Model of Child Socialization into the Islamic State, *Studies in Conflict and Terrorism*, 2016, p. 1-20.

Huggan, Graham. 2001. *The Post-Colonial Exotic: Marketing the Margins*, New York: Routledge.

Humphrey Thomas, Child Soldiers: Rescuing the Lost Childhood, Australian Journal of Human Rights, Vol. 13, No. 1, 2007, p. 113-148.

Huynh Kim, Bina D'Costa and Katrina Lee-Koo. 2015. *Children and Global Conflict*, UK: Cambridge University Pres.

Hybnerova Stanislava, Prohibition of Recruiting Child Soldiers and /or Achievable Obligation, *CYIL*, Vol. 1, 2010, p. 110-119.

India's Child Soldiers, A shadow report to the UN Committee on the Rights of the Child on the Involvement of Children in Armed Conflict, Asian Centre for Human Rights, 2013, p. 74.

International Criminal Justice and Children, No Peace Without Justice (NPWJ) and UNICEF, September 2002.

Iqbal Khuram. 2015. *The Making of Pakistani Human Bomb*, London: Lexington Books.

Jonasen Mary, Child Soldiers in Chad: A Policy Window for Change, *Intersection Online*, Vol. 10, No. 1, Winter 2009, p. 310-329.

Iweala, Uzodinma. 2005. *Beasts of No Nation*, New York: HarperCollins.

Jalloh, Charles C., Special Court for Sierra Leone: Achieving Justice? *Mich. J. Int'l L.*, Vol. 32, 2011, p. 395-460.

Kakhuta-Banda Francis Blessings, The Use of Child Soldiers in African Armed Conflicts: A Comparative Study of Angola and Mozambique, Unpublished Research Report, University of the Witwatersrand, Johannesburg, February 2014, p. 100.

Kageni Mbungu Grace, Good Intentions, Little Effect: International Norms and the use of Child Soldiers, Unpublished Thesis, Bowling Green State University, December 2009, p. 91.

Keairns Yvonne E., The Voices of Girl Child Soldiers, Quaker United Nations Office and Coalition to Stop the Use of Child Soldiers, October 2002, p. 30.

Khan Myra, International Laws Concerning the Recruitment and Use of Child Soldiers and the Case of Omar Khadr, January 27, 2011, p. 22.

Kim Grace, Eradicating Child Soldiers: Human Rights Approaches to Engagement with Armed Groups, Unpublished Research Paper, University of Ottawa, April 2012, p. 68.

Kirby Colleen, *Child Soldiers: An Innocence Lost*, Unpublished Thesis, Eastern Michigan University, 2015, p. 30.

Kuniewicz Anna, Case: *International Criminal Court Prosecutor v. Bosco Ntaganda*, *Chi.-Kent J. Int'l & Comp. Law*, Vol. 15, 2015, p. 11.

Kurth Michael E., The *Lubanga* Case of the International Criminal Court: A Critical Analysis of the Trial Chamber's Findings on Issues of Active Use, Age, and Gravity, *Goettingen Journal of International Law*, Vol. 5, No. 2,

2013, p. 431-453.

Lakhani Kalsoom, Indoctrinating Children: The Making of Pakistan's Suicide Bombers, *CTC Sentinel*, Vol. 3, Issue 6, June 2010, p. 11-13.

Lafayette Erin, The Prosecution of Child Soldiers: Balancing Accountability with Justice, *Syracuse Law Review*, Vol. 63, 2013, p. 297-325.

Lauren Ploch Blanchard Lauren Ploch, Boko Haram (The Islamic State's West Africa Province), Congressional Research Service, 12 April 2016.

Lee Ah-Jung, Understanding and Addressing the Phenomenon of 'Child Soldiers': The Gap between the Global Humanitarian Discourse and the Local Understandings and Experiences of Young People's Military Recruitment, Working Paper Series No. 52, Refugee Studies Centre, Oxford Department of International Development, University of Oxford, January 2009. p. 46.

Leveau, Fanny, Liability of Child Soldiers Under International Criminal Law, *Osgoode Hall Review of Law and Policy*, Vol. 4, No. 1, 2014, p. 33-66.

Lofgren Linda Harsta, Child soldiers from a legal perspective: A literature based case study of the Democratic Republic of Congo, Sierra Leone and Uganda, Unpublished Master Thesis, Uppsala University, December 3013.

Lonegan Bryan, Sinner or Saints: Child Soldiers and the Persecutor Bar to Asylum After *Negusie v. Holder, Boston College Third World Law Journal*, Vol. 31, Issue 1, 2011, p. 71-99.

Loren Raphaelle, Relevance and adequacy of the Optional Protocol to the CRC on the Involvement of Children in Armed Conflicts', *Global International Courts Review*, Vol. 5, Issue 1, 2004, p. 29–87.

Lorey Mark, Child Soldiers: Care and Protection of Children in Emergencies—A Field Guide, Save the Children, 2001, p. 84.

Louder Than Words: An agenda for Action to end state use of child soldiers, Child Soldier International, 2012, p. 162.

Machel Gracia. 1996. *The Impact of Armed Conflict on Children*, New York: UNICEF.

Machel Graca, *Impact of Armed Conflict on Children*, Report of the expert of the Secretary-General submitted pursuant to General Assembly resolution 48/157, A/51/306, 26 August 1996, p. 78. S-114.

Machel Study: 10-years Strategic Review, Children and Conflict in a Changing World, UNICEF, April 2009, p. 236.

Madsen Jessica Nann, The Sexual Exploitation of Child Soldiers in the DRC: A Victim- Centered Approach Utilizing Human Trafficking Principles, Contemporary Legal Institutions, St Thomas University, Florida, p. 23.

Madubuike-Ekwe, Joseph N., The International Legal Standards Adopted to Stop the Participation of Children in Armed Conflicts, *Annual Survey of International & Comparative Law*: Vol. 11, Issue 1, Article 3, 2005, p. 20.

Magali Maystre, The Interaction between International Refugee Law and International Criminal Law with respect to Child Soldiers, *Journal of International Criminal Justice*, Vol. 12, No. 5, 2014, p. 975-996.

Malsen Stuart, The Use of Children as Soldiers in Africa Report: A country analysis of child recruitment and participation in armed conflict, Coalition to Stop the Use of Child Soldiers, 2011, p. 109.

Manivannam Anjali, Seeking Justice for Male Victims of Sexual Violence in Armed Conflict, *International Law and Politics*, Vol. 46, 2014, p. 635-678.

Markovic Darija, Child Soldiers: Victims or War Criminals? Criminal responsibility and prosecution of child soldiers under international criminal law, 14 December 2015, p. 22.

May be We Live and May be We Die: Recruitment and Use of Children by Armed Groups in Syria, Human Rights Watch, June 2014. p. 37.

McBride Julie. 2014. *The War Crime of Child Soldier Recruitment*, Springer: Asser Press.

Merkel Annabel, Female Suicide Bombers: Recognizing media's gendered descriptions of women's violence, Human Rights Studies, Lund University, Autumn 2011, p. 53.

Minow Martha, Forgiveness, Law and Justice, *California Law Review*, Vol. 103, Issue 6, 2015, p. 1615-1645.

Monguno Abubaker, Yagana Imam, Yagana Bukar and Bilkisu Lawan Gana, Bad Blood: Perception of children born of conflict-related sexual violence and women and girls associated with Boko Haram in northeast Nigeria, Research Summary, 2016, International Alert/UNICEF, p. 28.

Monshipouri Mahmood and Kaufman Claire L., The OIC, Children's Rights and Islam, Human Rights Research Paper, No. 2015/6, The Danish Institute for Human Rights, p. 28.

Morini Claudia, First Victims then Perpetrators: Child Soldiers and International Law, *Especial*, Vol. 3, 2010, p. 187-208.

Mouthaan Solange, Barafooot, Pregnant and in the Kitchen: Am I a child soldier too? *Women's Studies International Forum*, Vol. 51, 2015, p. 91-100.

Mudimu Godknows, *Reparations and Child Soldiers in Africa: The Legal regime of reparations for Former Child Soldiers under the Rome Statute of the International Criminal Court*, University of Cape Town, Unpublished Thesis, February 2014, p. 85.

Mukhar Rose, Child Soldiers and Peace Agreements, *Annual Survey of International & Comparative Law*, Vol. 20, Issue 1, 2014, p. 73-100.

Munir Muhammad, Suicide Attacks and Islamic Law, *International Review of the Red Cross*, Volume 90, No. 869, March 2008, p. 71-89..

Mulira Dorcas B., International Legal Standards Governing Child Soldiers, LLM Thesis and Essays, Paper 88, University of Georgia School of Law, 2007, p. 69.

Odeh Michael and Colin Sullivan, Recent Developments in International Rehabilitation of Child Soldiers, Youth Advocate Program International Resource Paper, p. 7.

Okebukola Elijah Oluwatoyin, Training Children for Armed Conflict – Where Does the Law Stand? *International Criminal Law Review*, Vol. 14, 2014, p. 588-618.

Olidort Jacob, Inside the Caliphate's Classroom: Books, Guidance Literature and Indoctrination Methods of Islamic State, The Washington Institute for Near East Policy, August 2016, p. 92.

Olga Ziori, Child Soldiers: Deprivation of Childhood, unpublished research paper, University of Bristol, November 2010, p. 43.

Omilusi Mike, Weaker Sex as Aggressor: Suicide Bombing and Strategic Logic of Gender Mainstreaming in Nigeria's Boko Haram Terrorism, *Global Journal of Political Science and Administration*, Vol. 3, No. 5, September 2015, p. 59-74.

Ongoing Recruitment and Use of Children by Parties to the Armed Conflict in Afghanistan, Child Soldiers International, March 2016, p. 16.

Onuoha Freedom C. and Temilola A. George, Boko Haram's Use of Female Suicide Bombing in Nigeria, Report: Al Jazeera Centre for Studies, 17 March 2015, p. 1-9.

Oosterveld Valerie, Gender and the Charles Taylor Case at the Special Court for Sierra Leone, *Wm. & Mary J. Women & L.*, Vol. 19, 2012, p. 7-33.

O'Rourke, Lindsey A, What's Special about Female Suicide Terrorism? *Security Studies*, Vol. 18, 2009, p. 681–718.

Peace operations and conflict management, Chapter 7, *SIPRI Yearbook 2016: Armaments, Disarmament and International Security*, SIPRI. p. 269-319.

Peters Lilian, War is no Child's Play: Child Soldiers from Battle Field to Playground, The Geneva Centre for the Democratic Control of Armed Forces (DCAF), Occasional Paper No. 8, 2005.

Pupavac, Vanessa, Misanthropy without Borders: The International Children's Rights Regime, *Disasters*, Vol. 25 (2), 2001, p. 95–112.

Quenivet Noelle, The Liberal Discourse and the "New Wars" of/on Children, *Brook. J. Int'l L.*, Vol. 38, Issue 3, 2013, p. 1053-1107.

Ramgoolie Monique, Prosecution of Sierra Leone's Child Soldiers: What Message is the UN Trying to Send, p. 145-162.

Rawcliffe John T., Child Soldiers: Legal Obligations and US Implementation, *The Army Lawyer*, September 2007, p. 1-6.

Ray Jeffery R., Children, Armed Conflict, and Genocide: Applying the Law of Genocide to the Recruitment and Use of Children in Armed Conflict, *Barry Law Review*, Vol. 19, Issue 2, Spring 2014, p. 335-360.

Research Report - The Use of Child Soldiers in the Sierra Leone, Conflict, The Prosecutor against Alex Tamba Brima, Brima Bazzy Kamara and Santigie Borbor Kanu, Proceedings: Special Court for Sierra Leone, Case No. SCSL-2004-16-T, 11 October 2006.

Rivet Annabelle Karen, The Criminal Liability of Child Soldiers in International criminal law: Does Restorative Justice offer a balance between the Rights of the Victim and the Rights of the Child Perpetrator? Unpublished Thesis, University of Pretoria, 2014, p. 67.

Rosen David M., Who is a Child: The Legal Conundrum of Child Soldier?

Conn J. Int'l Law, Vol. 25, 2009, p. 81-118.

Rosen, David. M. 2005. *Armies of the Young: Child Soldiers in War and Terrorism*, Brunswick, NJ: Rutgers University Press.

Rosen David M., Child Soldiers, International Humanitarian Law, and the Globalization of Childhood, *American Anthropologist*, Vol. 109, No. 2, June 2007, p. 296-306.

Ross Hamish, Children's Rights and Theories of Rights, *International Journal of Children's Rights*, Vol. 21, 2013, p. 679-704.

Saenz Margarita Maria, Reintegration of Children Associated with Armed Groups in Colombia, Harvard Graduate School of Education, 2012, p. 36.

Sawicki Fr John, A Tragic Trend: Why Terrorists Use Female and Child Suicide Bombers, *Journal of the Catholic Health Association of the United States*, July-August 2016, p. 38-42.

Schauer Elisabeth and Thomas Elbert, 'The Psychological Impact of Child Soldiering', in Martz, E. (ed.). 2010. *Trauma Rehabilitation After War and Conflict*, Springer, p. 311-360.

Schmitt Michael N., Deconstructing Direct Participation in Hostilities: The Constitutive Elements, *International Law and Politics*, Vol. 42, 2010, p. 697-739.

Schmitt Michael N., The Interpretive Guidance on the Notion of Direct, Participation in Hostilities: A Critical Analysis, *Harvard National Security Journal*, Vol. I, May 2010, p. 40.

Scorched Earth, Poisoned Air, Sudanese Government Forces Ravage Jebel Marra, Darfur, Amnesty International, AFR 54/4877/2016, April 2016, p. 103.

Seneviratne, Lakmini, Accountability of Child Soldiers: Blame Misplaced, *Sri Lanka Journal of International Law*, Vol. 20, No. 2, 2008, p. 29-48.

Seneviratne, Lakmini, International Legal Standards Applicable to Child Soldiers, *Sri Lanka Journal of International Law*, Vol. 15, 2003, p. 39-50.

Serna Daniel Ruiz and Ines Marchand, *Agape*: a reconciliation initiative by members of civil society and former child-soldiers, War Trauma Foundation, *Intervention*, Vol. 9, No. 1, 2011, p. 35-43..

Seyfarth, Lucia H., Child Soldiers to War Criminals: Trauma and the Case for Personal Mitigation, *Kent. J. Int'l & Comp. Law*, Vol. XIV, 2014, p. 1-29.

Shanahan Fiona, Cultural Responses to the Reintegration of Formerly Abducted Girl Soldiers in Northern Uganda, *Psychology & Society*, Vol. 1 (1), p. 14 28.

Sherper-Hughes Nancy and Carolyn Sargent (eds.). 1998. *Small Wars: The Cultural Politics of Childhood*, Berkeley: University of California Press.

Silva, Jennifer R, Child soldiers: a call to international community to protect children from war, *Suffolk Transnational Law Review*, Vol. 31, No. 3, Summer 2008, p. 681–709.

Singer P.W. 2005. *Children at War*, New York: Pantheon Books. Book.

Singer P.W., Talk is Cheap: Getting Serious about Preventing Child Soldiers, *Cornell International Law Journal*, Vol. 37, 2004, p. 561-586.

Singer P.W., Caution: Children at War, *Parameters*, Winter 2010-11, p.157-172.

Sivakumaran Sandesh, War crimes before the Special Court for Sierra Leone: Child Soldiers, Hostages, Peacekeepers and Collective Punishments, *Journal of International Criminal Justice*, Vol. 8, 2010, p. 1009-1026.

Sommerfelt Tone and mark B. Taylor, Big Dilemma of Small Soldiers: Recruiting Children to the War in Syria, Norwegian Peacebuilding Resource Centre (NOREF) Report, February 2015, p. 8.

Spivak Gayatri Chakravorty, Righting Wrongs, *The South Atlantic Quarterly*, Vol. 103(2/3), 2004, p. 523–581.

Squires Cristina Martinez, How the Law Should View Voluntary Child Soldiers: Does Terrorism Pose a Different Dilemma? *SMUL.Rev.*, Vol. 68, 2015, p. 567-591.

Stephens, Sharon (ed.), *Children and the Politics of Culture*, 1995, Princeton: Princeton University Press.

Stern, Jessica and JM Berger, Raising Tomorrow's Mujahideen: The Horrific World of ISIS's Child Soldiers, *The Guardian*, March 10, 2015.

Storelli-Castro Luciana, How the War on Terror Frames Victim Ontology: A Comparative Analysis of the Case of Omar Khadr and Child Soldiers in Sierra Leone, *Journal of International Service*, Vol. 22, No. 2, Fall 2013, p. 1-18.

The Rights and Guarantees of Internally Displaced Children in Armed Conflict, Children and Armed Conflict, Working Paper No. 2, United Nations: Office of the Special Representative of the Secretary-General, September 2010.

Tan Joe, Sexual Violenece Against Children on the Battlefield as Crime Using Child Soldiers: Square Pegs in Round Holes and Missed Opportunities in *Lubanga, Yearbook of International Humanitarian Law*, Vol. 15, 2012, p. 117-151.

Taylor Mark B., Law, guns and money: regulating war economies in Syria and beyond, Norwegian Peacebuilding Resource Centre, report, July 2015, p. 11.

Thayer, B. A. and Hudson, V. Sex and the Shaheed: Insights from the Life Sciences on Islamic Suicide Terrorism, *International Security*, Vol. 34 (4), 2010, p. 37-62.

The Operational Guide to the Integrated Disarmament, Demobilization and Reintegration Standards (IDDRS), United Nations, 2014, p. 317.

The Paris Principles: Principles and Guidelines on Children Associated with Armed Forces or Armed Groups, February 2007, p.43.

Thomas Mara Achton, Malice Supplies the Age? Assessing the Culpability of Adolescent Soldiers, *California Western International Law Journal*, Vol. 44, Fall 2013, No. 1, p. 38.

Tiefenbrun Susan, Child Soldiers, Slavery and the Trafficking of Children, *Fordham International Law Journal*, Vol. 31, Issue 2, 2007, p. 417-486.

Udombana, Nsongurua J., War is Not Child's Play! International Law and the Prohibition of Children's Involvement in Armed Conflicts, *Temple International & Comparative Law Journal*, Vol. 20, No. 1, 2006, p. 57-109.

United Nations Security Council Resolution 1612 Adopted by the Security Council on 26 July 2005.

Ursini Brittany, Prosecuting Child Soldiers: The Call for an International Minimum Age of Criminal Responsibility, *St John's Law Review*, Vol. 89, No. 2, Summer/Fall 2015, April 2016, p. 1023-1048.

Valentine Sandrine, Trafficking of Child Soldiers: Expanding the United Nations Convention on the Rights of the Child and its Optional Protocol, *New Eng. J. Int'l & Comp. L.*, Vol. 9, No. 1, 2002, p. 109-176.

Vandenhole Wouter and Weyns Yannick, *Child Soldier and EU Policy on Children and Armed Conflict*, Policy Department DG External Policies, The European Parliament's Sub-committee on Human Rights (DROI), March 2014, p. 58.

Vandergrift K., Challenges in Implementing and Enforcing Children's Rights, *Cornell International Law Journal*, Vol. 37, No. 3, 2004, p. 547-553.

Vargas-Baron Emily, National Policies to Prevent the Recruitment of Child Soldiers, Ford Institute for Human Security, 2007, p. 31.

Vautravers Alexandre J., Why Child Soldiers are such a Complex Issue, *Refugee Survey Quarterly*, Vol. 27, No. 4, 2009, p. 96-107.

Verhey Beth, Child Soldiers: Preventing, Demobilizing and Reintegrating, Africa Region Working Paper Series No. 23, November 2001, p. 37.

Victims, Perpetrators or Heroes? Child Soldiers before the International Criminal Court, London: The Redress Trust, September 2006.

Vite Sylvain, Between Consolidation and Innovation: The International criminal Court's Trial Chamber Judgement in *Lubanga* case, *Yearbook of International Humanitarian Law*, Vol. 15, 2012, p. 61-85.

Wang Qianqian, The Crime of Child Soldier Recruitment, Unpublished Dissertation, University of Wien, 2012.

Waschefort Gus. 2015. *International Law and Child Soldiers*, Oregon: Oxford and Portland.

We Can Die Too: Recruitment and Use of Child Soldiers in South Sudan, Human Rights Watch, 2015, p. 75.

Webster, Timothy, Babes with Arms: International Law and Child Soldiers, *The George Washington International Law Review*, Vol. 39, No. 2, 2007, p. 227-54.

Weissbrodt David, Joseph C. Hansen, and Nathaniel H. Nesbitt, The Role of the Committee on the Rights of the Child in Interpreting and Developing IHL, *Harvard Human Rights Journal*, Vol. 24, 2011, p. 115-164.

Wells Sarah L., Crimes against Child Soldiers in Armed Conflict Situations: Application and Limits of International Humanitarian Law, *Tulane Journal of International and Comparative Law*, Vol. 12, 2004, p. 287-306.

Wessells Michael. 2006. *Child Soldiers: From Violence to Protection*, London: Harvard University Press.

Wessells Michael, Psychosocial Issues in Reintegrating Child Soldiers, *Cornell International Law Journal*, Vol. 37, No.3, 2004, p. 513-526.

Whitman Shelly, Tanya Zayed and Carl Conradi. 2013. *Child Soldiers: A Handbook for Security Sector Actors*, The Romeo Dallaire Child Soldiers Initiative, Canada, p. 200.

Wilkens Ann, Suicide Bombers and Society: A Study on Suicide Bombers in Afghanistan and Pakistan, FOI, Swedish Defence Research Agency, 2011, p. 65.

Winter Charlie, An Integrated Approach to Islamic State Recruitment: Special Report, Australian Strategic Policy Institute (ASPI), April 2016, p. 16.

Wounded Childhood, The Use of Children in Armed Conflict in Central Africa, Geneva: International Labour Office, April 2003, p. 98.

Yaregal Woineshet, Female Suicide Bombers: Desperation or Weapon of Choice? The Case of Palestine, Unpublished Thesis, Georgetown University, 2011, p. 188.

Zia-Mansoor Farkhanda, The Dilemma of Child Soldiers: Who Is Responsible? *King's College Law Journal*, Vol. 16, No. 2, 2005, p. 388-399.

Index